Choosing to LEAD

DENNIS WAGNER
JOHN SCANLON

Dedication and Acknowledgments

Choosing to LEAD is dedicated to all the leaders whose stories are chronicled in this work, together with many other colleagues who have chosen to team and lead with us and thousands of others on the initiatives detailed in these pages.

We are grateful for the talent, forceful leadership, and creative work of Lucille Tenazas who served as our Creative Director and Designer. She was joined in this work by Yu Fu, a diligent, hard-working, and highly skilled Designer in her own right. Lucille and Yu truly elevated this material, bringing life and snap to our stories, text, charts, and overall flow.

Many thanks to Carolyn Finney who served not only as our thoughtful and eloquent Developmental Editor, but who also joined with us in a robust and fast-paced final review of the edited versions of **Choosing to LEAD**.

Finally, we want to express our deep appreciation and loving gratitude to our spouses and family members who joined with us in the life-long journey that both preceded and included the times we spent in writing this book. Both of us are blessed with exceptionally gifted, kind, and wise spouses and adult children. Thank you.

Choosing to LEAD

INTENT

BEING

LANGUAGE

ROLES

Choosing to LEAD
INTENT BEING LANGUAGE ROLES

Copyright © 2025 Dennis Wagner and John Scanlon, Co-Authors
All Rights Reserved

We value copyright. Copyright supports innovation, free speech, entrepreneurship, and diversity. Thank you for buying an authorized version of this book and for complying with copyright laws by not reproducing, distributing or transmitting in any form or by any means, including photocopying, recording or other electronic or mechanical methods, without the prior written permission of the publisher/author, except in the case of brief quotations embodied in reviews and certain other noncommercial uses permitted by copyright law.

Publisher: Yes And Leadership, LLC
Alexandria, Virginia USA

Creative Director/Designer: Lucille Tenazas, NY/SF
Designer: Yu Fu

Developmental Editor: Carolyn Finney

Direct requests for permission to
Dennis Wagner of yesandleadership@gmail.com
ISBN: 979-8-9922288-1-6 (print)
Library of Congress Control Number: 2024926900

Although every precaution has been taken to verify the accuracy of the information contained herein, the authors and publisher assume no responsibility for any errors or omissions. No liability is assumed for damages that may result from the use of information contained herein.

Leadership   Public Service   Large-Scale Change   Business   Self-Help

Second Edition

- 6 **Introduction**
- 11 **CHOICE The Foundation of Leadership**
  - 12 Our Choices Define Us
  - 19 Leadership Choices in Four Domains
  - 25 Choosing to Lead: Use 12 Mindsets and Methods
  - 31 Do the Mindsets and Methods Support Malevolent Leadership?
  - 32 Learning From the Leadership Stories of Others
- 45 **We Choose Our Leadership INTENT**
  - 51 Project ECHO and the Democratization of Expert Knowledge, Sanjeev Arora MD
  - 62 Leadership Choices Lead to National Action and Results on Indoor Radon Gas, Dennis Wagner
  - 75 Compelling Vision as the Intended Future We Stand For
  - 82 Envisioning and Launching the "100,000 Lives" Campaign, Don Berwick MD, MPP
  - 104 Establishing and Achieving a Bold Aim on Organ Donation, Dennis Wagner
  - 117 Bold Aims as a Campaign to Realize Intent
  - 142 DNA: Decide-Notice-Acknowledge, A Joyous Way to Express Intent
  - 150 An Abundance of Opportunity for Large-Scale Transformation
- 153 **We Choose Our Ways of BEING**
  - 154 Becoming Conscious and Intentional About Our Choice of Being
  - 160 Be the Change You Want to See in the World, Bob & Barb Malizzo
  - 164 Choose to Foster Net Forward Energy in the Domain of Being
  - 174 Flip Negative Energy: A Great Way to Help Ourselves and Others
  - 183 Understanding and Activating Five Sources Of Resilience: A Personal and Professional Journey
  - 202 Establishing a Nationwide Bank for the Poor and by the Poor in Haiti, Anne H. Hastings
  - 220 Leadership and Choices in the Domain of Being
- 222 **We Choose Our Leadership LANGUAGE**
  - 223 Leadership Happens Through Language
  - 226 Choose to Use Leadership Speech Acts
  - 278 Leadership Stories: Language as a Narrative that Reaches and Engages Others
  - 288 Choose to Access Abundance
  - 299 Requests and Offers Generate Abundance, Susan McVey Dillon
  - 310 Choose To Speak The Language of Leadership
- 311 **We Choose Our Leadership ROLES**
  - 316 Switching Among Four Roles For Different Results
  - 339 Exercising Accountability Through 5 Dimensions of Action
  - 346 Leadership Choices in a Journey to Excellence, John Chessare MD, MPH
  - 372 Leaders Thrive on Pacing Events
  - 411 The Domain of Roles: Choices That Make Us Architects of Leadership Work
- 415 **We Craft our Own SIGNATURE STYLE of Leadership**
  - 416 All of Us Have A Signature Style
  - 418 Living a Leadership Signature Style
  - 425 Crafting and Practicing Your Own Signature Style of Leadership
  - 434 Choosing to Lead Through a Demotion, Dennis Wagner
  - 467 The World Needs More Leadership

- 472 About the authors
- 476 Photo credits

INTRODUCTION

People will forget what you said, people will forget what you did, but people will never forget how you made them feel.

MAYA ANGELOU

American Poet
Civil Rights Activist

Leadership Is A Choice We All Can Make

The world needs more leaders and more leadership. More of us need to recognize and embrace the opportunities and challenges that are calling each of us to choose to lead.

All of us remember that uplifting moment when a courageous boss, a charismatic teacher, a superb coach, a committed mentor, or a loyal friend helped us achieve something we never imagined we could do. Each of us has been inspired by others who worked against overwhelming odds to achieve extraordinary results. People who inspire and uplift us are people who choose to lead.

CHOOSING TO LEAD will help you step into leadership. It is a guide for creating the profoundly transformational experiences that you and your colleagues and associates will never forget. The leadership approaches outlined here come with a disciplined and systematic set of Mindsets and Methods that you can practice and adapt as you develop your own Signature Style of leadership. These Mindsets and Methods have been a transformative and enduring source of joy and results for ourselves and others.

CHOOSING TO LEAD is about understanding and applying leadership that uplifts. It's about how every one of us is capable of stepping into leadership today, and not only succeeding, but inspiring others to discover their own capacity for leadership. It's about gaining access to a Signature Style of leadership that will deliver meaning and purpose to our work and our lives.

We tend to think of leaders as key people with formidable positions such as Director or Chief Executive Officer. But leadership is really about the Choices that each of us can make at critical junctures, regardless of our job titles. We can choose to intervene rather than drift along when we see more productive and innovative outcomes are possible. We can choose to assist in times of disarray or impending failure when our colleagues need us. We can choose to help others visualize the unseen potential of what may appear to be a negative situation.

CHOOSING TO LEAD is about consistently seeing and making the daily tactical and longer-term strategic Choices necessary for transforming the worlds in which we navigate. This is our central definition of leadership. Leadership is not determined by our job title: it's determined by the Choices we make every day about our Intent, about our way of Being in the world, the Language we use, and our Roles.

Leadership as Choice is revolutionary.

Choosing to lead is a bold and transformative act.

Choosing to Lead is our invitation to be bold and transformative.

Mindsets and Methods Gleaned From Leadership Practice

This book equips each of us with a clear, straightforward set of proven Mindsets and Methods to help us succeed in making effective leadership Choices. These powerful concepts help us with the big Choices in our lives and careers, as well as in the little Choices we make in our meetings, in our emails, in our text messages, in our attitudes, and in many other aspects of our daily lives. We can learn to intentionally choose leadership responses—especially when confronted by difficult or negative situations—with sound decisions and actions. And when the world throws good things our way, we can consciously choose to magnify the good.

These Mindsets and Methods share several vitally important attributes:

Proven Effective: Our Mindsets and Methods have been applied by thousands of people to generate dramatic, rapid, quantitative, national, and international results in diverse sectors including healthcare, banking, and the environment.

Joyous and Uplifting: Leaders who have contributed to the initiatives chronicled here identify this work as one of the most rewarding highlights of their careers. Many of the participants in these initiatives share this view.

Easy to Learn and Apply: Mindsets and Methods of Bold Aims, Flip Negative Energy, and Access Abundance, among others, are clear, straightforward, and can be rapidly learned and shared with others.

Some of our Mindsets and Methods are well-known and have been written about for years, such as developing Resilience or using Effective Questions to lead change. But knowing and applying are two different things. Becoming more aware of our leadership Choices and learning how to apply the Mindsets and Methods will help us to make effective Choices that take each of us into the powerful and compelling futures that are ours to create.

**Leadership Stories Show How Choice Happens
And Is Carried Out**

The book profiles a number of leaders by sharing their vivid and inspiring stories. A Leadership Story is about the defining moments that generate opportunity for Choice, the compelling visions that gain traction in the world as a result, and the Mindsets and Methods that make up the nitty-gritty practice of leadership.

In the pages of this experience-based book we will encounter the stories of professionals, executives, managers, doctors, nurses, pharmacists, special education teachers, parents —ordinary people like all of us—who chose to lead and generated extraordinary results. We will see a common set of Mindsets and Methods in play as they apply their own unique Signature Styles.

Leadership stories have an important feature. They have an uplifting effect that we call the Upward Spiral. They trigger leadership possibilities in others. Listeners are inspired to join in and support the mission at hand. Some gain insights that surface their own opportunities to choose leadership. Others see how to support a colleague as he or she pursues leadership Choices.

Use the many leadership stories in this book to become inspired and to gain insight into your own leadership Choices and Signature Style. Get practiced in hearing and supporting the emerging Leadership Stories of those in your life.

Our Shared Vision: It's Important to Choose to Lead

We believe that while many of us are well-trained in the disciplines of management, administration, and analysis, effective leadership is rarely addressed or promoted.

Throughout our careers, as others would reach out to us for problem-solving and results, we would encounter situations where we were struck by the potential for innovative and transformative change. Yet management and administration were often content with operating at a scale and with an impact that fell far short of what was achievable.

Performance was weak, pedestrian, suspect. And always with rationalizations: "*We don't have the resources . . . It's not our mission . . . It's not my job . . . That isn't realistic . . . The goals are just aspirational . . . They won't let us do that . . . That's not allowed.*" When leadership is absent in these situations, the critical needs of our citizens and fellow humans go ignored and unaddressed.

We believe that we often have opportunities to fill that vacuum, to address suffering, and to help forge paths to greater health and prosperity for all of us. We can choose to consider the roles of leadership in our own daily Choices and in the bigger picture. We can learn to create and support teams, businesses, hospitals, government organizations, communities and systems that foster not just managers and administrators, but also people who deliberately and consistently choose to lead.

It's easy to get caught up in the current drift of the status quo. We need to get more comfortable with staking out what the late federal executive Mary Lou Andersen called "*the lonely place between the no longer and the not yet.*" We need to learn to take leadership actions to address the sometimes daunting scale of what needs to be done, and the capability to make the kinds of Choices needed to bring these possibilities into being. Pursuing leadership Choices requires a clarity and constancy of purpose, courage, resilience, and skill.

This book describes how to use a set of leadership Mindsets and Methods to make effective leadership Choices in the four domains of **INTENT**, **BEING**, **LANGUAGE**, and **ROLES**. One of the wonderful things we have discovered about using these Mindsets and Methods to make leadership Choices is that they lead not only to greater effectiveness and results, but also precipitate greater joy.

Join with us in creating the work and life experiences that others will remember.

Join with us in creating an Upward Spiral in work and life.

Join with us in Choosing to Lead.

CHOICE
The Foundation of Leadership

Between stimulus and response there is a space. In that space is our power to choose our response. In our response lies our growth and our freedom.

VIKTOR E. FRANKL

Neurologist
Psychologist
Holocaust Surrivor

Our Choices Define Us

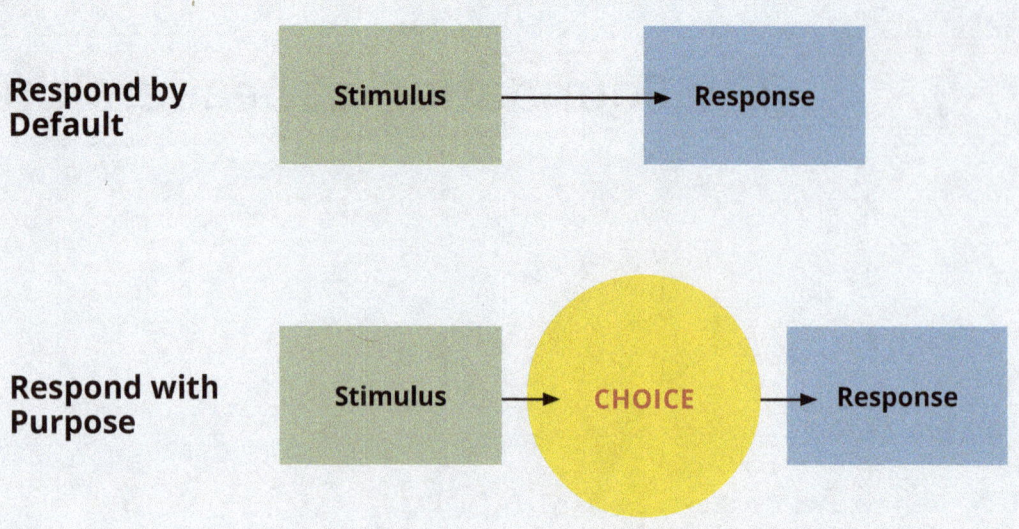

Choices Are Foundational Acts of Leadership

All day, every day, we make Choices both minor and major. We choose our Language, our goals, and our attitudes. Mostly though, we don't do it consciously. We act instinctively, out of habit. We have automatic, unconscious responses to whatever we experience in any given moment—"going with the current drift," as we call it. These default responses can mire us in worsening conditions and cause us to overlook higher and more fertile ground.

Default responses have deep sources: well-practiced routines when something unfortunate or unexpected happens, or patterns we learned in our families while growing up. Defaults are unconscious decisions often accompanied by quiet rationalizations or justifications. We experience a certain stimulus and we respond in a predictable way.

Much of the time, these predictable patterns can be a positive thing. We drive to work thinking about work, not about how to drive. When we see a stop sign (stimulus), it is to the good of the social order and our own that we stop at the sign (response). When someone provides us with a service, we automatically say "thank you." Much of our daily logistics and work are performed instinctively without thinking, a product of years of skill development and experience.

However as human beings, we also can choose our responses. We don't have to respond automatically and without thinking. Choice is the often challenging but liberating alternative to ingrained habit.

Understanding the freedom that Choice gives us is especially critical in choosing to take on leadership work. Leadership possibilities are often triggered by two stimuli: when encountering negative situations and when encountering new and unusual situations. Both situations can be intimidating, yet both are full of possibility.

How we respond to negative situations is always challenging. Hot button issues can elicit emotional responses with negative consequences. For example, when someone criticizes or insults us, the temptation is to be defensive, to go on the attack, or to stifle our response and nurture grievances.

Or, we can choose to take the high road.

When criticized, we can choose to respond positively to our critics, maybe by thanking them for the insight and requesting specific suggestions for learning and improvement. Most of us have responded irritably one time or another to disappointing service or an inferior product, only to be knocked for a loop when the agent or manager responds with attention and respect, completely resetting the transaction. With discipline and clear Intent, we can turn negative stimuli into opportunities for growth, learning, and fresh starts.

We need leaders who can respond to the negative with the positive. This is one of the essential ways we contribute to creating the better world we seek.

Then there are those "new and unusual" situations.

Leadership work naturally takes us into the realm of the new and unusual. As leaders, we need to be on the lookout for opportunities and possibilities for changing current practice, organizational relationships, and unproductive behaviors. But our instinct will often tell us to avoid the uncertainty and risk that accompany change, to default to habit and rote behaviors.

Our education, management training, work rules, and culture have effectively programmed many of us to avoid choosing leadership. The work of leadership requires us to be vigilant and open to Choice.

Our ability to choose with intention our response to any given stimulus is an extraordinary human endowment. Stephen Covey, author of *The 7 Habits of Highly Effective People*, wrote that making conscious Choices to stimuli is like "exercising the muscles of human-ness."

The more we exercise the muscle of Choice, the stronger it grows. Over time, we strengthen our humanity. We become more attuned to living with intention and goodness. Those we encounter get caught in this Upward Spiral of good things and are moved to join with us.

As we contemplate the Abundance of Choice and the leadership opportunities it provides, two Mindsets are vital to maintain:

Constant awareness of our unconscious responses and their potentially harmful effect.

Leadership is being ready to temper the negative effects of the rote response.
Options exist.

Constant awareness that we almost always have Choices and they involve others.

Leadership is recognizing those feelings of being boxed-in, powerless, or constrained as your signal to reach out to others and to think outside the box.
Options exist.

To adopt these Mindsets is to grant ourselves the freedom to choose leadership. We first learned about the importance of Choice from reading Stephen Covey's description of the compelling example of Viktor Frankl.

Choice and the Search for Meaning

Viktor Frankl learned about Choice the hard way.

Frankl was a psychologist and Director of the Neurology Department at a hospital in Vienna, Austria, until he and his family were rounded up by the Nazis in 1942.

During his internment, it dawned on Frankl that even in the most nightmarish of conditions, each day he was presented with a series of Choices. He realized that he could choose to comfort and help others who were experiencing the loss of loved ones, forced labor, torture, and starvation. He realized that he could choose to cultivate in himself and others an attitude of acceptance, forgiveness, empathy, and hope as powerful alternatives to anger, fear and despair.

"Everything can be taken from a man," he would later write, "but one thing: the last of human freedoms – to choose one's attitude in any given set of circumstances, to choose one's own way."

After surviving three years in four concentration camps, Dr. Frankl emerged only to learn that he had lost his young wife, his parents, and his brother to Nazi extermination. Frankl and his sister were the sole surviving members of their family.

Even in the face of these wrenching losses, he remained unwavering in his convictions and penned *Man's Search for Meaning*, his seminal work, in 1946. In this book Frankl advances key tenets of his philosophy of stimulus, choice, and response. He also dwells on the importance of identifying and nurturing a purpose in life, and then to intensely imagine the very outcome of that purpose. Imagining the realization of his own purpose was one of the key Choices that helped Frankl to survive the atrocities of the camps.

For most of us, our Choices will not be as dire as those faced by Viktor Frankl. Nonetheless his teachings and his example speak powerfully, as do his Choices to maintain his belief in humanity and to help others to sustain their own humanity throughout the despair and degradation of those three years. In a similar vein, Carl Jung reminds us, "We are not what happened to us, we are what we choose to become." By actively defining our purpose and maintaining the constant daily discipline of choosing what we become, we can inspire others to do the same. Naming and pursuing our purpose and ways of Being are acts of leadership.

Exercising the Freedom No One Can Take Away

This book is about a very specific set of Choices we can make in our lives. They may look and feel different and possibly even daunting.

Situations – stimuli – will definitely arise that point us towards a better future for ourselves and others. But taking action will raise the possibility of failure. There is risk. The default is to turn away from pursuing that future, for reasons that may be sound and defensible. We want to turn away because the Choices will often be fraught with accountability and with needs that appear far beyond our capability and influence. We may tell ourselves we lack the authority, or the resources, or the time, or the ability, or the permission to reach for that future. Yet even when we lack these things, there are options. We can imagine partnerships and larger cooperative efforts that would realize that future.

We still have that "last of human freedoms" to choose our response in any set of circumstances, to choose our own attitudes and Mindsets, our own ways. When we encounter a compelling Choice, we can learn to recognize it, to hold those default reactions in check, and consider how to accept the challenges that come with the Choice. We can learn how to take the often more difficult paths and, as leaders, invite others to join us on the journey. Choosing to pursue that future, with all the challenges it presents, is at the heart of leadership.

The notion of leadership as a series of Choices may run counter to conventional wisdom. But the wisdom of this truth will become evident in the powerful and instructive stories that follow.

As we encounter daunting leadership Choices and uncertain opportunities, we can step out and be on point ourselves – we can choose to be the first person who stands for the decision, for a new course of action, for the initiative, or for the Bold Aim. We also have the option to be the person who encourages and supports others who are ready to lead. We can align with the compelling leadership agendas and Choices of others. Consistently making leadership Choices that "exercise the muscles of human-ness" can become one of the most rewarding and defining parts of our lives.

First Lead Ourselves, Then Lead Others

Viktor Frankl tells us that Choice as a freedom can only be taken away from us by ourselves. Choosing to lead starts with taking on leadership of ourselves.

Leadership is first and foremost about self-accountability and Being in action today. Why wait to help a colleague who needs what we can give? Why wait to provide excellent customer service to someone who has a complaint? Why wait for a position to open? Why wait to solve climate change? Why wait to fix health care? Why wait to address rural isolation and poverty? Why wait to innovate? Why wait to address needs with an exciting new product? **WHY WAIT?**

Jonathan Haidt's book, *The Happiness Hypothesis*, uses the metaphor of a Rider and an Elephant to describe the challenge of using intentional rational thought to deal with our underlying desires and default responses. The emotional region of our brain, the Elephant, is much bigger and stronger than the rational part of our brain, the Rider. As Riders, we need to learn to channel and harmonize with the emotional power and energy of our inner-Elephant. Gaining mastery of this Elephant-Rider dynamic is key to making the Choices necessary to lead ourselves, especially when indifference, fear, suspicion, or scorn may lie in store as we seek to establish and implement **Bold Aims**.

Even as we encounter the inevitable challenges and negative reactions to our leadership, most of us have access to help. We don't do this work alone! As we grapple with setbacks and the unforeseen, reaching out for support will inevitably allow us to grow our circles of influence and our capabilities in addressing the needs of others. We will become practiced in leading ourselves, and over time we will develop the awareness, maturity, and skills necessary to lead others through risk and uncertainty to results that are life-saving, world-changing, and self-transforming.

Leadership as a Personal Choice, not an Assigned Title

A key message of this book is that leadership is a Choice. Unlike a management or executive position, we can't assign someone to be a leader. Leadership derives from our individual Choices: what we think, what we say, and the energy we spread to others. Leadership is something that each of us, at any level in our organization, can choose to assume; it is not limited to managers, CEOs, CMOs, or other executive Roles.

The traditional view of leadership relies heavily on organizational assignment. Through service to an organizational structure, someone is put in charge, and by virtue of their position, they are assumed to be leaders. We see this limited vision of leadership reinforced through unchallenged and limiting assumptions such as the following:

IF WE secure a job in an organization and provide meritorious service in various Roles, we'll eventually work our way up to a "leadership" position;

IF WE attend college to learn the Language and knowledge of a professional discipline—chemistry, engineering, law, philosophy, etc.—over time we'll become acknowledged as a leader in the field;

IF WE join a political party and run for office, soon we'll be seen out in front as a leader pursuing policy Intent;

IF WE join a church and actively participate, we can eventually become a leader in our religious community.

What these examples have in common is the notion that leadership is conferred by some external authority or consensus. In these scenarios, there's a well-worn path to follow, with leadership as an earned, formally acknowledged accomplishment. This is mostly a positive and motivating dynamic. People do good work and advance. At the same time, this traditional view of leadership can unintentionally lock us into ways of working and living that do not effectively respond to the Abundance of opportunities to lead that abound. There is so much more to the world—much more to live out, to give to others, to contribute. These leadership opportunities exist in the daily big and small Choices that we make.

Leadership Choices in Four Domains

If Leadership Is A Choice, What Does The Choice Look Like and Sound Like?

Hard work, lived experience, and intense study have shown us that leadership Choices available to each of us reside in four distinct domains: Intent, Being, Language, and Roles. The four domains provide us with practical, straightforward and relatively easy-to-recognize places for making our leadership Choices. They reduce the fairly daunting landscape of potential Choices into a manageable few that we can get our minds around.

The four domains are known fields of practice and knowledge. There is a logic to leadership that can be captured by the four domains.

Leadership is about moving ourselves and others toward a shared goal. A lot of people and many organizations come together, each in their own way, to realize a desired outcome, such as "put people on the moon" and "bring them back within the decade." There is **Intent**.

The way each of us thinks, feels, behaves, speaks and listens, and the response this gets from others, has a huge impact on our ability to more effectively align with the work at hand, and in the pursuit of our shared vision. There is a way of **Being**.

Working together with others, we have to talk in ways that are understandable, engaging and collaborative. We talk in a manner that enables collective action. There is the **Language** used.

As we come together in collective action, as people enter into agreements and partnerships, we draw on what we know about organizing enterprises for efficiency and effectiveness. There are ways to get complex things done. We consciously work to have the necessary accountabilities and responsibilities in place. We know a lot about how to set up and run enterprises, as organized efforts, that thrive by creating value. There are **Roles** that need to be performed.

Our leadership efforts can be viewed as the consistent and innovative application of Choices in these four fields of practice and knowledge. A sense of the depth and breadth of the knowledge base can be seen in the authors and best-selling books associated with each of them. Subsequent sections of this book will focus specifically on how to make effective leadership Choices in these four domains using 12 distinct leadership Mindsets and Methods.

Both strategic life Choices and tactical, in-the-moment Choices define our leadership

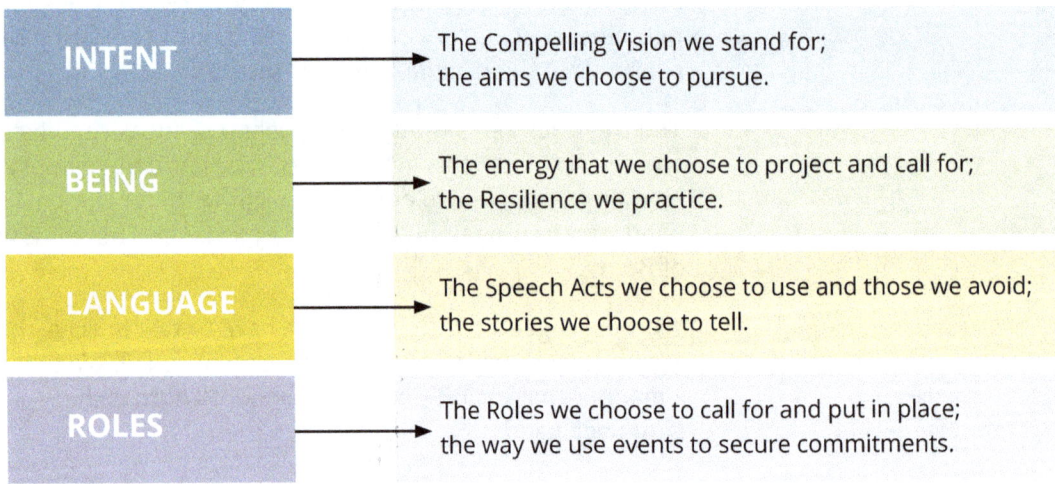

INTENT → The Compelling Vision we stand for; the aims we choose to pursue.

BEING → The energy that we choose to project and call for; the Resilience we practice.

LANGUAGE → The Speech Acts we choose to use and those we avoid; the stories we choose to tell.

ROLES → The Roles we choose to call for and put in place; the way we use events to secure commitments.

Understanding the Common Alternative Choices in the Four Domains

Each domain presents a range of Choices. Some are leadership responses. Others are instinctive reactions, and still others are learned, professional responses. To discern what leadership Choices are available to us, it helps to understand the instinctive reactions and learned responses we commonly encounter. The following table contrasts how leadership Choices compare with other instinctive and professional Choices in each of the four domains.

Distinguishing among Instinctive, Professional and Leadership Responses

Four Domains of CHOICE	Three Ways to Respond to the Life Situations We Encounter		
	Personal Instinctive Reactions	Learned Professional Choices	Self-Conscious Leadership Choices
INTENT	Response guided primarily by self-interest	Act according to the culture and perceived interests of the organization	Stand for a Compelling Vision that meets the true needs of others
BEING	Reactive responses to what others do or say triggered by our current mood	Maintain professional conduct: calm, logical, objective, defensive, stay in own lane	Open to and generating possibilities and opportunities
LANGUAGE	Unedited, habitual use of epressions that include idle chatter, opinion, gossip, blame and worry	Professional Language to share information, assign tasks, set standards, edit products, and perform critical review	Seek relationship and commitments through deliberate use of generative Speech Acts like Requests and Offers
ROLES	Pursuit of prescribed, instinctive, or comfortable Roles in work and life	Work from well-defined and focused job descriptions with acceptance of clear and achievable duties	Situational awareness to have self and others perform differing needed Roles at the right time

Review the columns in the Four Domains of Choice chart. Instinctive and professional responses are learned habits that often work well for us. However, it is easy to become stuck in them with no awareness that we may be limiting ourselves and others. We can waste precious opportunities by Being on autopilot with instinctive and professional responses. Becoming conscious of our instinctive reactions and learned professional response is a key initial step in choosing to lead.

People in organizational situations are taught to make Choices in the professional column. While these professional Choices are usually far better than the instinctive reactions, they frequently fall far short of the real need or our true calling or what might be possible if we stepped out and led.

In our experience, most of us have a constant stream of opportunities to make Choices between responses in the Professional column and responses in the Leadership column. We often don't perceive these Choices in the moment. Years of observation and first-hand experience have taught us that it is common to mistake Professional Behavior for Leadership and to let the true Leadership opportunities pass. While both are needed and valuable, understanding the distinction between the two is a tremendous asset in becoming more practiced in exerting leadership Choices.

Become Aware of the Distinctive Choices of Leadership in Each Domain

The following table provides examples of the leadership and non-leadership Choices that commonly show up in each domain. Each pair of Choices is not necessarily an "either-or" decision. In practice it can be "Yes, and …" Our effectiveness grows as we learn to recognize and act on leadership Choices in the four domains.

Domain	Non-Leadership Choice	Leadership Choice
INTENT	Satisfied with incremental progress	Committed to a Bold Aim
	Stay on task, finish on time	Working to meet true needs
BEING	This is happening to me	This is happening for me
	Upset with problems	Expecting challenges
LANGUAGE	Sharing information	Request commitments from others
	I disagree	Using "Yes, and …"
ROLES	An employee with a job to do	Switching Roles to fill the need
	A critical reviewer	Accepting accountability for action

Leadership opportunities that we fail to recognize don't get acted on. Understanding the habitual defaults and learned professional Choices can alert us that we may be locked into status quo or self-defeating patterns of behavior. The danger is that we fail to recognize that leadership Choices exist; we see ourselves as without Choices and therefore powerless. With intention, we can become more open to leadership Choices and to develop them over time into hardwired habits.

Leadership Choices Will Unleash Natural Abundance

There is an Abundance of energy and capability in the hearts and minds of our fellow human beings. People and organizations all over the world are deeply committed to making things better in some way. Most all of us want our contributions to add up to something important and meaningful.

Work at becoming conscious about this Abundance. Listen to colleagues. Listen to our youth. Listen to our seasoned elders. When we consciously listen, we hear common refrains:

"I want to make the world a better place."

"I want to have an impact."

"I want to spend my time, energy, and skills on things that really matter."

As leaders, we can channel these extraordinary gifts into meaningful Choices and results. But far too often we end up working in and unconsciously supporting systems and organizations where opportunities to make breakthrough gains are hidden, blocked, or ignored.

Unintended consequences and hidden costs are frequently discounted, leaving our colleagues, suppliers, customers, and others in some level of distress. Systems and organizations operating in this manner are insufficiently designed. They unintentionally advance dysfunctional patterns of behaviors and organizational processes that become the norm. Over time the processes affect us personally. They quietly sap our energy, weaken our commitment, and erode our skill sets. We can become stuck in jobs and organizational situations that fail to call for the highest and best expressions of our capabilities and desires. No one wants this, and yet it happens. It doesn't have to be this way. We and others can Choose to Lead.

Choosing to Lead:
Use 12 Mindsets and Methods

How We Learn To Make Leadership Choices

We have teamed with hundreds of effective leaders, in action and working to create positive change in the world. Careful observation of their work, together with our own practical application, have helped us to distill and codify ways of making effective, joyous leadership Choices.

In each of the four domains there are certain Choices that have proven to be successful in generating both joy and results. These Choices are practices—Mindsets and Methods— that have shown up across many different walks of life. They populate the stories people tell to share their leadership experiences. We have identified 12 Mindsets and Methods, three in each domain, that describe how to choose to lead.

Each is a Mindset. It's a way of looking at the world. All 12 are positive ways of understanding people and viewing the situations we find ourselves in.

Each is a Method in that one can become skilled in its practice. It's describable and teachable. For the most part many of us are already familiar with them in some way. The challenge is learning to consciously and consistently use them.

Individually, the 12 have utility. Taken together they create a powerful, high-energy leadership force. Taken together they can equip each of us with our own unique leadership Signature Style.

The 12 Mindsets and Methods are not definitive. There are many others that can be added. These 12 were sufficient to provide us with a robust Signature Style that enabled us to generate significant, joyous results and to understand how the leaders we encountered were getting results.

Each person will have his or her own leadership Signature Style. Our Intent with this book is to provide a framing and cases that will help you capture and develop your own leadership Signature Style.

Leadership Mindsets and Methods As Choices in Four Domains

We can choose to lead—and help others choose to lead as well—by gaining command of a series of practical and uplifting leadership Mindsets and Methods within the domains of Intent, Being, Language, and Roles.

An overview of each of the Mindsets and Methods follows. Each Mindset and Method is more fully elaborated upon in subsequent sections of the book and is accompanied by compelling examples of how we and other leaders have put these to use in transformative ways.

Four Domains of Choice
Twelve Leadership Mindsets and Methods

INTENT	BEING
Compelling Vision	Net Forward Energy
Bold Aims	Flip Negative Energy
Decide-Notice-Acknowledge	Resilience

CHOOSING TO LEAD

LANGUAGE	ROLES
Leadership Speech Acts	Role Switching
Leadership Stories	5 Dimensions of Action
Access Abundance	Pacing Events

INTENT

Compelling Vision
A compelling and actionable leadership vision comes from the intersection of our circles of influence and the needs of others. Gain insight into how leaders effectively marshal and grow our circles of influence to meet the critical needs of others.

Bold Aims
Aims create systems and systems create results. Establish big goals that lead to the systems necessary for generating results and impact at far greater scale. Pursuing Bold Aims is rewarding work that speaks directly to our desire for purpose and meaning.

Decide-Notice-Acknowledge
Systematically appreciating what we want as we encounter it will call more of it into the world. This is a better approach than telling people what to do. Acquire the uplifting and joyous habit of Acknowledgement to deliberately generate more of the attitudes, behaviors, actions, and results we want in the world.

BEING

Net Forward Energy
Leaders take accountability for the energy that we project and that we cultivate in others. Learn powerful ways to consciously generate positive Net Forward Energy in ourselves and others.

Flip Negative Energy
Negative energy often can be tremendous hidden asset. Discover how to see the positive potential in negative energy. Learn Methods for channeling this energy into progress for the benefit of both the source of the negative energy and the larger good.

Resilience
When times are tough, leaders strengthen and draw from our personal and professional Resilience. Learn how to get comfortable with Being uncomfortable in what Mary Lou Andersen calls *"the lonely place between the now and the not yet."* Gain insight and understanding on how to tap into five sources of Resilience to sustain ourselves while helping our colleagues, families, and others to develop and draw from their own reservoirs of Resilience.

LANGUAGE

Leadership Speech Acts

Leadership occurs through Language. Identify and eliminate undesirable gossip, blame, and insults that are almost always counterproductive. Gain command of the eight key Leadership Speech Acts that we can use with system and method to generate action and forward momentum:

Eight Leadership Speech Acts

1. **Make Declarations** of a vision in defining ourselves to the world;
2. Use evidence-based **Assertions** to show the vision is within our reach;
3. **Make Requests and Offers** to secure commitments from others;
4. Make, deliver on, and seek **Commitments** as the real work of leadership;
5. **Acknowledge** behaviors and achievements to appreciate, empower, and generate more of what we want in the world;
6. Gain control of our **Assessments** to be more interpersonally effective;
7. Learn to say **"Yes, and…"** to find ways to embrace the ideas and actions of others and to create synergy;
8. Create and use **Effective Questions** to generate productive Mindsets in ourselves and others.

Note: "Speech Acts" is an unusual expression. We initially thought it was a term originating with the article where we first encountered it. It turns out that there is an extensive body of literature about Speech Acts, which we have applied to our own work and study of leadership.

Leadership Stories

Leaders speak about their identity and intentions in certain ways. They tell stories that call on others to join with them and each other in pursuing a Compelling Vision. Learn to use the Speech Acts that provide the unique and powerful building blocks of your own story and enhance your ability to shine light on the stories of others.

Access Abundance

Leaders use two key Speech Acts, Requests and Offers, to access natural Abundance. They do it with system and method. Gain the necessary awareness, understanding, and courage to systematically make Requests and Offers to intentionally create greater Abundance in our work and our lives.

ROLES

Role Switching

In collective organized activity, leadership is markedly different from three other Roles of Management, Administration, and Observation. Discover the powerful distinctions in accountability for results, responsibility for resources, and access to knowledge that help to define and inform the deliberate practice of a leadership Role. Gain insight on the need to "switch" Roles, or to get assistance from others, depending on the situations we encounter.

5 Dimensions of Action

A gift of leadership is the freedom it provides to reach out to others. Leaders embrace accountability for action in five different dimensions where we encounter others: Up, Down, Sideways, Process, and Public. Gain insight on how to perform effectively in each of these key dimensions.

Pacing Events

Leaders intentionally and proactively use meetings and other events to bring the future we want into the world. Pacing Events are a way to organize our meetings to generate meaningful results in uplifting ways. They are a powerful and efficient way to apply many of the Mindsets and Methods synergistically. Each of us can choose to turn conferences, webinars, staff meetings, virtual calls, and other events into more joyous and uplifting "result engines." Pacing Events also provide each of us with an opportunity to experiment with hands-on development of our own unique Signature Style.

These leadership **Mindsets and Methods** are highly effective. Extraordinary results are documented throughout our book. We show how systematic use of the Mindsets and Methods has contributed to dramatic and lasting national increases in organ donation, micro loans lifting tens of thousands of the poorest women in Haiti out of poverty, improved indoor air quality across the nation, major national improvements in hospital safety, and more. We invite you to join with us and with thousands of other leaders in spreading the effectiveness and joy that comes from disciplined use of these **Mindsets and Methods.**

Crafting a Signature Style of Leadership

All of us have our own singular ways of interacting and engaging with the world. Some of us are focused on achieving bottom-line results—generating social impacts, amassing wealth, building businesses, making things, etc. Others are especially interested in service to others, some in collaborating with colleagues. Still others love the thrill of action and performance in high-stakes situations. We all bring something unique and different to the world. We all have our own style.

Leadership is no different. Certain Mindsets and Methods may hold special appeal. Leaders focused on bottom-line results may be drawn to the use of Bold Aims. Leaders who love interacting and engaging with others may be more drawn to Language like Acknowledgement, Requests, and Offers. Those of us motivated by service to others may be particularly drawn to Compelling Vision. Regardless of which come to us most naturally, we know they work, and they become even more effective and more joyous when we use them in synergistic combinations that align with our own Signature Style.

The final chapter in *Choosing to Lead* is designed to help each of us assimilate and devise ways of testing and adapting the Mindsets and Methods to our own diverse lives and work. The final section of the book will help readers to more consciously craft, refine and augment our own unique Signature Style of leadership.

Do the Mindsets and Methods Support Malevolent Leadership?

In this book we use the term "leadership" to denote a positive force in the world. Leadership is presented as a benevolent undertaking.

Yet we recognize that throughout history there are people seen as leaders who have taken their followers to dark and evil places. Adolf Hitler channeled the anger and grievances of the German people following World War I into inhumane and destructive ends that produced World War II and the Holocaust. He was terrifyingly effective in mobilizing his followers to these ends.

Can leadership be intentionally malevolent? No.

No, not the way we define leadership in this book. People like Hitler who stand out in front of a "malevolent" movement we would call "manipulators." A manipulator uses the vulnerabilities of one group to pit it against another group for his or her own benefit. Such a person frequently resorts to non-leadership Language such as blame, insults, toxic opinions, excuses, and fraudulent information. It's easy to distinguish leaders from manipulators. True leaders inspire the mindset of service and altruism; manipulators inspire the mindset of fear, resentment and sometimes hatred toward those perceived as weak, different, or questioning of authority.

What about the Mindsets and Methods profiled in this book? Can they be applied to nefarious ends? No.

Our leadership perspective is entirely oriented towards constructive, collaborative, and altruistic ends. The mission of *Choosing to Lead* is to help us to respond to stimuli, including negative stimuli, to the benefit of both ourselves and others. Making these Choices requires us to harness our own emotions and respond effectively to the emotions of others with thoughtfulness and discipline.

Automatic, blink responses to emotions such as fear and resentment are not consistent with our view of leadership. To use Jonathan Haidt's metaphor of the Rider and the Elephant, these automatic responses unleash and stoke the negative energy of our Elephant into destructive purposes. Fear, anger, resentment, and grievance are terrible allies.

Embrace the Good

If we find ourselves feeling helpless, or growing fearful of and angry at others, we should step back, examine the source of our negative feelings and understand the nature of the transaction that is occurring. Let's not allow the manipulative actions or the knee-jerk responses of others to dictate a harmful or self-punitive response on our part.

We try not to slip into the practice of calling people "leaders" simply because they hold positions of authority or are out in front. The leadership Mindsets and Methods profiled here can help each of us and many leaders-in-the-making to pursue intelligent Choices of service, collaboration, and altruism to the benefit of all.

Learning From the Leadership Stories of Others

Many of the Mindsets and Methods profiled here derive from our experience in working with hundreds of other highly effective leaders. Don Berwick MD, the Founding CEO of the Institute for Healthcare Improvement and former Administrator of the Centers for Medicare and Medicaid Services, taught us and hundreds of thousands of others how to use Bold Aims to generate exhilarating rapid improvement and results. Bob and Barb Malizzo taught clinicians, hospital executives, and others how committed leaders can transcend tragedy, and, drawing from the domain of Being, become catalysts for life-saving improvements for millions of patients. Some of these leaders were the source of Mindsets and Methods, while others provide examples of these Mindsets and Methods in action.

These Leadership Stories take us out of the hypothetical and into the real-world challenges and rewards of leadership. *Choosing to Lead* relates true and vibrant Leadership Stories in the domains of Intent, Being, Language, and Roles. Some of these stories are riveting first-person accounts by the leaders as related to us and others in a series of training sessions in 2021. Some are first-person accounts by Dennis, who teamed with John as Dennis's executive architect and leadership coach on this work, dating back to 1991. Other stories are our own descriptions of the insightful and moving examples of leaders we have encountered over decades of shared work.

Look for Defining Moments

In studying these stories, we encounter some of the key Defining Moments which helped these leaders embrace their true callings. In many cases, these Defining Moments resulted in deeply personal leadership Choices that helped guide the direction of lives and careers. Readers will learn that Defining Moments can arise from a conversation with a stranger on an airplane, as a flash of insight during an annual meditation, through a reassignment and demotion in a large federal agency, and in other surprising venues and situations.

Through the examples of others, we see how Defining Moments can manifest through both conscious re-direction and decision-making on our part, and through our leadership Choices in response to unexpected and unforeseen situations. We can learn to discern when defining moments show up in our lives; are we seeking them, ignoring them, resisting them—or are we embracing them?

In-Depth Leadership Stories

We provide in-depth examples of the Leadership Stories of seven leaders whose work and contributions are especially aligned with one of the four leadership domains:

INTENT

SANJEEV ARORA MD is a thoughtful, caring medical specialist in New Mexico who spent many years caring for patients with liver diseases like Hepatitis. Propelled by deep concern for patients who were not able to gain access to his life-saving treatments, he made leadership Choices that would not only transform his life but would also transform the lives of patients and clinicians throughout the world.

DON BERWICK MD, MPP is one of the world's foremost leaders in healthcare quality improvement. A passionate medical expert and committed healthcare provider, he and his leadership team at the Institute for Healthcare Improvement made a leadership Choice in 2004 to engage nearly all of the nation's hospitals in a nationwide campaign and to get the country on a rapid pathway to saving 100,000 lives.

BEING

BOB AND BARB MALIZZO are two committed, thoughtful parents who suffered the tragic and unexpected death of their daughter to a grievous and preventable medical error. They made extraordinary and deeply personal leadership Choices to channel their loss into service and action aimed at helping others.

ANNE H. HASTINGS is an organized, hard-driving, smart consultant who left a highly successful practice in the nation's capital, determined to make an impact on the lives of others less fortunate than herself. She chose to move to one of the poorest nations on earth—where she didn't speak the language—and entered into an entirely different profession of international banking. Learn how she used Resilience and other Mindsets and Methods to generate transformative and lasting results for tens of thousands of the world's most vulnerable women and families.

LANGUAGE

SUSAN MCVEY DILLON
is a committed, caring, no-nonsense special education teacher from Pennsylvania. She and her family suffered the catastrophic loss of a loved one, which led to her resolute choice to help several other parents to avoid the loss of their children. Her passionate and clear requests and offers helped transform medical practice—first in her own local community, then in her home state, and later across the nation.

ROLES

JOHN CHESSARE MD, MPH
is a practical and visionary pediatrician and hospital executive. Seeing lots of committed medical professionals who were trapped in poorly designed systems, he made a leadership Choice early in his career to pursue the development of systems needed for ensuring top quality healthcare. He ultimately helped thousands of clinicians and staff throughout an entire hospital and health system in Baltimore to commit and act on the constant daily Choices necessary to dramatically transform and improve the quality of care for their patients.

Leadership Stories by Authors

There are several in-depth Leadership Stories throughout the book that describe co-author Dennis Wagner's own learnings and experiences throughout his 30+ year career of leading large-scale change initiatives for the United States government. John Scanlon teamed with Dennis on much of this work as his executive architect, leadership coach, and fellow implementer.

Dennis describes leadership efforts he helped to launch and implement in several agencies. As a new employee in a staff position, low in the Environmental Protection Agency hierarchy, he and his colleagues move the larger federal structure into more effective policy and action to address serious public health hazards associated with radioactive radon gas in homes. A dormant campaign is made successful. In a second agency, the Health Resources and Services Administration, he leads a team that seizes an opportunity to increase organ donation rates in hospitals. The initiative transforms the nation's donation system. It increases the number of organ donors and saves several thousand more lives a year. A chapter near the end of the book chronicles Dennis's journey through a disruptive reassignment and demotion in a large federal agency. It shines a light on how, through a series of Defining Moments, sometimes we can transform what we consider to be the worst that could happen into an opportunity to create one of the most enriching experiences of our lives.

Leadership Stories Draw from Multiple Mindsets, Methods, and Domains

Each of these key stories is grounded in the Mindsets and Methods profiled in the four domains. At the same time, it's important to recognize that each of the Leadership Stories and vignettes are not confined to a single Mindset and Method nor only to the domain with which they are associated.

For example, while Anne H. Hastings' leadership story is a stirring illustration of Resilience and appears in the Being domain, it also serves as an example of a leader who expanded her circle of influence in pursuit of a Compelling Vision that has helped create micro loans for the most impoverished and vulnerable women in the Western Hemisphere. Anne's story, like others profiled here, cuts across multiple domains and draws on multiple leadership Mindsets and Methods.

Diverse and Compelling Vignettes from Exemplar Leaders in All Walks of Life

In addition to these in-depth case studies of leadership in action, we have included shorter stories and vignettes from still other colleagues and exemplary leaders who have contributed to shared learning, action, and transformational results.

To give you a sense of the range and depth of their leadership, a few of the extraordinary individuals listed below are profiled in brief on the next four pages.

INTENT	Joe McCannon	100,000 Lives Campaign Manager
	Tom Evans MD	CEO, Iowa Healthcare Collaborative
	Marilyn Gaston MD	Assistant Surgeon General and Bureau Director, Health Resources and Services Administration
	Mary Lou Andersen	Deputy Bureau Director, Health Resources and Services Administration
	Phyllis Busansky	Chairwoman, Hillsborough County Commission
	Alan McKenzie	Executive Director, Buncombe County Medical Society
BEING	Doug Krug	Author, Leadership Coach, and Thought Leader
	Carolyn Candiello	Vice President, Quality and Patient Safety, Greater Baltimore Medical Center
	Marie Schall	Senior Director, Institute for Healthcare Improvement
	Jeneen Iwugo	Deputy Center Director, Centers for Medicare and Medicaid Services
	Phyllis Busansky	Chairwoman, Hillsborough County Commission

LANGUAGE	Tracy Enger	Program Manager, U.S. Environmental Protection Agency
	Paul McGann MD	Deputy Chief Medical Officer, Centers for Medicare and Medicaid Services
	Jade Perdue	Federal Program Leader and Mother of Twins
	Paul O'Neill	CEO of Alcoa and Principal, Council for Excellence in Government
	Howard Nathan	CEO, Gift of Life Donor Program
	Ginny McBride	Collaborative Improvement Advisor, Health Resources and Services Administration
ROLES	Mark Abramson	Founding President and CEO, Council for Excellence in Government
	Carolyn Candiello	Vice President, Quality and Patient Safety, Greater Baltimore Medical Center
	John Mitchell & Brenda Doroski	Program Managers, U.S. Environmental Protection Agency
	Steven Chen	Associate Dean for Clinical Affairs, University of Southern California Mann School of Pharmacy
LEADERSHIP STYLE	Karen Minyard	CEO, Georgia Health Policy Center
	Zandra Glenn	Pharmacist and National Leader in Quality Improvement
	Elizabeth "Betty" Duke	Administrator, Health Resources and Services Administration
	Frank Zampiello MD	Captain, U.S. Public Health Service and National Leader in Quality Improvement
	Helen Bottenfield	Nurse and National Organ Donation Leader

JOE MCCANNON

Former Director of the Institute for Healthcare Improvement's 100,000 Lives Campaign, Joe describes how his disciplined approach to systematic quality improvement to precipitate large scale change required a clear focus on Bold Aims, Resilience, and learning in the face of adversity.

TOM EVANS MD

An extroverted, likeable, and engaging family practice physician and medical system leader, Tom recounts how collaboration and teaming with others has revealed the natural Abundance that surrounds all of us. He demonstrates the ability to surface the possibility and opportunity that flows from a Compelling Vision.

ALAN MCKENZIE

A focused, disciplined, and deliberate manager and leader, Alan describes how he and his colleagues used DNA (Decide-Notice-Acknowledge) to great effect in organizing and connecting medical doctors in smart ways to have dramatic impacts on healthcare for uninsured low-income people in Buncombe County NC, and then in more than 50 communities across the nation.

DOUG KRUG

A best-selling author and national thought-leader, Doug taught us and thousands of our colleagues about the conscious and intentional cultivation of Net Forward Energy, the use of Effective Questions, and the systematic practice of DNA (Decide-Notice-Acknowledge) to call more of what we want into the world.

MARIE SCHALL

Marie is a thoughtful, open-minded, and committed national quality improvement expert who served for many years as a key leader in the Institute for Healthcare Improvement. All of us have much to learn from the Mindsets and Methods that Marie uses to effectively Flip Negative Energy and thorny challenges into opportunities, constructive action, and next steps.

TRACY ENGER

A talented, bold, and vivacious facilitator, coach, and senior analyst at the US Environmental Protection Agency, Tracy shares how she learned about the powerful use of Language in a collaborative initiative to help leaders in Thailand's Pollution Control Department in their work.

BRENDA DOROSKI and JOHN MITCHELL

Serving as the foundational leaders of a global initiative to improve cook stoves for millions of the poorest families on the planet, Brenda and John used their platform with the US Environmental Protection Agency to organize and knit together initiatives from countries throughout the world; they drew on many of the leadership Mindsets and Methods—including especially the systematic use of Pacing Events—to build positive "can do" energy and to spread best practices among their hundreds of worldwide partners.

STEVEN CHEN

A disciplined and hard-working Associate Dean at the University of Southern California Mann School of Pharmacy, Steven describes how learning about the Mindsets and Methods—particularly the distinctions between management and leadership—has helped him to step out and assume accountability for results, especially when resources are lacking.

KAREN MINYARD

Karen is a highly skilled state and national leader and policy expert. She and her team at the Georgia Health Policy Center have been effective in developing and testing policies and practices in Georgia, and then teaming with others to spread them nationally, especially throughout vulnerable communities and rural America.

ZANDRA GLENN

An outgoing, collaborative, and insightful pharmacist and national quality improvement leader, Zandra shares how adopting a Signature Style has influenced all aspects of her life, including with her children.

Every one of these exemplars—and many others contained in these pages—provide us with vivid illustrations of leadership in action. Learn from the expertise, wisdom and experience of these talented leaders who hail from diverse walks of life.

These Leadership Stories are a source of rich learning and practical application, told by ordinary people who chose to lead in extraordinary ways. We invite you to learn from their efforts, and to explore your own capacity for generating uplifting, unforgettable and extraordinary results.

Learn to make smart, non-default Leadership Choices.

Choose action.

Choose effective, joyous, rewarding careers and lives.

Choose to lead.

We Choose Our Leadership
INTENT

*What You Can Do,
or Dream You Can, Begin It;
Boldness Has Genius, Power,
and Magic in It*

JOHANN WOLFGANG VON GOETHE
German Writer
Polymath

translation of Johann Wolfgang vonGoethe
by Irish poet John Anster

INTENT

Compelling Vision

Bold Aims

Decide-Notice-Acknowledge

Leadership Intent is the bold, compelling change we desire to create for a better future. But that future is almost always beyond what a leader can achieve on their own. To realize the future, the leader must choose to team with others and bring the collective means into play.

Intent is exciting and self-defining. It's voluntary. It's public. It's marked by action and commitment to the long run. The leader stands for the chosen future to be realized, giving their Intent both clarity and energy. There is nothing casual or occasional in choosing to lead with Intent.

In this chapter on Intent, we demonstrate how this particular domain of leadership Choice is expressed through three powerful Mindsets and Methods. Intent can be a Compelling Vision to be shared with others; Intent can be a Bold Aim that we and others commit to achieve; Intent can be the commitment to Decide-Notice-Acknowledge (DNA) those things that we seek to bring more of into the world. These Mindsets and Methods help define our leadership Intent and provide proven ways to tackle daunting challenges.

Compelling Vision is not just imagined, it is experienced. It exists at the intersection of the circumstances within our control and the serious, unmet needs that are beyond our ability to address single-handedly. These unmet needs grab our attention and make the Vision compelling.

Our first Leadership Story in this chapter describes how Dr. Sanjeev Arora, a physician and professor in New Mexico, was driven by a Compelling Vision to remedy a major and sometimes deadly service gap in local health care. Our second Leadership Story relates the Compelling Vision that inspired Dennis Wagner and a team of employees in the federal Environmental Protection Agency to address dangerously elevated levels of radioactive radon gas in millions of homes across the nation.

These two stories demonstrate the necessity of tapping into our circles of influence, the people with whom we are already in relationship, enabling them to contribute and magnifying their influence and impact. The expansion of our circles of influence to address compelling needs is a defining element of leading with Intent.

As you read Dr. Arora and Dennis's stories, watch for the dynamic between activating one's circle of influence and how the circle's embrace of a Compelling Vision can snowball and expand.

Bold Aims are a powerful, attention-getting Method for expressing Intent. With Bold Aims, a leadership team translates a Compelling Vision of the future into specific targets that ourselves and others commit to achieving by a specific date. Bold Aims enable a leader to organize and activate a leadership campaign involving multiple players and organizational units into a major community of integrated action.

A second set of Leadership Stories in the chapter shows how Compelling Visions are translated into Bold Aims and how campaigns are launched and implemented to achieve those Aims. In the first story, Don Berwick MD, recognizes hospital safety as an urgent problem requiring an organized national effort to engage thousands of hospitals. In the second story, a federal team led by Dennis Wagner uses their access to hospital performance information to craft a Bold Aim that achieves a dramatic increase in national organ donation rates over a multi-year campaign.

Decide-Notice-Acknowledge (DNA) drives the achievement of Bold Aims and Compelling Vision by energizing our circles of influence. Leaders actively notice and appreciate the practices, behaviors, results, and performance outliers who are already bringing us closer to our intended future. DNA embodies the principle of "beginning with the end in mind."

The practice of DNA makes leadership work easier and more rewarding. It is based on the belief that the answers we seek are already in the room, and the future we strive for already exists somewhere, waiting for us to reach for it. In addition to performing the traditional heavy lifting of solving difficult problems, inventing solutions, convincing others, we add to our repertoire the joyous activity of recognizing and celebrating already existing examples of what we want. We find people doing these things and bring them forward.

In our section on DNA, we cite specific examples of how leaders and small teams brought entire communities of practice to new and better places through practical application of DNA. These cases were set in motion by the 100% Access and Zero Disparities campaign led by Dr. Marilyn Gaston of the Health Resources and Services Administration (HRSA) and directly supported by the co-authors. In the first case, we describe a sales tax campaign to help finance health care for the poor in Hillsborough County, Florida led by County Commissioner Phyllis Busansky. In the second case, Project Access, a volunteer medical care program for the uninsured poor in Asheville, NC, is led by one of our key partners, Alan McKenzie. Alan's narrative recounts the many ways DNA can be a force in creating real assets and results. A third case touches on the use of DNA "change packages" in the Organ Donation Breakthrough Collaborative led by Dennis and a federal team.

All together, these Leadership Stories and cases illustrate how Compelling Vision, Bold Aim, and DNA guide our Choices and actions within the leadership domain of Intent. As we are reminded at the top of this section: *Boldness has genius, power, and magic in it.* Compelling Vision delivers the genius; Bold Aim, the power; DNA, the magic. It is by actively engaging and expanding our circles of influence that we gain the knowledge and resources we require to address serious unmet needs at a level that is truly transformational.

Begin it now.

Dr. Sanjeev Arora's Leadership Story:
Project ECHO

In 2015, Dennis was poised to deliver a presentation in Santa Fe, New Mexico, to the Board of Directors of a large health care Quality Improvement Organization (QIO) serving the southwestern US. Over 100 senior officials from the region and the executive team from the Quality Improvement Organization were in attendance. Dennis was representing the Centers for Medicare and Medicaid Services (CMS), the federal agency that funded and provided oversight for quality improvement in tens of thousands of hospitals, nursing homes, clinical practices, and other organizations.

Directly before presentation, Dennis was introduced to another speaker, Dr. Sanjeev Arora, a professor of medicine at the University of New Mexico and a practicing liver disease specialist. Why, Dennis remembers wondering, would a liver disease specialist be addressing the Board of a Quality Improvement Organization?

A Leader with a Riveting Agenda

Dr. Arora spoke first, and "why" became immediately clear. He described the far-reaching impact of Project ECHO (Extension for Community Health Outcomes), which he had founded in response to the life-threatening problem of access to specialty care in New Mexico. Dr. Arora related ECHO's singular impact on patient health, achieving extraordinary, life-saving results which were backed by peer-reviewed journals. Given its success, Dr. Arora was now expanding the ECHO model nationally and internationally, employing its innovative approach which he described as the "democratization of expert knowledge."

In the following pages, Dr. Arora describes the formative period of his Project ECHO leadership story. It is a story of personal discovery and growth achieved by transforming the ineffective system he found himself in.

As you read about his journey, look for three powerful leadership dynamics at work:

1. Dr. Arora in his every-day work becomes aware of a need to transform a significant part of New Mexico's health care system. He chooses to pursue a vision of a better future for a large patient population in the State.

2. Despite a total lack of authority or resources, Dr. Arora solicits and secures commitments from others to put in place a transformative platform managed and administered in an Intentional way to realize the vision. The platform makes an important medical specialty in short supply more readily available through a leveraging innovation.

3. As Dr. Arora encounters others, the vision expands and the platform spreads nationally and then internationally. Others step forward into leadership Roles and partner with Dr. Arora. The vision grows from saving thousands to serving millions. Dr. Arora's leadership actions generate an upward spiral of life-saving specialty care throughout the world.

Consider how these leadership dynamics in Dr. Arora's story show up in our own lives and in the lives of others we know.

LEADERSHIP STORY

Project ECHO and the Democratization of Expert Knowledge

by **Sanjeev Arora MD**

In 2001, a 43-year-old woman showed up in my clinic seeking treatment for Hepatitis C, a condition she had been aware of for eight years. She was a single parent with two children, a 14-year-old boy and 9-year-old girl. With concern, I asked why she had waited so long to get treatment.

Hepatitis C is a liver infection caused by the hepatitis C virus (HCV). Untreated it causes liver damage, cancer and even death. Hepatitis C is spread through contact with blood from an infected person. In the 1990s and early 2000s, the treatment regimen for patients was more complex than it is today. Hepatitis C is now treated using direct acting antiviral (DAA) tablets. Over 90% of people infected with Hepatitis C virus can now be cured of their infection, regardless of HCV genotype, with 8–12 weeks of oral therapy.

"I called but was told there was an eight-month wait for an appointment," she explained. But the real problem was that there was no specialist in her hometown; she would have to make 12 weekly trips for treatment. As a single working mother living 200 miles away with a one-year-old baby, there was no way she could take off time from work and make the 400-mile round-trip each week.

A severe pain in her abdomen had finally brought the patient into the clinic that day. An ultrasound revealed a cancer on her liver the size of a tennis ball. We commenced treatment, but it was too late. She passed away six months later, leaving two children alone in the world.

A Leadership Vision Surfaces

Pondering this tragic death, I asked myself: "Why did she die when we know how to treat this disease, when we have medicines that work, and when we live in the richest country in the world?"

The answer came right back to me: She died because the right knowledge did not exist at the right place at the right time. This was an important insight for me; even with all the medicines and the treatment regimens at hand, none of that matters without the right knowledge in the right place at the right time to serve the needs of our patients.

The mother who died was just one of many patients with similar conditions seeking treatment from my gastroenterology and hematology practice. There were no specialists in New Mexico's rural areas who could treat Hepatitis C at the scale necessary to save the lives of the thousands of people who needed treatment. I calculated that in New Mexico, with a population of about 2 million, nearly 28,000 patients had been diagnosed with Hepatitis C, yet fewer than 1,500 were receiving treatment.

I was struggling to find a way to help, but being an expert in liver disease made no difference if I couldn't reach people; the only people I could treat were the ones who were able to show up in person. I felt trapped by my clinic calendar and by the geographic distance between me and the people who desperately needed my care.

Bringing more highly trained specialists into rural areas was not a plausible option. Even doubling or tripling the number of hepatologists in New Mexico would not solve the problem. This was not just a matter of more efficient administration or more effective management of existing resources. Compared to currently available resources, the need was extraordinary and could not be adequately addressed with a business-as-usual approach.

A Flash of Insight, And A Choice

In 2003, I turned 46 and found myself at a stage where I was exploring how to spend the rest of my career. My life had been blessed: I had a family, a fulfilling career, financial security. Resorting to my daily practice of meditation, I petitioned the universe for guidance on what to do with the second half of my life.

The Answer came: "You have earned so much in the first half of your life; devote the next half of your life to giving back." It was a message akin to, "to whom more is given, more is expected." I had been provided a unique set of skills, and these were the skills I needed to use in service to others.

It was over the holiday season some months later, during my annual tradition of a longer, six-hour meditation, that I envisioned the model that would allow me to perform that service. The model wasn't derived through logic—it came as a flash of insight. Literally from that day onward, my life changed. The answer was: *moving knowledge, not people.*

Using My Experience and Relationships to Address a System Shortfall

It was through a university fellowship in Boston that I had become an expert gastroenterologist and hepatologist by seeing patients and then presenting their cases to my professor. More patients, more presentations, and so on. I also learned from the cases of my fellow residents. After two years of seeing individual patients, presenting to my professor, and teaming with other residents, I became a specialist.

The way forward became clear to me: I could use the same educational approach to train new Hepatitis C specialists in New Mexico. I would reach out across the entire state and invite local primary care doctors and nurse practitioners of patients with Hepatitis C to join the mission of becoming specialists in the treatment of the infection.

These local doctors and nurses would not have to travel to the university to train; we would use video-conferencing to present cases and share treatment protocols, and a web-based database to monitor patient outcomes. (While the use of video conference might seem ordinary in the 2020s era of pandemic-inspired virtual platforms, such a widespread approach was a novelty in 2003 and had not been applied to training and treating a disease on such a scale.)

Persistent Asking Enrolls Clinicians

Although the expertise and training model were available, funding and organizational support for this approach were nonexistent. And I still had the obligation of my full-time role at the Academic Medical Center.

But I did have weekends. And so I started driving around the state of New Mexico, using my own resources to present to doctors, nurses and physician assistants in primary care settings. "Look," I would tell my sparse audiences, "people are dying of hepatitis in this community. I need one of you to train with me. I will mentor you so that you can take care of them."

I was asking local doctors and other clinicians to devote a few hours a week for six months to be mentored, becoming experts via a two-hour video conference every week to help their community. Initially,

I had no takers. Clinicians would say, "This is too complicated, it's too dangerous. We haven't had fellowships like yours to learn this."

But as a professor, giving talks came naturally to me. I was persistent; I was recruiting; I was evangelizing the model. Ultimately, I spoke to over one thousand clinicians, and in the end, I found my first 21 enrollees, clinicians who were located in health centers in rural areas and in the state prison clinics.

Launch of Project ECHO in New Mexico

Project ECHO, Extension for Community Health Outcomes, was launched in 2003 with our first 21 participating clinicians. I recruited university faculty—liver specialists, psychiatrists, and pharmacists—to team with me and volunteer two hours a week to extend liver treatment across the state. Our intent was to democratize the expert knowledge of the university faculty and myself using video-conferencing to leverage our expertise.

ECHOs clinics occurred weekly, Wednesdays from 2-5 PM. The clinic greatly resembled the web-based meetings that are now a fixture of our covid-era professional lives. Clinicians from the 21 practices would convene by video with the university team and present the Hepatitis C cases of their patients, with approximately eight cases under discussion. Faculty kept their lectures to 15-minutes and shared treatment protocols. It was important to keep the sessions about real cases so that we could help practitioners solve the real problems of their patients.

New Mexico ECHO Demonstrates Quality, Performance, and Adaptability

Studies were showing that within 12 months of participation, these local doctors were becoming experts. On a scale of 1 (no skill) to 7 (able to teach others), their competency scores shot from 2.8 to 5.5, a remarkable increase.

Later research published in scholarly journals would show that our mostly rural ECHO sites provided the same level of care with viral suppression outcomes comparable to academic medical centers. The approach was working! By 2022, there were several hundred peer-reviewed publications documenting the performance of ECHO programs across a wide variety of conditions.

The New Mexico ECHO succeeded by giving expertise to clinicians on the ground and by supporting them with case review and performance monitoring of their patients. Once it was demonstrated that ECHO participants could absorb so much complexity, it was clear that this same methodology could be applied to other disease areas. Today in New Mexico, there are ECHO programs throughout the state for 29 disease conditions including HIV/AIDS, Rheumatology, High Risk Pregnancy, Diabetes, and Cardiovascular Disease.

It also became clear to those of us supporting Project ECHO that we had a model that could be spread to other States, and maybe even to other nations.

Hub and Spoke: Spreading a Force Multiplier Across the United States

As soon as ECHO launched, I began applying for grants to expand ECHO's capabilities and reach. After running ECHO for quite some time as a volunteer, I realized that I needed help and the program needed infrastructure. Our growing staff constantly wrote proposals, and today the expansion of ECHO is supported by a wide variety of public and private donations, contracts, and grants.

ECHO took off nationally upon winning a 2007 global Disruptive Innovations in Health and Health Care competition, sponsored by Ashoka's Changemakers and the Robert Wood Johnson Foundation's Pioneer Portfolio. Project ECHO received a $5 million grant to expand into other specialty areas and to spread the model. We began cultivating a relationship with the University of Washington Medical School to implement ECHO in Washington State.

With the award money, my team and I set up the needed infrastructure to spread the model to other disease conditions throughout the nation. We packaged the videoconferencing technology, the data system software, and the training program. More staff were hired to assume the more administrative tasks on behalf of the expert doctors and nurses who were willing to democratize their knowledge.

To enable our expansion, we took the step of organizing ECHO into a replicable hub-and-spoke system. The hub is the center of expertise, usually an academic institution; the spokes are local clinicians serving the population. This structure creates a "force multiplier," with each expert enabled to endow dozens of practitioners with expert knowledge in a disciplined and managed way.

Other universities started following the University of Washington to establish hubs. A number of federal agencies worked with our team to create ECHOs to support their own programs, and soon several institutions became "super hubs," helping us establish and support other hubs in their regions.

Project ECHO In India and Beyond

I was curious to test the ECHO model in a low-income country. I had grown up in India before leaving at the age of 23, and it seemed logical to me that the country of my birth might benefit from this program. Lacking any outside funding, my wife, also a doctor, and I decided to fund the effort ourselves.

There is a massive need for better specialty care throughout the world. Countries like India have far less medical technology available than the US; they have less of everything. At the outset, we found that best-practice guidelines from the US were far too expensive to implement. For ECHO to succeed, we needed to start with a different question: "How do experts in India solve problems in India?" The task became clear, to democratize the best practices already in place.

ECHO administrators gained insight into how to operate in low-income countries by bringing in local care providers to solve local challenges. We also learned that the poorest people typically receive care only through government agencies funded by taxes. Foundations and philanthropy can jumpstart this work but cannot provide it over the long term. So we shifted our focus onto convincing government agencies that ECHO was a viable training program.

Often the governments or medical establishments in these countries were initially skeptical that their systems could replicate the ECHO model, so we worked to support them closely in their first tests; as the model revealed its effectiveness, the governments often chose to adopt it.

This global work continues and requires a lot of evangelizing on my part; I travel five to six months a year and deliver hundreds of talks. Today ECHO boasts 684 hub partners and learners in 179 countries around the world.

Project ECHO Becomes an International Force Multiplier with a Bold Vision

Once the effectiveness of the ECHO model became apparent, I realized that the program had the potential to be significantly more ambitious and could be adapted to treat other diseases. The level of avoidable death throughout the world is staggering; with Hepatitis alone, there are 350 million people in the world who require access to the right knowledge at the right place at the right time; 50,000 people die every day from the disease, even when medicine is available to treat them.

ECHO is not an academic mass-training exercise; it is a delivery system that can mean the difference between life and death. And although there are millions of specialists in the world, even if we doubled or tripled the number, we would still lack enough specialists in the right place at the right time to treat conditions. Once again, we needed a force multiplier.

I sensed that world-wide, there are thousands of people – not only clinicians, but teachers and other experts – who would be willing to dedicate two hours a week to help change the world. But they had the same problem that I struggled with at the beginning of my own journey: time and distance. ECHO could be adapted to give these specialists the platform to wield impact by devoting as little as two hours a week. I decided to do with Project ECHO what we had done with our expertise in Hepatitis C, only now, we would democratize our expertise in broadcasting ECHO far and wide by making it available to every university in the world.

ECHO now offers specialists the platform for free, with this simple message: "We will give you the technical assistance to run ECHO. Use it for your mission in life, no matter what that mission is. You can be a force multiplier for addiction treatment, for math and science education, for leadership development, whatever your expertise is, and to spread it at scale."

ECHO is now organized to accomplish the democratization of knowledge internationally, with a team in place to support experts and link them with clinicians and other specialists in their field. It is force multiplication at global scale.

In 2021, Project ECHO's vision became to "Touch the lives of one billion people by 2025." Given our past results, we believe this goal is completely within our grasp.

COVID-19, Seizing an Opportunity to Contribute and Grow

When the coronavirus pandemic struck in March of 2020, the entire global ECHO network pivoted resources to meet the COVID-19 threat around the world. Since 2020, ECHO programs have trained hundreds of thousands of health professionals in COVID-19 response.

In Africa, the pandemic has disrupted routine care and treatment for conditions such as HIV and tuberculosis, as well as screening for cancer and other diseases. We have partnered with local Ministries of Health, Centers for Disease Control, World Health Organization, and others to launch ECHOs and respond to the massive need for up-to-date information. In India, we have partnered with national and state governments to launch ECHOs to teach health workers across the country about COVID-19, from prevention to vaccination to the treatment of long-COVID.

Although the pandemic has been difficult for all of us, one bright spot is that ECHO has grown massively, reaching millions more within just the last two years and with adoption across Africa, India, Latin America, Southeast Asia, and around the world. These new ECHO networks will not only address the current needs arising from COVID-19, but will also address the pre-existing health disparities that these regions face, with the goal of strengthening the health systems most in need.

Each Step Creates New Possibilities

Today, my role is primarily focused on raising money and extending Project ECHO's capacity to support others. So many of us want to do good; ECHO gives us a way to do just that.

Since 2003, ECHO has added 644 hubs in 51 countries, and now has 28 super-hubs around the world. Globally ECHO has launched over 1600 programs across dozens of disease areas and other disciplines such as education, climate change, and many more. Project ECHO has raised over $200 million and worldwide partners have collectively raised over $2 billion to support these programs.

At ECHO, the mission is to democratize implementation of best practices for health care and education to underserved people all over the world. ECHO is well on track to reach its goal of touching one billion lives by 2025, saving the lives of millions in the process.

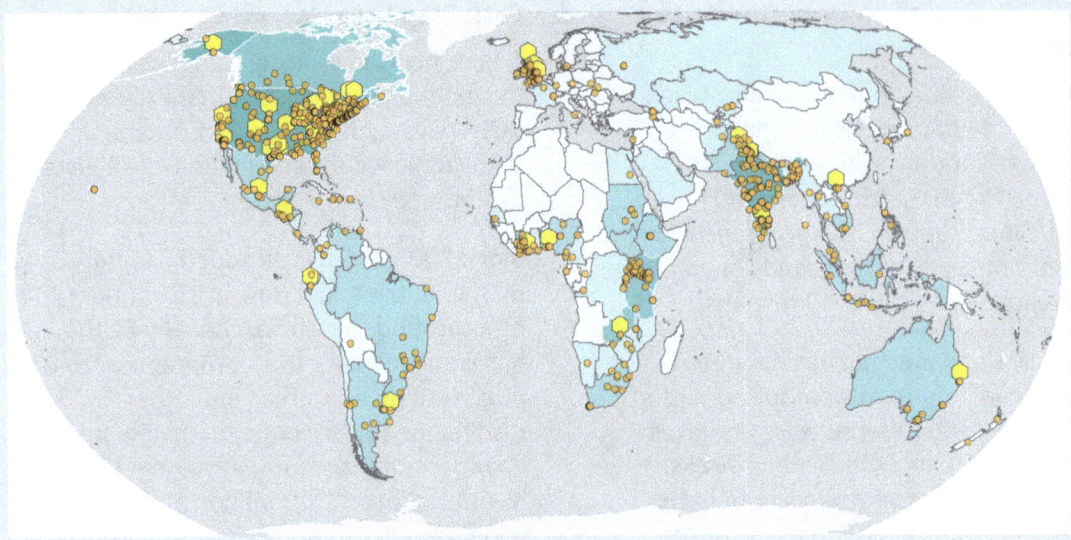

Global Footprint of Project ECHO

Project ECHO Team

Reflections on Dr. Sanjeev Arora's Leadership Story

Dr. Arora's leadership story is remarkable for where it begins, how it evolves, and how it continues to expand and democratize expertise amid a global health crisis. Teaching a medical specialty and practicing as an expert in the field would be a full career for most of us. But when Dr. Arora discovered a compelling need in his field that no one owned, he was called to act.

Choosing to Lead on Needs that Required Action

The larger healthcare system in New Mexico was falling far short of his and other's best efforts to care for a patient population. He saw patients who were in trouble because they did not have access to needed specialty care in their communities. From where he stood, Dr. Arora could see the problem was not going away and that no one was naturally accountable for solving it. There were, and would continue to be, too few specialists to meet the need. The source of his vision was the intersection of the compelling needs of patients and his own circle of influence as a teacher and medical specialty physician.

Transformation Requires Leadership; Management and Administration are Not Enough

Incrementally better management and more efficient administration of the current healthcare system was not a solution. This inability to respond to a problem situation is common in large systems made up of multiple, independent organizations with distributed authority. Problems suddenly emerge for which no one is accountable or responsible. Dr. Arora realized that he faced a challenge that required the region's delivery system to be transformed.

Dr. Arora turned to the arena he knew, his colleagues in academia and clinicians in the field. From his own training to be a specialist he saw a way to spread specialized knowledge into everyday clinical practice. He created a Compelling Vision where patients get the specialty care they need through their primary care physician, physician assistant, or certified nurse practitioner. It was the democratization of expert knowledge through a force multiplier structure.

Leadership Behavior Surfaces Abundance

Successful system transformation is often transferable to like systems. Addressing the New Mexico Hepatitis C care gap inspired Dr. Arora to apply the ECHO model to other diseases needing specialty treatment. He made the platform infrastructure transmittable to other universities and potential hub organizations across the nation. Dr. Arora then chose to take ECHO into countries across the world. The requests and offers triggered by that insight opened a world of Abundance, enabling Dr. Arora to establish a new Bold Aim: "Touch the lives of one billion people by 2025." (Further detail on how leaders can use requests and offers to generate Abundance is detailed in the chapter on Language.) As a system transformation, Project ECHO not only improves the lives of the patients it touches, it also improves the lives and careers of the clinicians who step up to provide new, expanded, higher levels of treatment for their patients. For healthcare providers who care deeply about the needed life-saving treatments available to their patients, Project ECHO is truly a lifeline.

The career transformations experienced by healthcare providers is on full display at the global MetaECHO Conference that is hosted at the original home of Project ECHO in Albuquerque, NM. Nearly a thousand healthcare leaders, government officials, clinicians and others convene every few years in an electrifying four-day event to hear from world-renowned speakers, to share cutting-edge research and evaluation methods, and to increase shared momentum for sustainable change. Participants converge from across the world including Uruguay, India, the United States, South Africa, Europe, and Australia. Session titles like "Scaling ECHO India: Lessons from the World's Largest Democracy" give some insight into the reach, energy, and impact of ECHO's work.

We Can Apply These Insights in Our Own Lives

Leaders like Dr. Arora are showing us how the big social economic systems we live and work in can be transformed for the benefit of those in need. In our own fields of work, each of us can choose to become more aware of the opportunity for creating transformative management and administrative systems that achieve a leadership vision. By applying lessons from Dr. Arora's story, we may be able to better see ways to introduce the missing accountability and responsibility into our own systems—large and small— through leadership efforts.

We can ask ourselves:

What are the unmet and compelling needs of others I am encountering in my own work and life?

What are ways I can use my own circle of influence to address these needs?

What new relationships can I establish to help others achieve their leadership visions?

As we surface leadership Choices, we may or may not step into a career-altering journey on the scale of the one pursued by Dr. Arora. If we are not ready to choose to lead ourselves, then we can encourage and support others who are interested and ready to lead. We can call for the systems we work and live in to be open to the kind of leadership driven innovation and programming of Project ECHO. We can call for it, expect it, and celebrate it when we see this kind of leadership appear.

Compelling Vision:
From Health Care to Environmental Policy

Dr. Arora's story illustrates how a Compelling Vision grows out of his lived experience. In the following section, a second Leadership Story is presented showing the same defining dynamic in a different setting and situation. While Dr. Arora's story takes place in a professional service setting, the Radon story occurs in the federal government and involves a variety of organizational units and policy makers. Dennis Wagner and a team of federal leaders in the EPA move into action to address a serious public health issue. Watch for how circles of influence are used to grow a Compelling Vision, and how in turn the vision expands the leaders' circles of influence. Following the Radon Leadership Story, we describe how to use the Mindset and Method of Compelling Vision to create the future we stand for.

LEADERSHIP STORY

Leadership Choices Lead to National Action and Results on Indoor Radon Gas

by **Dennis Wagner**

"Generating meaningful results on bold Intent is a great way to live and lead."

One of the most important and exhilarating achievements in my fledgling career at the US Environmental Protection Agency (EPA) came to fruition in September of 1988. At that time, I was working in EPA's Radon Division. Looking back on this formative experience, I now see how we can use our own small circles of influence to have big impacts.

As a young, fairly junior federal civil servant, I had staff-level leadership accountability for programs to educate the public about indoor radon gas. Radon is an invisible, odorless, carcinogenic, naturally occurring gas that comes from the radioactive decay of uranium in the soil. It is the second leading cause of lung cancer in the nation. The mission of our newly established EPA program was to reduce the public health risks of indoor radon gas.

Discovery of Deadly Radon Levels in Homes

The agency had unexpectedly discovered high levels of radon in homes in 1984 as part of an emergency response incident impacting a cluster of neighborhoods in Pennsylvania and New Jersey. An engineer named Stanley Watras set off radiation detection monitors at the Limerick nuclear powerplant in Pennsylvania while the plant was under construction and no fuel was in the reactor. How was that even possible?

The radiation exposure was eventually traced back to the Watras home where our EPA team detected alarming levels of naturally occurring radon gas. Initial emergency response surveys showed that many homes in surrounding neighborhoods throughout parts of Pennsylvania and New Jersey also had high levels of radon gas.

The EPA worked quickly to develop cost-effective methods to test for and reduce elevated radon levels. This was accomplished through straightforward methods of sealing residential foundations and installing fans to ventilate the aggregate building material underlying the homes.

Through subsequent statewide surveys, EPA established that homes in many areas throughout the nation, not just in Pennsylvania and New Jersey, had deadly concentrations of this naturally occurring gas in basements and first floors. The elevated radon levels in millions of these homes posed risks to the occupants that were comparable to smoking one to four or more packs of cigarettes a day. That is a lot of risk. Lots of children had bedrooms in the basements of these homes.

New Radon Mission Comes with Responsibility for Careful Messaging

When the radon problem was first discovered, EPA was extremely concerned about preventing widespread public fears and panic about this invisible, odorless, cancer-causing gas that was present at elevated levels in millions of American homes. The Agency crafted straightforward public education materials to inform the public and to convey the underlying science of radon health risk, testing, and mitigation. The EPA public education materials were scientific and benign and used statements like "If you are concerned, you should consider testing your home for radon."

Federal Environmental Policy to Reduce Radon Health Risks is Stalled

Four years later, however, it was clear that the public education problem EPA was confronting wasn't one of "panic in the streets" but "public apathy everywhere." The evidence was clear: few Americans were testing their homes for this widespread public health hazard. This was true despite the availability of relatively low-cost tests of $10 to $25, and proven methods for reducing elevated radon levels that cost around $900 to $2500 per home. In the first four years of radon public education, only about 600,000 of the nation's 70-80 million homes had been tested for radon, or less than 1%.

The weak response was impossible to ignore. As the staff leader for public education on radon, I knew we had to change the Agency's messaging to achieve our program's risk reduction mission. To further complicate matters, the earlier messaging strategies were now fully baked into the policy and programs of the Agency. Like most policies of large federal agencies, changing these ineffective bedrock messages would not be easy.

Engaging a Formative Circle of Influence on the Vision

Here I was, a new employee in a junior position with no policy-making authority. My experience was quite limited. Neither of my parents had ever worked in a professional office setting. I was the first person in my family of origin to get a college degree. I had grown up on a small eclectic ranch in rural Montana, far from work in a large federal agency in the nation's capital. I was a relatively recent graduate student who joined EPA in 1986, immediately after matriculating with a Master of Public Administration degree. My degree had a special emphasis on mass communications.

Although a relatively low-level employee at the agency, my small circle of influence and academic training in communications provided sufficient background for me to know that EPA, its Radon Program, and the public all required much more proactive messages. I was not willing to spend my days cranking out ineffective policies and messages. I began turning over every rock in pursuit of the needed change.

In reviewing options, it was clear to me that my chain of command had to be on board with the needed change in policy and messaging. I began to argue forcefully, with sound evidence and reasoning, that we had to figure out how to change the EPA policy and the messaging that went with it. Honestly, it didn't take much convincing on my part. My bosses recognized that change was needed.

My immediate supervisor was a politically astute and savvy young federal manager named Steve Page. Steve was a master at navigating and managing the bureaucracy. He gained some of this expertise in the Carter White House while serving as Special Assistant to President Carter's Chief of Staff. Steve's new boss at EPA was a hard-charging federal executive named Margo Oge, who had recently assumed leadership of the EPA Radon Program. She was committed to using her first assignment as a member of the Senior Executive Service to deliver important program results.

Steve and Margo also knew that her boss, the head of the EPA Office of Radiation Program, a Captain in the US Public Health Service named Richard J. Guimond, could request and get an audience with the head of the US Public Health Service, the Surgeon General of the United States. This gave Rich some important access to weighty authority that extended way beyond our own limited circles of influence. And Captain Guimond was not only firmly committed to the program's mission of reducing the public health risks of radon but was also the main architect of this mission! Rich Guimond was a health physicist, a nationally known expert on radon, and a candid, plain-spoken leader. He was also a man of action.

A Leadership Team Forms to Champion a Change in Policy

C. Everett Koop MD
Surgeon General
1982-1989

Lee Thomas
EPA Administrator
1985-1989

Persistent and forceful advocacy had surfaced a cadre of leaders in EPA who were ready to play co-leadership Roles in changing the Agency's policy on how to pursue the Radon mission.

C. Everett Koop, the current Surgeon General at that time, was a medical doctor with a reputation for action—the kind of leader who might team with EPA to take bolder action on the public health risks of indoor radon gas. Dr. Koop had led aggressive and forceful federal actions to stem the rising tide of HIV-AIDS, despite relatively lukewarm political support from the Reagan Administration. The evidence showed that Surgeon General Koop was not afraid to stand up for public health policies that made sense.

Offering a Bold Message to Move the Nation into Action

Steve, Margo, and I reached out to Rich and advocated that he brief Surgeon General Koop on the most recent round of compelling new data from 17 statewide surveys. The surveys documented elevated radon levels in homes throughout each of these states. We asked Rich to recommend that Dr. Koop team with EPA Administrator Lee Thomas to issue a National Radon Health Advisory that all US homes get tested for radon. A joint public health advisory to proactively urge that all US homes be tested for radon was a bold move. Such an action would fundamentally transform our federal policy from "consider testing if you are concerned" to "get your home tested for radon." We reasoned that both Captain Guimond and Surgeon General Koop were inclined toward bold moves. Rich Guimond gave us the go-ahead.

Steve and I teamed with Margo to develop the briefing materials and joined with Rich when he met with the Surgeon General. The briefing was crisp, focused on science and data, friendly and professional. Dr. Koop paid close attention.

At the end of the briefing, Dr. Koop agreed that—if the EPA Administrator would join with him—he and the US Public Health Service would issue the National Radon Health Advisory.

Our next stop immediately became a briefing for EPA Administrator, Lee Thomas. Our leadership challenge was to enroll him into the emerging vision.

Administrator Thomas was known as a technically savvy, data-based, factual leader who acted on clear science and logic. Captain Guimond and our team presented the Administrator with the latest statewide radon survey data, reminded him of the clear and compelling health risk assessments documenting radon as a Known Human Carcinogen, summarized the evidence of apathetic public response, and shared the Surgeon General's willingness to team on a joint EPA-Public Health Service Advisory. Administrator Thomas gave the green light to the proposed Advisory! All systems were go.

Unexpected Challenges Nearly Wreck a Major Environmental Policy Shift

We worked closely with Surgeon General Koop's team over the summer. We crafted the language of the Joint National Radon Health Advisory, finalized an EPA press release, and wrote talking points for the major press conference to be held in the EPA Auditorium. Concurrently, we developed new, more proactive radon public education materials to be issued with the new policy, and geared up our regional, state, and private partners to participate in a major new push on radon public education. The workload was intense. Our EPA radon team invested a tremendous level of effort into the impending announcement and policy change. We had innumerable meetings to share evidence and plans with scientists and policy experts at the Agency – many of them were naturally worried and somewhat resistant to the planned new messaging and policy change. The scientists and experts were worried that the strong, clear messages about the need for radon testing and action wouldn't contain all the details, caveats, and nuances that were such a major part of the earlier agency communications. Preparations for the National Health Advisory were a huge lift.

Then, in the week prior to the big announcement in September, an unexpected call from Dr. Koop's office nearly gave me a heart attack. The voice on the other end of the line apologetically informed me that Dr. Koop would no longer be available to participate in the unprecedented announcement.

"What!? How can this be!?" I asked Koop's special assistant.

The Public Health Service Officer on the other end of the line explained that it had nothing to do with the subject matter of the announcement. Under fierce questioning, she eventually revealed that Dr. Koop remained personally and professionally supportive of the recommended National Radon Health Advisory. After more pleading, she indicated that the reason for the cancellation was unfortunately confidential, and that no additional information would be available.

The call ended. This was not good. This was bad, really bad.

This was by far the most difficult call that I had taken in my first two years of service at EPA. I instantly relayed the devastating news to Steve, Margo and Rich. They were just as stunned as I was.

We immediately resolved to do everything in our power to sustain the planned announcement. Months of planning and work with the EPA Administrator's office and other partners had occurred to ramp up our outreach and education activities to generate life-saving public action. We were determined to salvage something from all of the preparation and hard work.

Repeated calls by Captain Guimond to the Office of the Surgeon General finally resulted in an offer for him to meet with the Deputy Surgeon General. The Deputy Surgeon General was reportedly charged by Dr. Koop to see if something could be worked out.

Now we were cooking with gas!

A flurry of negotiations with the Deputy Surgeon General resulted in an agreement that an Assistant Surgeon General from the Centers for Disease Control (CDC) would be deployed to Washington to join with our EPA Administrator. Consistent with Dr. Koop's support, the Deputy Surgeon General agreed that the planned National Radon Health Advisory could go forward and would be issued jointly by the EPA and the U.S. Public Health Service. Rich informed EPA Administrator Thomas of the unexpected change in plans, and he agreed to proceed with the planned announcement, press conference and policy change.

EPA and the US Public Health Service issued a National Radon Health Advisory on September 12, 1988, recommending that virtually all US homes be tested for indoor radon gas. Assistant Surgeon General Vernon Houk of the Centers for Disease Control joined with EPA Administrator Thomas in the press conference to issue the joint National Radon Health Advisory. I counted 29 TV cameras in the EPA Auditorium for the historic announcement.

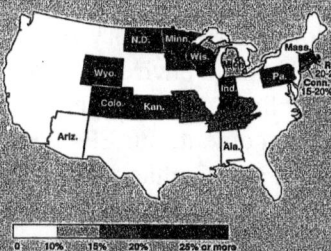

Radon Health Advisory was Headline News throughout the Nation

New Radon Policy Triggers Structural Changes in the Housing Market for Dramatic Impact

The evening after our huge press conference, I switched on the TV in our apartment to watch the news. All three of the major network news anchors – Dan Rather of CBS, Peter Jennings of ABC, and Tom Brokaw of NBC – opened their evening newscast reporting on the "tough new Federal radon warning." Our policy change shouted from the front page of the New York Times, the Washington Post, and USA Today, and ran as headline news for days.

The National Radon Health Advisory was a major, needed shift in US environmental and public health policy. In the six weeks following the announcement, our EPA Radon Program estimated that 1.5 million homes were tested, nearly three times the number tested in the prior four years combined. The increases were a major victory in our work as public education leaders for the radon program.

Thanks in large part to the proactive new, "you should test" public messaging, our EPA team was successful in getting the Ad Council to partner with us in launching a major pro bono multi-year media campaign aimed at mobilizing the public to act. Serving as the government point person for EPA's first Ad Council campaign opened up exciting new vistas of public service for me. I began traveling from the nation's capital to New York City every two weeks to team with top executives and creative team members at the Ad Council and our TBWA advertising agency. We developed hard-hitting public service announcements and other materials to generate increased public action on radon. Some of our advertisements won prestigious national ADDY awards. Our work appeared in TV, radio, outdoor, and print media throughout the nation. We received lots of free publicity when a sheriff in Missouri tore down one of our EPA Ad Council billboards. He didn't like the message that "radon was a problem in this area."

The new, straightforward radon testing recommendation eliminated ambiguity that had depressed needed action in real estate transfers and new home construction. For example, prior to the shift in EPA's radon policy, the real estate industry provided mixed messages to home buyers and home sellers about the need for radon testing. Following the announcement and shift in federal policy, radon testing rapidly became common practice as part of real estate transfers. In a similar fashion, our EPA radon housing experts worked in close partnership with the new home construction industry and building code organizations to make sure they followed suit in proactively responding to the new national Health Advisory. Today, most new homes in higher-risk radon areas are routinely built to be radon-resistant. Over time these two structural changes in real estate transfers and new home construction have resulted in millions of radon tests and mitigations, and in millions of radon-resistant new homes.

Assuming Leadership Roles Led to Larger Circles of Influence for EPA Staff and Executives

My supervisors and key partners, who were part of my own small circle of influence, went on to much greater accountabilities and achievements. Rich Guimond was promoted to Rear Admiral and Assistant Surgeon General in the US Public Health Service not long after the historic announcement. He went on to lead a major, successful EPA effort to transform action and progress in the Agency's previously stalled Superfund waste cleanup program. He then transferred to the Department of Energy where he became accountable for leading more successful work to clean up the nation's radioactive weapons production sites.

Both Steve Page and Margo Oge became two of the highest-ranking civil servants in EPA. Margo's distinguished career led to many important policy and program results as the nation's chief environmental regulator of cars, trucks, airplanes, and other mobile sources of air pollution. Steve gave many years of dedicated and effective service as the senior leader of the Office of Air Quality Planning and Standards at Research Triangle Park in North Carolina. Steve served as the nation's chief environmental regulator of stationary sources of air pollution, such as factories and electric utilities.

The National Radon Health Advisory work also impacted my own career trajectory in major ways. It taught me about the importance of staying focused and true to the bottom-line mission and program Intent – in this case, of reducing radon health risks. This lesson on the importance of Intent served me well as I assumed greater accountabilities on ever larger policy and public sector missions. Over the next 30 years, I would become responsible for national leadership to increase organ donations and transplants, to increase healthcare access for some of the nation's most vulnerable people, and to improve patient safety in all US hospitals.

The radon campaign also laid the groundwork for a longstanding partnership with my co-author John Scanlon. I shared the story of how we made this dramatic change in EPA policy as part of a 1990-91 leadership development initiative called the Council for Excellence in Government Fellows Program.

John Scanlon was the executive architect in charge of coaching and mentoring our group of Fellows. John loved this story about the challenges in messaging an urgent public health danger and helped me to understand that Bold Aims such as the one we had recommended to Rich and the Surgeon General were key to effective, results-based federal leadership. John has always been an advocate for Bold Aims. His constant advice to Fellows was, "You lead large programs in the US Federal Government – don't play checkers on this football field. Play football!"

Sharing and refining my own leadership journey on this work ultimately led to what became a 30-year collaboration and career partnership with John. Dr. Scanlon and I have been teaming and working together as leadership students, practitioners, and mentor/mentee ever since.

Epilogue on What Almost Stopped the New Radon Policy

Many years after we issued the National Radon Health Advisory, I encountered the Public Health Service Officer who had placed the devastating call to me from Dr. Koop's office early in September of 1988. She apologetically relayed—more than a decade later—that Surgeon General Koop had been contacted by the White House and was confidentially requested not to participate in any significant press activities or announcements in the months of September and October. This was due to the lead-up to the Presidential election that was held in November. This made sense. It was important to the Reagan Administration that visible leaders like Dr. Koop not rock the boat in any way that might cause a public relations issue for the Bush Campaign at this sensitive point in time.

Resistance is not always personal or policy. But it's almost always present. Persisting through the obstacles posed by Surgeon General Koop's required cancellation was an essential element in achieving our leadership Intent. Effective leadership in pursuit of bold Intent almost always requires persistence and resilience.

Nearly 17 years later, on January 13, 2005, Surgeon General Richard H. Carmona joined with EPA to issue a second National Radon Health Advisory. The agency finally got an Advisory that was formally issued by the Surgeon General himself!

Organizational Missions Give Us Access to Leadership Choices and Multiplier Effects

Reflections by
John Scanlon

Organizational missions are expressions of important aspirations: clean up the environment, provide access to quality health care, end health disparities, lift millions out of poverty. Organizational missions enable us to see situations that are full of leadership opportunities. Situations like the radon problem emerge that show the need for significant changes to the status quo.

Laying the painstaking groundwork for the National Radon Health Advisory was the result of Choices that Dennis and his supervisors made about their leadership Intent and their agency's mission. The missions of EPA, the Surgeon General and Public Health Service involved protecting and advancing the health of the nation and reducing environmental risk. These institutions are accountable for developing and providing sound evidence-based guidance that all parts of society need to manage health and the environment. All of this can be seen and heard as a call to action sufficient to address the risks encountered. Missions open the door to leadership Choices.

As an EPA staff-leader for radon public education, Dennis had a circle of influence that clearly intersected with the need for stronger messaging and public action on radon testing and mitigation. Understanding that Vision is born from the intersection of the needs of others and our own circle of influence opens up an incredibly powerful multiplier effect. When leaders Intentionally work to address the needs of others, their circle of influence expands dramatically. New partnerships can be formed. New knowledge is acquired. People whose needs have been met become powerful advocates for further and expanded action into new domains.

To get into action in similar ways, we can ask ourselves straightforward, effective questions:

Concern
What urgent need is not being met?
What makes it compelling to others?

Influence
What is the field of action I have access to?
What elements of my own circle of influence can I bring to bear on this compelling need?

Action
Who will I engage and enroll?
What Requests and Offers can I make?

British writer William Hazlitt put it like this: "The more you do, the more you can do." We grow the capabilities of our partners as well as our own through teaming on our shared Intent.

This Leadership Story shows that assuming leadership accountability as a Government Service grade 11 federal civil servant can lead to new national environmental policy and dramatic outcomes. If Dennis could make major contributions to these kinds of changes in national policy as a GS 11 civil servant, so too can others. Get clear on Intent in your own work. It will help get you on a powerful trajectory where one good thing leads to another.

Compelling Vision
as the Intended Future We Stand For

INTENT

Compelling Vision

Bold Aims

Decide-Notice-Acknowledge

What Makes Leadership Vision Compelling?

What makes a leadership Vision compelling is its source: people in great need, or the vexing challenge that demands our attention or calls for action.

As a young person, Dennis thought that Vision might be some kind of personality trait. He wondered whether charismatic, big-picture leaders were born with this trait or if it could be developed in himself and others. The Founding Fathers of our nation had the vision of democracy. Martin Luther King Jr. had the vision of racial equality. Rachel Carson, author of Silent Spring, had the vision of environmental protection.

This curiosity about vision caused Dennis to snap to attention while participating in a leadership training session in the early 1990s. The training was conducted by the best-selling author and thought leader, Stephen R. Covey, in a large hotel ballroom in downtown Washington, DC. Dennis and his entire EPA team were staunch fans of Dr. Covey and had benefited immensely, along with millions of others across the world, from the lessons of Covey's blockbuster book, *The 7 Habits of Highly Effective People*. Dr. Covey asked the audience to turn to the workbook page on the Source of Vision. The page displayed a simple diagram with two nested circles called Circle of Influence and Circle of Concern. Pictured below is our adaptation of the original diagram.

Leadership Vision Emerges As We Choose to Bring Together Two Forces We Encounter In Our Lives

Graphic is adapted from Covey Institute training materials

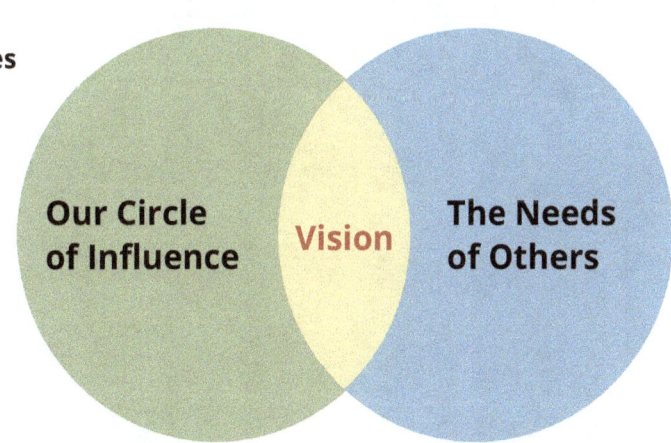

75

The Source of Vision is the simple intersection of two spheres:

1. Our own Circle of Influence; and,
2. The Needs of Others.

Needs of Others is the genuine concern for others, including but extending beyond our own self-interest. Internalizing and authentically owning these needs is key to the practice of leadership and is what makes a leadership Vision compelling.

Our Circle of Influence can be thought of as the people we know and can effectively engage with in a meaningful way. These relationships are the product of our personal and professional histories, our organizational resources and positions, our skills, the energy we choose to project, our ways of Being, the Language we use. A Vision of the future becomes clearer and more compelling as we engage our Circles of Influence in addressing the serious unmet Needs of Others.

A leadership Vision of the future is one where the needs of others are met through plausible—and usually challenging—pathways of action. The paths begin with our own Circle of Influence.

"It's easier to act your way into a new way of thinking than to think your way into a new way of acting."

Jerry Sternin and
Richard Tanner Pascale
Harvard Business Review
May 2005

Leadership Vision is Crafted through Action with Others

Vision emerges through shared action. Big, serious, challenging needs are not usually resolved by individuals. We don't put a man on the moon or address global warming by working alone. The pathways of action that ultimately emerge are shared pathways.

Initially, the Vision is almost always far beyond the reach and capability of our own small circle of influence. However, those in our circle have their own circles of influence. And the people in those circles also have circles. By reaching out and enrolling others into the Vision, we create a multiplier effect that grows our collective ability to realize the vision. It's an exciting and energizing leadership challenge—to grow our circles of influence and to add the circles of influence of others. We accomplish this through modeling the action and commitment we seek, and by making Requests and Offers to others.

"Action without vision is rote, turning the crank. Vision without action is daydreaming. However, a powerful vision, combined with disciplined action, will move the world."

Mary Lou Andersen

In the next Leadership story, we learn how a leader with a Compelling Vision activated his extensive circle of influence to address the large-scale problem of poor patient safety in US hospitals. From that Vision emerged a Bold Aim: to save 100,000 lives across thousands of hospitals within a period of 18 months.

Management Vision versus Leadership Vision

Management:

As managers, the job of crafting vision is matching our readily available assets to address the needs of our organization and its customers. It starts with the manageable and practical question, "What part of the need can I address with the resources at my disposal?" The response can be ambitious. Our teams might use their skills and assets to provide new, exquisite products that fulfill and delight our organization's customers. The management vision is within our reach.

Leadership:

A leadership vision is different. A leadership vision starts with the question, "How do we address the full scope of a need that is beyond our reach?" A leadership situation arises when the resources at hand are far from sufficient. One of the key elements of leadership work is to develop relationships and other assets that bring those needed resources into play. Much of the work is about accessing the circles of influence of others, and gaining their active involvement in pursuing the leadership vision.

Don Berwick's Leadership Story:
100,000 Lives Campaign

Donald M. Berwick MD, MPP co-founded the world-wide Institute for Healthcare Improvement (IHI), and later served as the Administrator of the Centers for Medicare and Medicaid Services (CMS) to launch its implementation of the landmark Affordable Care Act. He is a member of the Institute of Medicine and has led and served on many of their influential national committees and studies, including the renowned *Crossing the Quality Chasm* and *To Err is Human* reports. Don has authored books and contributed to thousands of medical and scientific articles in the published literature. Dr. Berwick was even knighted by Queen Elizabeth II for his leadership and contributions to transform Britain's National Healthcare System.

Encountering Dr. Berwick and Large-Scale Transformation

We met Dr. Berwick in the late 1990s when the Institute for Healthcare Improvement was teaming with the federal Bureau of Primary Health Care (BPHC) to improve healthcare quality across the national network of federally qualified health centers. Marilyn Gaston MD, the Bureau Director, and Frank Zampiello MD, Director of its Quality Center, introduced us to Don and his innovative approaches to leadership and large-scale quality improvement.

Dr. Berwick co-founded IHI primarily as an educational institution to improve health care quality and practice. Don and his team quickly learned that education alone was not sufficient to generate meaningful change. As a consequence of this learning, in the early 1990's IHI developed the Breakthrough Series Collaboratives, which go well beyond traditional education and information dissemination approaches. The Breakthrough Series Collaboratives introduced clarity of purpose, high energy events, structured action periods, and accountability for results by providers on the ground to create more effective improvement campaigns.

In Breakthrough Collaboratives, healthcare organizations would sign up to work together to achieve a specific, bold goal within a period of 12 to 24 months. An example of a bold goal would be to establish specific quantitative targets for significantly reducing patient waiting times in health centers, while simultaneously increasing the patients' time with their physicians. Participating organizations each formed a team to test and adapt proven practices for achieving the goals.

The platform for change was a series of three to four in-person, multi-day Learning Sessions with all teams, each session followed by Action Learning Periods in which the teams would test and make changes back in their organizations. Teams transparently reported and shared data on process and outcome measures. This was a major advance in improvement practice. It was designed to create rapid, dramatic, and measurable change among participating organizations.

In the Leadership Story that follows, Dr. Berwick and his team were able to break the traditional mold of small, incremental improvement projects. We see how Dr. Berwick activated his extensive circle of influence and applied it to the large-scale problem of poor patient safety in US hospitals. We see how Dr. Berwick's circle of influence in national forums like the Institute of Medicine, coupled with his on-the-ground experience with Breakthrough Collaboratives, enabled him to see and act on the needs of others at a national scale.

From this Breakthrough Collaborative model, a Vision and a Bold Aim emerged: to save 100,000 lives across thousands of hospitals within 18 months.

Dr. Berwick describes how he and his team developed the Aim, mobilized the infrastructure needed to voluntarily enroll thousands of hospitals, and managed a nation-wide campaign. The 100,000 Lives Campaign wielded a major impact on hospital safety and led to a number of highly consequential follow-on national campaigns.

Bold Aim of 100,000 Lives Campaign

In interviewing Don Berwick, we learned that one of his leadership mantras is to "never go alone." The 100,000 Lives campaign was a team effort. In this section we will also hear from Joe McCannon and Tom Evans, two of the many co-leaders in the campaign. Dr. Berwick teamed closely with Joe McCannon, the 100,000 Lives Campaign Director, to effectively apply principles of large-scale change to this national initiative.

Joe comments near the end of this Leadership Story on how IHI enlisted ownership of the Bold Aim across national organizations. He also describes how resistance surfaced and was used to generate further improvement.

Tom Evans MD, Director of the Iowa Healthcare Collaborative, describes how his organization served as a "campaign node" and brought the entire Iowa hospital community on board with on-the-ground implementation across the State. Dr. Evans shows the kind of independent leadership efforts already in place that made Iowa ready to co-lead on 100,000 Lives in Iowa.

As you read about this ground-breaking campaign, watch for the Choices that Don Berwick, Joe McCannon, and Tom Evans made as they performed leadership Roles:

A Compelling Vision, based on the integration of Dr. Berwick and IHI's circle of influence with the needs of others;

A time-limited and quantitative Bold Aim, providing clear and compelling Intent, and communicated to enroll and engage others in a national movement;

Positive energy, deliberately and intentionally cultivated in the campaign through celebratory, well-designed campaign events.

Watch for the use of invitation, acknowledgement, celebration, parties, and these leaders' Choices of Language and stories. And watch for how negative energy is effectively channeled to deal with challenges and criticism.

An Upward Spiral of more energy, better hospitals, safer results, and new opportunities for follow-on campaigns was created by the breakthrough leadership Choices made by Dr. Berwick and his campaign team.

LEADERSHIP STORY

Envisioning and Launching the "100,000 Lives" Campaign

by **Don Berwick MD, MPP**

"Here is what I think we should do. I think we should save 100,000 lives. And I think we should do that by June 14, 2006—18 months from today.

Some is not a number; soon is not a time. Here's the number: 100,000. Here's the time: June 14, 2006, at 9 AM."

By 2004, the Institute for Healthcare Improvement (IHI) was a seasoned and successful quality improvement organization. The Board, executive staff, and faculty of IHI were looking for ways to take health care improvement to a larger, national scale. We were considering how to work with many more hospitals to create a national impact on hospital safety.

The Institute of Medicine (IOM) report, *To Err Is Human* (1999), had made the country aware of medical errors in hospitals. Errors were common, resulting in an estimated 44,000 to 98,000 deaths per year. With thousands of hospitals involved, the scale of the patient safety problem felt overwhelming. It's a big country. Quality improvement projects tended to be local, focused, and small scale.

Improving patient safety across the entire US health system looked daunting. However, I have always been drawn to take on hard things. This is an intrinsic motivation of mine. It's kind of an addiction, and not always a good thing. I noticed this trait in myself early on.

For my 8th birthday, my parents gave me an Erector Set. It came with a booklet about all the things you could make with the set, with each thing becoming progressively harder as you proceeded through the booklet. I remember turning immediately to the last page and started working on the most difficult item you could make with the set. This pattern has repeated itself throughout the decades of my life.

Using Bold Aims to Release the Positive Spirit of Others

How do we get the attention of several thousand hospitals? How do we work with them? The answer to this scale challenge came to us from an encounter with the nation's presidential campaign that was underway. My son Dan, a volunteer for the campaign, explained that in Florida he and his team had on a recent weekend "knocked on 60,000 doors." I was intrigued. The scale of the activity was impressive. In looking into the design of political campaigns, I was struck by two factors: the specificity of Intent, and an infrastructure from which to operate.

Specificity of Intent and Operating Structure

Political campaigns have specificity of Intent. Get 50% of the vote plus one by the close of election day and your candidate wins. The goal is riveting. This is key to running a campaign.

The underlying rule for specificity that my son Dan recited to me was: "Some is not a number. Soon is not a time." Our aim had to be specific and to drive everything we did. Then, to operate effectively, five components had to be in place: an action platform, a communication system, field operations, a measurement system, and enough money.

Five Components of a Campaign

Action platform
state what the campaign stands for and offer sound solutions

Communication system
be able to listen to and talk with the world

Field operations
leverage knowledge and action in a geometric way

Measurement system
some is not a number; soon is not a time

Money
have sufficient resources to act

At IHI, we decided to act and to use our own program delivery infrastructure. Our work gave us an action platform to address safety. We saw a way for hospitals to reduce errors.

The 100,000 Lives Bold Aim emerged from several months of activity, driven by the needs we observed. It built on our own experience. Back-of-the-envelope calculations showed that if several thousand hospitals implemented six proven changes in care (see Platform insert), 100,000 lives could be saved each year. There was not a lot of calculation involved. The care changes were known and quite well documented. The challenge was taking the six interventions to scale in all hospitals.

Specificity called for a date—"soon is not a time." We set 18 months from launch to achieve the result. In December of 2004, we launched the campaign at IHI's annual national forum. With our partners, we called on hospitals to save 100,000 lives by June 14, 2006.

To Err Is Human had made the topic compelling to a national audience. The Aim was plausible. The six proven care changes that follow provided a clear line of sight for achieving the Aim. We were ready to build the field operations, a communication strategy, and a measurement plan to launch and run the campaign. And, most important, our team chose to run with it!

100,000 Lives Platform: Six Practices that Save Lives

1. Deployment of Rapid Response Teams
2. Delivery of Reliable, Evidence-Based Care for Acute Myocardial Infarction
3. Medication Reconciliation
4. Prevention of Central Line Infections
5. Prevention of Surgical Site Infections
6. Prevention of Ventilator-Associated Pneumonias

Making Requests to Enroll 3,100 Hospitals

The IHI staff swung into action. An innovative and fast-moving "skunkworks" team led by campaign director Joe McCannon was formed (see Joe's narrative on 3000 Hospitals, One Common Aim). The charge was, "Go for it." The spirit was "Make it happen. There are no rules."

We saw this spirit in action when staff showed up with a tour bus that had been shrink-wrapped with the campaign motto. Our team planned a cross-country, 15-city tour. At each stop they would hold rallies to enroll hospitals. The Campaign team did not ask permission to do this; they just did it. And the IHI executive response to this unusual approach was "Why not!" We trusted our team and knew the energy they were projecting into this work was infectious and needed.

Everywhere the team went, hospitals stepped forward to commit. In Madison, Wisconsin hospital leaders met the bus in a stadium with 1,200 seats outlined with yellow balloons to illustrate the 1,200 lives they were committing to save.

The campaign released this kind of celebratory energy everywhere. People showed up saying "This is what we are going to go for, this is what we are going to do." The plans they shared were often focused on specific practices they were testing, important harm areas that needed attention, the numbers of lives they projected would be saved by their work, patients or key clinical leaders that were part of their efforts, and more. These frontline healthcare providers gave the effort heart and meaning. IHI did not issue commands. We uncovered what people already wanted to do. We created free, downloadable toolkits and other resources to explain the effective clinical changes and helped the providers to master quality improvement methods to gain traction. The campaign offered a way for them to take action and to do the things that needed to be done to make their hospitals safer.

Over the course of the 18-month period, 3,100 hospitals enrolled and participated from all over the United States.

Institute for Healthcare Improvement Campaign Bus Tour

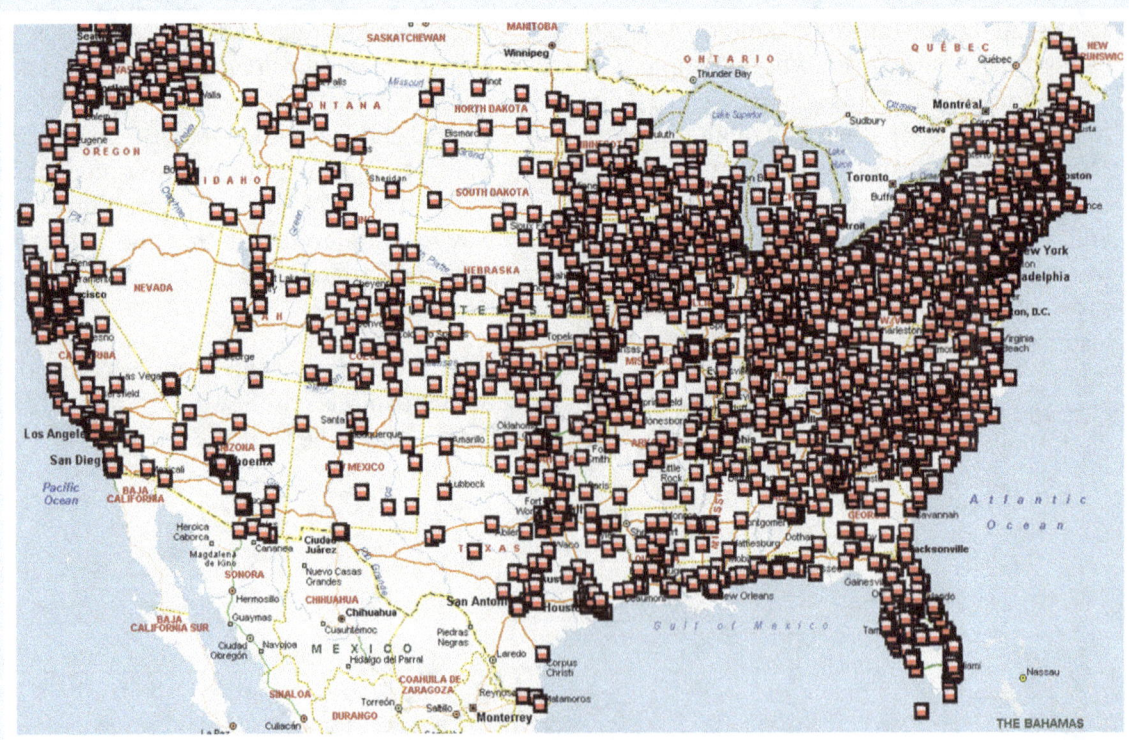

3100 Hospitals Participated in the 100,000 Lives Campaign

Hospital Team in Wisconsin
Yellow Balloons Outline 1200 Stadium Seats to Show Impact of 1200 Lives Saved

A Collaborative Platform Generates Action and Captures Results

100,000 Lives in 18 months was designed to attract others. All hospitals were invited to join. We had a standing Request and Offer: "Please commit; be part of a community in action and be supported and acknowledged." And "If you want to join – welcome!"

A node-and-spoke infrastructure was established. Organizations serving as nodes supported and guided a set of hospitals that they were connected to, one way or another. The nodes included organizations like State Hospital Associations, large health systems with multiple hospitals, and affinity groups of hospitals such as children's hospitals. These organizations stepped forward and volunteered. They just showed up. There were also hundreds of "mentor hospitals," local exemplars, whom the nodes could tap for peer-to-peer exchange and sharing of proven best practices.

Evidence was frequently brought forward to show that success was possible. Data was drawn from high-performing hospitals that had already succeeded in reducing harm to patients. The process systematically spread the use of best practices from the high performers to other hospitals in the campaign. IHI was offering a bold goal, evidence-based methods, and a way forward.

Progress was tracked through voluntary self-reporting by hospitals. Our rough measurement model estimated that in the 18 months, there were 122,000 fewer hospital deaths. While the exact number was debated, the level of national action was unprecedented, and major improvements in safety on the targeted conditions were made by hospitals across the country. The 100,000 Lives Campaign generated a new level of systemic activity on hospital safety. The work released phenomenal energy. Over time, richer and more textured approaches to reducing harm also showed up.

The "5 Million Lives" Platform

Original six practices to save lives

1. Deployment of Rapid Response Teams
2. Delivery of Reliable, Evidence-Based Care for Acute Myocardial Infarction
3. Medication Reconciliation
4. Prevention of Central Line Infections
5. Prevention of Surgical Site Infections
6. Prevention of Ventilator-Associated Pneumonias

Six additional practices

1. Prevention of Pressure Ulcers
2. Reduction of Methicillin-Resistant Staphylococcus Aureus (MRSA) Infection
3. Prevention of Harm from High-Alert Medications
4. Reduction of Surgical Complications
5. Delivering Reliable, Evidence-Based Care for Congestive Heart Failure
6. Getting Boards on Board

Leadership Campaigns Can Generate More Leadership Campaigns

The hospital safety movement grew internationally. Health systems from other countries asked IHI to teach them how to run their own campaigns. We worked with hospital groups in Denmark, Sweden, UK, Japan, and South America. For example, in Brazil, the 116 public sector hospitals set a Bold Aim to reduce by 50% three major hospital-acquired infections over 36 months: Central Line Associated Blood Stream Infections or CLABSI; Catheter Associated Urinary Tract Infections or CAUTI; and Ventilator Associated Pneumonia or VAP. After learning how to use the IHI action platform and architecture, the hospitals hit every goal well before their own 36-month target.

The 100,000 Lives Campaign was a turning point for IHI and a breakthrough for the nation, not just in hospital safety, but also in more general healthcare quality improvement. In the United States the 100,000 Lives Campaign led to a series of expanding campaigns that extended the reach and impact of the hospital safety movement.

The 100,000 Lives Campaign was immediately followed by IHI's 5 Million Lives campaign. We asked the hospital sector to join with us and with each other to prevent five million incidents of medical harm over a period of two years, from December 12, 2006 through December 9, 2008.

The node architecture of the 100,000 Lives Campaign was re-used to implement the work of the follow-on campaign. Additional hospital-acquired conditions and methods were added to the action platform (see insert). The hospital safety programs became more robust. In 2008, at the Campaign's closure, 4,050 hospitals had enrolled (at that time there were about 5,100 hospitals in the nation).

Following the 5 Million Lives campaign, President Obama asked me to serve as the Administrator of the Centers for Medicare and Medicaid Services (CMS). During my tenure at CMS, we established the CMS Innovation Center, one of the key provisions of the Affordable Care Act. The Innovation Center invested $500M in a Partnership for Patients campaign with a Bold Aim of reducing preventable harm in hospitals by 40% between 2010 and 2014.

A rigorous measurement system showed the 2010 rate falling dramatically from 145 harms/1000 hospital discharges to 121/1000 in 2013 and to 86/1000 in 2017. The comprehensive measurement system established for this large federal patient safety campaign documented big improvements in hospital safety.

Learning How Campaigns Work

The 100,000 Lives campaign and its follow-on efforts have built up our knowledge of how to lead and how to operate large-scale change in health care. The political campaigns we encountered showed us some of the structure needed for large-scale efforts: an action platform, communication system, field operations, measurement system, and money.

At the same time, we also learned that a danger with campaign methods is that their stewards can let them become "cookbook" or commercial. It is important not to turn things into a standardized approach that allows the methods to produce rote behavior. Commercial approaches make the campaign contractual and transactional. We need the generalizable theories and methods to guide us, but we have to be open to embracing the improvisational nature of the world. The elements of our methods always look different when we pursue practical application. We need to maintain an openness to improvisation and to the varied nature of the things we encounter in the real world. Our campaign methods have to be adaptable and inviting.

We brought our experience from IHI's Breakthrough Collaboratives to help supply an Action Learning Platform. In the Collaboratives, healthcare organizations sign up to work together to achieve specific, bold goals over 12 to 24 months, such as eliminating or sharply reducing waiting times for patients in health centers and increasing time with the physician. Teams test and adapt proven practices for achieving the goal. The platform for change is a series of three to four in-person Learning Sessions, each followed by Action Learning Periods in which the teams would test and make changes back in their organizations. Our work on 100,000 Lives gave us a way to dramatically scale-up this kind of work.

We stumbled into 100,000 Lives in 2004 and several years later came out with at least nine major lessons learned (see insert on adjoining page). The first three are about creating a Bold Aim: *Go Big, Specificity Works, and Structure Helps*. Three are about the enabling environment that leaders can create: *Suspend the Rules, Invitation Beats Command, Always Say Yes*. The last three are about encountering others in ways that generate Net Forward Energy: *Celebrate, Run from Fights, and Tell Stories*. We learned that these are important qualities to live by when we pursue Bold Aims.

Lessons From Large Scale National Campaigns To Improve Health Care

Be Driven by Bold Aims

Going Big is a Success Factor: A form of timidity comes from thinking that we will demoralize people if we set big goals. We find just the opposite happens. The big goals produce high morale. Big goals are what people want to do with their lives. The timidity and incrementalism we encounter comes from fear, not from the spirit. It's easy to find and engage the spirit to go big.

Specificity Works: "Some is not a number. Soon is not a time." People appreciate specificity. People can buy into even arbitrary goals. There is a sense of gratitude for clarity.

Structure Helps: It helps to have communication systems, action platforms, field operations, measurement, enough money. All these structures were appreciated. Especially the two-way communication system, when we were making scientific knowledge available in a usable form and listening back actively to what people were telling us. People were eager to download tools, and eager to help others.

Create An Open Culture

Suspension of Rules: This was not a project that involved getting permission. The IHI team shrink-wrapped the bus and went at it. This is how change happened in hospitals all over the country. Breaking rules to achieve better care matters and can be a good thing to do. Just be smart about it … and people are smart. Help people go for it.

Invitation Beats Command: The biggest lesson overall from the Campaign may be that when you work with invitation it changes everything. All we did was open a door and say, "if you want to come in, welcome." Invitation beats command every day. We had no command center; we could not issue orders. We had no power, there was no control structure. The power that grew was the power of involvement – collective action.

Always say Yes, never say No: Never reject a gift. People offering to help are giving us something precious. My colleague, Maureen Bisognano, phrases this as "Waste no will."

Create Positive Energy

Celebration is as Good as Invitation: We had parties. The hospital sites had parties. When we showed up there were celebrations. There was an unabashed willingness to say we went for it, and we had success.

Run From Every Fight: Don't ever waste time fighting with someone. There is too much positive energy in the world for us to spend much, if any, of our limited time fighting anybody. Yes, take on evil, fight crime. But I will not fight with friends. If they disagree with me, fine. We can go do different things. Avoid wasting time looking for obstructions and arguing about them.

Lead with Stories: We remember the story of the person whose life was saved.

Envisioning the Next Series of Bold Aims: A Call to Action

I would like to turn to another challenge and opportunity for health care that we don't know how to make happen just yet. We first introduced this emerging vision at the 2019 IHI National Forum. There I laid out my sense of frustration with the fact that we know so much about the social determinants of health and how to keep people healthy, yet we don't systematically address the underlying issues of food insecurity, housing, transportation, and more. We continue to invest heavily in expensive healthcare delivery to the point where it crowds out investment in the true generators of health. Healthcare is, of course, noble and worthy of significant investment. However, we are neglecting adequate investment in addressing the causes of illness, injury, and disability.

We have a list of transformative agenda items we need to work on, both as a nation and as a healthcare industry. There are seven items that I call the *Moral Determinants of Health*. The first thing we have to do is declare our goals. We envision doctors, nurses, pharmacists, practices, stepping forward and saying "Yes, we will deliver health care, but we will do this too: help create health!" That is a big ask of a busy and already stressed industry. However, I think we are best positioned to do it. We have the moral platform, the knowledge base, the gravitas, and the resources. We can make it happen if we choose to work on the causes of ill health, not just the symptoms of illness.

Look at number four: "Achieve radical reform of our nation's criminal justice system." This is about the prisons and jails. While running for office in Massachusetts, I became familiar with the criminal justice system.

A Campaign for the Moral Determinants of Health

1. Achieve US ratification of major human rights treaties;
2. Make health care unequivocally a human right in our nation;
3. Restore American leadership to reverse climate change;
4. Achieve radical reform of our nation's criminal justice system;
5. End policies of exclusion and achieve compassionate immigration reform;
6. End hunger and homelessness in our nation;
7. Restore order, dignity and equity to our democratic institutions; assure the right of every single person's vote to count equally.

Nationally about 2 to 3 million people are incarcerated—with 10 million cycling through the system each year. Our system is very, very broken. It's not fair and it's not just. The incarceration rates of African Americans and Latinos far exceeds that of whites. In addition, it is a big health problem. Over 70% of inmates have mental health and substance abuse problems.

Our system fails in three big ways:

1. We have too few alternatives to incarceration, so we use prisons way too much, more by far than any other developed nation;

2. Inmates don't get the health care they need in prison;

3. On reentry into society, former inmates don't get the support they need.

Other countries have solved these problems. They have successful restorative justice systems. And we have some great, local models in the US as well. It's all fixable.

We can ask a difficult question: ought the health professions and their institutions take on this redirection of prisons and jails?

Honest and compassionate people disagree about health care's proper role in improving social conditions, countering inequity, and fighting against structural racism. Some say health care should remain focused on the traditional "caring for illness." I believe that it is both important and appropriate to expand the role of physicians and health care organizations into both demanding and supporting societal reform.

We in health care should help fix the criminal justice system. It is a symbolic and important example of something gone terribly wrong. The health care system should lead that fix because it can. Physicians, nurses, and other health care professionals can speak out, write opinion pieces, work with community organizations devoted to the issues listed, and, most important of all, vote and ensure that colleagues vote on election days.

We would have to do it locally. I am thinking of the way Tom Evans picked up the 100,000 Lives campaign and brought it into Iowa (see story that follows). Every community, led by the local health care institutions, could carry out the transformation.

> *"Healers are called to heal. When the fabric of communities upon which health depends is torn, then healers are called to mend it. The moral law within each of us insists that we do so. Improving the social determinants of health will be brought at last to a boil only by the heat of the moral determinants of health."*

The Moral Determinants of Health,
Journal of the American Medical Association
by Donald M. Berwick MD, MPP, July 21,
2020 Volume 324, Number 3

Three Thousand Hospitals, One Common Aim

by **Joe McCannon**
100,000 Lives
Campaign Manager, IHI

"Successful movements don't dictate what to do. Instead, they uncover passion and skill – and then unleash it."

Creating an Atmosphere for Commitment, Ownership and Action

When I look back on the 100,000 Lives Campaign, I remember the wonderful teammates I had at IHI and the great relationships we formed with colleagues across the country. We shared exciting and challenging moments and really learned together.

A lot of that learning is captured in Don's reflection – the power of shared aims, for example, and the importance of creating a structure networked for exchanging information and ideas. Providers around the country felt a shared accountability to the goal we had established – they really believed in trying to avoid 100,000 unnecessary deaths – and they shared generously and transparently with one another to try to make that happen.

With a little distance and perspective, I also think a major factor in the initiative's success had to do with how we understood our own role in orchestrating national action. Initially, my mental model was ineffective: from our office in Cambridge, MA, IHI would tell hospitals around the country how to avoid harm. My image of leadership was directive – we were in charge. As it turns out, that approach doesn't generate much engagement and energy. People might come and listen to a webinar or download a document from your web site, but that's mostly passive. And then they'll just move onto the next thing. There is no evidence to suggest that a webinar or a paper will lead to behavior change.

Over time, what we realized is that the way you really bring people on board is to both set a thrilling aim that they co-own, and then empower them to take action within their spheres of influence. Successful movements don't dictate what to do. Instead, they uncover passion and skill – and then unleash it. We had national partners (the American Medical Association, the American Nurses Association, the Leapfrog Group, the Centers for Medicare & Medicaid

Services, the Centers for Disease Control and Prevention) and field offices (so-called "nodes" including state hospital associations, quality improvement organizations and large private health systems) and we told them that they needed to make the campaign work for them and for their constituents. What's meaningful to a group of rural hospitals, for instance, will be different than what's meaningful to a network of academic centers. We supplied the evidence-based content and expert faculty, and they then channeled that in a way that was locally appropriate and effective for their audience. As long as their adaptations are taking us closer to our aim, that's not a bad thing – it's a source of improvement and learning. It's how spread happens.

This insight held true in our interactions with hospitals and individual providers. They all had moving personal stories of witnessing harm to patients and the pain they felt as a result; and they also had incredible ideas to avoid that kind of harm from ever happening again. We just needed to invite them to test their innovations and share their results. Our job wasn't to prescribe their actions – it was to go out in the field to find the bright spots and celebrate them, to distill and redistribute their ingenuity. We held up a mirror to them and said, "Look at what you're building. This is all about you —your passion, creativity, and courageous leadership." We designated a number of the most successful facilities as mentor hospitals, and they regularly coached and guided their peers.

In that atmosphere – where we had a clear, shared aim combined with an invitation to innovate – amazing things started to happen. Participating nodes and hospitals became co-leaders of the initiative. They really embraced a common goal and held one another accountable for success and progress. When aims and motivation are aligned, outside inspectors aren't needed to drive action.

In addition to the evidence base we shared, the free how-to guides and toolkits we supplied, and the national training sessions we offered with experts (some attended by the thousands), we saw a proliferation of local events happening in different states and regions around the country. Different approaches were being used in different places. It started to feel like every node was a laboratory, testing different methods to drive change—from collaboratives to extension agencies. At some point we started to have a hard time keeping track of every event and realized that this kind of spontaneous action, even though it worried us at times, was the sign of a healthy movement.

We reinforced this activity by actively and intentionally limiting fear. We knew that if participants felt we were going to embarrass them or call them out when they shared their struggles, that would seriously limit their questions and their learning. One key area we focused on in this respect was measurement and data collection. A system was designed to collect self-reported hospital data in a way that did not expose individual hospitals. This allowed us to go out and study interesting performance (good or bad) and also to create a national estimate of change in mortality. The approach encouraged data-driven learning and assessment while limiting potential for embarrassment or shame. We knew that payers, accreditors and quality organizations would be measuring that in time, but we wanted to first create a safe environment for learning. Most participating hospitals (86%) submitted data, and many discussed performance with their supporting campaign node. I think that helped everyone get better faster.

We also limited fear – and increased joy and learning – by spending a lot of time out in the field. Don mentioned the Bus Tour – this was one element of a much larger effort where we were constantly visiting states and hospitals to identify breakthroughs, understand challenges and develop responsive content. One week in our second campaign, we actually had nearly every staff and board member visit a facility in every state. We were deeply focused on building relationships with those we served, and we used what they told us to continuously adjust. We were learning and improvising in the same way we hoped they would.

Learning From, Improving With, and Responding to Criticism

Of course, the campaign wasn't perfect – not by any stretch of the imagination. Our effectiveness varied from facility to facility, state to state and system to system and, in hindsight, I wish we had thought more about disparities in care and harm for long-neglected communities and individuals. That's something I would do differently today.

We also experienced criticism and pushback along the way. Despite Don's incredible leadership and our constant effort to share recognition with others, some felt that IHI got too much credit. Others dismissively said that IHI was good at generating activity but were skeptical of the campaign's impact. And probably the biggest challenge of all came in June 2006, shortly after we announced the campaign's results.

Over the 18-month period, the hospital participants had exceeded their goal and we estimated they saved 122,000 lives. Exceeding the campaign goal generated great excitement and quite a bit of media coverage—it was a celebratory moment for all of us. But a few weeks later two very respected physicians thoroughly critiqued us in a paper. They said that although the 100,000 Lives Campaign succeeded in catalyzing efforts to improve safety and quality in American hospitals, the promotion of rapid response teams as an evidence-based best practice was problematic, and they raised methodologic concerns regarding the "lives saved" calculation, making it difficult to interpret the campaign's true accomplishments in their view.

It was hard to hear, and our team was upset. I certainly felt personally embarrassed and lost a lot of sleep. We were proud of the measurement system we had created, which took a lot of thought and creativity from our measurement team and other IHI experts, and we felt we had explained our approach very clearly in the lead-up to announcing our outcomes. We felt that much of that had been ignored, and that some of the feedback was simply incorrect.

It was hard to know how to react. I definitely made some missteps. It's easy to get angry or defensive and sometimes you just want to walk away. Ultimately, I think the key was in returning to our aim: avoiding medical harm. With that as a starting point, we learned to say, "Okay, what can we learn from this that will help our cause and our next campaign? What's valid in the feedback we got and how can we improve from that? Is there any way the debate about our results can draw more attention to the important work we're doing? Might we even team up with our critics to get it better the next time?" That's hard but you always have a choice to manage constructively and, ultimately, we felt like we owed that to the caregivers, patients and families who were such integral parts of the larger effort.

In a nutshell, we chose to take three steps to avoid an argument and to put the criticism to constructive use:

1. Clarify points in the article that we felt were not correct;

2. Use the critique to learn how to do better, and share insights with the campaign community;

3. Get on with the work of improving hospital safety.

In the spirit of the health profession's scientific peer review culture, the critical paper triggered a conversation about important policy and program design factors. The critique covered the evidence required to introduce a safety intervention, risk adjustment, extrapolation, and use of self-reported data. Over the next ten years, hospital safety campaigns by IHI and the federal government continued to build and deploy more advanced approaches to hospital safety measurement. I think this discussion helped make that work more effective.

Although dealing with a public critique can be uncomfortable and even painful, the process surfaced several IHI values: maintaining our focus on our life-saving purpose, using this focus to sustain resilience, learning fast, and showing improvement on the ground.

Ready to Co-Lead in Iowa

by **Tom Evans MD**
CEO of the Iowa
Healthcare Collaborative

An Invitation to Tap into Abundance

"First do no harm" is more than simply not making errors. It's a challenge for the healthcare field to adopt a vision, plan, and actions for continuous improvement. Don Berwick has taken up this challenge throughout his life and career. He invited the healthcare industry to lead the transformation of hospital safety. The solutions were at hand. However, hospitals weren't deploying them. Don believed that clinicians and organizations shouldn't simply meet standards of care – "checking the boxes"—but should also be constantly innovating toward higher and higher levels of performance.

As a participant in the campaigns Dr. Berwick helped launch, I came to understand how the principle of Abundance enables transformation to occur in situations that seem overwhelmingly resistant to change.

Don offered us a platform to work from. The Institute for Healthcare Improvement (IHI) launched the 100,000 Lives campaign in 2004. I had the privilege of serving as a faculty member. Extremely innovative at that time, the campaign proposed that the hospital safety results we were getting were simply not good enough. It envisioned a new future by recognizing that most medical complications were dependent upon the processes of care delivery, and that the adoption of well-known best practices was inconsistent across the country. It boldly stated that many of these complications can be improved, and that healthcare providers had an obligation to make the improvements.

Dr. Berwick and his IHI team invited hospitals to join a national campaign of change and improvement. We were challenged to deploy an identified set of best practices and save 100,000 lives within 18 months. In doing so, Don tapped into the secret of Abundance.

There are people out there who see that something needs to be done, are ready to act, but don't know how to proceed. They may even have tried, without getting very far and becoming frustrated. I was one of these people. Don and his colleagues gave people like me permission to act on instincts we already had. They gave us an open forum to engage with others on a common vision. Instead of focusing on the barriers to change, he asked us all, "Why not?" Turned out, there were a lot of us ready to act. An abundance of people, energy and action emerged in response to Don's invitation and request.

A Strong Circle of Influence for Hospital Safety in Iowa

I know I was ready. I had just finished a six-year period as the Chief Medical Officer of a large health system in Iowa. Much of my time was spent trying to convince executives to move ahead on quality and safety. I was not having much success. Though everyone agreed quality and safety were important, I was pushing up a very steep hill. The focus at that time was on efficiency and financial performance. While the CEO and the Board expressed support for our work, financial constraints signaled by our Chief Financial Officer always managed to prevent any real progress. Though frustrated, I knew that this work had to go forward. We had the answers. We just needed the will and an avenue for proceeding.

About this same time, another experience confirmed our Abundance and that we had what we needed to proceed. While serving as the president of our state's medical association, I used my leadership platform to bring together the three big health medical systems in our state to share quality strategies and experience. All three systems had previously publicly stated that we were interested in quality and safety. We convened to explore those efforts, and to have a professional exchange – a show and tell. When we got together, however, a whole new concept of collaboration emerged.

I presented first. I was eager to showcase some innovative patient safety work that my system was doing and was certain that the other systems would be impressed. The talk was very well received, and my competitors were a bit envious of our progress. The next system presented, and while their patient safety strategy wasn't as good as ours, their cardiology strategy was much better. I made a note to myself to get together with them to explore this. Finally, the health system with an academic medical center presented. I was certain that, with all of those medical students and residents, their patient safety strategy couldn't be as good as ours. As expected, it wasn't. Nor was their cardiology strategy as good as our competitor.

However, their infectious disease strategy was by far the best of the three.

It suddenly dawned on us all: "Why don't we all work together, share our best practices, and build a total quality system across all three healthcare systems?" I called Dr. Berwick at that point to ask whether IHI had state chapters to do health care improvement. His reply was, "No IHI doesn't have a chapter program. But why don't you just do it anyway?"

Two years later I left my healthcare system to create the Iowa Healthcare Collaborative.

Through an initial partnership between the Iowa Hospital Association (IHA) and the Iowa Medical Society (IMS), our provider-led transformation effort was launched. I am proud to share that Iowa was the first state with 100% of our hospitals committed and participating in the IHI's 100,000 Lives campaign. We continued this work through the IHI 5 Million Lives Campaign and into the Centers for Medicare and Medicaid Services Partnership for Patients initiative. Sixteen years later, we continue to work with hospital systems in Iowa, and now across the nation to improve the effectiveness, safety, and efficiency of health care.

Working with Don Berwick and his IHI team taught me to live with an attitude and expectation of Abundance. Focus on what we have rather than our barriers. There are always people out there ready to co-lead with you.

Federal Sequel to 100,000 Lives Campaign Earns a Rare Public Acknowledgement

In 2011, the Department of Health and Human Services and the Centers for Medicare and Medicaid Services (CMS) announced the Partnership for Patients (PfP). CMS and its partners drew on learning from IHI hospital safety campaigns and adapted them to launch a national policy and health system improvement initiative. The Partnership was launched while Don Berwick was serving as CMS Administrator for an 18-month period, 2010 – 2011, with Joe McCannon as his Senior Advisor. The White House and its Office of Management and Budget (OMB) approved a requested $500 million investment to reduce preventable harm in hospitals by 40% over four years – another Bold Aim. Dennis, together with his colleague Paul McGann MD, took over as Co-Directors of the Partnership shortly after Secretary Kathleen Sebelius, Administrator Berwick, Joe McCannon, and many partners launched the national change initiative.

In designing the Partnership for Patients, a cross-cutting group of experts called a "tiger team" from CMS, the Agency for Healthcare Research and Quality (AHRQ), and the Centers for Disease Control (CDC) collaborated on the development of a national measurement approach to assess overall progress on the ten greatest hospital harms targeted by the Partnership, including adverse drug events, pressure ulcers, falls, and surgical site infections, among others. The product of the tiger team's work became known as the AHRQ National Scorecard. Most of the data in the scorecard is collected by the CMS Medicare Patient Safety Monitoring System (MPSMS). A random sample of approximately 30,000 patient charts each year are pulled from hospitals, and then chart abstractors go through all the charts to physically count every instance of hospital harm.

People who study and count medical impacts believe that chart review is one of the strongest ways to truly measure what happens to patients during health care. This data was the principal source of the top-of-the-line federal measurement system. The CMS chart review data was further augmented by administrative data from AHRQ, and infection data from CDC's National Healthcare Safety Network.

The new system was designed to measure changes in hospital safety and established that there were 145 harms to patients per one thousand discharges in the campaign baseline year of 2010. The Partnership for Patients enrolled and teamed with nearly four thousand of the nation's five thousand hospitals to systematically reduce harms to patients. As the graph in Don Berwick's leadership story shows, by the end of calendar year 2017, the AHRQ Scorecard showed that patient harm in US hospitals had declined to 86 harms per thousand discharges, a 41 percent reduction in overall harm.

Over the 12-year period from the beginning of the 100,000 Lives Campaign through 2017, we can see how leadership generated significant national improvements in hospital safety, and continuously generated innovative systems to deliver that performance. As leaders, Don, Joe, and their successors anchored themselves in purpose, said "Yes, and..." to criticism, avoided fights, and stayed resilient. They continuously improved their work and persisted in deliberate, Intentional leadership action.

A Public Assertion and A Challenge

In an ironic but affirming twist of fate, a question about hospital patient safety results came into the national spotlight again in April 2015. President Barack Obama had convened a national meeting of healthcare leaders at the White House and charged them with assessing and making recommendations to improve the government's implementation of the landmark Affordable Care Act that was signed into law in 2010.

As part of President Obama's speech, he noted that "more than 50,000 lives had been saved" as a result of programs implemented through the legislation. At that time, the AHRQ Scorecard showed that patient harm had declined to 121 harms per thousand discharges, saving an estimated 87,000 lives. Glenn Kessler and his team at the Washington Post Fact Checker column leapt on the President's remarks and immediately contacted the Department of Health and Human Services to investigate the accuracy of the assertion.

The Fact Checker column's signature assessment of challenged facts was to award 1, 2, 3 or 4 long-nosed "Pinocchios" depending on how bad the inaccuracies or outright lies were for the statements that they challenged. It is never a good sign when the Washington Post Fact Checker calls your federal communications office.

Dennis joined with Paul McGann MD and Rick Kronick MD, the Director of the Agency for Health Care Research and Quality (AHRQ), for a lengthy, intensive meeting with Kessler and his team. Following the extensive conference call, they forwarded the published peer-reviewed paper on the Partnership for Patients measurement approach, a summary of the extensive underlying chart review data, and the detailed AHRQ analyses that substantiated the National Scorecard findings.

As anticipated, several days later the Washington Post Fact Checker ran a column on the President's claim.

The Washington Post Fact Checker awarded Obama's statement the coveted Geppetto Checkmark, indicating that Obama's statement reflected "the truth, the whole truth, and nothing but the truth." The federal agencies' communications offices didn't know that such an outcome was even possible! None of them had ever experienced or encountered the extremely rare Geppetto Checkmark. The facts checked out.

The Resilience of Don Berwick MD, Joe McCannon, and the original Institute for Healthcare Improvement team paid off. Their decision to anchor themselves in the compelling purpose of Bold Aims, while learning from and addressing the measurement criticisms leveled at their work, informed the federal Partnership for Patients initiative, and resulted in further life-saving improvements. National improvements in patient safety were validated through the new measurement system.

Partnership for Patients Initiative Earns Rare "Geppetto Checkmark"

The Washington Post

Fact Checker, by Glenn Kessler

Obama's claim the Affordable Care Act was a 'major reason' in preventing 50,000 patient deaths

✔ **The Geppetto Checkmark**
"The truth, the whole truth, and nothing but the truth"

 One Pinocchio
Mostly True with Shading of Facts

 Two Pinocchios
Half True with Significant Omissions

 Three Pinocchios
Mostly False with Factual Errors

 Four Pinocchios
Flat-out Untrue

President Obama uses the Agency for Healthcare Research and Quality (AHRQ) analysis of Partnership for Patients impact in remarks on 5th anniversary of ACA.

The Washington Post Fact Checker confirms accuracy of the President's remarks in April 2015 with a coveted red "Geppetto" Checkmark (above).

Pinocchio graphic courtesy of Steve McCraken

INTENT

Compelling Vision

Bold Aims

Decide-Notice-Acknowledge

Establishing and Achieving a Bold Aim on Organ Donation

Former Wisconsin Governor Tommy Thompson came to Washington, DC, in 2000 to serve as Secretary of the U.S. Department of Health and Human Services. He was committed to improving the practice and frequency of organ donation. As Governor of Wisconsin, he had participated in a legal argument over organ donation policy with the Department he was now charged with leading. As Secretary, Thompson resolved to increase organ donation nationally. He brought a leadership vision and translated it into program action. A public information campaign encouraging people to register as organ donors was launched.

However, after two years of extensive public education and public relations efforts, the nation's organ donation numbers were still relatively flat, and the waitlists for organs were increasing.

Cabinet Secretary's Leadership Vision Creates Opportunities for Federal Team

Late in 2002, Dennis took on leadership of a small team of federal civil servants and contractors responsible for implementing some of Thompson's organ donation initiatives at the Health Resources and Services Administration (HRSA), one of the agencies in the Department of Health and Human Services. In studying hospital data, our team saw an opportunity to create a Bold Aim that could significantly increase the number of organ donors and lives saved through transplantation.

HRSA Team Builds a Bold Aim Grounded in Performance Data

The data we analyzed showed the distribution of organ donation rates for the 300 largest trauma centers in the nation. This important variable is the number of eligible donors in a trauma center who become actual donors. When a patient on life support experiences the tragedy of brain death, the family is typically asked for permission for the patient to become an organ donor. The national average showed that less than half the families said yes – only about 46 percent of the eligible organ donors were becoming donors.

We looked at the variation in these rates among the nation's largest hospitals and specifically, the performance outliers. In the following graph, about 30 of the nation's 300 largest trauma centers and their associated organ procurement organizations (OPOs) already had organ donation rates above 70% (see the green columns to the right in the graph below).

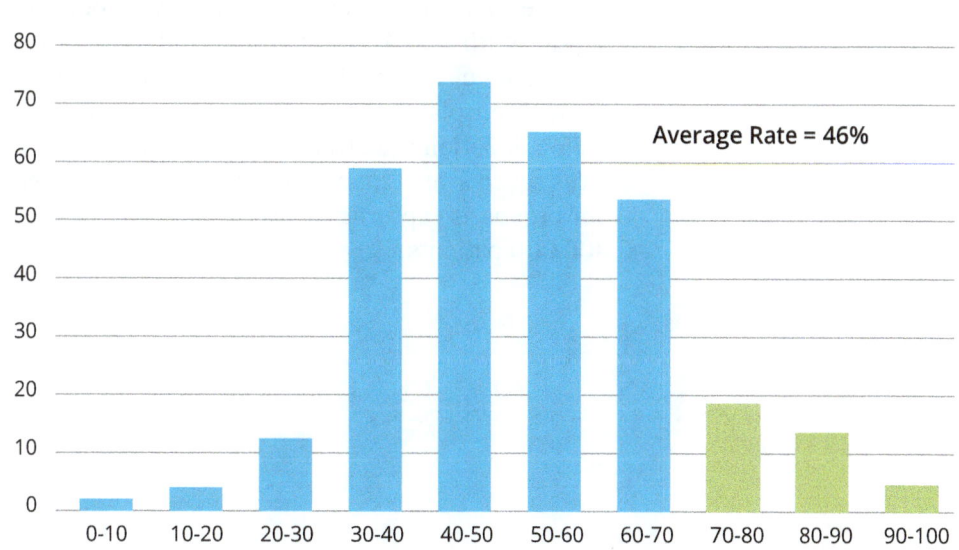

Source: Organ Procurement and Transplant Network data

Interestingly, this graph was not seen by many in the community of practice as showing differences in the performance of the hospitals. People attributed the differences to the environment. Hospitals and OPOs in the blue columns considered their rate to be appropriate given their populations and local situations. When asked, these hospitals almost always had explanations for why their results were different than the hospitals at the extreme right. The explanations were not grounded in data and evidence.

By contrast, centers with the highest rates, like Boston Medical Center and Memorial Hermann hospital in Houston, could explain how they achieved the higher performance. Further investigation found that clinicians and other practitioners in these high performing outlier hospitals and their affiliated organ procurement organizations (OPOs) had command of the practices that led to the high rates. The practices appeared to be imminently transferable. Our federal team realized that high donation rates in large trauma centers were more uniformly possible. The best practices of these leading hospitals and their organ procurement organizations could show the way.

Moving the national system to a 75% donation rate would have major, life-saving impacts. In 2003, the number of eligible deceased donors was about 12,000 a year. With a 50% donation rate, and three organs per donor, about 18,000 life-saving and enhancing deceased donor transplants were performed each year. But with a 75% donation rate, transplants would result in 27,000 lives saved a year, many thousands more. The demand for organs as captured by waitlists was on the order of 100,000 patients.

Take Advantage of Variation: Raise All Boats to Levels of High Performers

In developing and committing to Bold Aims, our team learned the importance of going beyond assessing average performance and setting incremental targets. Incremental goals don't capture the attention and excitement needed by the people who have frontline accountabilities for improvement. Incremental goals have us simply aligning available resources to the task at hand.

Instead, we need to rethink the work. We need to study the activities already in place that are producing high performance and take advantage of the implicit knowledge behind their numbers.

Why settle for improving performance just a little? Instead, help everyone move to the levels already proven possible by the high-performing outliers.

Intentionally Grow Commitment To, and Accountability For, the Bold Aim

Our small federal team had no legal or statutory authority to require action or compliance with a 75% donation rate. We had no management vehicle through which to move OPOs and the 500 independent trauma centers in the US to a higher donation rate. The Bold Aim of a 75% rate was not yet on the radar screen of the Office of the Secretary.

Our team in the Division of Transplantation had to build commitment to the Bold Aim of a 75% rate at three levels. First, the proposed Aim had to be accepted in the Department of Health and Human Services as a way to achieve the Secretary's priority. Second, the senior executives of the professional organizations associated with organ donation and transplantation would be asked to call for action on the proposed Bold Aim. Third, and possibly the most challenging, we had to convince a critical number of the 500 trauma centers and their partner organ procurement organizations to voluntarily commit to the Bold Aim. These were big challenges.

Backed by immediate supervisors, our team presented the Bold Aim and supporting data to Department officials as a new way to contribute to the Secretary's vision for increasing organ donation. Through staff discussions with his office, our team urged Secretary Thompson to add a new component to the ongoing public relations approach. We offered an intensive, large-scale national quality improvement initiative by spreading the best practices of organ procurement organizations and large trauma centers (including those in Wisconsin, the Secretary's home state) that already had high rates of organ donation.

Galvanized by Camille Haney, a trusted Senior Advisor who also hailed from Wisconsin, Secretary Thompson used his presentation at a groundbreaking ceremony for the new building of the United Network for Organ Sharing to embrace a Bold Aim: an organ donation rate of 75% in the nation's largest trauma centers.

Our federal team worked hard to make sure Secretary Thompson wasn't alone in committing to this Bold Aim. We reached out to key leaders in the organ donation, transplantation, and healthcare quality improvement communities. Executives and elected leaders of key national organizations agreed to join with the Secretary in committing to the organ donation donation rate of 75%.

Senior Leaders Commit to the Bold Aim

A decision was made to capture these commitments into a formal Contract for Results. Organizations like the Association of Organ Procurement Officials, the North American Transplant Coordinators Organization, the Institute for Healthcare Improvement, and others, all joined with Secretary Thompson in committing to the new Bold Aim. The Contract for Results was frequently displayed at events in the form of signatures on a six-foot poster board (see facing page).

Two of the high performing field executives who helped to create the Bold Aim also signed the contract. Teresa Shafer, a nurse executive then at the Life Gift Organ Procurement Organization in Dallas/Fort Worth, was one of the key sources of best practices leading to high donation rates.

Teresa was joined in the work to spread proven best practices by John Chessare MD, then Chief Medical Officer of the Boston Medical Center. (For Dr. Chessare's Leadership Story on improving patient care quality, see the chapter on Roles.) Dr. Chessare was a key leader in supporting the team in his hospital that generated its high rates. Shafer and Chessare, a nurse and a doctor, ultimately served as the volunteer Faculty Co-Chairs of the Collaborative. As voices of leading-edge practice that produced high donation rates, their early commitment gave the proposed campaign credibility across the board.

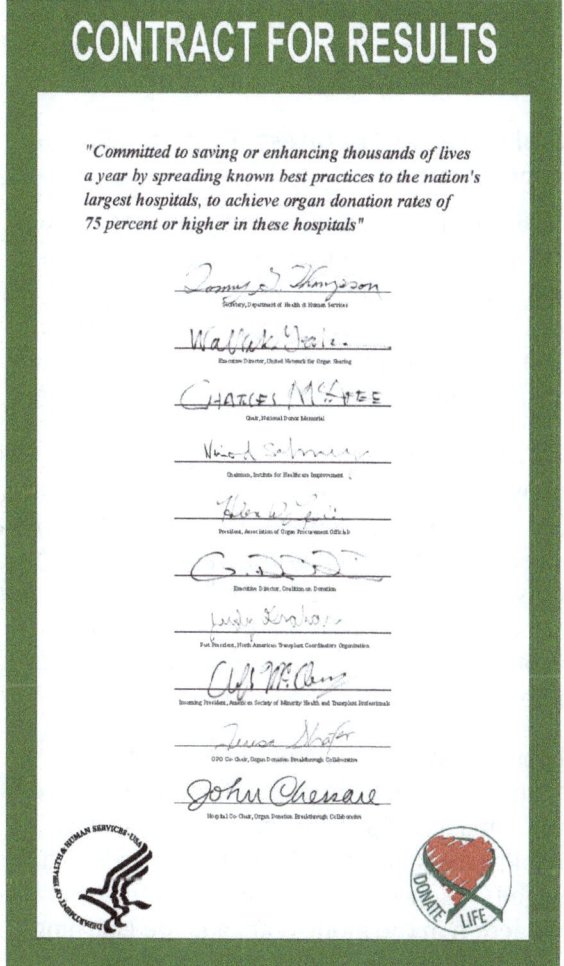

Circles of influence committing to a common goal: increase hospital organ donation rates from under 50% to over 75%.

Health and Human Services Secretary Tommy Thompson commits to a Bold Aim on organ donation at the groundbreaking ceremony for the United Network for Organ Sharing in April of 2003 in Richmond, Virginia.

In background is Vinod Sahney, Board Chairman of the Institute for Healthcare Improvement

Enrolling Responsible Organizations onto a Managed Platform for Improvement

A critical mass of OPOs and large trauma centers were attracted to the life-saving possibilities of the Bold Aim and the influential leaders and organizations who had committed to it. In September 2003, the players convened in Washington, DC for the first time in a special event, our first Learning Session. The Organ Donation Breakthrough Collaborative was formally launched with 800 people in attendance. Initially, 43 Organ Procurement Organizations (OPOs) and 95 trauma centers enrolled. Those numbers increased to 50 OPOs and 131 additional trauma centers the following year and continued to grow to eventually involve nearly 500 of the nation's largest trauma hospitals over the course of the next four years.

HRSA Establishes and Operates an Action Learning Collaborative Platform

The 75% Bold Aim represented a major departure from the current drift and would require major changes and new systems. It required breakthrough thinking and large-scale testing and adaptation by teams from across the nation's 500 largest hospitals and their affiliated organ procurement organizations.

The federal team chose to use the collaborative methodology developed by Don Berwick of IHI as described earlier. The IHI Breakthrough Collaborative Framework was ideal for this work because it was built around a shared commitment to Bold Aims and used an All Teach, All Learn engagement strategy, where frontline practitioners learn best practices from each other in organized collaborative learning events and activities.

OPO and hospital staff joined forces to establish collaborative teams. Teams met in person every three to four months for several days to share insights, learning, and results. Progress on commitments was reviewed and acknowledged. Teams developed new commitments for testing and action in the months ahead. The Learning Sessions were well designed Pacing Events ranging from 800 to 2500+ participants. Key leaders from high-performing Organ Procurement Organizations and trauma hospitals served as faculty. Monthly webinars were held to maintain focus, learning, and action. Teams carried out rapid cycle testing and implementation between Learning Sessions.

As a packaged method, the Action Learning Collaborative program gave all of us a management platform with several key features:

- **Continuous rapid learning is the engine.**
  Teams met regularly to share results and practices. Trial and error enabled rapid learning. Barriers and failures did not leave teams stuck. The answer was always in the room.

- **High energy is created and maintained.**
  The Collaborative convenings were designed as Pacing Events designed to nurture the positive energy needed to keep everyone moving forward. Transplant recipients and donor families were featured. High performers were acknowledged. All sessions were highly interactive. Participants made public commitments.

- **Performance information gives common focus and makes teams accountable.**
  Processes to collect data and information were established. Progress at the participant level was tracked and managed. Review of performance trends and differences generated action and energy. There was public accountability for commitment to results at multiple levels.

- **Gains are spread and sustained for system impact at scale.**
  The Collaborative was intentionally made highly visible to non-participating hospitals, national professional organizations, federal policy makers, patient advocates, and others. This made it more likely that success would be hard-wired into the nation's organ donation and transplant system.

The Collaborative was a high-energy intensive effort carried out in stages over several years. As the initial group of collaborative teams succeeded in achieving higher levels of performance, additional waves of activity were added so that new teams could join. It was a modest but important investment in transformation by the government and the participants. HRSA financed the series of Learning Sessions and the necessary staff support to organize and conduct the initiative with a budget of about $4 million annually.

A New Normal is Created

Over a four-year period, the Organ Donor Breakthrough Collaborative reached the critical mass necessary to make the effective new practices a new normal for the organ donation and transplant field. A culture of improvement, consent rate tracking, systematic use of clinical triggers, huddles, and widespread use of Donation after Circulatory Determination of Death were among the many elements of the higher-performing system. Together these new system elements have contributed to constant year-after-year growth in organ donation and transplantation.

The Improved Systems Generated Life-Saving Results

The Organ Donation Breakthrough Collaborative met and in some cases exceeded our expectations. The number of large trauma centers with donation rates of 75% and higher grew rapidly.

The Collaborative's first organized Learning Session took place in September 2003. Over the next four years, the nation's rapidly improving organ donation system routinely established new records month after month. Donation increased from approximately 525 organ donors per month to approximately 650 organ donors per month—an increase of 125 per month, or 1,500 donors per year, translating to roughly 4,500 additional lives saved each year. Many waitlisted patients—mothers, fathers, children, grandparents among them—received lifesaving and life-enhancing transplants.

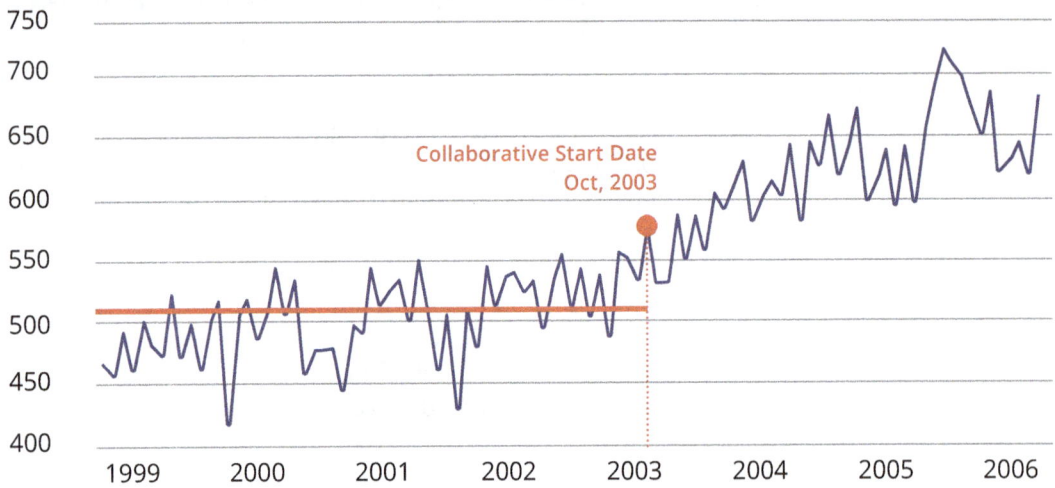

Source: Organ Procurement and Transplant Network data

Acknowledge Commitments, Demonstrate Impact, Celebrate Results

Transformative change is challenging and stressful. An effective way to energize people through challenge and stress is to acknowledge their good work on the road to change. Building celebration into Learning Sessions was one way the HRSA team accomplished this; organizing special, stand-alone celebratory events was another. The Organ Donation Breakthrough Collaborative team took several steps to build acknowledgement into the practices of organ procurement organizations and hospitals, creating a new form of national recognition for those achieving the Bold Aim.

Linking Transplant Recipients with Hospital Clinicians and Staff

As the work of the Collaborative progressed, one of the things that many of us involved in the work began to understand was that clinicians and staff in trauma centers were not connected with the lifesaving impacts of their organ donation work. The organ donation process is intricate and time sensitive. It occurs amid difficult and heart-wrenching communications with families who have lost or are in the process of losing a loved one. We learned that hospital providers rarely if ever got to see the lifesaving consequences of their organ donation work. They didn't naturally encounter transplant recipients during the course of their work. Their only experience was typically limited to the devastating loss of the patient. For a healthcare provider, nothing is worse than the loss of a patient.

To address this gap, involvement of transplant recipients and their families became a standard feature of our Collaborative Learning Sessions. We began to close the loop so that providers in trauma centers could see the impacts of their lifesaving work. ICU nurses and trauma surgeons started meeting and interacting with recipients whose lives were saved by their improved organ donation processes. This closing of the loop led to other ideas aimed at recognizing the providers who were so central to enabling and supporting the lifesaving work of donation.

Establishing the Organ Donation Medal of Honor to Acknowledge High Performing Teams

Secretary Tommy Thompson was scheduled to make remarks at a Collaborative Learning Session in Dearborn, Michigan in the Spring of 2004. The Secretary had originally pursued the idea of establishing a Congressional Organ Donation Medal of Honor but had not succeeded in getting Congress to adopt this proposal. Now charged with drafting the Secretary's remarks, our team decided to take the initiative on a slightly different approach.

As the person in charge of drafting the remarks, Dennis embedded an important announcement into the Secretary's draft speech. The communications officials approved it. The Secretary's staff approved it. At the Learning Session in Dearborn, Thompson announced:

> *In one year's time, the Department of Health and Human Services will confer its first-ever Organ Donation Medals of Honor on hospital and OPO teams who achieve a 75% organ donation rate among the eligible donors in their large trauma centers.*

Large Hospitals with 75% Donation Rates Receiving HHS Medal of Honor

Pre-Collaborative	<30
May, 2005	184
October, 2006	371
October, 2007	392

The HHS Organ Donation Medal of Honor became a powerful way to officially recognize the lifesaving work of dedicated OPO and hospital providers who excelled in their organ donation practices. Teams from 184 hospitals and their affiliated OPOs were awarded Medals of Honor in 2005 with more Medals awarded in 2006, 2007, and beyond. The federal team used the Medals of Honor to make the needed connection between the work of healthcare providers involved in organ donation, and the lifesaving results that flowed from their use of effective donation practices.

Locking in the New Normal

The Organ Donation Breakthrough Collaborative had transformed the nation's practice and performance on the dimensions of eligible donors and organ donation rates. All the key organizations in the field of donation and transplantation were engaged as owners and co-owners of the initiative. The work spanned from on-the-ground OPOs and hospitals to many national professional associations. A transformative level of engagement had been achieved, and collaborative participants were eager to lock in this new normal.

During the course of the Collaborative, national organizations with a stake in the donation and transplantation work were convened every four months as a Leadership Coordinating Council. They agreed to align their work with the Bold Aim of the Collaborative. This helped to ensure that Council member conferences, publications, continuing education, advocacy, and other programs were aligned and supportive of the collaborative teams participating in the work.

As the Collaborative began to transition to new and less intense phases of work, the Leadership Council decided to create a new not-for-profit organization to continue its work. The Organ Donation and Transplant Alliance was chartered in 2006. The Board of the new organization drew its membership from participating organizations like the American Hospital Association, the American Society of Transplantation, the Association of Organ Procurement Organizations, the Joint Commission, and others.

This dynamic and influential organization has continued the work of identifying innovative concepts and working to spread and hardwire best practices across donor hospitals, organ procurement organizations, and transplant centers. The Alliance, now under the leadership of Executive Director Karri Hobson-Pape, recently celebrated its 15th Anniversary.

The Health Resources and Services Administration has incorporated ongoing, sustained support of quality improvement into its oversight and work with the national Organ Procurement and Transplantation Network (OPTN). The number of donors has continued to increase since the Collaborative. In 2020 and 2021, the United States led the world with the highest rate of donors per million people. This is quite remarkable given that in some countries such as Spain, donation is compulsory for all deaths unless the citizen has taken prior specific actions to prevent the donation of their organs.

The National Academy of Sciences, Engineering, and Medicine (NASEM) issued a report in February of 2022 that called attention to the achievements of the Organ Donation Breakthrough Collaborative. The report of the National Academy urged the US government to establish new, higher goals, providing sustained support for quality improvement work at national scale. With strong support from HRSA, the OPTN's Board of Directors followed suit by committing to a new Bold Aim in December of 2023: Achieving 60,000 Deceased Donor Transplants in 2026. More recently the World Health Organization's Donation and Transplantation Global Report for 2023 ranked the US as #1 in the world for patients transplanted per million population.

The 2003 Contract for Results and the Collaborative were voluntary efforts, grounded in a shared commitment to a Bold Aim. The Organ Donation Breakthrough Collaborative was able to secure authentic commitment from participants. Many of those involved frequently shared a common message with us: "Participating in the Organ Donation Breakthrough Collaborative was one of the most meaningful experiences of my entire career." They mean it. Authentically and genuinely committing to challenging Bold Aims that are much bigger than ourselves is profoundly rewarding and meaningful work.

Bold Aims as a Campaign to Realize Intent

A Near Term Aim Far Beyond Current Capability

A classic example of a Bold Aim was put forward in President Kennedy's address to Congress in 1961:

I believe this nation should commit itself to achieving the goal, before this decade is out, of landing a man on the moon and returning him safely to earth.

Back then, the United States lacked the necessary technology or systems to rocket to the moon and back. Much of it had not been invented or imagined. Achieving President Kennedy's Aim required hundreds of organizations and tens of thousands of people to invent, build, and deploy completely new systems. The plausibility of the moon program's Bold Aim was grounded in the Soviet Union's and the United States' success in orbital space and the advances in rocketry and communication after World War II. The aim was plausible and compelling. But it was far beyond the reach of existing management and administrative systems.

A Bold Aim statement is simple, but it's loaded. As shown by President Kennedy's leadership declaration, it has key defining characteristics:

- A well-defined performance target;
- A near-term time period in which the Aim will be realized;
- Clarity about who sees themselves as accountable for achieving the Aim;
- Evidence in the world that the Aim is plausible;
- Means to achieving the Aim are not typically available at-hand;
- A conceivable overarching strategy and program to pursue the Bold Aim; and
- A way to see and track the Aim being realized.

We use the term Bold Aim for a particular leadership approach to expressing and pursuing a Vision. As we observed in the two previous Leadership Stories—100,000 Lives and the Organ Donation Collaborative—the approach is especially striking in situations involving networks of independent organizations with similar missions and performance expectations. We will refer to these two stories in the following discussion of the Bold Aim Mindset and Method.

Seven Campaign Dynamics to Establish and Achieve Bold Aims

The leadership stories presented here are part of a body of evidence showing that Bold Aim-driven campaigns can be highly effective. These stories also provide insight into the proven practices associated with doing this kind of work. Methods and principles emerge. Don Berwick MD, for example, describes how the Bold Aim to establish the 100,000 Lives campaign came from watching his son participate in a political campaign. He was struck by two factors: the specificity of Intent, and an infrastructure from which to operate:

Political campaigns have specificity of Intent. Get 50% of the vote plus one by the close of election day and your candidate wins. The goal is riveting. This is key to running a campaign. Specificity called for a date and a number – "soon" is not a time. We set 18 months from launch to achieve the result: 100,000 lives saved – "some" is not a number.

At IHI, we decided to act and to use our own infrastructure. Our work gave us an action platform to address hospital safety.

From the Leadership Stories profiled in this book and from our own experiences, we have identified a pattern in successful Bold Aim campaigns. The following table summarizes Seven Dynamics that leaders have used to establish and effectively pursue Bold Aims. The seven are referred to as dynamics rather than steps because they happen concurrently, and they typically interact with each other. At the same time, there is a sequence to the seven and they represent discrete types of work and skill sets. All seven are necessary to establish and realize Bold Aims. The whole set calls for a team. One person working alone is not going to achieve big Bold Aims like going to the moon and back. Leadership to achieve Bold Aims requires teamwork.

Achieving a Bold Aim Through a Leadership Campaign Approach

	Seven Dynamics to Establish and Achieve a Bold Aim	How the Seven Dynamics Appear in Action
1	Observe Leading Edge Practice and Craft a Bold Aim	Performance outliers set a compelling, actionable vision; are presented as faculty
2	Through Circles of Influence, Generate Partners to Pursue the Bold Aim	Core team accesses and leverages the connections, resources of interested others
3	Craft, Secure, and Manage a Dynamic Learning Platform	Effective convening and collaboration will yield rapid adaptation of best practices
4	Voluntarily Enroll Those Organizations Ready to Commit to the Bold Aim	Early adopters are engaged; they increase the interest of others in the campaign
5	Regularly Use a Platform for Learning, Collaborative Execution, Accountability	Participants share, adapt practices and systems; breakthroughs realized and spread
6	Acknowledge Emergent Systems and Progress on the Aim; Celebrate Results	Acknowledgement creates new norms and systems; incentivizes achievement
7	Establish Accountability & Responsibility for Emergent Systems and the New Normal	The transformation envisioned by the Bold Aim is institutionalized and sustained

DYNAMIC #1 Observe Leading Edge Practice and Craft a Bold Aim

Establishing Bold Aims is a group process that is grounded in experience and data. It is not "pick a big number and hope for the best." Bold Aims are authentically constructed based on data analysis and modeling of experience with leading edge practice and performance outliers.

Many of us encounter situations where we see the possibility of breakthroughs and transformation. Our life experience and circles of influence gives us access to seeing what is possible. As we open ourselves up to possibilities, a leadership vision forms. Crafting a Bold Aim can capture and make actionable some key feature(s) of that vision.

The construction of a Bold Aim is frequently informed by what we call performance outliers, individuals, or organizations with exceptional and relevant performance in the field of practice or in a comparable field. We can make it a habit to watch for and study leading edge performers. Learn how they have command of a set of practices producing the results and whether those practices can be modeled and spread.

Prior to the Organ Donation Breakthrough Collaborative, national donation rates averaged 46%. However, several dozen high-performing trauma centers had donation rates above 70%, and we learned that they had command of the practices that produced those results. At that point the leadership action was straightforward: transform the national system's performance by spreading leading-edge practice and performance to all 500 large trauma centers.

Building a Bold Aim is exciting work. It brings us into contact with interesting and successful practitioners. They are self-aware and excited about what they do. These leaders often turn out to be a valuable source of knowledge and inspiration for pursuit of the Bold Aim. They are the living embodiment of what they have already shown to be possible. They can be enrolled as experts and faculty for campaigns to realize the Bold Aim. In addition to their knowledge base and as evidence of what results are possible, these leading practitioners are an important source of energy for driving a campaign. The first dynamic, then, is to find such people and work with them and other partners to construct a Bold Aim.

DYNAMIC #2 **Through Circles of Influence, Generate Partners to Pursue the Bold Aim**

Each of us has a circle of influence. As we craft a Bold Aim, a related dynamic is to reach out and engage with our circle of influence. Seek the feedback and support of those who will be our partners. That feedback makes them co-designers of the aim. That support can increase access to their resources. Support could come as endorsement, referral to others, access to information, funding, staffing, or commitments to participate. With the help of others, highly influential organizations and those with authority and resources can sign up to pursue the Aim.

The Organ Donation Breakthrough Collaborative team engaged circles of influence in multiple dimensions. As the Bold Aim statement took shape, the federal team from the Division of Transplantation began by approaching the Office of the Secretary. The Intent was to have Secretary Thompson endorse the Bold Aim of a 75% organ donation conversion rate at a groundbreaking ceremony for a national organ donation organization. This was a very unusual way to proceed. Each of several organizational levels between the Division of Transplantation and the Office of the Secretary had some review and approval process, making each review a potential No. The Bold Aim would be viewed by most as risky, not likely ever to be realized. Executives do not want these chancy targets in their performance plans. However, a working relationship between the Division of Transplantation team, and a key person in the Office of the Secretary, helped to truncate review and leverage the Bold Aim into the Secretary's speech. Note how the upward exercising of circles of influence within the DHHS organizational structure resembles the approach used to gain support for the leadership vision described in the EPA Radon story.

The Division of Transplantation team went on to exercise leadership outside their federal department. The team leveraged the Secretary's support to help enroll influential national organizations such as the Association of Organ Procurement Officials, the Institute for Healthcare Improvement, the Joint Commission, and others. The team secured commitments from executives to join in signing the Contract for Results that defined the campaign Intent.

As we shall see in Dynamic #4, the federal team created enough national influence behind the Bold Aim that they were able to sign up the large number of trauma centers and OPOs required to generate national results. The second dynamic builds the necessary influential support under the Bold Aim.

DYNAMIC #3 **Craft, Secure, and Manage a Dynamic Action Learning Platform**

Enrollment of multiple organizations requires a platform for people and organizations to work together. The platform enables the systems and convenings necessary to drive group learning, execution, and accountability. Establishing the platform and securing the resources to operate it are part of running with Bold Aims. Expanding our circles of influence creates more opportunities to attract the resources needed.

The platform can be a series of regular convenings designed with a theory of change, a collaborative learning method, and an accountability space. The platform becomes an organized effort of collaborative change with the Bold Aim as its brand. An existing Action Learning Platform can be adapted and used, or a new platform can be built.

Don Berwick MD and the Institute for Healthcare Improvement team needed a way to manage performance on their Bold Aim across thousands of autonomous hospitals. They adapted their quality improvement collaboratives into a nation-wide action learning campaign for hospitals, introducing a hub-and-spoke model for an Action Learning Platform that paced participants toward the Aim. Performance reporting systems were established to track progress toward the goal. A similar type of platform was established and operated with the organ donation collaboratives.

A formally resourced collaborative program has a big payoff. Action Learning Platforms enable all participants to pace themselves to success. Rapid cycles of Plan, Do, Study and Act (PDSA) can be used to learn and adapt what works. Participants can be routinely convened in work sessions called Pacing Events. These events are purposefully designed to produce effective collaboration, to generate visible positive energy, and to secure new commitments for further testing and action. The events are aggressively managed to maintain high positive energy in a community of common purpose with accountability for the Bold Aim.

In all the Leadership Stories presented here, the Action Learning Platforms are managed aggressively to move participants toward the Vision and the Bold Aim. Administrative systems are created to support convening and to work with performance data. Observation programs are used to identify progress and breakthroughs. In the chapter on Roles, the distinctions among leadership, management, administration, and observation will be addressed in depth.

With the third dynamic we put in place the infrastructure the core team needs to reach and work with participants across several dimensions of action.

DYNAMIC #4 Voluntarily Enroll Those Organizations Ready to Commit to the Bold Aim

Establishing a Bold Aim is a revolutionary way to transform a network of independent organizations. The members voluntarily form a cohesive community of practice with a common vision. A new level of accountability is created across the field of practice, not by hierarchical authority, but rather through widespread voluntary commitment by individuals and organizations. Our circle of influence is expanded to include those whose operations will be transformed. They commit to using a well-defined platform to collaborate on the Aim.

Because participation is voluntary and self-directed, it is possible for participants to align their contributions and work in ways that a centralized authority would never even imagine. People and organizations bring all sorts of innovative angles to their contributions when invited and challenged to do so.

Enrolling a critical mass of participants requires an intense social marketing effort. Enrollment can be pursued by turning public events into a defining moment. The Organ Donation Breakthrough Collaborative used the Contract for Results and signing ceremonies to call for, acknowledge, and celebrate commitments being made. By enrolling into the collaborative, participants make themselves accountable for achieving the Bold Aim. Common purpose and mutual accountability draw people together. With Dynamic #4, we recruit the right participants in sufficient numbers for an organized collaborative effort that can be managed and administered to achieve the Bold Aim

DYNAMIC #5 **Regularly Use a Platform for Learning, Collaboration, Execution, Accountability**

A campaign naturally evolves. Its evolution can occur over 12 months, 60 months or more. It takes time and it's managed with persistence and intensity. Hundreds of participants are making complementary and synergistic changes. A lot happens! And where does all the direction come from?

Years of experience have taught us that there is a tremendous body of knowledge and wisdom among the individuals and organizations who participate in leadership campaigns. Our colleague and fellow leadership author, Doug Krug, often observes that "the answers are in the room." Well-designed events can release the answers while exercising accountability for results. We see this collaborative action learning dynamic at work throughout each of the leadership stories profiled on Intent.

Over the course of 2003 through 2007, participants in the Organ Donation Breakthrough Collaborative met in large Learning Sessions of 800 to 2500 participants every four to five months. The frequent organized learning sessions provided a venue for profiling known and emergent best practices among the campaign participants. The sessions also established accountability for action and results. Participants in the learning sessions were routinely asked to process what they learned from the presentations of peers, and then to commit to taking actions to put their insights to work. The cadence of frequent, regular learning sessions also created an expectation of progress for spread, action, and results stemming from the work of campaign participants between each session. Take, for example, learning how to substantially increase organ donation through the pursuit of Donation after Circulatory Determination of Death (DCDD). Gaining command of existing and emergent best practices in this area led to more than 46,000 additional DCDD transplants by the end of 2020.

As part of Don Berwick's leadership story about the 100,000 Lives Campaign, Tom Evans, MD, described how his fellow Chief Medical Officers in three of the largest healthcare systems in Iowa discovered that each of their systems had effective best practices in certain medical areas that could be adapted and used by the other systems. This generative discovery in a collaborative event among the three large systems ultimately led to the birth of the Iowa Healthcare Collaborative in 2004, a not-for-profit organization that now supports 277 hospitals, 8,000 clinicians, and 24 communities with systematic quality improvement initiatives across 18 states.

Supporting campaign participants in the day-to-day work of learning from each other, and then helping them to make commitments to apply the learning to their own work, is the results-engine of campaign work. Dynamic #5 is where the lion's share of the work of a campaign occurs.

DYNAMIC #6 Acknowledge Progress and Emergent Systems; Celebrate Results

It is common for good work to go unnoticed. Special improvement efforts often end without leaving a footprint. Participants move on to the next assignment. Acknowledgement is a way to create footprints and trigger the adoption of new systems. To acknowledge is a powerful Speech Act.

Acknowledgement for delivery on commitments happens across all the stories profiled in this chapter. The acknowledgement occurs through public recognition and celebration. It is about creating special events and honors such as the Organ Donation Learning Congress where Medals of Honor were personally handed to representatives of high performing hospitals and OPOs by donor families and transplant recipients.

In those cases where a deadline has expired and the Aim is not yet achieved, acknowledgement can also play an especially important role. Leaders know that our efforts don't always result in stunning successes. In such a case, the spirit of commitment calls for us to reset. First, acknowledge the commitment and where the team is—how far we have come and how far we still have to go. Build on the experience and the learning. Bring forward additional benchmark models of success. Establish a new near-term target date and re-commit. And finally: celebrate the progress made and the commitment to reset. These actions will help the whole community get into a better place and ready to make the next advance.

Acknowledgement as public recognition and celebration sends a message throughout a system. Dynamic #6 reinforces the value and acceptance of new practice and the new performance expectations.

DYNAMIC #7 Establish Accountability and Responsibility for Emergent Systems and the New Normal

In the future, Dynamic #7 may require the most development and creativity. Even successful campaigns end with still more to be done and new possibilities and opportunities to pursue. The challenge is to sustain gains and to continue to pursue further improvement.

In every Leadership Story in this chapter, efforts were made to sustain the transformations and to pursue the new opportunities that surfaced. The actions taken vary and include: establishing new organizations to play an oversight role; maintaining the leadership platform and spreading it to cover more fields of practice; encouraging and supporting efforts to install institutional mechanisms; and follow-on campaigns to further the vision.

The 100,000 Lives campaign had a remarkable set of follow-on efforts. The leadership team was able to expand the 18-month campaign (2004) into a 5 Million Lives campaign (2006 – 2008). Later, key members of the leadership team joined the Obama Administration where they established the Partnership for Patients (2011-14) to reduce preventable harm in hospitals by 40%. This impressive run of leadership campaigns left the nation's system of independent hospitals in a much better safety situation. Following the Partnership for Patients, the Centers for Medicare and Medicaid Services (CMS) funded a group of national, regional, and state hospital associations and health system organizations to serve as Hospital Improvement Innovation Networks (HIINs) for another four years. This work continues at a much more modest level through the present as part of the institutional Quality Improvement Organization (QIO) program.

Emerging from the Organ Donation collaboratives, the independent non-profit Organ Donation and Transplant Alliance was chartered in 2006 to continue an organized program of improvement work towards ever-increasing organ donation and transplantation. The Alliance expands on the work of the national Organ Donation Breakthrough Collaborative through the consistent leadership of national organizations associated with the three estates of donor hospitals, OPOs, and transplant centers. Start-up funding and other resources to create the Alliance were provided by members of the Collaborative's Leadership Coordinating Council, along with a number of organ procurement organizations and others.

The hot, hyper energy of a leadership campaign naturally gives way to the cooler systematic energy of managed and administered systems. At some point, a new kind of engagement will be needed to hold the gains and move forward. Leadership teams will have to ask, "What are the more institutional vehicles that will sustain these gains? What further leadership work is needed to achieve those parts of the vision not yet realized?" Our own experience and that of others shows that there are lots of different and effective answers to these kinds of questions. Dynamic #7 recognizes the need to secure the gains and a build on experience to again define and own the future.

Bold Aims Generate Shared Achievement, Celebration, Joy —Don't Wait, Start Now

A Near Term Aim Far Beyond Current Capability

The Leadership Stories profiled here showcase Bold Aims as a powerful way to be in action. While the opportunities to pursue Bold Aims are often present in our work and our lives, the reasons not to pursue them can appear overwhelming. We offer four observations that can help us develop the strong leadership mindset that is necessary to pursue Bold Aims:

1. *Make and Share Personal Choices For A Better Future*:
   We are never alone in this work.

2. *Jump In, Then Figure It Out*:
   Realize how "aims create systems, systems create results."

3. *Plan and Practice Resilience*:
   Expect to overcome the common resistance and breakdowns that can scare and frustrate.

4. *Celebrate The Action and Results of Others*:
   Take advantage of what is ultimately joyous, high-energy work with exciting results.

These experience-based observations are somewhat counter-intuitive. Lurking behind each of these four lessons are common default practices that take the opposite, less risky path. We offer these four enabling practices to help generate possibilities and deeper understanding of the leadership Mindsets necessary for using Bold Aims effectively.

Personal Mindset: Make and Share Personal Choices for a Better Future. It is easy to become absorbed in the drama and mechanics of a Bold Aim campaign. We all want to learn how a Bold Aim is accomplished, but a key question is often overlooked: why was there a Bold Aim in the first place? The answer is: a series of personal Choices were made by a number of people – people who look just like each of us. A Bold Aim is the result of many people making and sharing personal Choices about the future. The Bold Aim is co-authored and evolves.

Don Berwick MD and the Institute for Healthcare Improvement team made a bold decision in 2004 to mobilize and support healthcare providers to transform hospital safety throughout the nation. This Bold Aim was not a product of federal legislation, lawsuits, big grants, or new regulations. The personal and organizational leadership Choices of Dr. Berwick and the IHI team were central to the establishment of the Aim and the program of work necessary to achieve it.

In the case of organ donation, prior to the beginning of the Organ Donation Breakthrough Collaborative in 2003, all the assets that were needed to increase organ donation rates were present in the world in some way. However, everyone throughout the national system was already busy doing other serious work. Everything was tied up, committed, floating along on the business-as-usual drift toward predictable and less than ideal donation rate results. Then, suddenly, a Bold Aim was established. How did the Bold Aim come into being? Here is where some of the most important leadership insight lies: personal choices were made!

The 75% Bold Aim and its associated program of work was initiated by mid-level civil servants, without formal authority, specific guidance, or resources. This is remarkable. The implications of this can inspire hope in all of us. It means that folks in any position and situation can truly make a difference. Dennis Wagner, Ginny McBride, Jade Perdue, Donald Coleman, Frank Zampiello, Rich Durbin, Joyce Somsak, and their colleagues stepped up and made personal choices that resulted in the declaration of a Bold Aim by executives throughout the organ donation system. These civil servants chose to act. Their choices, and the choices of those they encountered going forward, made all the difference in the world. Each of us has access to such Choices in our own work, in our own lives.

A key lesson is that leadership Choices on the foundational Mindsets and Methods of Bold Aims and source of Vision are not limited to those at the top of established hierarchies. This is true even in large, traditional, bureaucratic federal agencies and departments. Many at all levels can step forward to make personal Choices to lead.

Proactive Mindset: Jump In, Then Figure it Out. Avoid wasting time trying to get ready . . . instead, grow the resources and systems you need. Don't wait, act! Leverage the leadership principle that "aims create systems, systems create results." Help the new and necessary systems emerge.

We used to think that to establish Bold Aims, we had to get ready. We thought we had to have the capability needed to achieve the Aims before committing to them. We thought we needed authority, control, resources. This seemed like the prudent, practical way forward – systematically managing our way into change and improvement. And all that might be efficient and true for traditional management tasks and objectives. However, our experience is that it doesn't usually work when we seek to achieve big, meaningful, dramatic changes.

Achieving bigger things often means taking the leadership action to commit to Bold Aims when we do not have what is needed to achieve them. The leadership required is both challenging and somewhat counterintuitive. We have learned that knowing this counterintuitive truth makes it easier and more sensical to act on it. Once we accept this difficulty of committing in the absence of resources and certainty, it actually paves the way for us to see and step into the leadership work that is required. In many cases, the needed leadership work involves lining up the relationships and resources needed to achieve the Bold Aim.

The work of resourcing and creating new systems is a product of pursuing Bold Aims. In leadership work, "Aims create systems and systems create results." This is counterintuitive for most of us who are trained in the disciplines of management and administration.

In the more traditional discipline of management, we use known systems to achieve predictable results. With leadership, we evolve and build our way towards achievement of the Aims. This is system-building work. For those of us trained in management, it can even feel uncomfortable or even somewhat unethical to commit to Aims in the absence of required resources.

Aims create systems. We don't first build the systems and then work to achieve the Aims. We first commit in the absence of the necessary systems. This is hard to do.

Committing to Bold Aims in the absence of the necessary resources to achieve them involves risk, uncertainty, ethical considerations, and a commitment to lots of hard work. Leaders who pursue Bold Aims need to get comfortable with Being uncomfortable. Jump in, and as you figure it out, expect that you will often feel uncomfortable. In time, you may even come to enjoy the discomfort!

Anticipatory Mindset: *Plan and Practice Resilience.*
Leaders build Resilience into Bold Aim campaigns. The Seven Dynamics listed in the earlier table may sound and look straightforward. The clear, straightforward seven-item process makes the work of Bold Aims appear much tidier and easier than it turns out to be.

Each Dynamic takes time and a great deal of energy. The work is performed through collaboration. It's work without a detailed master plan. It means taking action and asking people to do things when the outcomes are uncertain. It takes courage to act and learn, and then to act on the learning.

Each of the Dynamics is likely to create anxiety in our leadership teams. In our own experience, we have vivid memories of the many different times in this work where it appeared that all was lost and that things were going to hell in a handbasket. Enrolling line organizations was harder than we thought. Often there were moments when the results were not as clear or powerful as we expected. Sometimes the data even suggested we were going backwards, actually making things worse through our interventions. We sensed that some partners were not sufficiently committed.
A multitude of competing mindsets and philosophies were demanding attention. Disagreements and debate surfaced to sap energy. Outside factors and forces seemed to be showing up and taking precedence. Yet our partners and team members usually successfully worked through all of these bumps in the road. We learned to be resilient and came to see it as necessary to deliberately and intentionally foster Resilience in ourselves and others. Resilience is presented as a key leadership Mindset and Method in the chapter on Being.

Most important, you and your team members can anticipate that pursuing Bold Aims will ultimately be joyous, high-energy work.

Celebratory Mindset: Celebrate the Actions and Result of Others. Make celebration a habit . . . It is our experience that Bold Aims open up joyful and effective ways to work and live. Leaders who work with Bold Aims can have tremendous impact in at least three major sectors:

1. The lives of those impacted by progress towards the Aim;

2. The professional development of the many who become involved in this work, including our own personal and professional development;

3. Societal recognition and community-wide acknowledgement of the extraordinary future realized.

Each offers opportunities to celebrate success and acknowledge those who have made it happen. We have opportunities to showcase success in all three sectors to help set new values, higher expectations, more pride, and greater joy.

Always celebrate action when people emerge better off! Achievement on the Compelling Vision means the serious needs of others are being met. Imagine your work is helping people graduate from the organ transplant waiting list, or making hospitals safer, or enabling complex health care to be delivered to underserved patients, or being assured that an invisible, major health risk has been brought under control, or that the poor in an undeveloped region are receiving life-changing access to capital and health care. These kinds of compelling outcomes represent phenomenal advances in societal welfare that can and should be showcased and acknowledged.

In addition to the extraordinary outcomes that come from achieving Bold Aims, the personal and professional growth that results among all of those involved is just as compelling. For example, thousands of nurses, physicians, organ procurement coordinators, hospital administrators and others were involved in the organ donation collaborative. They produced the dramatic national increases in organ donation and transplantation that are profiled in the case study. Many of these people said then—and still say today —that their work in the Organ Donation Breakthrough Collaborative was one of the most exciting and meaningful parts of their professional lives.

Those involved were growing a stronger culture of leadership and performance in a major sector of the nation's health care system. That impact on professional culture and performance should be showcased and acknowledged.

Realizing and then recognizing these individual and societal benefits most definitely adds value in many ways. It more than compensates for the uncertainty and anxiety that often accompany leadership work. The insights gained and the relationships developed in this proactive work make it personally rewarding. As we look back on those times where a long and challenging journey produced great results, it was the celebratory actions to acknowledge people that stand out the most for us.

Choosing to Run with a Bold Aim . . .

Bold Aim opportunities are always there, percolating just below the surface, ready to be triggered by leadership. When that opportunity shows up, we should ask ourselves: What's it going to be—incremental, predictable, safe progress with realistic management goals? Or something bold and transformative?

As your leadership calling begins to emerge, you will find an abundance of resources to help clarify and energize your Intent. We urge you to boldly engage your circle of influence and those of others. Stay alert to the potential for leadership Choices and Defining Moments. And work to say "Yes" to opportunities for collaboration, system creation, resilience, and celebration that will allow you to lead the way to transformational change and a bold new normal.

. . . and Choosing to Run With DNA

Dr. Berwick's Leadership Story shows how Intent as a Bold Aim was used to bring together independent organizations, with similar missions and practices, to participate in an exciting, well-managed national improvement campaign. The following sections will show how Intent can also be developed and spread in a different, more organic way. The practice of Decide-Notice-Acknowledge (DNA) is featured as a central Mindset and Method used in the Bureau of Primary Health Care's 100% Access and Zero Health Disparities campaign. Watch for how leadership Intent is built by singling out and aligning a number of distinct high-performing innovations. Using DNA to celebrate success surfaces innovation leaders, and those leaders go on to use DNA to further develop their own networks of leaders. Following the 100% Access/ Zero Disparities review in this chapter, DNA is described as a Mindset and Method for intentionally creating the future we stand for.

The 100% Access/Zero Health Disparities Campaign

by **John Scanlon**

Marilyn Gaston MD
Assistant Surgeon General and Bureau Director, Health Resources and Services Administration 1990-2001

Mary Lou Andersen
Deputy Bureau Director, Health Resources and Services Administration 1996-1999

A full decade prior to the Affordable Care Act of 2010, a charismatic and influential pediatrician named Marilyn Gaston MD launched a campaign in 1998 designed to help communities across the nation achieve a bold shared vision of 100% Access to Healthcare and Zero Health Disparities. Dr. Gaston was serving at the time as the Director of the Bureau of Primary Health Care at the Health Resources and Services Administration (HRSA) in the federal Department of Health and Human Services (DHHS). She was a highly accomplished physician, a nationally known researcher, and a Rear Admiral in the United States Public Health Service. Dr. Gaston was a leader with an extraordinary background. As an African American woman, she had grown up in housing projects in Cincinnati, and was determined to use her Community Health Center and National Health Service Corps programs and influence to help others get the healthcare they needed.

Her Deputy Director was Mary Lou Andersen, a renowned pharmacist, 67 years old, who had been in the federal government since the mid-70s. Early in her career she took a new set of federal health programs into Appalachia and West Virginia and rapidly got them in place where they were desperately needed.

Mary Lou had a knack for putting things together on the ground even when there was high political resistance. A natural community organizer, she believed in community-based organizations and community-based health care as the key to social justice and effectiveness. The way to get things done, she believed, was to "just do it," one of her favorite expressions.

The 100% Access/0 Health Disparities campaign was not mandated by legislation, or by the Department or even by Dr. Gaston and Mary Lou Andersen. It emerged from a group of mid-level bureau managers who Dr. Gaston and Mary Lou had enrolled into a leadership development program at the Council for Excellence in Government. The Council was supporting federal leaders and advocating for the use of Bold Aims to achieve extraordinary results. Mary Lou created a safe space in the Bureau for this group to convene and establish a bold goal. They named themselves the "Just Do It" Group—ten people who were seasoned and senior in position. All had full time jobs with responsibility for managing Bureau programs. I supported Dr. Gaston, Mary Lou and the federal team as a leadership consultant.

The bureau was responsible for assuring access to preventive and primary care for vulnerable populations through community health centers, and by deploying clinicians into rural and underserved parts of the county. Its programs provided health care to some of the most vulnerable communities and populations, reaching about 20% of the 45 million uninsured and vulnerable people in the nation. Dr. Gaston had a larger vision. She wanted to make the Bureau's penetration into the universe of need a policy issue. She thought access should be universal. To achieve it through expansion of Bureau's programs would cost many additional billions in federal funding. That was not going to happen. Internal department planning and budgeting only considered incremental growth with relatively modest funding increases. She wasn't finding a receptive audience.

Dr. Gaston, Mary Lou Andersen, and the "Just Do It" Group saw another path. They believed that communities could achieve health care access for 100% of their residents by restructuring resources already present in the community. Doing so could not only reduce health disparities but could actually eliminate them. Major progress could be achieved across the nation without the huge increases in federal funding that federal policy makers feared. Dr. Gaston held that "communities can do this because I have been out there, and I have seen some of them doing it. If a few can do it, others can too. This is an issue of local will and determination." The solution to her and Mary Lou was clear: go find out what works and do more of it.

The "Just Do It" Group, feeling empowered by Dr. Gaston and Mary Lou, and emboldened by the DHHS Healthy People 2010 goals, committed to a vision where the county's 3,000 communities would develop integrated health systems delivering 100% access and 0 health disparities. They established a Bold Aim to enroll and support 500 communities over three years.

Initially the Group's vision and bold goal were not well received by many in the Bureau. When they briefed the Bureau executive team there was support from a few, but caution and rejection from most. The resistance was strong: "*It's not practical . . . We don't know how to do it . . . It's not ethical because it takes attention away from our legislated programs . . . It's too much additional work.*" In weekly meetings, Mary Lou guided the "Just Do It" Group to avoid arguments, respect the different views, but to move ahead. The "Just Do It" Group rapidly evolved into the team that established and led the Campaign for 100% Access/0 Disparities.

Healthy People 2010: Legitimizing The 100%/0 Campaign

Developed by the Office of Disease Prevention and Health Promotion of the Department of Health and Human Services, Healthy People 2010 established national objectives to improve health, increase access to healthcare, and eliminate health disparities over the decade. As one decade ends, progress is assessed and new objectives for the next decade are established. There was no funded program behind Healthy People 2010. The Intent is to provide objectives in a format that enables states, communities, organizations associated with health and health care to combine efforts and collaborate. The Healthy People 2010 agenda legitimized the 100%/Zero Vision and gave the Bureau team a feeling of permission to go for it.

Social Marketing Principles Secure the Partnerships Needed to Engage Communities

In the fall of 1998 Dr. Marilyn Gaston and May Lou Andersen recruited Dennis Wagner to join the Bureau of Primary Health Care and work on the 100%/0 campaign. Dennis was brought in on detail from EPA as an expert in social marketing. The 100%/0 team met weekly, often with Dr. Gaston and Mary Lou. The team was dynamic. There was never one person in charge. They saw the world from the perspective of an important mission that all of them were committed to implementing.

The team had to address two key questions: how do they, the small 100%/0 Team, reach 3000 communities and enroll 500 without program authority or funding to do it? Then once enrolled, what do local communities do on their own and with bureau support to make 100%/0 happen? There was no federal manual to consult on this work!

The goals were far beyond the resources at hand. The work had to be about developing relationships to align resources in the bureau, and to deploy other organizations' resources and interests. Rather than perform traditional management of "plan, allocate, do" the team had to "declare, discover, enroll, and support."

Dennis introduced a social marketing principle where the team began to systematically use the communication channels of bureau programs and national organizations to reach people of influence in targeted communities. A national organization with state and local chapters can reach thousands of influential members, and these kinds of organizations naturally do a lot of convening. The team supported Dr. Gaston and Mary Lou in systematically reaching out to receptive national organizations. The bureau was able to enter into low-cost performance arrangements with multiple organizations that had influential membership located in communities including, for example: United Way, International City and County Managers Association, National Association of Counties, American Academy of Pediatrics, and others.

The bureau's own programs also had grantees and contractors working on the ground with large numbers of communities. Over a three-year period, the federal 100%/0 team used a number of program platforms to reach out to communities. Existing grants to State Primary Care Associations, the health center program's Models That Work initiative, site development for the National Health Service Corps, and a new federally funded Healthy Communities Access Program proved to be effective channels through which to engage, enroll and support important community leaders. Over the 1998-2002 period these partnership networks of national organizations and federal program infrastructure proved to be energetic and effective advocates of 100%/0.

Finding and Acknowledging What Is Working Creates Models for Spread

The team and its partners were constantly on the hunt for examples of successful community healthcare systems that could show Methods and progress on the 100%/0 goals. This turned out to be easier than expected. Early in the work, the 100%/0 team learned of two very different and highly effective community initiatives through the Harvard and Ford Foundation Innovations in American Government Awards program. They were stunned by the comprehensive and well-documented impacts of these incredible community healthcare systems. One was in Buncombe County (Asheville), NC and the other in Hillsborough County (Tampa), FL.

Buncombe County (Asheville), North Carolina

Project Access is a volunteer care program led by the Buncombe County Medical Society. It is an organizing force for, and critical part of an integrated community delivery system. In 1996, the leadership of Project Access worked to develop and organize volunteer specialty care, and then to integrate this care with a comprehensive set of primary care, pharmaceutical and hospital services. The leaders of Project Access were crystal-clear on their Intent: provide a comprehensive set of medical services to approximately 25,000 residents per year who were uninsured with income under 200% of the federal poverty level. About 3,000 of these patients are served with donated specialty care each year. Over 700 physicians (85% of Medical Society members) volunteer to provide the care for a specified number of patients per physician or per physician practice.

The initiative provides specialty care valued at $3M to $5M in donated services each year. The medical society and participating physicians team with the local county commission, the hospital, pharmacists, health centers and free clinics. These partners agreed to provide the primary care, pharmacy and hospital services needed by enrolled patients. Having an integrated system of care that "covered all the bases" produced high quality healthcare for the patients served by Project Access. Alan McKenzie was the diligent, hard-working, and highly effective executive director of the Medical Society. He and his community partners worked with our HRSA team to successfully establish Project Access in more than 50 other communities in 1998-2002 as part of the 100%/0 campaign.

Hillsborough County (Tampa), Florida

Hillsborough Health Care is a comprehensive managed care program for Hillsborough County residents with limited income and assets who do not qualify for other health care coverage. The program is administered by the county government. It has a sustainable source of funding: a local sales tax of up to one half of one percent, authorized by the State legislature and enacted by the county in 1991 in response to a local financial crisis. Florida county governments were responsible for indigent care, using property taxes as the state-mandated local government funding source.

The healthcare bill for care in Hillsborough County was in the millions and growing rapidly, soon to exceed the property tax caps. A bold, caring, persistent and persuasive County Commissioner named Phyllis Busansky led a successful sales tax campaign to finance this health plan for the poor. She believed the local community could solve its own problems with political will, and that it could be done with a local campaign. Phyllis often said, "It's all about people, politicians, and press." Commissioner Busansky showed that local elected officials could be a leadership force in creating a 100%/0 delivery system through local financing. Phyllis and her colleagues in Hillsborough County were grounded in clear Intent: replace a fragmented, short term, emergency-driven delivery system with a comprehensive, coordinated and managed continuum of care network, that provided care for those in need. Of the estimated 39,000 potential enrollees, the program was seeing 34,000 people by 1998.

As a formal county program, its costs and results were well documented and audited. The managed care network had a track record of remarkable reductions in costs, together with improvements in population health. Phyllis teamed with HRSA to support other communities as part of the 100%/0 campaign to help these communities develop similar innovative funding and managed care solutions.

Using What Works to Generate Energy and Spread

These two examples, along with many others, were strategically featured and celebrated at local, state and national events organized by Dr. Gaston's 100%/0 team. Everywhere we sent them, Alan, Phyllis, and their community partners generated interest and action among local healthcare leaders across the nation. An organized volunteer effort by a community's physicians, and an organized program of managed care funded by a sales tax, showed the exciting range of possibilities that could be tested and adapted by other communities. As the juggernaut campaign moved forward, our team strategically sought out and showcased many other examples of successful organizational and community strategies—for example, a triple payer insurance plan in Muskegon County, Michigan, provided coverage for employees of small businesses. Similarly, the Jessie Tree in Galveston, Texas, organized and managed a central safety net referral and assistance network supported by more than a hundred local faith-based organizations.

Shift in National Policy Ends the Federal 100%/0 Initiative; the Work and Lessons Live On

In 2001-2002, several changes occurred that pulled the 100%/0 Team out of their leadership role. Dr. Gaston and Mary Lou retired, and a new Presidential Administration came into office. The administration assigned the Bureau of Primary Health Care a management initiative to implement a major legislated expansion of community health centers. The federal legislation represented another path to increasing health care access and addressing disparities. Team members took on new roles and Bureau attention and resources were focused on implementing the FQHC expansion.

While the federal leadership of the 100%/0 Campaign was ended, many of the community-based systems of care created by Alan, Phyllis, and the 100%/0 Team continue to this day. The focus of leadership for 100%/0 moved from the federal team to several new intermediary organizations outside of the federal government. Communities Joined in Action, CJA, a nonprofit organization, was formed to continue collaboration among community-based leaders in health care transformation. Today CJA has an administrative home in the Georgia Health Policy Center.

Many of the leadership Signature Style Mindsets and Methods began to surface in the work of hundreds of federal and private partners who were part of leading the Campaign for 100% Access/0 Health Disparities. The Pacing Event Mindset and Method profiled in the chapter on Roles emerged as a new and important way to generate relationships and results. The incredibly valuable lesson of using acknowledgement to generate energy, action and results was a lasting gift. The leadership Mindset and Method of Decide-Notice-Acknowledge (DNA) profiled in an upcoming segment is a powerful tool for accessing this almost magical gift.

Being Acknowledged Makes Project Access Sustainable Locally and Spreads It Nationally

by **Alan McKenzie**
Executive Director,
Buncombe County,
North Carolina
Medical Society

Our Medical Society's Project Access initiative won a Ford Foundation Innovations in Government Award in 1998. Project Access used volunteer physician services to provide integrated care for the uninsured low-income residents throughout our community. We proved that this approach could close the chronic access to health care gap. The scale was significant, with over 700 physicians volunteering to provide medical specialty care to 3,000 patients per year as part of an organized system of care that served 25,000 low income and uninsured people.

The award brought us to the attention of the federal government as a community that was successfully providing 100% access to healthcare. This attention emboldened us. The federal team provided a national platform and modest funding that enabled us to coach other communities in establishing similar Project Access programs across the country.

While being acknowledged and featured as expert faculty in events across the nation was exciting, my primary focus remained on Buncombe County. Project Access was a volunteer program with hundreds of physicians and dozens of partners donating time. We had to remain focused on sustaining all of the effort necessary to keep our program operating effectively back home in Buncombe County. How do you keep such a large volunteer program viable over the long term? Starting a program is one challenge, but sustaining a program over time is an even bigger challenge. In 1998 – 2003 this was my primary concern. Systematic acknowledgement and appreciation turned out to be a powerful way to make Project Access an essential and enduring part of our community.

We learned that if we wanted more of something (like volunteer specialty care), we needed to find ways to systematically notice and then acknowledge and appreciate it. To get more of what you want: know what it is, be on the lookout for it, and when it shows up—acknowledge it.

We wanted our doctors to continue to volunteer to provide care for a given number of patients. As physicians signed up and served patients, we decided to publicly recognize their contributions. Each year we featured their names in a full-page section of the local newspaper. This helped to both increase and sustain enrollment in the program. Physicians were honored to be on the list. And it served as a powerful reminder for physicians to re-enroll each year.

Because of the Ford Foundation award and the attention from Dr. Gaston's team at the Health Resources and Services Administration (HRSA), other communities called to learn more about what we were doing. They wanted to visit our community to see how it worked. I treated the calls as an asset. I used the visits to showcase our local physicians, community partners and participants. We would feature different physician practices in each visit. The site visits were a meaningful way to celebrate and sustain the contributions of our valuable community partners! We kept visibility high through outside recognition. The visits showed the community that Project Access was something special – something for them to be proud of.

Our federally supported work to encourage and guide other communities had the same effect. Our County Commissioners, specialty physicians, health centers and others all became part of an organized effort to mentor their counterparts in other communities. Our efforts to replicate Project Access became a way to publicly acknowledge the individual and organizational leadership of our community partners. We were able to launch more than 50 community initiatives like Project Access over three years!

As I saw how acknowledgement kept interest and energy high, I actively worked to nominate our partners for national awards in their own arenas of work. Our county commissioners were recognized with national awards by the National Association of Counties. Our pharmacists won national awards from the American Pharmacists Association. Celebration and recognition of others was central to our work, every step of the way. All this continuous notoriety made the community aware that Project Access was something necessary and important enough to sustain locally and spread nationally.

The systematic appreciation and celebration of people was an essential part of our success. I am proud to share that 25 years later, Project Access is still going strong.

INTENT

Compelling Vision

Bold Aims

Decide-Notice-Acknowledge

DNA: Decide-Notice-Acknowledge:
A Joyous Way to Express Intent

Leaders achieve their Intent by sharing and pursuing Bold Aims and Compelling Visions. A third powerful and uplifting way to bring our Intent into the world is to acknowledge and publicly appreciate the people, the behaviors, the results, and the organizations that routinely deliver the things that we want more of in the world. Acknowledgement helps us to engage with and energize others towards our shared vision. The intentional practice of this leadership Mindset and Method is called DNA:

Decide what we want to see more of in the world;
Notice it when it shows up in our work and life;
Acknowledge it when we see it.

Our colleague Doug Krug, co-author of *Enlightened Leadership*, introduced this easy-to-remember tool that we use to call more of what we want into the world. DNA can be spontaneous, strategic, or even theatrical. It's a leadership tool that harnesses an especially joyous part of leadership work: celebrating the success of others.

DNA is another way to express Intent along with Compelling Vision and Bold Aim. It is also a powerful way to do leadership work. Expressing Intent and doing leadership work are two qualities that make DNA especially attractive and powerful However, applying DNA does take courage.

Using DNA to Express Intent

Decide can mean deciding we are going to look for already existing cases or examples of the things we want to see more of in the world, including those who are already achieving our vision and bold goals. **Decide** becomes a declaration to personally commit and to involve others in the search. **Decide** is not telling, teaching, or supervising a person or group to deliver on a goal, but rather a constant readiness to remain open to seeing the changes and results we seek, in whatever form they might take.

Notice is when we encounter something that fits the initial decision. There is an eureka moment of recognition—"That's it!" Or "that's a significant part of it!" We have prepared ourselves to check it out, to understand and capture the important features, and to engage the players involved. We acquire real-life examples of progress and results toward our shared vision.

Acknowledge is the public expression to an audience that those we are acknowledging are doing something special. We have the courage to say, "Here are people doing great things. Let's learn from them." Properly communicated, each acknowledgement can produce energy and momentum for our teams and expanding circles of influence.

ACKNOWLEDGE can have payoffs with three groups:

1
The acknowledgers.

We become clearer about our Intent and more and more proficient in finding what moves us toward it. We become more open to seeing the good practices and intentions of others, more appreciative of what they are doing and the possibilities they represent. The result is expansion and growth of the desired practices.

2
The acknowledged.

They are hearing their work embraced and appreciated by us. Acknowledgement further energizes the recipients and adds to their professional capital. They are motivated to continue stepping forward and are better able to see how their work fits with envisioned futures. Others seek them out.

3
The observers.

Acknowledgement also ripples out among all the involved networks of people and organizations who witness or learn of the acknowledgement. Those who are part of our larger effort see the acknowledgement and are influenced. Because of the acknowledgement, the observers see progress, possibility, opportunity, and sources of help.

Using DNA to Do Leadership Work

In our leadership work, we have used and observed DNA being used in at least three productive ways: in our everyday personal coaching of others to *create a culture*; as a strategic way to *network for content and partners*; and with the *investment in spread infrastructure*. The three ways come at work from different perspectives—as personal, as strategic, as investing. They complement and can be combined for synergy.

Use DNA as Personal Coaching to Create Culture. How can we move each other into action? In our professional, educational, and religious lives, we benefit from the effective management and administrative cultures of organizations. We are told what to do, and in turn we tell others what to do. This "telling" takes many forms, with styles ranging from command-and-control, assignment-and-audit, to teaching-and-preaching and telling-and-selling. Underlying these styles is an authoritative structure grounded in tradition, credentials, and reputation.

However, this traditional approach is far less effective in our leadership roles. Many of the resources and relationships we need to achieve our shared Vision lie outside our authority. The knowledge we need is often initially unavailable. DNA is a proven, joyous alternative to the traditional authoritative structure and approach.

In everyday life we often casually use a form of DNA. If a son or daughter unexpectedly mows the lawn, we notice the good job done and then show appreciation by lending the car or treating to pizza. If a colleague takes the initiative and brings people together to fix a problem, we may think to publicly thank them. We know what we want, we notice it when it happens, and we sometimes remember to acknowledge it. As leaders, we can choose to bring greater awareness and intention to these occasional behaviors.

If we intentionally **Decide** we want to see greater teamwork, for example, this decision will help to train our minds to **Notice** the teamwork when it shows up. When we publicly **Acknowledge** others for these behaviors, the reinforcement will cause more of these behaviors in those acknowledged, as well as in the behaviors of others who see the acknowledgement occurring. The same is true of actions, results, and all manner of things that we want to see more of in our lives and our work.

Deciding Leads to *Noticing*
by **Dennis Wagner**

When I first began to apply DNA to my own life and work, I was astonished at how **deciding** impacted **noticing**. My first conscious memory of this phenomena was actually not associated with the practice of DNA. It happened when I gradually came to a decision that my next car would be one of Chrysler's PT Cruisers. I liked the retro look of the car and wanted a roomier vehicle for our growing family of five. I decided that when it was time to get a new car, I would buy the PT Cruiser.

All of a sudden, I began to notice PT Cruisers everywhere! Were they there before?!

The act of **deciding** really tunes our minds to **noticing**. DNA capitalizes on this feature of human awareness and makes it easier for leaders to deploy the powerful speech act of Acknowledgements. With Choice, DNA can become a formidable leadership habit.

DNA deploys the Speech Act of acknowledgement in a special way in the pursuit of our Compelling Visions and Bold Aims. As leaders, we are always at some point between "the no longer and the not yet." The vision is something still in progress or yet to be fully realized. In this stage, the overriding questions are "what does that future really look like?" and "how do we get there?" There is enormous value in being able to answer these questions with real-life examples of progress and momentum. Part of our work as leaders is to identify, foster, foment, and help to generate these examples. DNA does just that.

DNA is a Mindset that we can deploy every day to coach those we encounter. DNA has us looking for reasons to celebrate success, no matter the scale. It has us moving toward the future we want to realize. DNA is joyous leadership work, such a rewarding way of doing business that it is easy to forget that this is actually work—it's like routinely looking for and finding gifts.

Use DNA as a Strategy to Network for Content Partners.
DNA can also be used strategically to build and convey powerful examples of the leadership vision. We can break the vision down into a number of defining elements and seek out places performing as envisioned in each element. As we find these high performers, we practice DNA and bring them forward to be acknowledged and celebrated. The acknowledged players become seen as benchmarks to guide others. As described earlier, Alan McKenzie (Project Access) and Phyllis Busansky (sales tax financing of indigent health care) were showcased in this way by the federal 100% Access, Zero Health Disparities campaign. Both sites became knowledge assets for community action, and both became contributing partners with the 100%/0 Team.

As a later example, consider a national program like the Partnership for Patients funded by the Centers for Medicare and Medicaid Services to make hospitals significantly safer over the four- year period of 2010-2014. The vision was to achieve a major reduction in hospital acquired conditions – harms caused to patients by their hospital, such as surgical site infections and pressure ulcers. Ten specific hospital acquired conditions were identified as collectively generating very high national harm rates (145 harms per 1,000 hospital discharges). Each of the 10 hospital acquired conditions had evidence-based programs that could be used to eliminate them. However, the needed and available safety programs were not in place in most US hospitals. One of our DNA strategies was to find hospitals that had best-in-class performance for one or more of each condition.

These high performers were identified and celebrated as the equivalent of our "all-star" sports team. We routinely DNA-ed their examples in national webinars and events with thousands of their peers. Acknowledging the initial best practice models made each of these hospitals an asset to the campaign. They demonstrated that safety was achievable, and they could show others how to do it. They were deployed as "faculty" in training events to spread the practice where they excelled. The acknowledgement of these high performing hospital teams enhanced and solidified each of their local reputations and influence. Moreover, these high performers became campaign partners who played leadership Roles in the national effort.

We quickly found best in class performers for one or several conditions. However, we soon needed examples of hospitals that were good at preventing patient harm in far more than one or two of three of the hospital acquired conditions. We needed examples of hospitals that could grow their success rates to best-in-class performance on 8, 9 or all 10 of the key harm areas. As the campaign progressed, more and more US hospitals got better and better at addressing more and more of the patient harm areas. Using the practice of DNA, we consistently called attention to the pattern of ever-increasing performance of hospitals. In time, we got to a place where we were routinely celebrating hospitals who were highly effective in "reducing harm across the board" on all 10 hospital acquired conditions.

DNA as part of a campaign strategy calls for an intentional search for performers out in the world that in some way represent the future we want when the vision is realized. This is planned work, performed with system and method. It's a step beyond the more spontaneous and improvisational personal coaching version of DNA. DNA as a strategy can be built into our work and can draw on the many vehicles in place to seek out and honor innovation and extraordinary performance.

Use DNA with Investment in Ambitious Spread Infrastructure. DNA as investment is a level beyond DNA as strategy and several levels beyond DNA as personal coaching. As our DNA practice identifies people and organizations with the kind of extraordinary performance we seek, it becomes practical to consider investing resources to codify and spread the best practices of high performers. DNA can be carried out in a systematic way as part of an aggressive management system to capture and spread what works.

An example of this is the development of a *change package* to support collaboration among multiple, independent organizations working to achieve a Bold Aim. This concept package concept was introduced to us by the Institute for Healthcare Improvement as used in their Breakthrough Series. A *change package* is essentially a document that systematically codifies the best practices of high performers. It is an easy-to-use decision tree that captures high-level strategies, medium-level concepts, and often more than a hundred specific testable actions used by people and organizations with a track record of results. It is a synthesis of best practice across a number of sites with exceptional performance. It is a potent tool for spreading best practices.

In the Organ Donation Breakthrough Collaborative, our federal team developed a change package that codified the best practices associated with high organ donation rates. As part of this work, we conducted site visits to organ donation hospitals, transplant centers, and Organ Procurement Organizations to document the best practices of high performers. Analysis of performance data showed the sites selected for visits were exceptionally high performers on donation rates and organs transplanted per donor. Three findings stood out from these visits:

- ***The identified sites were verified as high performers.***
  They were aware of their performance and could demonstrate it with documented data.

- ***The sites could describe how they achieved the performance.***
  They were in some way managing their operations to intentionally achieve the measured outcomes.
  What they were doing was transferable, teachable.

- ***The sites were surprised and then excited to learn they were performance outliers.***
  Although they understood their own performance, the on-site personnel were often not aware that their performance was exceptional, compared to others. They were often surprised to learn that what they were doing made them high performance outliers.

On the last point, the site visit team was frequently asked by site personnel, "why are you all here to interview us?" After learning why, they became excited. And these feelings of excitement were often accompanied by slight embarrassment at Being singled out. They felt what they were doing was just the right thing to be doing. The opportunity to share their stories for replication by a national audience excited them and that too was viewed as the right thing to be doing. It was always a joyous experience for the Collaborative's site visit team to first see the exceptional work Being performed, and second to see the effect on the practitioners as they were acknowledged for their best-in-class performance, and in the end to see them step into national leadership Roles.

This site visit process was carefully designed and managed with three ends in mind:

- **Capture the visited site's own description of how it delivered exceptional performance,**
- **Identify candidate faculty from the visited organization's people responsible for the performance,**
- **At the end of each site visit, convene a work session with representatives from the site and from several other high performers to craft the critical elements of the change package.**

As faculty to the improvement initiative, the high-performing practitioners were deployed into a series of in-person learning sessions involving hundreds and sometimes thousands of practitioners from the organ donation and transplantation field. The whole process was driven by the systematic use of DNA.

Significant resources were invested in the site visit reviews, in the synthesis across sites, in the development of faculty from high performing sites, and finally in the action learning sessions to spread best practice across all donor hospitals and OPOs. Using the Mindset and Method of DNA assured that the investment had a high payoff in rapid spread of best practices. It delivered great content and faculty from high performance sites playing national leadership Roles.

DNA Takes Courage

DNA is an easy practice that can quickly become a wholesome habit. At the same time, it requires courage. As leaders, we are vouching for the people who are Being acknowledged. We are implicitly or sometimes explicitly calling on others to see them as a model.

In our professional lives, many of us tend to shy away from such public endorsements. We worry that we might be wrong, that we might not know enough, that others may disagree. It's safer to look for holes in the data, flaws in the logic, and needed improvements. It's easier to call for further study. However, as leaders, we should expect to be part of decisions and conversations where we will need to "stand for" the leading-edge actions and performance of others. Few endeavors are complete; most are a work in progress. We need courage to call out and recognize the behaviors, actions and performance of others as they show up.
We must bring forward the breakthroughs, and those things

that work. At the same time, we can learn to account for limitations and uncertainties and figure out how to discuss and address them publicly.

DNA equips us to step into an uplifting and effective way of organizing our leadership Choices on Intent. It helps us to bring more of what we want into the world. It provides us with a wonderful way to be a source of leadership and joy in the lives of others. Look for the people who are already doing what you want more of in the world. Have the boldness and courage to acknowledge their good work.

An Abundance of Opportunity for Large-Scale Transformation

The four Leadership Stories in this chapter illustrate how leaders were able to produce transformative change in major fields of practice by standing for a Compelling Vision of the future with Intent. All the leadership stories in this book emerge out of the unique situations the potential leaders find themselves in. These are the same kinds of defining moments that can show up in each of our own lives. Consider the range of situations in the first four stories. Each of these examples are regular human Beings who make intentional Choices to address the compelling needs of others.

Wide Range of Situations Where Leaders Made Choices on Intent

With Project ECHO, Sanjeev Arora mobilized a sector of the medical profession in New Mexico to reset how it served Hepatitis C patients. As a professor in medical school and a practicing specialist, he sees Hepatitis patients are in crisis because there are too few specialists in the region. He envisions how the Methods of medical specialty education can equip primary care clinicians who are already in place to provide specialty care for hepatitis patients. Sanjeev Arora commits to the vision and takes to the road on weekends in his home state to enroll primary care physicians. A far-reaching cycle of system transformation has begun.

In the radon story, we hear how a junior hire in EPA's Radon Division helps to transform federal policy on a serious but little-known public health issue. The federal program in place is insufficient to address the radon public health problem. By engaging the people in his chain of command and in expanding circles of influence, a more proactive federal policy is established. A serious public health problem is addressed with more effective and lasting national policy and messaging.

In the "100,000 Lives" story, Dr. Berwick and his co-leaders working from national expert committees and a successful quality improvement organization that he co-founded, see high rates of avoidable errors across hospitals with no vehicle in place to move hospitals into action at the right scale. Dr. Berwick stepped forward with others to enroll the nation's hospitals into an intense, voluntary campaign to transform patient safety practice. This work becomes the model for future highly effective quality campaigns in hospital patient safety and health care more broadly.

In the Organ Donation Breakthrough Collaborative story, Dennis Wagner finds himself in a federal Division with a mandate from Department executives to increase life-saving organ donation rates. The federal programs in place were not on track to generate significant results. A federal team forms and decides to establish a Bold Aim and enroll donor hospitals and Organ Procurement Organizations in a collaborative quality improvement initiative to increase donation rates. They work at multiple levels to get the Bold Aim adopted by Department officials, professional organizations, and the national community of practice. The nation's organ donation system is placed onto a path for transformation, ultimately saving tens of thousands more lives.

Throughout the book you will encounter people who found themselves in situations that called out for leadership. The situation presented itself, and they chose to take action. The platforms they worked from, the resources they controlled, the formal authority they had were not sufficient. Yet each person and team featured here chose to assume a leadership role in addressing the situation. They did it with Mindset and Method. They began with Intent.

Using the Mindsets and Methods to Make Leadership Choices on Intent

Compelling Visions, Bold Aims, and DNA provide us with proven strategies for making good Choices when leadership opportunities arise. These opportunities are everywhere. We only have to look and, when a situation resonates, avoid saying "it's none of my business." Instead, make it our business. Intervene in the current drift.

As you leave this chapter, stop, and examine the possibilities present in your own life for expanded leadership Choices on Intent. Consider how you might advance a Compelling Vision, how you might team with others to establish a Bold Aim, and how you might begin to use the practice of DNA to bring more of what you want into the world. Intent is a key trigger for releasing the leadership within each of us. Reflect on questions like these:

- ***The real possibility of transformation:*** What is the most compelling need of others that moves me today and how might I express it?

- ***Others who would be interested:*** Who in my circle of influence (family, friends, colleagues) am I ready to share my concern and interest with tomorrow?

- ***The example of what's already present:*** Who can I publicly acknowledge for their encouraging work to address the need?

- ***The next conversation that can follow:*** What would be the easy and effective way for me to engage someone in my circle of influence who would likely enroll another?

Keep accumulating the insight and energy needed to release the leadership within you. Leadership Choices on Intent are powerful agents for change. Live life to the fullest. Actively work to transcend the very natural fears that accompany commitment to big Intents. As the leadership stories in this chapter show us, each of us can commit to and deliver on important, meaningful Intents. And as Goethe reminds us,

"At the moment of commitment,
the entire universe conspires to assist you."

We Choose Our Ways of
BEING

Be the change you want to see in the world.

MAHATMA GANDHI
Indian Lawyer
Anti-colonial Nationalist
Political Ethicist

BEING

Net Forward Energy

Flip Negative Energy

Resilience

Becoming Conscious and Intentional About Our Choice of Being

Every day, we face an abundance of Choices, opportunities large and small, to choose how we lead and act. It is in these countless Choices that we can weave the fabric of our lives and choose to lead in the Domain of Being.

We use the term *Being* to encompass the way each of us thinks, feels, behaves, speaks, and listens, and the responses that these elicit from others. As leaders, we choose our state of Being to align with the work at hand and to pursue our shared vision.

We present here three Mindsets and Methods for cultivating intentional Choices in the Domain of Being: Net Forward Energy, Flip Negative Energy, and Resilience. Along with two inspiring Leadership Stories, we share transformative examples from our own professional and personal experiences that demonstrate how to bring good energy, how to deflect negative energy, and how to persist through the inevitable challenges of leadership.

Net Forward Energy. Leaders take accountability for their energy and the energy of others we work with. Net Forward Energy is a way to generate and manage the energy in our meetings and in our interactions. In this section, we relate how we learned about the powerful concept of Net Forward Energy from a colleague, and provide examples of what this looks like in practice.

Flip Negative Energy. The energy of a person or group can be positive or negative. Net Negative Energy tends to move players apart while generating noise and chaos. Yet negative energy is still energy. It does set people in motion, just not in the directions we need. Any leadership enterprise will by its nature generate issues and resistance.

We can anticipate Negative Energy, and when we encounter it, we can flip it into positive energy. In this section, we share a dramatic example in which a leader named Marie Schall turns a potential ethical crisis into a leadership breakthrough by using a proven toolkit for Flipping Negative Energy.

Practicing Resilience. Leaders have to get comfortable Being uncomfortable. Gaining command of the five sources of Resilience—Purpose, Choice, Perspective, Partners, and Problems—is an essential and powerful leadership capability that we can foster in ourselves and in others.

It's the ultimate ability to effectively manage energy in a leadership movement. We share important techniques that have been effective in enabling ourselves and our colleagues to bounce back from the inevitable setbacks and breakdowns that come with leadership. We also profile a number of testimonials and three case examples to illustrate the practical application of the resilience Mindset and Method: the Kersting Family case example, the "Has Anybody Called Bill?" case example, and the story of Dennis and his family's experience on the 500-mile Camino de Santiago pilgrimage.

Become Intentional About Our Choice of Being

It takes effort to gain intentional control of Being. Awareness of our own state of Being is the first step in gaining that control, and it empowers us to make effective leadership choices with intent. We often fall into Being choices by default. The defaults are our moods, our habits, our deeply ingrained patterns.

A driver in another car honks when we don't immediately accelerate after the traffic light turns green. This may cause us to default to feelings of anger, irritation, or guilt at being a slow starter. Gaining awareness of our moods and default reactions is a key initial step in consciously seeking to choose our state of Being.

When we wake up in the morning, some of us may unconsciously default to worrying about all the problems, challenges, and undone tasks facing us in our day. But we don't have to default to the habit of worry or any other ingrained habit of Being. We can learn to choose other ways of Being with intention.

Gaining intentional control of our own state of Being may seem a daunting task. It's doable. And it gets easier with practice. For example, when we find ourselves in a negative state of Being precipitated by external events or ingrained habits, we can pause, take a deep breath, and reflect on the state of Being that would better align with our current situation. We can use simple exercises to take ourselves and others to the desired state of Being.

Instead of worry, maybe you want to start your day with gratitude. Make a mental list of five things you're grateful for. Spending a few minutes to create and reflect on this list will produce gratitude, a much more positive mode in which to start our day.

Establishing a state of gratitude is just one of hundreds of intentional ways of Being that are available to us. Angry about something? Launching into your next activity or meeting in a state of anger is usually counterproductive. Instead, ask yourself generative questions to actively deal with the anger: *What's good about this seemingly bad situation? What are the potential benefits of releasing this anger? Who could I talk with to gain greater perspective on this anger?*

Over time, practice in making these kinds of Choices of Being turn into habit. To make these Choices is to truly exercise the muscles of human-ness central to cultivating impact and joy.

Helping Others Choose Effective States of Being

As leaders, we can also take the important next step of helping our colleagues to align their states of Being with the work at hand. This isn't complicated, but it is unusual. And, it does require courage—a willingness to put ourselves out there in order to lead the collective Being of others.

Try it. Create a state of appreciation for colleagues:

1. Direct participants in an upcoming meeting to take two minutes to write down two or three things they appreciate about another person;

2. Then ask each participant to turn to another person and share their list with each other in two minute's time;

3. Take another two minutes to invite a few participants to quickly share their list with the full group.

A feeling of mutual appreciation for others will become the Being vibe of the entire gathering. Think of it! As leaders, we can have a profound impact on the state of Being in a meeting or large event with these three straightforward requests in a mere six minutes. This is an especially useful exercise if the work at hand is something like team-building.

We can use this approach to foster many impactful states of Being—Acknowledgment, Resilience, testing new ideas, alignment to build on the work of others, and problem-solving—tailored to the specific tasks of our meetings. Six minutes to intentionally manage collective Mindsets is a worthwhile investment for leaders.

Helping others access a productive state of Being is an invaluable yet under-utilized leadership asset. We can call for certain states of Being, whether in our team meetings, in our families, with friends, or at conferences with tens, hundreds, even thousands of participants. We've done this many hundreds of times—and it works.

Three Challenges and Approaches to Gaining Intentional Control of Being

Knowing how to lead in the Domain of Being is a profoundly influential leadership asset, with at least three key challenges that leaders routinely confront:

1. Dealing with our own personal default habits and current moods;

2. Leading others who have habits and moods that are not aligned with the shared work at hand;

3. Encountering negative and even tragic circumstances that are beyond our control and can sometimes stop us cold.

Once these three challenges are recognized, we can prepare ourselves to recognize and meet them by cultivating three leadership ways of Being:

1. ***Proactive leadership of ourselves:*** We can become more aware and self-conscious of what state of Being is needed for our leadership work. The Choices we make about our own state of Being are a vitally important first level of practical application. Leadership starts with leading ourselves.

2. ***Proactive leadership of others:*** We can become attuned to identifying and influencing the state of Being of others. As leaders, we can choose to help establish intentional Mindsets in groups that can lead to uplifting and effective group action.

3. ***Reactive leadership for self and others:*** We can master the natural fear, anger, and other negative responses that surface in ourselves and others as we encounter challenges in our leadership work. For example, by learning to respond effectively to Negative Energy, which is covered in the following pages, we can be prepared to meet this and other difficulties the world will invariably throw our way.

The leadership stories and three Mindsets and Methods presented in the following pages show us how to gain greater command of our leadership Choices on Being.

Leadership Stories Show How Being is a Defining Choice

Before launching further into methodology, we share a stirring, real-life example of Net Forward Energy, Flip Negative Energy, and practicing Resilience in action. The Leadership Story of Bob and Barb Malizzo is one of how two heartbroken parents chose Being of service as their response to an immense personal tragedy. Moving through their grief and anger, these parents ultimately made leadership Choices that were unlikely yet exceptional, with extraordinary results.

We also hear from renowned thought-leader Doug Krug on how to harness Net Forward Energy; we learn how Marie Schall averted a potential ethical crisis through Flip Negative Energy; and Dennis shares how an arduous pilgrimage tested his family's resilience and resulted in emotional and spiritual deepening.

Our Being chapter ends with the leadership story of Anne H. Hastings who chose to embrace leadership in a mid-career transition by creating partnerships to address poverty and ultra-poverty in rural Haiti. Anne's story illustrates how Choices in the Domain of Being can make extraordinary things happen when using Net Forward Energy, continually Flip Negative Energy, and practicing Resilience to overcome setbacks and breakdowns. Anne's story shows how Being open to possibilities helps us to both generate opportunities and to act on unseen opportunities waiting to be seized upon.

LEADERSHIP STORY

Be the Change You Want to See in the World: Bob & Barb Malizzo's Leadership Story

Bob and Barb Malizzo, along with daughter Kristina Chavez and her son Adrian, visit their daughter, Michelle Ballog's grave at Graceland Cemetery in Valparaiso, Indiana. Michelle died after a medical error was made during surgery.

Choosing to Respond to Tragedy with Service

Imagine losing a child—your daughter, a mother with two young children—during a straightforward hospital medical procedure. And then emerging from the grief and loss to help that same hospital correct its safety protocols so that other patients would be safe.

Bob and Barb Malizzo lost their daughter, Michelle Malizzo Ballog, to an anesthesia error at the University of Illinois Hospital and Health Sciences System in 2008. Their grief at this unexpected death of their daughter was total. Their anger at learning it was caused by an avoidable medical error was deep.

Moving through their grief and anger, they ultimately made leadership Choices that were unlikely and extraordinary. Bob and Barb joined with Tim McDonald MD, the Vice President of Quality and Safety at this same hospital, and worked with him and other hospital staff to correct the system errors that led to Michelle's death. Bob and Barb became active members of the hospital safety review committee, helping to create a program to eliminate medical errors and promote transparency.

The hospital leadership, to their credit, went above and beyond the deny-and-defend strategy common in health care. When hospitals make errors, they often are dealt with legalistically: avoid admission of guilt and limit information to families. Punish the caregivers and providers who were involved. If necessary, use the punishment as proof of corrective action.

The University of Illinois Medical Center did something different. They admitted the error that caused the death of Michelle. They apologized to Michelle's family for the error. They offered compensation. And then they went to work with Bob and Barb to improve their safety processes and track record. The leadership Choices made by this hospital became a powerful example for many other hospitals across the nation.

Extending Their Patient Safety Service to the Nation

In 2011, the Malizzo's work with Tim McDonald and University of Illinois Medical Center was brought to the attention of our federal hospital safety team at the Centers for Medicare and Medicaid Services. We were connected by an influential and empathic safety advocate named Martin (Marty) Hatlie, CEO of Project Safe Care and a national leader in hospital safety.

After learning about Bob and Barb's phenomenal work with UI Medical Center, our team asked them to join with the Centers for Medicare and Medicaid Services, the Agency for Healthcare Research on Quality, and healthcare leaders from nearly 4000 of the nation's 5000 hospitals, to mount what became a successful national push to achieve dramatic reductions in hospital harms such as the event that killed Michelle. Bob and Barb joined with the federal agencies, improvement contractors, national associations, and hospital teams, and formally committed to a shared Bold Aim of generating a 40% reduction in preventable hospital harm by 2014.

Bob and Barb Malizzo speaking at National Patient Safety Conference

As part of the work to achieve the 40% reduction in harm, our team worked with Marty and Project Safe Care to deploy Barb, Bob, and Dr. McDonald at many state hospital association conferences and other events with large numbers of hospital leaders. Together they advocated for hospitals to implement the federal government's Project CANDOR (Communication and Optimal Resolution) initiative, which was being tested at the University of Illinois when Michelle died.

Hospitals adopting CANDOR follow a straightforward protocol when a serious medical error occurs: 1) disclose the error, 2) accept accountability, 3) offer compensation, 4) provide support to caregivers involved, and 5) work to fix the underlying system(s) that led to the error. Many hospitals adopted CANDOR because of the work of this persuasive and influential team.

We Can Respond to Bad with Good

The Choices and reactions to pain and suffering made by Bob and Barb Malizzo are an inspiration for all of us. They responded to one of life's deepest tragedies by choosing to help others. Their commitment to Being of Service, and all their subsequent decisions and actions, helped prevent deaths and the accompanying grief for tens of thousands of other families.

The leadership Choices of the University of Illinois Medical Center were also significant, with the hospital becoming a model for hundreds of other hospitals across the nation. They too, like Bob and Barb, chose to respond to bad with good.

Bob and Barb eventually arrived at a place of appreciating the actions and safety improvements at the University of Illinois Medical Center where they had lost Michelle. In 2013, they presented engraved watches to the medical team to acknowledge improvements in their safety of care. This is both poignant and astonishing. The leadership lesson on Being is profound: each of us can consciously choose to respond to the problems, difficulties, and bad things that happen to us with intentional, positive responses that help both ourselves and others. Bob and Barb chose to be leaders in improving patient safety at the hospital that caused the death of their daughter, and for millions of other people throughout the nation.

National Results Flow From Leadership Choices On Being

In 2015, the federal government released a report showing that dramatic reductions in hospital harms had resulted in an estimated 2.1 million fewer harms, $19.8 billion in cost savings, and 87,000 lives saved as a result of improvements over the period 2011-2014. The results represented a 39% reduction in preventable hospital harm. Bob and Barb, along with many other committed people, were a big part of achieving these extraordinary life-saving results that impacted tens of thousands of patients and families. New Bold Aims, continued work, and further results followed through 2017.

Hospitals in the US Became Much Safer from 2010 to 2017

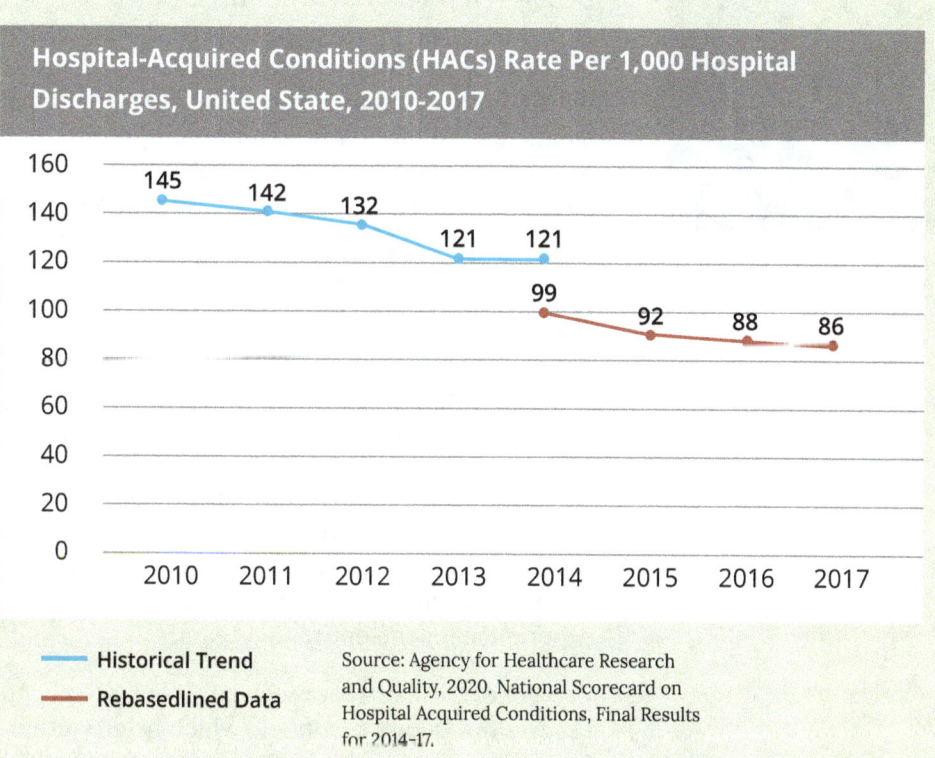

Source: Agency for Healthcare Research and Quality, 2020. National Scorecard on Hospital Acquired Conditions, Final Results for 2014-17.

BEING

Net Forward Energy

Flip Negative Energy

Resilience

Doug Krug
Author
Leadership Coach
Thought Leader

Choose to Foster Net Forward Energy in the Domain of Being

A Coach With a Concept Called Net Forward Energy

Dennis is forever grateful for having met Doug Krug, a fascinating person. Doug has served as a policeman in Miami, a record store owner in Denver, the author of numerous leadership books, a management consultant, a radio talk-show host, and more. Dennis met Doug in 1995 through Bud Ward of the National Safety Council, a friend and colleague who called one day to say that he had participated in a life-changing leadership workshop with his senior executive team at a two-day event in Chicago. Bud wanted Dennis to meet with the man who led the event.

Dennis and Doug met the following week in Washington DC and clicked immediately. Doug is upbeat, authentic, confident, experienced in the ways of the world, and fun to be around.

Shortly after meeting, Dennis and his team contracted with Doug to conduct a two-day leadership retreat at the US Environmental Protection Agency (EPA). The leadership retreat conducted with Doug was a genuinely transformative experience for the entire EPA team.

Everyone at the retreat received a copy of *Enlightened Leadership*, Doug's first book, which he co-authored with Ed Oakley. More recently, Doug teamed up with Christine Kahane to write *UNLearning! Leading Change without Resistance*. We highly recommend both books to our readers.

One of the many things learned from Doug was the concept of **Net Forward Energy**. Put simply, Net Forward Energy is when positive thoughts, statements, and actions outweigh negative thoughts, statements, and actions. Net Forward Energy gets a group moving forward, together.

Doug did more than just explain this concept. He gave the team permission to encourage each other to call for Net Forward Energy in our meetings and in our work. This simple strategy didn't come naturally to many at EPA. EPA is filled with scientists and lawyers, and the culture is grounded in deep scientific analysis and fierce debate. EPA staff and their constituents routinely fought about the underlying environmental science as well as the regulations that flowed from this science. Conflict was a routine way of Being. When the EPA issued a new environmental regulation, it was common for the business community to sue the Agency for having gone too far, and for the environmental community to sue the Agency for not having gone far enough. This contentious way of Being weighed heavily on everyone.

Doug's coaching on Net Forward Energy helped participants wake up to the impacts of the Agency culture, and to bring much-needed positive and productive energy to the team and even beyond, to the larger agency.

Guided to Focus on Goals and the Future Instead of Problems and the Past

Doug's coaching came at just the right time. Prior to encountering Doug, Dennis's team had spent several weeks identifying, documenting, and prioritizing problems with their work that needed attention. This focus on problems had sucked the energy right out of the team. The more problems the team looked for, the more they found. Long and tedious conversations ensued about which problems were highest priority. It was demoralizing and exhausting.

Doug introduced the technique of using Effective Questions with team members: "What works?" and "How to get more of what works?" The team went from focusing on problems to focusing on goals and strengths, a simple change that made all the difference. While we cannot and should not ignore our problems, powerful strategies and cultures are not built by focusing on problems. Humans gravitate towards what we focus on. Problems may call our attention and deserve correction action, but it is far better to focus on our assets, on what works, and on our goals. Focus on problems and we get closer to our problems. Focus on our goals and we get closer to our goals.

What Dennis's team learned from Doug about Effective Questions, focus and the conscious spread of Net Forward Energy became powerful building blocks in all their subsequent work. Focusing on goals and the future has had a remarkable impact, not only on the team's way of Being, but for thousands of colleagues at EPA and throughout the nation.

Understand How Energy Shows Up and Moves a Group Forward or Backward

People interacting create energy. As a group interacts, an observer can sense and actually measure and track the kind of energy being produced. We can categorize the energy as positive in that it moves us forward into the future we seek, or as negative in that it moves us backward into a past that we want to leave behind. As shown in the figure below, the energy we create can move us in two directions. To the right has us focused on what we can do to realize our goals; to the left, on what we can't do because of the problems we have.

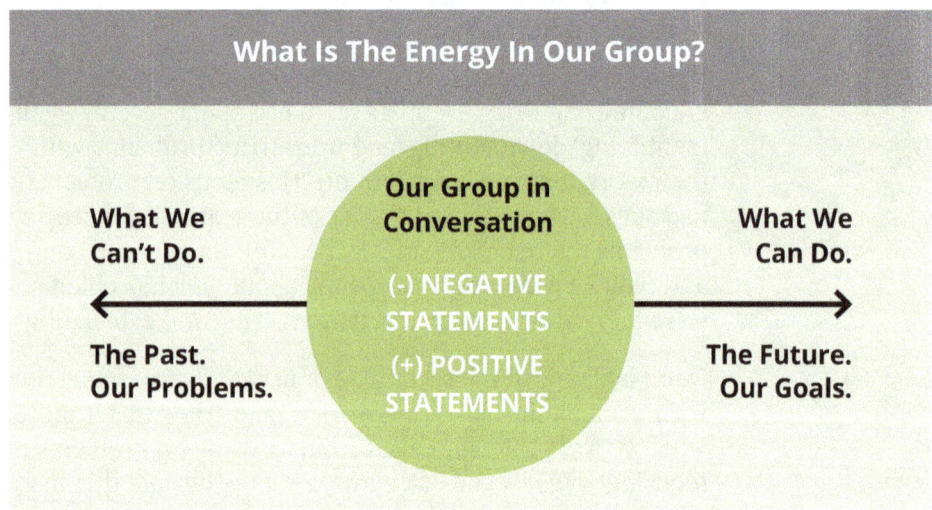

Adapted From Ed Oakley and Doug Krug, *Enlightened Leadership*

Positive energy may show up as insights about what works and steps that we can take to make real progress. Negative energy may show up as reasons why we failed, barriers we face, and complaints we have. These critical diagnostics may be necessary to explore and deal with at some level, but they are not likely to move us forward.

Our thoughts and statements generate energy and direction. As leaders, we must be self-conscious about the kind of Being we model and the effect this has on others.

Two Kinds of Energy from Different Thoughts & Statements	
Positive (+)	**Negative (−)**
Taking Responsibility	Blame, Complain
Opportunities	Problems
What We Can Do	What We Can't Do
Acting	Waiting, Wishing
Being Proactive	Waiting, Wishing
Good Stories	Bad Stories
Open	Judgmental
Testing Ideas	Arguing Opinions

The above figure illustrates thoughts and statements that tend to generate positive energy and those that tend to generate negative energy. Just reading the terms in the column on the right can make us feel uncomfortable, while those on the left instill feelings of hope and possibility.

The following two figures illustrate the Method behind Net Forward Energy. Each plus or minus sign represents a way of Being by a participant in a meeting. The more we choose to dwell on the positive side of the table, the more positive energy our group generates. When the positive exceeds the negative, we have Net Forward Energy. And of course, when the negative exceeds the positive, we have Net Negative Energy.

With Net Forward Energy, participants leave meetings with insight and ready for action. We have a positive outlook which makes us and our work appealing to others.

Net Forward Energy operates as conversations about goals and what we can do. The group moves forward into the future.

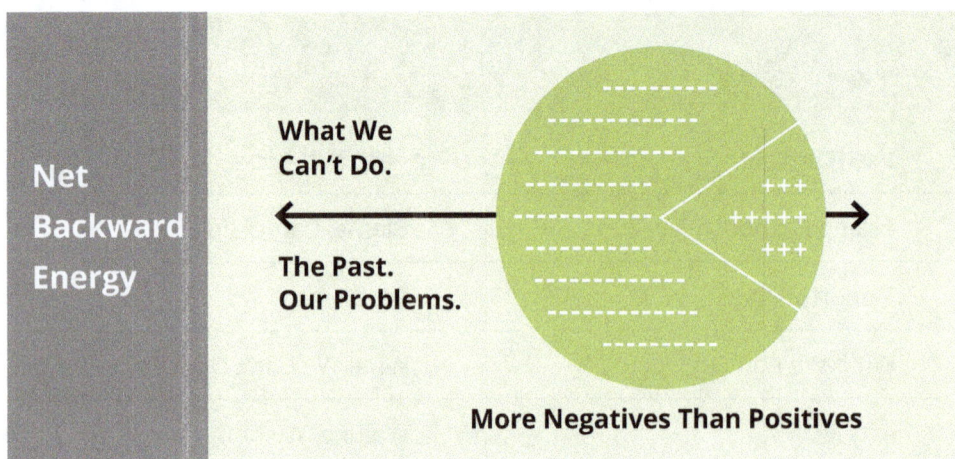

Adapted From Ed Oakley and Doug Krug, *Enlightened Leadership*

With Net Backward Energy, the danger is spending too much time assigning blame, arguing causes, looking for fixes to small problems, and perpetuating the status quo. Net Backward Energy often shows up as conversation on problems and what we can't do. The group dwells on the past and how to fix it.

It's not uncommon to find ourselves in situations where it feels like there's little or no energy, or where the energy becomes negative. This can happen professionally, socially, or in the other day-to-day interactions of our lives. It's easy for us and our colleagues to accept the weak energy state we find ourselves in.

In the following section, we show how making leadership Choices in the domain of Being can generate the kind of energy needed to achieve our Compelling Visions.

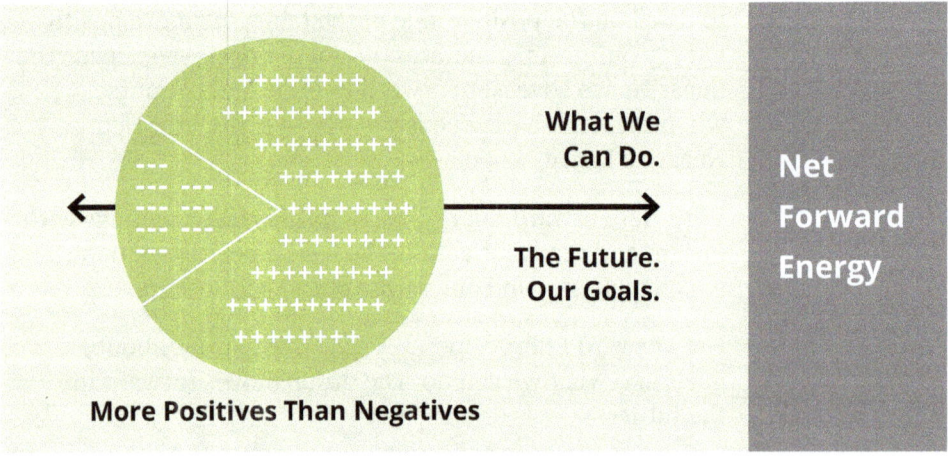

The Net Forward Energy Mindset and Method

We want to establish situations with others that generate Net Forward Energy. Leaders seek to both model Net Forward Energy and to call for it in others.

Net Forward Energy is a way of Being that can be attained with the three-part Mindset and Method presented below. We can orchestrate the energy we need by Being accountable, aware, and authentic.

Being Net Forward Energy: Orchestrate the Energy Around Us

1. **Be Accountable.** Assume accountability for the energy in the group situations we are in.

   - *Prepare An Abundance Mindset.* Show up with a positive mindset of Abundance; address the mindset of scarcity when it naturally emerges.
   - *Make Requests.* Ask that others adopt a mindset of Abundance.
   - *Use Effective Questions.* Guide others into a positive conversation by asking questions that generate productive responses.

2. **Be Aware.** Monitor our own energy state. Keep a mental log of the type and level of energy in play from meeting to meeting, event to event. Act to create a positive trend.

3. **Be Authentic.** Cultivate Net Forward Energy as an authentic way to find opportunities in painful and problematic situations. Avoid masking real problems with false or empty positive expressions.

We have in our own practice intentionally nurtured the positive energy needed to move many different groups forward in pursuit of Compelling Visions. We have witnessed hundreds of colleagues and partners do this as well.

This approach has become a standard, uplifting, and effective element of more than a dozen large national and international initiatives that we have participated in or led. We have consciously and intentionally cultivated Net Forward Energy at every opportunity—in our conferences, learning sessions, monthly conference calls, webinars, Zoom meetings, and even weekly staff meetings. This is a central feature of our work, and it has made all the difference in the world.

Be Accountable for Net Forward Energy

A key element of the Net Forward Energy Mindset and Method is to take accountability for the energy in the activities and initiatives that we lead. The energy we bring into the world doesn't just happen. We can exercise accountability as we engage others by following a simple three-step method of preparing an Abundance Mindset, making Requests of others, and using Effective Questions.

Preparing an Abundance Mindset for ourselves is a way to become conscious and intentional about the energy being generated by the situations we are in. Abundance is a belief that the resources and solutions we need are out in the world and can be accessed. Its opposite is a scarcity mindset which sees limits and boundaries that deprive us of access to what we need. (For a more detailed discussion on Abundance as a Mindset and Method, see the chapter on Language.)

Our Choices matter. The energy we choose to bring into the world matters. A first step in exercising accountability for Net Forward Energy is to choose a Mindset of Abundance for the situation we are in. Experience teaches us what that Mindset looks and feels like. The adjacent table contrasts common Choices we face between scarcity and Abundance thinking.

Alternative Mindsets	
Scarcity = Negative Energy	**Abundance = Positive Energy**
Frustrated with Problems	Problems as opportunities
Finding Fault	Looking for the Good
What we don't have	What we do have
What we don't like	What we do like
What we can't do	What we can do
Why is this happening to me?	Why is this happening for me?

Accountability for Net Forward Energy begins with our choosing to be open to Abundance. But it doesn't end there.

Make requests of others. Ask them to join with us in adopting an Abundance mindset.

Others are making their own Choices, too. Stay aware of these Choices and help others become aware as well. We can help others become conscious of their energy Choices by calling them to their attention and by modeling these approaches ourselves. Then we can ask our colleagues to deliberately and intentionally choose the positive.

Most of us have far more influence and power than we recognize. We can start our next meeting by describing the positive energy we want to bring into the world. We can ask our participants to join with us in generating more positives than negatives as a deliberate way of Being.

This business of asking others to choose positive ways of Being may feel odd at first. Give it a shot. Our experience with this is that people begin to appreciate it. We aren't telling folks things they don't already know; we're simply bringing it to the front of their brains so that all of us can remember to live life together with positive energy, intentionally and fully.

Ask Effective Questions. In a later chapter on the Language Domain, we will learn more about the power of certain ways of speaking that include Requests, Offers, and Effective Questions that generate accountability for Net Forward Energy in the moment. Asking Effective Questions is often an elegant way to orchestrate the creation of Net Forward Energy. These are questions designed to generate substantive, thoughtful responses (instead of yes-or-no opinions) that open up possibilities and opportunities. *"What most excites you about the presentation? What worked and what caused it to work? What parts of their example could help us to improve our own operations?"*

Be Aware Of The Energy

High energy meetings propel us forward. Low and negative energy meetings leave us feeling unproductive and perhaps frustrated. As we move rapidly from meeting to meeting, we tend to lose track of the overall trend in the quality of our events and the impact that quality has on ourselves and others.

Once being accountable for Net Forward Energy is chosen as a way of Being, it becomes necessary – and easier—to become conscious of how energy is showing up in our activities and encounters. This energy manifests itself in several observable ways:

- *Attention:* Participants in an event or other situation are present in the moment. They are paying attention and not mentally drifting off to other matters.

- *Insight:* Learning is taking place and being shared. More than just transferring information, we and our colleagues are processing understanding, possibilities, and opportunities.

- *Deal making:* At some level, Requests and Offers are being made and Commitments are being generated. Real leadership work is being performed. Participants are in action.

As we participate in an event, we will automatically have a sense of the energy that is present. We can inquire about it; it can be measured. On occasion we have asked participants in our meetings to rate the energy of the meeting on a quality and outcome scale and to comment on what worked and what could be done better.

In our leadership events, we often work to build in participant exercises to surface insights and to foster dealmaking. These exercises are formal and visible. On multi-day events, at the end of each day, we often ask participants to fill out a short survey to describe what worked, what to change, and what to add. Our event team processes the surveys in the evening. Next day opens with a report-back to the audience on what we learned and a list of actions we are taking in response. By becoming aware of the energy present in our interactions, we are better able to manage our events to produce high Net Forward Energy in pursuit of our shared vision.

Be Authentic

Be authentic in our Requests and Offers for Net Forward Energy. Most all of us want to participate in meetings or simply experience our days with interactions that are filled with more positives than negatives. We understand, of course, that there will be hard days, big problems, major setbacks, and unexpected losses, all of which need be acknowledged and dealt with. Troublesome things cannot and should not be glossed over with a facade of positive energy. Ignoring or denying the negatives is not effective. One of the many things we learned from Doug is that avoiding doesn't work.

However, at the same time, leaders can choose to cultivate Net Forward Energy as an authentic way to find the possibilities and opportunities in painful and problematic situations. As Winston Churchill advised, "Never let a good crisis go to waste." Crisis alters conditions, perceptions, and attitudes, making it possible to accomplish what appeared to be impossible before.

Leaders do not mask real problems with false, empty, positive expressions. Leaders can choose to deal with these setbacks and problems in effective and proven ways. Two Mindsets and Methods for dealing with these negatives are profiled in the following segments on Flip Negative Energy and Resilience.

Choosing to generate positive energy and asking others to join with us in positive ways to perform the work at hand will help create productive conversations and uplifting feelings that people won't ever forget. This straightforward practice can contribute to making the ordinary into something quite extraordinary. It is a powerful way of Being in the world.

BEING

Net Forward Energy

Flip Negative Energy

Resilience

Flip Negative Energy:
A Great Way to Help Ourselves and Others

The leadership Mindset and Method of Net Forward Energy previously profiled demonstrates how to generate and spread positive energy as a deliberate way of Being. However, anyone who has ever tried to lead anything knows that sometimes our leadership is met with stiff resistance, anger, challenges, adversarial questions, and other forms of negative energy. Leadership is rarely a bed of roses. How do we learn to handle these situations?

Even Negative Energy Can Be an Asset

The first and possibly most important thing is to recognize that strong negative energy... is energy. People care. And they care enough to express it, sometimes with great force.

For leaders, energy is an asset. Harness that energy in service to our aims, in service to the person expressing it, and we are on the road to good places. Even helping someone to a state of Being that is more neutral and not in opposition is a gain.

We need to understand and act on this important Mindset: **energy is good, even when it is being expressed in negative ways.** When negative energy crops up—and it almost always does – recognize that this could be the source of good things going forward. This view is at the heart of the Mindset we cultivate as a key step in learning to flip negative energy.

Kevin O'Connor, former CEO of LifeCenter Northwest in Seattle, coaches us to think of negative energy like sailing and the wind. Sailors learn how to sail to their destinations, no matter what direction the wind is blowing. The wind is energy to be harnessed. As leaders, our challenge is to find a way to accept the negative energy, to go beyond tolerating or diffusing it, to embracing and channeling it to constructive ends.

This is all easy to say. It is harder to do. But not too hard.

The Toolkit for How to Flip Negative Energy

The encouraging reality is that there are Methods—specific leadership Speech Acts—that we can apply to our ability to Flip Negative Energy into forward movement, all while helping and supporting the people who are surfacing the negative energy. We can pursue and help to generate an Upward Spiral of good things, even when seemingly bad things are cropping up. How about that!

Our leadership tool kit for how to Flip Negative Energy includes three powerful Speech Acts shown in the chart on the following page. (For a more detailed discussion of Speech Acts, see the chapter on Language.)

To Flip Negative Energy is Like Harnessing the Wind

Flip Negative Energy: A Kit

Say "Yes, And …"	Listen for Requests & Offers Just Below the Surface	Process The Negative With An Effective Question
Accept what is offered (Yes), then add to it what we need (And). Don't fight. Say "Yes" and figure out later how to include it.	Listen to complaints and criticism as calls for help, as possible offers to create a solution. Secure a commitment to address the issue.	Create questions that cause ourselves and our partners to generate positive possibilities around a negative situation that is stopping progress.

Say Yes, and …
Learning to use the two powerful words of **Yes, and…** is a highly effective way to create forward motion in situations where negative energy arises. We have learned a lot about leadership, synergy, and teamwork by studying improvisational comedy. One of the first rules of comedy improv is to learn to say *yes*. Yes, always *yes*, to your partner or group. The second rule is to not only say *yes* but to also say *and*. Work to accept and expand on the original offering. Don't be afraid to accept potential solutions. As ideas are offered, suspend judgment. **Yes, and…** keeps things going, builds on what's already there without blocking others.

Leadership as improv—who knew?

Listen for Requests & Offers Below the Surface.
Many times, complaints and other forms of negative energy can be viewed as an awkward way of formulating what may actually be a Request or Offer from the person expressing the negative energy. Listening for Requests and Offers below the surface is about distinguishing a person's analytic and personality style from their good will and potential interest. They could be negatively critical and still want to help. They may see problems and may be willing to own and act on them.

One of the habits in Steven Covey's 7 *Habits of Highly Effective People* is to "seek first to understand, then to be understood." As leaders, we can learn to be open to negativity while also working to understand what is behind it. This attitudinal shift, all by itself, can create a different kind of relationship with the source of the negative energy. The source of the energy will sense that they are being listened to and heard.

What sounds like negative energy could potentially be thought of as a Request for you or others to help the person expressing the negative energy to solve a vexing problem. In some cases, we might in fact be able to discern an Offer from the person expressing negative energy. They may want to be called on or be invited to put forward a solution or to take actions to address the problem.

Work to turn complaints into Offers. We have been in large conferences of 3000 people where someone in the audience takes the floor to ask a question or share a comment, and then proceeds to go off on a negative rant about some aspect of the issue at hand. In a few situations, a simple question back to them, "Is that an Offer?" will result in the person pausing, thinking, and saying, "Yes, actually, maybe it is." We've had this very experience on multiple occasions, connecting with the person during a break and eliciting from them a plan to follow-up and go into action on their Offer. As leaders, we can become proficient in helping problem-identifiers become problem-solvers. This is a gift both to them, and often to many of their colleagues.

Process the Negative with Effective Questions.
Using Effective Questions when confronted with negative energy is like having the power to turn lead into gold. This is something a leader can do in a group process. It is a way to steer a boat through a challenging set of rapids.

Breakdowns in plans and operations, public criticism, partners withdrawing – in the work of leading, there are many occasions that can be heart-breaking and demoralizing. On these occasions, one possible solution in your toolkit is to bring your colleagues together and process the negative situation with an Effective Question. Consider the following examples of effective questions: Miller's Law, Congressman Elijah Cummings' "Why," the McGann Effective Question, or your own personal version of a question such as the one posed by Carolyn Candiello.

Miller's Law

"To understand what another person is saying, you must assume that it is true and try to imagine what it could be true of."

George Miller
Professor of Psychology
Princeton University

Miller's Law has had a big impact on us. The Effective Question is: If this statement that I dislike were true, what would it be true of? The question invites us to understand a person's frame of reference and the way they are thinking. This equips us to better deal with the issue and converse in their Language and framework.

When we respond this way with a person who is saying something we disagree with or dislike, we find the "what is true" approach often enables us to see the person in a positive light. A much better and sometimes very productive situation is created.

The "McGann Effective Question" to Flip Negative Energy

"What is good about this seemingly bad situation?"

Paul McGann, MD
Deputy Chief Medical Officer, Centers for Medicare and Medicaid Services

An executive team at the Centers for Medicare and Medicaid Services (CMS) ran into to what appeared to be a devasting setback in a long-term effort to move a proposed program through to Departmental approval. The team was meeting in a conference room and its members were despondent. Dr. Paul McGann, the CMS Chief Medical Officer for Quality Improvement, showed up and asked what the problem was. The team shared the breakdown. Dr. McGann asked them to consider "What is good about this seemingly bad situation?" They responded, "Absolutely nothing." Dr. McGann persisted. "What is good about this seemingly bad situation?" The team began to talk about it.

The team stuck with Dr. McGann's question, and much to everyone's surprise, ideas began to surface, people began to build on each other's ideas, and potential solutions started to emerge. We have learned time and again that effective questions are somewhat irresistible – we humans are attracted to answering them. Before Dr. McGann left, the team was re-energized, and had an initial game plan for moving ahead. Frequent use of the McGann Effective Question became a regular feature of our shared work on problem-solving at the Centers for Medicare and Medicaid Services. We and many others use this powerful and effective question constantly.

When confronting difficult, painful situations:

Elijah Cummings
Former Congressman

"Instead of asking:
Why is this happening to me?
Ask:
Why is this happening for me?"

"Why is this happening to me?" This is a lesson Congressman Elijah Cummings shared in a 2019 public congressional hearing. Change the ineffective question, "Why is this happening to me?" to an effective one: "Why is this happening for me?" In processing the two questions out loud, we can feel our mindset shift from victim to someone with new possibilities. We begin to search for the potential benefits embedded in our difficulty.

As setbacks emerge, as they inevitably do:

Carolyn Candiello
VP Quality &
Patient Safety, GBMC

"Given this situation, what do we have to do better to have a chance at achieving the Baldrige Award"

Leaders in the middle of a mission or pursuit of a vision can create their own personal Effective Questions. Carolyn Candiello, Vice President of the Greater Baltimore Medical Center, devised a customized Effective Question in partnership with CEO John Chessare, MD, as they pursued the prestigious Malcolm Baldrige Quality Award. Their 10-year journey to achieving the Baldrige Award provided many occasions for them to apply Carolyn's question above. (Dr. Chessare's full Leadership Story is presented in the section on Roles.)

As leaders, each of us can practice crafting our own personal Effective Questions to flip negative situations.

Case Study in Flip Negative Energy: Marie Schall Leads Us From an Ethical Crisis To a Breakthrough Solution

Marie Schall
Senior Director,
Institute for Healthcare Improvement

A Call to Action to Save Lives

In September of 2003, the US Department of Health and Human Services Organ Donation Collaborative was deeply immersed in a two-day Learning Session with 800 healthcare leaders and clinicians, in a hotel ballroom 10 blocks from the U.S. Capitol. A defining moment for the collaborative occurred in the middle of a high-energy session on the morning of day two.

Six panelists were seated on stools in a semicircle, facing the packed and highly engaged audience. The panel was discussing the need for hospitals to call their designated organ procurement organization (OPO) when it became clear that death was imminent for a patient who could potentially become an organ donor. Being ready to act quickly in circumstances like these can save the lives of other patients waiting for a lifesaving transplant.

One of the panelists pointed out that new federal regulations buttressed the need for early referral and rapid response as a lifesaving best practice for increased organ donation when the death of the potential donor was imminent.

An Ethical Issue Threatens a Veto

The discussion appeared to be going smoothly, when suddenly, a distinguished medical doctor from Johns Hopkins University Hospital stood up in the audience, becoming visibly angry as he rejected the proposal on ethical grounds:

> You folks are suggesting that I need to do something which is clearly wrong, and which poses serious problems to the oath I took as a doctor. I don't give up on my patients and accept the imminent death language of this federal regulation. No way am I doing this!

The room went silent. The energy shifted. Other clinicians in the audience were nodding their agreement. Clearly, this was a serious development. The best practice of early referral and rapid response as a source of high performance in lifesaving organ donation suddenly seemed highly problematic, possibly even fundamentally wrong. Our hearts sank.

"Yes, and ..." Creates a Conversation

The panel chair, Marie Schall from the Institute for Healthcare Improvement, responded to the situation. She said,

> Yes, this is important. I also care deeply for the patients we serve. You are raising a vitally important issue. And, am I hearing a request that we address this serious issue?

The physician nodded.

Marie was expert in the "All Teach, All Learn" style of our Learning Session, which engages frontline providers in the room to foster peer learning and action. She turned to both the panel and the audience and asked, *"Has anyone successfully addressed this important concern in some way?"*

Marie's Effective Question Surfaced Potential Solutions

A young woman stood up in the audience. She introduced herself as a nurse from an organ procurement organization in the Midwest. She gave a one-minute speech from the floor.

> *Yes, we've dealt with this issue many times. I share the doctor's concern about the "imminent death" language in the new federal regulations. Imminent death is a subjective decision and it is highly problematic. Instead of citing the regulations, we use objective clinical triggers to determine when a hospital should call their Organ Procurement Organization (OPO). For example, when the patient meets two out of three medical conditions such as: 1) brain flow tests are below a certain level or 2) the patient is on a ventilator, or 3) there has been a discussion with the patient's family about the possibility of removing life support, then the OPO is called. These objective, fact-based clinical conditions permit doctors and clinicians to continue doing everything possible to save the life of the patient. They also enable the OPO to be called and be present and in action immediately if the patient dies and can become an organ donor. This practice also fulfills the federal regulatory requirement.*

One of the panelists and several other audience members chimed in to share that they were using similar kinds of clinical triggers to guide their work. Others began to request that the triggers be shared with the full audience of nation-wide attendees.

Listening for the Underlying Request and Offer Creates Closure

Maria Schall wasn't finished. She turned back to the doctor and said,

> *Thank you so much for raising this critically important issue. Would you be willing to test and possibly adapt and improve one of the available clinical triggers in your own practice?*

The doctor said, "Is that a Request?" Marie affirmed that it was. The doctor replied, "Yes, I'll try it. This could work." It was an incredible moment for everyone in the room. We all knew that something important, something very good, had happened.

Today, clinical triggers are a common practice across the nation's trauma centers and in all the OPOs who support these hospitals. Marie's confident, thoughtful, empathetic leadership set the stage for national improvement.

Flip Negative Energy Is Essential to Leadership Work

On that day in 2003, we saw a leader in healthcare improvement, Marie Schall, masterfully use all three Speech Acts in the Flip Negative Energy toolkit – *Say "Yes, and…," Listen for Requests and Answers below the Surface*, and *Process the Negative with Effective Questions*. She did this all in the moment as the difficult situation and negative energy emerged. She successfully avoided a number of pitfalls that could have resulted in an impasse or a veto of a best practice

The answers are in the room is a principle of the collaborative method. In this case the answer was a fully developed, ready-to spread-solution. We will not always be that fortunate. However, we have learned over and over that the Flip Negative Energy toolkit can help us to reliably generate positive outcomes.

These Methods Work

Hundreds of leaders have used the Mindsets and Methods profiled here to Flip Negative Energy in their individual interactions, email responses, work sessions, conferences, and events.

The three Methods profiled here are just the tip of the iceberg. When we share these Methods in working sessions, we often ask questions like: "*What are your own best practices in effectively dealing with negative energy?*" There are lots of great answers to this question. There is tremendous wisdom in the All Teach, All Learn approach to work and life.

Perhaps even more important, flipping this energy is a gift that leaders can give to those who are jammed in some way that produces the negative energy in the first place. We can help those who are stuck to get unstuck. We can help ourselves and others to get onto an Upward Spiral where one good thing can lead to another.

The leadership Speech Acts embedded in the Flip Negative Energy toolkit set forces in motion that can surface all sorts of solutions. We urge leaders everywhere to try this powerful approach to flipping and more effectively dealing with the negative energy that naturally arises in our work and our lives. Negative energy is still energy. Learn to harness it for good.

BEING

Net Forward Energy

Flip Negative Energy

Resilience

Understanding and Activating Five Sources Of Resilience: A Personal and Professional Journey

by **Dennis Wagner**

Leadership is challenging. Standing for Bold Aims, enrolling others, persisting through big problems, securing commitments from others, delivering on the commitments we make, sustaining the energy of ourselves and others over the long haul – this is the nuts and bolts of leadership work. It can be difficult.

A close working partner of mine and senior executive at the Centers for Medicare and Medicaid Services, Jeneen Iwugo, sums it up nicely with seven words:

"Leaders have to get comfortable BEING uncomfortable."

Jeneen M. Iwugo
Deputy Center Director,
Centers for Medicare and
Medicaid Services

Jeneen is an outgoing woman of action and accomplishment. She is a leader who gets things done, time after time, often in thorny, challenging situations. When Jeneen worked for me, I knew I could go to her with practically any difficult problem and she would somehow figure out how to make headway with it. Later, when I reported to Jeneen, this was an even greater asset. She was an outstanding boss who I could turn to for help on challenging problems.

Jeneen's take on leadership is spot-on. And those who've worked closely with her have learned that she is, in fact, comfortable Being uncomfortable. This is a habitual state of Being for Jeneen.

How in the world do leaders get comfortable Being uncomfortable?

As members of the federal government's Senior Executive Service (SES), both Jeneen and I were well-trained. SES are the "general" grades of the US Civil Service; like military generals, SES members have been exposed to some of the finest leadership training in the world. We both learned a lot about how to get comfortable Being uncomfortable at the Federal Executive Institute in Charlottesville, Virginia. We learned that developing and nurturing Resilience is at the heart of the solution.

Cultivating Resilience in ourselves and others is an essential leadership asset. Resilience is what allows individual leaders, teams, federal agencies, military units, and entire networks to bounce back from the unpredictable but inevitable breakdowns and setbacks that are encountered when pursuing bold leadership goals.

When we step out and lead, the uncomfortable problems and breakdowns that come our way generally don't decrease, they increase. Resilience helps leaders like Jeneen bounce back from the ever-increasing onslaught of breakdowns. We cannot expect or hope that these problems will decrease or go away entirely. Rather, as leaders, we have to learn to get comfortable Being uncomfortable with these ever-present challenges and breakdowns.

Five Key Sources of Resilience

Early in my own career when I encountered what we now know to be a resilient leader, I thought they were tough. I have since learned that Resilience is not about developing a thick skin or getting tougher. Rather, it is about intentionally accessing and tapping into the resources that enable us to be resilient.

The sources of Resilience listed on the facing page—Purpose, Choices, Perspective, Partners and Problems—are the very things that bring us closer to our humanity and our authentic selves. Having a clear sense of Purpose, making the Choice of positive action, gaining Perspective on the big picture, drawing strength from our Partners, and expecting and embracing Problems when they inevitably arise – all of these things enrich our own humanity.

They help us to become even more human. Because the sources of Resilience are so clear, we can learn to take the actions that allow us to tap into these powerful sources. Awareness of these allows us to take the necessary actions to draw upon them when we need to bounce back. In the next few pages, we will explore some real-life examples of what it looks like to access and draw upon the sources of Resilience.

Five Sources of Resilience

PURPOSES
Turn to a compelling, emotionally charged sense of purpose

CHOICES
Know there are choices for positive action in difficult situations

PERSPECTIVE
Gain perspective on the bigger picture and what may underlie, affect, or be affected by our hardships

PARTNERS
Draw strength from our partners when the situation is down

PROBLEMS
Anticipate problems that inevitably show up and embrace the possibilities they reveal

Purpose as a Powerful Source of Resilience

Alexa Kersting

Monica and Loren Kersting, and their daughter Alexa, clarified Purpose as a source of Resilience for 1500 healthcare leaders one morning in Birmingham, Alabama, in 2005.

Key leaders and staff from the nation's largest trauma centers, together with their affiliated organ procurement organizations, had convened in Birmingham to share best practices, progress, and to address persistent obstacles in our work to increase organ donation across the United States. After nearly a year and a half of fast-paced, successful work to increase donation, the community of leaders were concerned that our increases were plateauing.

We were all tired. It was challenging work to rapidly learn, spread, adapt, and test practices that would be effective in one large trauma center to another. Big trauma centers are filled with bureaucracy, clearances, layers, egos, financial challenges, legal issues and more, just like any other large institution. Testing and installing new practices and procedures to increase organ donation wasn't easy. Many felt stuck.

It had become a regular practice at these large collaborative learning sessions to showcase success. The healthcare providers were introduced to the patients and families who benefited from the life-saving work of organ donation and transplantation. Seeing the vibrant healthy people whose lives and families were restored through transplant was very motivating.

When Monica and Loren took the stage in Birmingham, the audience anticipated learning of another successful transplant.

Instead, in a low quavering voice, reading from a script in her shaking hand, Monica shared photos of her 14-year-old daughter, Alexa. She was the light of their family. Her brother adored her. She was a vibrant, kind young woman. She loved to jet-ski on lakes near their home in Fargo, North Dakota.

Then we learned that she died six months prior, in Loren's arms, waiting for a lung transplant that never came.

At the close of their short talk, Monica and Loren shared how they had heard numerous times from people at the learning session how 17 people die every day on the national organ donation waiting list. They reported how mentally jarring it was for them to hear this compelling statistic, as they tearfully observed, "It's incredibly painful to hear that 17 people die each day waiting for an organ transplant when one of them is your beautiful 14-year-old daughter."

Monica and Loren concluded by requesting, on behalf of all the parents with sons and daughters on the transplant waitlist, that the assembled doctors, nurses, surgeons, administrators, and organ procurement specialists stay committed to their purpose of systematically spreading proven best practices in organ donation.

The audience in the huge hotel ballroom rose as one to honor these two courageous, grieving parents. The extended ovation was far more than the sound of 1,500 people clapping. It was the sound of genuine, heartfelt renewal of purpose and commitment to this work.

Those of us in that ballroom left with a fierce commitment, filled with energy aimed at doing absolutely everything possible to continue to increase organ donation and to prevent deaths on the transplant waiting list.

From that time on, when setbacks and obstacles showed up in our organ donation work, we would think of Monica, Loren, and Alexa. To this day, nearly two decades later, colleagues and professional friends in the organ donation and the transplantation community still remind ourselves of waitlist patients like Alexa who are relying on each of us to overcome the obstacles that stand in the way of increased donation and transplantation. These patients need the clinicians and leaders in the organ donation and transplant system to be Resilient.

Commitment to the purpose of preventing deaths on the transplant waiting list is a powerful source of Resilience. It propels the daily actions of the tens of thousands of healthcare providers who work to ensure that no child on a waitlist must die in the arms of their parents.

Learn to Activate Purpose as a Source of Resilience

There are lots of ways to anchor to purpose. At work, an entire community of practice drew strength from purpose when we heard from Monica and Loren Kersting in Birmingham. Beginning a team meeting with the round robin question, "Why is this work so important?" before tackling a potentially demoralizing hardship is another hands-on, practical way to foster Resilience by connecting with purpose. When your own teams and colleagues are facing a tough problem, try launching your meetings with a question to help everyone present to connect back to shared purposes.

Choice as a Ready Source of Resilience

We saw Monica and Loren Kersting bring Resilience to a professional community of practice by renewing our collective sense of purpose. Monica and Loren also experienced Resilience in their own lives by the Choices they made following Alexa's death.

Their response to this loss, the greatest loss any parent can experience, was to choose to take action to increase organ donation. Instead of bitterness, anger and resentment, Monica and Loren made the Choice to tell Alexa's story in service to others. They chose to give and to care for others.

Our organ donation collaborative leadership team first learned about Alexa when Monica contacted the federal Division of Transplantation in December of 2004. She was calling to request permission to use the federal shattered heart with green ribbon logo that was used to promote organ donation.

Over the course of her call to our agency, we came to gradually understand that Monica was creating and selling posters, cards and other artwork in memory of Alexa. All the proceeds were donated to organizations and activities aimed at increasing awareness and action on organ donation. Monica wanted to experiment with incorporating the federal green ribbon and shattered heart logo into her artwork. After jumping through various bureaucratic clearances with our federal agency's legal department, we clearly established and communicated back to Monica and her printer that she could use the logo in her charitable artwork.

Our federal team was impressed with Monica, this mother and artist who had lost her young daughter waiting for a transplant that never happened. Here she was now, working to use her artwork to help increase organ donation for others. A deep respect and appreciation for Monica's actions led the team to invite her and Loren to present to the audience of 1,500 in Birmingham several months later.

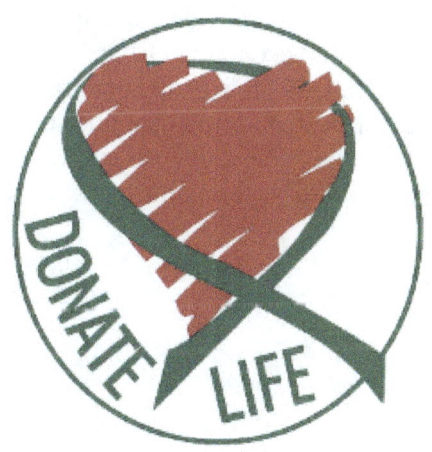

We knew her story would help all of us stay focused on our life-saving purpose. It was only as we became closer to this thoughtful couple that we came to understand how these two parents also gained Resilience by choosing to help others.

Following the Kersting's presentation in Birmingham, trauma centers and organ procurement organizations from across the nation began to call on them to participate in regional, state, and local events to promote organ donation. Although it was always painful for them to talk publicly about the transplant that never came, Monica and Loren continued to share their daughter's story, whether during Grand Rounds in hospitals with ICU nurses, trauma surgeons, chaplains, and others, or thanking runners who had just completed a 10K to raise funds for organ donation awareness.

Learn to Activate Choice as a Source of Resilience

Monica and Loren's Choice to give back to the very system that failed to provide a lung transplant for Alexa is a vivid, almost startling, example of the power of Choice. Instead of choosing bitterness and anger, Monica and Loren chose to help others. So often when we encounter hardships, we feel boxed in, as if we had only one unsavory and unacceptable option. Remembering that we almost always have options and Choices is a powerful way to deal with our difficulty.

Most of the Choices in action and attitude that we will make do not rise to the level of Monica and Loren's example. Thankfully, most of our daily Choices are a whole lot easier. In our experience, the three key challenges with activating Choice as a source of Resilience are:

1. To remember that we almost always have Choices, as hard as that may be when we're feeling boxed in;

2. To work with partners and colleagues to generate options; and,

3. To act on the attitudinal shift that often comes with making the Choice.

This attitudinal shift is often a mark of Resilience. It may involve forgiveness, personal resolve, or challenging ourselves to think very differently about the challenge at hand.

Fostering Resilience in Ourselves and Others Has Payoffs

Following Monica and Loren's presentation in 2005, the work to spread best practices on organ donation in large trauma centers and organ procurement organizations continued to produce results. The feared plateau in increases did not materialize, possibly because the teams assembled in Birmingham leaned in and chose to redouble their efforts.

As shown in the chart below, the organ donation community continued to sustain increased rates of donation compared to the same month of the prior year for all but the month of December in 2005 (purple line). The community continued this pattern of increased donation for all but January and November in 2006 (red line).

Organ donation rates have continued to increase in the years following the conclusion of the government-sponsored Organ Donation Breakthrough Collaborative. The practices of systematic quality improvement, coupled with leadership practices like those associated with cultivating Resilience, have helped to propel greater and greater increases in organ donation year after year.

A not-for-profit organization called the Organ Donation and Transplantation Alliance was created by private leadership organizations involved in the Collaborative to continue the improvement work. The Alliance celebrated its 15th Anniversary in 2021 under the leadership of Karri Hobson-Pape.

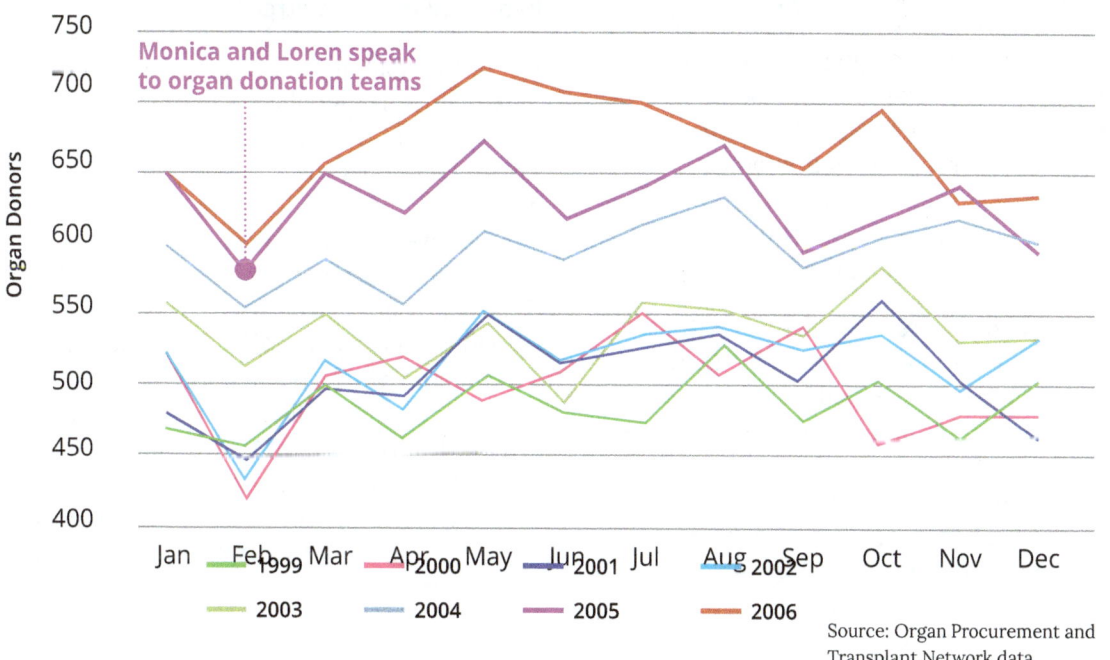

Source: Organ Procurement and Transplant Network data

Perspective as a Source of Resilience

Choosing over and over again to promote organ donation also helped Monica and Loren gain perspective. They gained a deeper, more informed understanding about the hard work and genuine caring of the people involved in the nationwide system of organ donation and transplantation. They saw, up-front and in person, that transplant surgeons, transplant coordinators, ICU nurses, social workers, organ procurement coordinators, and others routinely worked to move heaven and earth in the pursuit of life-saving organ donation and transplantation.

Contact with the people who constantly went the extra mile to secure consent from heartbroken families who had unexpectedly lost loved ones also deepened Monica and Loren's perspective about what happened to Alexa. They came to realize that, although the organ donation and transplantation system was imperfect, as virtually all systems are, there are many thousands of people working hard every day to ensure that every potential organ is made available for transplant into waiting patients. This increased knowledge, this expanded perspective, was incredibly helpful to Monica and Loren. It strengthened their own Resilience and their ability to improve the larger system that had not produced a lung transplant for their daughter.

We have had the great privilege of witnessing Monica and Loren and others who made similar Choices and gained similar increased perspective from their actions. We have met and worked with people who lost loved ones due to hospital errors, who turned around and gave back to improve the very systems and hospitals that had failed them.

Recall the example of Bob and Barb Malizzo that was presented at the beginning of this chapter. It's inspiring and humbling to witness and learn from people who consciously and intentionally choose to turn their own loss into service for others.

Learn to Activate Perspective as a Source of Resilience

Communication is at the heart of developing perspective as a source of Resilience. Listening to others who share their challenges and difficulties helps us to put our own problems into better perspective.

Similarly, sharing our own challenges and difficulties also helps. The simple act of naming them out loud somehow helps to make them more manageable.

Monica and Loren's involvement in the organ donation and transplantation community created greater perspective, both for them and for all of us who engaged with them. Perspective as a source of Resilience is a beneficial two-way street.

As another example, organized world-wide movements like Alcoholics Anonymous, Narcotics Anonymous, and AlAnon are driven by regular meetings that are based on sharing and listening to gain greater perspective and help in dealing with addiction. These meetings are attended by those who suffer from addiction or those who love others who suffer from addiction. The meetings are a tremendous source of perspective and Resilience for those who attend. The two acts of 1) listening to others share their experiences, thoughts and feelings, and 2) sharing our own experiences, thoughts and feelings are the key elements of these meetings.

One of My Most Prized Possessions

Several years after we met Monica and Loren,
in a private moment following a large collaborative
learning session in Los Angeles, they presented me
with original framed artwork. It depicts an angel
presenting a gift and incorporates the federal organ
donation logo of a heart with green ribbon.
The artwork is one of my most prized possessions,
a reminder of compelling purpose in my life and
a source of Resilience when times are tough.

—*Dennis Wagner*

Partners as a Foundational Source of Resilience

Although it seems obvious now, the idea of seeking partners was not a significant part of my Resilience toolkit until a training session at the Federal Executive Institute specifically identified partners as a source of Resilience. As someone who leads large national efforts to generate change, progress, and results, I mainly thought of partners as influential colleagues with platforms, programs, and resources that could be brought to bear on the challenges and goals that we pursued together.

By virtue of my long career with the federal government, I have acquired literally hundreds of smart, thoughtful, influential partners. I count as partners executive leaders of state and national associations, business owners, city and county elected officials, hospital CEOs, health center managers, state and local health department leaders, nursing home executives, transplant surgeons, federal executives, organ procurement organization leaders and staff, foundation staff, academic leaders, members of the boards of directors of healthcare organizations and many others. There is an abundance of partners in my life.

Learn to Activate Partners as a Source of Resilience

Two transformative encounters opened my eyes to understand that these incredibly talented partners and colleagues could be a source of Resilience.

"Never Worry Alone"

I really learned how to call on partners as a source of Resilience when a mentor and colleague, Don Berwick MD became the Obama Administration's designated Administrator of the Centers for Medicare and Medicaid Services (CMS). Dr. Berwick came to CMS from his prior role as the Founding President and CEO of the Institute for Healthcare Improvement (IHI), where I had previously worked with him and some of his talented managers and staff on a host of national healthcare quality improvement initiatives. IHI is widely regarded as the foremost healthcare quality improvement organization in the nation and throughout the world.

Dr. Berwick came to CMS determined not only to implement the new Affordable Care Act rapidly and effectively, but also to influence the culture of the agency. As a senior executive in the organization, I had the great privilege of working with Dr. Berwick for much of his tenure as Administrator. Don frequently commented, "Culture eats strategy for lunch." He wanted to do everything he could during his time leading the agency to share the cultural lessons and strategies that he and his IHI team had learned in implementing highly successful healthcare improvement initiatives throughout the world.

Because of my prior history of teaming with Don, he frequently called on me and other members on my team at the Office of Clinical Standards and Quality to join with him in conducting all-hands meetings with the entire 5000 executives, managers and staff of the federal agency. One of the crystal-clear methods that Don would share in these sessions was a straightforward, three-word best practice on partners and Resilience: *"Never worry alone."* Don knew that worrying alone can take us onto a downward spiral. He wanted to imbed this highly effective best practice into the culture of the agency.

Don's three-word best practice is the action we can take to trigger the Resilience that partners can provide. From that point forward, whenever my team and I realized that one of us was worrying alone, we would reach out to each other.

Never worry alone is the clear and implementable tactic that our team learned to routinely use in our shared work to implement challenging provisions of the Affordable Care Act. We applied it to every aspect of our work at the agency, revising the Conditions of Participation that are used to enforce healthcare quality standards, developing the measures and metrics used to pay for value in the Medicare program, improving hospital patient safety, and much more.

"Has Anyone Called Bill?"

Phyllis Busansky
Chairwoman,
Hillsborough County Commission

In addition to providing much needed emotional support when we worry, partners now rival purpose for the Number One spot in my Resilience toolkit. Partners bring so much to the table when the heat is on. Phyllis Busansky, the former Chairwoman of the Hillsborough County Commission in Tampa, Florida, served as a key partner when she helped members of our team to not only not worry alone, but also addressed an expensive problem with major help. And she did it fast.

While leading an effort to generate major increases in healthcare access for underserved populations, I had encouraged a good friend and professional colleague in an influential national association to guarantee a room block at a prestigious Washington DC hotel venue. Sandy was working with John and me as part of a small group who were organizing a large first-of-its-kind healthcare conference. Because our government contract was not yet in place to handle the logistics for the event, Sandy agreed to sign the contract with the Marriott Wardman Park hotel, guaranteeing that 500 rooms would be reserved along a certain timeline in advance of the big event.

Due to a series of unexpected setbacks, we were unable to fill the hotel rooms in accordance with the schedule of advance hotel reservations. Further, our federal contract was still not in place. A General Manager with Marriott contacted Sandy to let her know that she would need to pony up $100,000 in the coming week to cover the shortfall in room reservations. Her association employer was not financially prepared to cover the shortfall. She was panicked, and our team was panicked right along with her. Sandy's job was literally on the line.

John and I quickly mobilized the small team of 8-10 government and private sector colleagues who were at the center of the effort to conduct the conference. We convened our team to meet the very next day for an intense all-day working session to try and resolve the shortfall.

Our initial efforts were aimed at calling potential participants to fill the room block. After four hours of intense work on the phones, it appeared that while we were making decent progress, this strategy would not be sufficient to meet the hotel reservation target by the deadline.

Suddenly, in a moment none of us will ever forget, one of our core team members named Phyllis Busansky swept in to join the effort. Phyllis was a flamboyant, persuasive, personable, and confident leader. We had met Phyllis through the Ford Foundation's prestigious Innovations in American Government awards program. Phyllis was one of their national award winners. During her tenure as the Chairwoman of the Hillsborough County Commission in Tampa, she had conceived of and secured for funding for the Hillsborough County Health Plan, a local government initiative that provided an organized system of managed care for 50,000 low income and uninsured residents of Hillsborough County. Phyllis was a force of nature who generated action and results everywhere she went. Our plan was to put Phyllis immediately to work making calls to fill the rooms, as she was well-connected and very respected by many of the anticipated but currently un-registered conference attendees.

We brought Phyllis up to speed on the current room shortfalls and our lackluster progress in getting rapid reservations. Instead of leaping into action on her phone, she inquired:

"Has anyone called Bill?"

"Bill who?" we asked.

"Bill Marriott" she replied.

We explained that we were dealing with the General Manager of the hosting Marriott hotel, and he had summarily denied our request for an extension on filling the room block.

It turned out that Phyllis had a close personal and professional relationship with Bill Marriott! She had met Bill during the course of her successful effort to site the New York Yankees' spring training facility in the Tampa area. Within minutes, Phyllis rang up Bill Marriott, got him to work with the hotel's General Manager, and secured a reprieve on the $100,000 payment. Just like that, our problem was solved!

Phyllis was an energetic partner with a powerful network. Her emotional energy and confidence immediately buoyed our team when she arrived on the scene to help. Ringing up Bill Marriott would never have occurred to those of us working the phones in that room. Because of Phyllis' intervention, we could now get back to the business of organizing and planning the event, this time with a keen eye on turning out the required number of registered participants.

And as it turned out, we ultimately exceeded our 500 room block and filled up the hotel with 700 participants. The conference was a huge success.

Next time you encounter a big problem or situation that requires Resilience, take Don Berwick's advice to "Never worry alone." Let Phyllis Busansky be an example of the hidden resources waiting for you to call upon. We've found that in addition to providing the emotional support to deal with our worries, the perspective our partners can unleash is a truly extraordinary example of Abundance.

Life Partners Are a Remarkable Source of Resilience

My partner in life, Diane M. Hill, has been a steadfast source of Resilience for me during our 38+ years of marriage. When I give thanks for the many blessings in life, Diane is always at the top of my list. I am incredibly fortunate to be teamed with her in all aspects of my life. Diane is a wise, strong-willed, determined, adventurous and thoughtful mother, spouse, and leader. A talented professional with extensive experience on Capitol Hill, she not only is always there for the big things, the challenging life-events, but also has supported her friends, our family and me in all the daily worries, problems, and frets that arise in caring for loved ones, maintaining a home and cars, finding work, balancing budgets, raising children and more. However, it wasn't until I got executive training in Resilience that I realized that I had always interpreted Diane's support of me—and my support of her—as something that just comes with being married. In my mind, the Resilience that flowed from our partnership was something that I associated with a strong marriage. I did not connect her constant and unwavering support for me as a source of Resilience, even though it most definitely was exactly that. I work to do the same for her (but I'm not as good at it).

Dennis Wagner & Diane Hill

Problems, Anticipated and Praised, as a "Graduate Level" Source of Resilience

John Scanlon loves challenging and complex problems. For many years his consulting practice specialized in crisis management. John's coaching and problem-solving attitude and abilities have helped many executive teams to prosper from the challenges and changes precipitated by crisis. John's mindset and approach of embracing problems is rare, but not unique. Some people have a special, natural, or learned ability to anticipate, and then to embrace problems as an inevitable, expected fact of life.

It just makes sense. Anytime we pursue challenging leadership work and step out of our comfort zones, we should expect that big problems will eventually show up as part of the package. Knowing this is a key step onto the pathway of getting comfortable being uncomfortable. As M. Scott Peck reminds us in the opening paragraph of his international best-selling book, *The Road Less Traveled*:

> *Life is difficult. This is a great truth, one of the greatest truths. It is a great truth because once we truly see this truth, we transcend it. Once we truly know that life is difficult – once we truly understand and accept it – then life is no longer as difficult. Because once it is accepted, the fact that life is difficult no longer matters.*

We can learn to expect problems. However the next step is harder. How do we learn to actually embrace and then act on these problems when they materialize?

One key strategy involves recognizing that problems can generate growth. We almost always learn, grow, and benefit from working through difficulties and failure. But getting our hearts and minds around this fundamental reality isn't necessarily easy. Learning to embrace problems when they show up is truly the pathway to "graduate level" Resilience. Getting to this place of seeing problems as a source of learning and growth is a powerful tool in our Resilience kit.

Another strategy is, of course, *Never worry alone* when these inevitable problems reveal themselves. Do you know someone who possesses a deep, abiding, internal calm and Resilience, even in the face of daunting and unexpected problems? If so, make them your mentor or partner straightaway. Then, when you reach out with worries, they will help you learn to embrace the problems.

Embrace Problems As A Source of Resilience

1. Accept that problems will happen and get comfortable with Being uncomfortable
2. Remember that problems often generate growth.
3. Seek out partners to "worry" with!
4. Make a habit of anticipating and praising problems.

We can learn to better understand and learn the benefits of anticipating and praising problems as a source of Resilience.
A personal experience with my family helped me to learn about and deeply internalize the benefits of praising problems as a fifth source of Resilience.

Hiking the 500-mile Camino de Santiago Pilgrimage

by Dennis Wagner

On a Sunday afternoon in 2016, my family of five went to see the movie *The Way* starring Martin Sheen. In the midst of deep personal trauma, Martin Sheen's character makes the decision to hike the 500-mile Camino de Santiago Pilgrimage from France across Northern Spain, ending at the awe-inspiring Cathedral of St. James the Apostle in Santiago de Compostela near the Atlantic coast. The journey was a transformative, physically challenging, and spiritual experience for the pilgrims, set to a soundtrack composed by James Taylor. Inspired by this story, our family made our own decision to hike the Camino.

We set out from France in July, 2017. However, our Pilgrimage turned out to be a lot more challenging than it looked in the movie.

Ever hike 15 miles a day, every day for 34 days in a row, rain or shine, with your whole family? With heavy backpacks and no uplifting James Taylor score kicking in?

On day four of our Camino journey, our son Grant casually observed that this was our first family backpacking excursion. We agreed that it was.

He then drolly intoned, "Don't you think most families might've started their backpacking experience with a three-day trip on a long weekend?"

"Thanks, Grant," we muttered, as we continued our slog through the final miles to our next stopping point.

We experienced blisters, meltdowns, tendonitis, joint pain, multi-mile detours due to missed turns on the path, occasional conflicts, blistering hot days, wind, wet and slippery descents on rocky mountainous paths, and more. It was challenging. Really challenging. At the same time, we experienced beautiful mountains, authentic and fulfilling camaraderie with other pilgrims and with each other, hearty pilgrim-menu meals with simple Spanish wines, majestic cathedrals, blessings from strangers, and more. The good things and the difficult things were all mixed together in our pilgrimage, just as they so often are in life.

Musician Busking on the Camino

**Leonard Cohen
Singer, Song-writer**

Learning to Say Hallelujah for Life's Challenges and Triumphs

While walking The Way, we would often hear a familiar song lilting through the forests, hostels, churches, and streets. Musicians busking along Camino would frequently be playing Leonard Cohen's song *Hallelujah*.

"Hallelujah," or "God be praised," is an expression of gratitude and rejoicing. And though I thought I knew the song well, hearing it over and over along the Camino made me focus more on the lyrics. As I listened more carefully, I learned that the song actually celebrates brokenness, pain, defeats, failures and setbacks in life, with praise and hallelujah.

This was truly thought-provoking. Celebrating and praising hardship and failure had not previously been part of my way of Being. I had always seen these as things to be prevented or avoided, certainly not welcomed with praise or thanksgiving.

The more I pondered this and discussed Cohen's *Hallelujah* with my family and others, the more we began to better understand that these difficulties are truly the parts of life where so much of our growth and humanness comes from. Life's challenges can become the source of greater caring, compassion, learning, maturation. *Hallelujah* celebrates these difficulties and failures. Learning to embrace and even praise these difficulties can help to develop the Resilience that enables us to get comfortable being uncomfortable. Cohen's lyrics celebrate that at the end of life, he will stand before the Lord and celebrate even the things that all went wrong in life. Wow. This is what the practice of graduate level resilience might look like.

Reaching the Destination and Gaining Insight

Our family set out together early the morning of August 21, 2017, from nearby Lavacola and hiked the final several miles into Santiago de Compostela. It was a happy, anticipatory morning. As we arrived in the outskirts of the city, we began to join with throngs of other Pilgrims converging from multiple routes—from St. Jean Pied de Port, from Lisbon, from Ferrol—who were arriving that same day.

As we approached our destination, feelings of thanksgiving, joy, anticipation, and a bittersweet ending began to swell in the hearts of each of us. As we came down a narrow street under an archway that fed into the plaza at the front of the Cathedral of St. James, tears were streaming down our faces, and we saw the same was true of most other Pilgrims who were arriving along with us. These final steps on our 500-mile journey were an incredible upward-spiraling moment for our family, and for the hundreds of other Pilgrims converging in that place at that time.

We celebrated the Pilgrim's Mass at noon that great day with other Pilgrims and guests. Two Spanish ladies seated in the pew next to where our family stood kept trying to give up their seats to us because we were tired pilgrims. We declined the seats and took photos with them afterwards instead. Out of our journey's hardship and pain, joyous moments of true thanksgiving had emerged.

Entering the final days of our pilgrimage, I realized that success and failure in leadership work are often two sides of the same coin. They go together. Looking back on the many campaigns that have been part of my life's work, it is clear now that failures were often the necessary precursors to future success. And even success itself enabled us to see other things that were not working, and that needed to be tackled next. I began to appreciate that failure and success, together, can put us on an upward spiral.

The implications are profound. The insight means we can temper being drained or disabled by problems and breakdowns. We can learn to treat our difficulties as natural sources of learning, growth, and progress, acquiring greater inner calm and Resilience when the inevitable problems make their appearance.

**Margo, Dennis, Grant, Diane & Tess
Breakfast on the Camino de Santiago**

**Grant, Tess, Margo & Diane with
Spanish Colleagues after Mass**

Learn to Activate Problems as a Source of Resilience

Our family's Camino de Santiago pilgrimage was incredibly rewarding. Persevering through the many daily, physical, social, and mental challenges of the Camino ultimately resulted in bonds of mutual joy and accomplishment. Our challenging 34-day journey helped make us a stronger family in the end. We became more empathetic, open, appreciative, accomplished, and happy, and we did it together as a family.

The key lesson of the Camino was a richer and more authentic understanding that working through difficult challenges made us stronger and more Resilient in the end. I learned, possibly not for the first time, that challenges and setbacks are inevitably bonded to joys and successes. These things go together. Knowing this, expecting this, and working to learn to praise the problems, can help us to access the Resilience we need as leaders.

Foster Resilience in Ourselves and Others

Purpose, Choices, Partners, Perspective, and Problems are all highly effective sources of Resilience. We can deliberately and intentionally trigger the actions necessary to access these sources.

We can build Resilience into our own lives. We can act from Purpose, look to act on a Positive Choice, reach out to Partners for help, seek Perspective, and anticipate and embrace Problems when they show up. We can learn to use the feelings of being down, boxed in, lost or overwhelmed, to trigger our Resilience gameplans.

We can hardwire the habit of Resilience into our families, relationships, organizations, networks and campaigns. Leaders like Jeneen Iwugo, Monica and Loren Kersting, Don Berwick, and Phyllis Busansky have helped entire national communities of practice learn to use the sources of Resilience in shared work.

Nurturing our own Resilience while helping others to do same can help us create upward spirals of progress. Taking the actions that enable us to become more Resilient is key to the leadership practice of *getting comfortable with Being uncomfortable.*

Anne H. Hastings Leadership Story: Introduction

In the late 1990s, Anne H. Hastings made the bold decision to leave consulting and commit herself to a mission she could wholeheartedly pursue: ending poverty for the rural poor in Haiti, one of the world's most desperately poor countries.

Anne H. Hastings and John Scanlon had worked as business partners in the late 1980s and early 1990s, providing crisis management services to government and not-for-profit organizations. Anne was exceptional at assembling and managing rapid action projects to solve complex problems, from salvaging a major evaluation of the Federal government's newly formed Senior Executive Service, to managing a crash process to address a serious gap in annual Law School Admission Test questions.

But in mid-career, Anne walked away from consulting and stepped into a stark situation in a country where she had no personal network, no knowledge of the language, and no resources. Her new business partner: a Catholic priest who invited Anne, despite her lack of expertise, to join him in creating a "bank for and by the poor." What was intended to be a one-year experiment blossomed into a 17-year journey with great rewards for the Haitian people and for Anne herself.

Anne's story shows how new and transformative results can emerge from our leadership choices. Look for several dynamics of leadership that guided Anne's actions and resulted in a diverse and supportive array of players. Keep in mind the way Anne is "Being" throughout, learning to say Yes to formidable leadership opportunities and challenges, and seeking the trusted Partners who will come forward to help address them. Her story is an example of how the three leadership methods of being—Net Forward Energy, Flip Negative Energy, and Resilience—can be an everyday practice.

LEADERSHIP STORY

Establishing a Nationwide Bank for the Poor and by the Poor in Haiti

Summarized Conversations with Anne H. Hastings

Anne H. Hastings and Father Joseph

A Call to Action and an Urgent Mission

In 1995, after 15 years of working in Washington, DC as a management consultant with nonprofits and federal agencies, I found myself increasingly frustrated by the difficulties of making real change, especially in government agencies. There was always someone who could block change. Now in my mid-40s, I wanted to make a difference in something that mattered.

Undeterred by my lack of experience in international development, I submitted an application to join the Peace Corps. Before I could even work my way through the entire process, a Peace Corps executive put me in contact with a Haitian priest he described as doing groundbreaking work in addressing poverty.

Father Joseph Philippe had a vision to build a bank "for the poor and by the poor" in Haiti. He was looking for someone with experience as a bank director, fluent in English, French, and Creole, to commit to a minimum of three years to this project. I met none of these conditions. Even so, I faxed a letter offering to help for one year.

I came home hours later to find this message on my answering machine:

"Anne, thank you for courage. You are the Director of our new bank."

I bought a ticket to Haiti and flew down to meet Father Joseph. Little did I know the impact that meeting would have in my life.

When we met, I felt it important to be completely transparent about my lack of experience.

"Father Joseph, I don't know anything about banking."

He held my gaze, seeing something in me I was unable to see in myself. "I am sure you will figure it out."

"I can't speak Creole."

"Not a problem. You will learn it in two months." He went on to say, "You will begin by organizing a meeting in Miami with at least one Haitian from every Haitian community in the US, Canada, and the Caribbean nations to develop support for a bank."

"But—you're the only Haitian I know!"

"Not to worry. Here is a list of every Haitian I know in these communities."

It was time to wrap up our meeting. Father Joseph discussed the money I would need to live on for my year in Haiti, which he estimated to be about $12,000. As I walked out the door, Father Joseph called after me:

"Anne, I have no way to finance $12,000 for your stay in Haiti."

"Are you kidding?! I'm going to have to pay to come and work with you?"

He approached and put his hand on my shoulder "I think you'll find a way." He knew he had me.

In spite of what seemed insurmountable requests, Father Joseph was somehow making it easy for me to say yes. It dawned on me: here was a person who had a clearer vision than all my consulting clients put together. I had found the urgent mission I was looking for. I committed to returning in May 1996 to begin my year in Haiti.

But there remained the quandary of supporting myself for the year. On the flight home, I found myself disclosing my new commitment and financing dilemma to the woman sitting next to me. A perfect stranger, she listened intently, then replied: "The money will come. Tell everyone you know that you're going to Haiti. This is going to transform your life. Everyone who loves you will want to be part of that transformation."

Once home, I wrote to all my friends and family telling them of the commitment I had just made. I didn't ask for money. Yet over the next few days, I received checks that covered my first year, the first of which came from my business partner of 15 years, John Scanlon. My fellow passenger was right – people want to be part of a transformation, even if indirectly. One hurdle down. So many more to come.

Fonkoze as a Compelling Vision

A bank that the poor could call their own. A bank that would help hard-working people in rural areas develop their communities and give their families the tools they needed to escape poverty. A bank that would serve women supporting their children through their own small businesses. A bank called Fondasyon Kole Zepòl Shoulders Together Foundation—Fonkoze for short. This was Father Joseph's vision.

Arriving in Haiti in 1996 and settling into my new role, I asked Father Joseph what services he wanted Fonkoze to provide. "Oh, the normal things: savings, credit, money transfers from their families living outside of Haiti." I thought to myself: challenging, but doable. The goal, he went on, was to cover the entire country with bank branches, especially in the rural areas where 80% of the population lived. That's when the magnitude of the challenge began to sink in. It would soon become more striking as I encountered Haiti's huge rural population of underserved persons and the lack of roads, telephone services, and security. There was no infrastructure!

Father Joseph went on to explain that we would not simply give women their loans and send them on their way; we would have to "accompany them" in their struggle out of poverty. We would need to teach them how to read and write, as well as other skills needed to run their small, informal businesses, which were largely invisible to standard economic metrics. A bank that not only does banking, but teaches its clients to read and write. The challenges kept growing.

Father Joseph envisioned creating a democratic society and a democratic economy that would give poor families a way to lift themselves out of poverty. He was not interested in projects or demonstrations. He was building a foundational institution to end poverty. We would accomplish this standing shoulder-to-shoulder with the people we served. I left our discussion overwhelmed yet driven to action.

By the time I left Haiti in 2013, 17 years following that initial meeting with Father Joseph when I promised to stay only for one year, Fonkoze would boast 46 branches spread all over the country and growing. "I'm sure you will figure it out," Father Joseph had assured me in the beginning. Those 17 years were a crash course in leadership and saying yes to formidable challenges and transformative opportunities I could never have "figured out" on my own. Even if I didn't know it at the time, there would be supportive partnerships that would prove essential to building the Fonkoze vision.

Scarcity, Stress, and Resilience

I had abandoned the comfort and certainties of the American workforce to show up as the director of a bank in a foreign country knowing nothing about banking and speaking not a word of the native language.

Instead of well-resourced government and private sector clients, my clients now consisted of seven million people who were poor, with 50% going hungry every day and whose children also went hungry and didn't go to school. My job was to improve their lives by giving them loans and teaching them to save, all while introducing literacy and other important life skills and providing access to health care. This was to be accomplished by giving out hundreds of thousands of $25 loans from several million dollars in financing that I was personally charged with raising.

Diving into the Fonkoze mission was stressful. One of our board members called our approach "Guerrilla Banking." It was small actions every day in every direction in the face of overwhelming challenges.

Colorful bus making its way on a dusty dirt road in rural Haiti.

Our team had to manage constant stress. To succeed, we had to cultivate sources of resiliency.

Contributing to the challenge was the near total lack of infrastructure in the countryside. Each weekend Father Joseph, a group of colleagues, and I would travel to the far parts of Haiti to learn about the needs of rural communities. We would drive ten or twelve hours to attend a meeting, with as many as seven other people accompanying us in a pickup truck with no air conditioning and on dirt roads so dusty you couldn't even open the windows.

When we finally arrived at our one-room host household, the family would move out so I could sleep on the one mat on the dirt floor in case it rained. We would awake the next morning with a large audience already gathered and eager for our message. I marveled that more than one hundred hopeful men, women, and children somehow knew to show up for the meeting, having walked barefoot for two or three hours, with no phone service and no mobile phones to alert them.

However overwhelmed I felt, my sense of purpose became increasingly compelling as I got to know the Haitian people. Witnessing the urgent need for action became its own source of energy for me. The deep connections Father Joseph had with the people and the constant interaction with our hardworking clients instilled in me a much deeper knowledge of the problems at hand.

Early on in my tenure, we would arrive at a meeting and Father Joseph would introduce me in Creole, saying, "This is Anne. The Holy Spirit has sent her to help me build a bank the poor can call their own." Had I understood Creole back then, I would've been floored.

It also began to sink in how cultural and mission differences between organizations providing assistance and partners could be disabling. For example, one provider of banking technical assistance only trained in French. However, as Fonkoze is a truly Haitian organization, our official language was Creole, not French. We held to our mission and effectively teamed with others to bridge these chasms over time.

And indeed, I did learn to speak Creole, although not in the two months optimistically promised. Father Joseph arranged for me to be tutored for three hours a day by youngsters, and after a year's time I was finally able to make myself understood as well as to mostly understand our clients.

What a blessing that was! Speaking Creole allowed me to truly learn about their aspirations, their hopes, and their dream to be able to care for their children, keep them healthy, send them to school. To truly understand how they would get up at 3 am to walk several hours to get to the marketplace with their merchandise on their head or, if they were lucky enough, on their donkey's back. To truly understand how they would sometimes go a whole day or two with nothing to eat so that their children could have a little something. When one of them finally learned to write her name, how the others would cheer her on, while continuing their own struggles to learn to read and write.

And the successes were many. Seeing their children leave for school with their uniforms on; covering their dirt floor with a slab of concrete; pitching in to help another woman make her loan payment; watching the solidarity grow in their meetings with one another.

Their struggles appeared unbearable, but their accomplishments were genuine. And they always made me and my staff feel respected and loved. If they didn't like one of our policies, they were never afraid to speak up and let us know.

We listened. Fonkoze staff were Creole-speaking Haitians from the rural areas and always out in the countryside with our clients. I was engaged in the field with clients and field staff around the frequent disruptions we were encountering. We worked with our clients. We learned to take advantage of what showed up. In my last few years in Haiti, we realized all clients had recently gained access to cell phones. We set up a toll-free number to handle complaints and setbacks. The calls were recorded, and, in a weekly meeting, the leadership team and I would decide how to address any that required a special response. It was truly a bank for and by the poor.

The needs of our clients were significant and far-reaching; we had to move quickly and in every direction. Haiti's 70% unemployment required that the women we served commit to becoming day-to-day entrepreneurs to feed themselves and their children. Without access to affordable loans, they were constantly at risk and in debt. In addition to granting a microentrepreneur an affordable loan, we knew they could not be successful unless we helped them learn to read and write and develop their business skills. But along the way we discovered that mothers with sick or malnourished children can't easily repay their loans, so we began to add some basic health care for the family. It seemed that no sooner had we solved one challenge, another would rise to the surface.

Partnering Our Way Forward

Raising money for the bank required heavy lifting. With no preexisting structure, we realized we needed a US-based fundraising partner, so we created Fonkoze USA. With a limited recruitment budget, I ended up hiring Leigh Carter over a bowl of ice cream to lead Fonkoze USA. It turned out to be one of the best decisions I would make. A talented fundraiser, Leigh would accompany me every step of the way, frequently traveling to Haiti from Washington, DC as my trusted advisor. Our friendship has endured to this day, and now she even doubles as my memory bank.

At the outset, Father Joseph considered granting loans from savings being deposited. But we realized early on this was not an effective strategy. Savings from our clients were not sufficient to meet demand, and to rely on savings was too risky. At the same time, we were seeking donors to contribute capital expense and to fund human development work. In the first year, we identified a donor who agreed to help us establish five branches. Father Joseph challenged us to do more; we ended up opening ten branches with the money. However, donations often came with strenuous conditions, requirements, and reporting, often making the funding process long and arduous.

Fonkoze was a not-for-profit organization, but nowhere close to being a legally licensed bank. Building a dependable, stable institution in Haiti meant responding to the demands of players much larger than we were: donor agencies, potential investors, and the Haitian government. These other players often presented hazards we could not control—their own missions, requirements, and conditions that often did not work for us. We had to work our way around them as best we could.

Over time, I came to learn microfinance and banking by developing relationships and seeking out partners who became advisors, donors, and champions. As my seatmate on the plane had so wisely counseled, people were drawn to the mission. But to pull them in we had to reach out relentlessly. When stress arose, we used it as a signal that it was time to engage with our existing partners and to seek additional partners. This pattern of seeking, engaging, and being inspired by our partners would itself become a source of our durability.

Fonkoze started with nothing but purpose, vision, and the everyday needs of the women we wanted to help. Each challenge, each need, was a call to improvise and innovate. By developing relationships and partnerships, we were able to cultivate sources of resiliency. Stress became not the problem but the trigger to seek the help that was so often right at hand. All we had to do was reach for it.

Banking on Partners

There was no master plan for building Fonkoze. But there was a method to master, and I applied it almost from day one.

We had to generate the opportunities and strategies we needed. A key solution to our lack of a master plan was to disclose what we needed, to ask for feedback and ideas, and to ask for help. We continued to develop relationships and take advantage of the connections that each relationship surfaced. In other words, I had to create partnerships to secure the pieces we needed. I learned that creating partnerships is not a task that gets checked off a list: it's a way of working that must be engaged at all times.

Even before I moved to Haiti, Father Joseph had decided we should organize a meeting of Haitians in Miami. Without a single dollar in our budget, we somehow found supporters to donate space and to volunteer. To gain access to expertise in microlending, I invited Carter Garber who was known for his microfinance work in Nicaragua. Carter not only showed up, he opened a new path for us.

As an alternative to giving out loans from the limited savings deposited in Fonkoze, Carter introduced us to the concept of socially responsible investment. His microlending institution made use of loans from religious orders of primarily Catholic nuns. These orders were well-organized, with money to invest in good works. Spurred on by Carter, Fonkoze USA reached out to several of these religious orders, inviting them to witness our work in action, and indeed, after visiting our operations in Haiti, they agreed to support us. Their commitment took us to a whole new level of operation.

Yet even with the vital support of socially responsible investing, we were still lacking a business model that would support the growth we aspired to. On a trip back to the US, I was asked to pay a visit to one of our major donors, Gordon McCormack, who jokingly referred to himself as a "vulture capitalist" due to his success in buying and then turning around bankrupt companies. Over dinner, I mentioned that in some parts of the world, not-for-profit microlending organizations were turning themselves into commercial, for-profit banks. Gordon got very excited. "This will allow us to move beyond donations and loans to equity investors! It will make Fonkoze a stronger bank."

I wasn't sure what all that meant, but Gordon offered to come to Haiti to write the investment business plan. A result of this plan was the decision to split the financial services from the human development work of the foundation, creating a financial service organization which we called Fonkoze Financial Services (SFF, in Creole). The foundation became a shareholder in SFF. Gordon instructed us to go back to our benefactor nuns and ask them to change their loans to equity in the SFF. Many of the nuns willingly agreed.

Putting aside my fear of seeming presumptuous, I then approached another major donor, Julian Schroeder, to ask him to become an equity investor. Before I even had a chance to explain our new approach, Julian exclaimed, "Anne, don't you understand? I have two pockets in my suit: one for philanthropy, the other for investing. I'll continue to donate to Fonkoze, and I'm happy to invest in SFF." Julian went on to become a member of the Board of Directors and continues to serve in that role.

This equity approach added a vital new layer to our financing strategy. Investors became a new source of capital. Partners like Gordon McCormack and Julian Schroeder were also a tremendous source of Resilience. Turning to these partners helped keep us strong in the face of constant adversities and generated a synergy that produced a successful bank at the necessary scale.

Fonkoze Uses Banking With Solidarity Groups To Build A Democratic Economy

As a lender, Fonkoze makes tens of thousands of $45 to $75 short-term loans to poor women. Women use these loans to operate micro-businesses and lift themselves and their families out of poverty. However, the banking is done in a way that builds community and support.

Integrating Haiti's poor into the struggle for a democratic society meant building leadership and solidarity within the poor communities. Fonkoze was designed as a membership organization, not for individuals but for organizations. It was open to the multitude of peasant associations in the country, women's groups, youth groups, groups of any kind. And it was open most especially to solidarity groups of women micro-entrepreneurs.

Fonkoze banking clients in a village receive loans in solidarity groups. Each group consists of five women, creating a built-in system of accountability and support. The loans start small and increase over time. It is similar to the model created by the Grameen Bank, a leading micro-finance organization in Bangladesh. Five or six Solidarity Groups from a common geographical area join together to form a Solidarity "Center" of 25-30 women. Centers meet monthly to make and repay their loans, build community and participate in education and training activities.

Multiple Centers in the same region meet together twice a year and elect their representatives to go to a national assembly, where the members of the Board of Directors of Fonkoze are elected. Fonkoze's Board is made up of representatives of the peasant associations and of the female borrowers, as well as several of the founders of the institution. This incredible process is a training ground for building democracy from the ground up.

The Opportunity That Comes With Crisis

The earthquake in 2010 was a catastrophe for Haiti. The government and society were paralyzed, with banks and businesses completely shut down and no access to money for basic necessities. Haitians outside the country couldn't send money to their families. All the banks in Haiti, including the Central Bank, were shut down. Fonkoze had dollars in its bank in New Jersey, but no way to bring that money into Haiti.

The day after the quake I received a call from the Inter-American Development Bank (IADB), one of our donor agencies. My contact asked how we were doing and what we needed. "We have money in the US, but can't get it into the country," I lamented. "All institutions are shut down." My contact replied, "Let me think about this."

He did more than think. He contacted his boss, who contacted the State Department, which then contacted the White House, which authorized military support. The President and CEO of our New Jersey bank, who was Haitian, located a bank in Miami that had the needed cash. On January 22, an armored car delivered $2M in 34 packages to Homestead Air Force Base, and a U.S. military C-17 transport flew the funds to a base in Haiti where two Marine helicopters delivered the packages to ten regional locations. Branch directors on motorcycles met the helicopters and delivered the money to their own branch and to the other nearby branches.

Our openness in sharing our urgent need led to a solution we could not have imagined on our own. And when the Central Bank of Haiti learned of the effectiveness of our SFF network in a crisis, they were impressed and began collaborating with Fonkoze on common interests. Previously we had never fit into the country's regulatory banking framework; suddenly, we were a player at the table. Soon our Chief Financial Officer (CFO) and a former employee of the Central Bank, Georgette Jean Louis, was appointed by the President of Haiti to the Board of Governors of the Central Bank. I had hoped she would become my successor at SFF, but her position at the Central Bank ultimately allowed her to do far more for us.

Over this 17-year odyssey, we would learn that every encounter was an opportunity. We spent every day developing relationships, which in turn generated our financing. Even without a master plan, there was a practice to master: disclose what we needed, then ask for feedback, ideas, and help. Fonkoze was built not only by adopting strategies of socially responsible investing and equity investing; it was built with partners.

Gradually, we found ourselves building a staircase out of poverty. At each step we offered clients a different mix of financial, educational, and health services that together would help them take the next step. Our job was to assess a client's needs upon entry, help her get on the staircase, and be there for her whenever she stumbled so she could recover her footing and resume her ascent.

And we've had so many women succeed, starting at the very bottom, graduating from one step to the next, and gradually make their way to the top. As they climb, important things start to happen: they enroll all their children in school; their health improves; their living conditions improve.

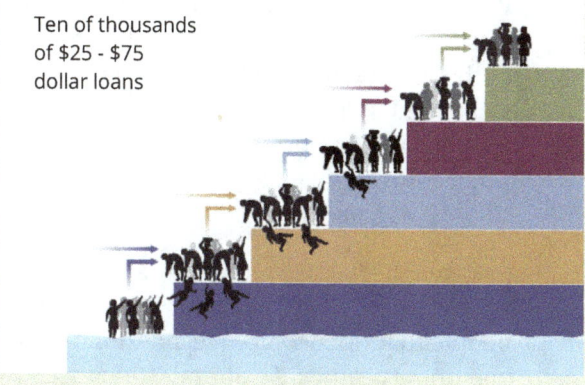

Staircase Out of Poverty

"At each step, we offer clients a different mix of financial, educational and health services that together will help them take the next step. Our job is to diagnose where the client is upon entry, help her get on the staircase, and be there for her whenever she falls so we can help her get back up and continue."

Building the Staircase Out of Poverty
The Process works!

The house where Wilna used to live **Wilna's new home: after 6 solidarity loans & 1 home loan**

Witnessing the success of clients like Wilna was a tremendous source of strength for both staff and fellow clients, providing a constant stream of evidence that our purpose was important and that we were succeeding in helping our clients find a way to prosper in life.

My time in Haiti seemed to be a never-ending series of encounters with special people that opened up new possibilities and opportunities. As our microfinance operation developed, we had four significant breakthroughs in understanding rural poverty that helped us generate new solutions: we were developing the capability to address health care, the ultra-poor, micro insurances, and jobs—each a significant barrier to ending poverty.

Extending the Fonkoze Impact on Poverty By Linking With Healthcare

Dr. Paul Farmer was an infectious disease specialist and co-founder of Partners in Health (PIH), known as Zanmi Lasante in Haiti, which is the country's leading non-governmental provider of rural primary medical care.

I decided to reach out to Paul when he was in Haiti to ask him to review a sexual and reproductive health module a consultant had developed for Fonkoze's education program. Although he found the module impressive, what he really wanted to talk about was Fonkoze. "Anne, we need a much bigger partnership. I'm so tired of treating people who are dying of tuberculosis, AIDS or other diseases, bringing them back to good health, only to watch them die because they go hungry. If you can help them find a way to make a living, I'll help you build Fonkoze branches everywhere we have a clinic."

The great potential in Paul's offer excited me. Fonkoze and Zanmi Lasante joined forces to bring health care and banking together to address the poverty of our clients. We started a joint campaign called *Breaking the Cycle of Disease and Poverty in Haiti*. This vital collaboration would launch my search for solutions to the most extreme forms of poverty.

Supporting the Poor Not Ready for a Loan

Through market research in 2001, we discovered that many of the poorest Haitian women were not reaching out to Fonkoze. These women had no assets; their children were not in school; they went without food for one or more consecutive days. Dealing with banking or a business loan was beyond what they could imagine; they had lost all hope of a better future. And Fonkoze had inadvertently created barriers such as requiring a savings account before getting a loan. The women were afraid to make an application to Fonkoze, and our Fonkoze solidarity members quite frankly didn't want them for fear they wouldn't be able to repay their loans.

This realization took me in 2004 on a global search for the best method to help these women restore their dignity and provide a living for themselves and their children. Along the way, I traveled to Bangladesh where I met Sir Fazle Hasan Abed, founder of BRAC (originally the Bangladesh Rural Advancement Committee). Engaging Sir Abed and the BRAC ultra-poor program run by Rabeya Yasmin was a major turning point in my life.

On my first visit, I was struck by BRAC's effectiveness in addressing this form of poverty. They understood that the poorest are not just poorer than the poor. Ultra-poverty is not a continuum of deprivation but a structural break. A large section of those who fall into this form of poverty remain there for long periods of time, sometimes over generations. The poorest have been shut out of most development approaches, microfinance included.

After many years of researching this type of poverty, BRAC initiated a program, Challenging the Frontiers of Poverty Reduction: Targeting the Ultra-Poor, or TUP for short. TUP families are brought into a two-year investment program that involves a transfer of assets: goats or chickens that they can use to generate income; intensive enterprise training and coaching; health care, temporary cash stipends; and, social development. The larger community commits. BRAC's goal is to enable the ultra-poor to develop new and better options for sustainable livelihoods, thereby graduating out of ultra-poverty. Today, this program is often referred to as the Graduation Program for the ultra-poor.

BRAC targets the poorest communities in a country; the program team mobilizes into those communities to plan the program in collaboration with the community; the team organizes each community into two-year campaigns to elevate the ultra-poor from poverty and into sustainable personal businesses. The process is staff-intensive, but it works.

Studies, including many with experimental controls, showed that BRAC's Graduation Program not only graduated women out of ultra-poverty, with graduation rates of over 90%—it was also cost-effective. Sir Abed and Rabeya were masters at taking the program to scale. In Bangladesh, BRAC has served millions of households and is currently engaged in more than 70 countries worldwide, bringing millions of households out of extreme poverty every year.

But would the Graduation Program for the ultra-poor work in Haiti?

After my trip to BRAC, I convened a weeklong Global Anti-Poverty Summit to determine whether the BRAC Graduation Program could be applied in Haiti. I invited four seasoned practitioners from Asia, Africa, and Latin America to gather in Haiti to address the challenge of Haiti's poverty. For three days, they visited rural Haiti, meeting Paul Farmer and people living with HIV, talking to the Zanmi Lasante staff, and visiting the hospitals. They also visited Fonkoze clients in their homes, in their markets, in their literacy centers, and with their children. This international survey team listened to the clients' stories, heard their pain, and used what they learned to evaluate what services would be most appropriate for them. The last three days were dedicated to intensive, facilitated work sessions with Fonkoze and Zanmi Lasante staff and with our partner organizations on the ground in Haiti.

BRAC's Graduation Approach to Ultra-Poverty in Haiti was greeted with enthusiasm. We concluded the summit by announcing a new global partnership and by eliciting commitments to ultra-poverty programs in Haiti with a testing and start-up schedule that promised dramatic impacts. We would take the leap!

The Summit was a dream come true. I had wanted to explode the myth that there was no solution to ultra-poverty in Haiti. The success of BRAC's model had strongly suggested that all that was needed were the commitment and resources for implementation.

Fonkoze Services to Address Poverty

Financial Services

- Savings
- Loans
- Currency Exchange
- Money Transfers
- Payroll Services

Fonkoze

- Literacy
- Health Care
- Business Education
- Health Promotion
- Crisis Response Programs

Resourcing the initiative was of course a challenge, but after a concerted effort, we were able to gather the resources to pilot an adaptation of BRAC's approach in Haiti. The first step was to send our team to Bangladesh to train with Rabeya Yasmin's and learn the essentials. After a full month of training, Rabeya and two of her staff came to Haiti to work with us. BRAC had a sequenced set of interventions tailored to the local situation. The approach was well defined and adaptable to the Haitian situation. Three years following my visit, Fonkoze implemented our very own program entitled *Chemen Lavi Miyò* (The Pathway to a Better Life).

In 2009, I was given the honor of standing on stage at the Clinton Global Initiative with Sir Abed and Dr. Paul Farmer, two visionaries I was proud to bring together in this work, to introduce the world to our Commitment to Break the Cycle of Disease and Poverty in Haiti. This two-year initiative united BRAC, Fonkoze, and Zanmi Lasante (Partners in Health), in a comprehensive effort to eliminate extreme poverty in the Central Plateau of Haiti. The effort represented a tremendous collaboration of different missions and proven approaches, all working to alleviate some aspect of poverty.

By 2020, despite a continuing onslaught of hurricanes and earthquakes, Fonkoze had successfully served 9,726 of Haiti's poorest women and their families, enabling them to emerge from ultra-poverty. There is a way to solve extreme poverty!

Protecting Our Clients from Disaster

Over the years, as our strategy expanded from financial services to education, health care, and ultra-poor services, I came to realize that asset building doesn't mean much without asset protection. This lesson stemmed as much from our failures as our successes. I've seen women start at the bottom of the staircase make it to the top, only to be knocked back down because of the need to pay for a funeral or to rebuild after four hurricanes in the space of three months. In fact, I've seen the same women fall down and start again two or three different times within a six-year period.

Just as it pained Paul Farmer to witness his patients succumbing not to disease but to hunger, it pained me to see my clients strive to save regularly, reinvest their profits back into their business, use credit wisely, only for them to lose everything because of a hurricane, fire, or a death in the family.

And given the trauma to our national psyche inflicted by the earthquake in 2010, the issue of anticipating large-scale disasters was more important for Haiti's future than ever. Accordingly, we began working with the Swiss Re Group and Mercy Corps to create the Microinsurance Catastrophe Organization (MiCRO), a first in Haiti, and began putting it to the test. In the first years, it worked reasonably well, but after Hurricane Sandy in 2012, we realized that while Fonkoze's clients were well protected, design flaws meant big losses for Fonkoze. In the face of the losses, the board decided that Fonkoze would no longer offer such insurance after I left Haiti. Today the design has been fully corrected, is working well, and is operational in El Salvador, Mexico, Colombia, and Guatemala with plans to expand further.

Forging Different Pathways Out of Poverty: Jobs and SMEs

We soon discovered another larger structural issue: not everyone is a microentrepreneur. Many of the very poor just need jobs.

There are pathways out of poverty, but there is not a single pathway. Some motivated and fortunate women run straight up the ladder held out for them; we call them the "fast climbers." Then there are the slower climbers who may trip on the rungs, women who simply aren't suited to becoming entrepreneurs. They just need a job to support themselves and their families with dignity.

With unemployment at 70% and higher during my tenure in Haiti, job creation was absolutely critical for those not oriented to small business ownership. But those very jobs, especially jobs in rural areas, were often most effectively created by small and mid-sized businesses. Without access to credit, these businesses cannot grow and create jobs. It becomes a self-perpetuating cycle of defeat.

I kept asking myself: could it be that to solve extreme poverty, we needed to also focus on Small and Medium Enterprises (SMEs) as job creators? Fostering SMEs is not simply a matter of providing credit. Small business owners need to be legally registered; they need audited financial statements; they need technology support; they need insurance.

As a mission-driven organization focused on Haiti's poorest, Fonkoze had to be very careful as we considered moving "upmarket" into the SME space. We weren't able to fully resolve this question before my tenure ended, but SME support has become a major initiative of Fonkoze Financial Services (SFF) since I left in 2013.

My Upward Spiral

Twenty-seven years ago, I went to Haiti as a volunteer for one year to help build a bank for the poor and by the poor. When I arrived in 1996, Fonkoze was a three-volunteer office open a few hours a day, with 32 savings accounts and a handful of loans to women's groups in the neighborhood.

Once I realized the depth and scope of Father Joseph's vision and saw how quickly we were able to make changes in people's lives, I ended up staying for 17 years. He, and maybe I as well, believed the Holy Spirit was leading us through all the troubled waters.

Creating a microlending bank was an all-consuming undertaking. It would have been easy to walk away after my one-year commitment, to surrender in the face of endless detail and inevitable challenge. But I learned how commitment to vision and leadership gives rise to new opportunities and new partnerships. This was not a one-off project or program; we were building a democratic and economic development institution in what is the most fragile and impoverished country in the western hemisphere.

By my departure in 2013, despite the challenges of political instability and natural disasters, our remarkable team had established a successful microfinance bank and an effective program to address ultra-poverty. Fonkoze had amassed over 250,000 savers, approximately 65,000 borrowers, a loan portfolio of $16.5 million, 46 branch offices, and more than 800 employees throughout the country.

Our services included well-performing health and education systems, and a huge step forward in addressing the challenge of ultra-poverty. Two new issues had emerged: helping clients to protect their assets and determining how Fonkoze might go about stimulating SMEs for job creation while staying true to our mission.

Despite the fact that Haiti is currently facing one of the most challenging periods in its troubled history, both Fonkoze and Fonkoze Financial Services (SFF) continue to perform strongly. While the country is grappling with criminal violence, political instability, and widespread disruption to daily life, SFF continues to grow and remain modestly profitable. The fiscal year ending September 30, 2021, showed increases in deposits in the aggregate loan portfolio and in the number of both Solidarity and Business Development borrowers. And most importantly, for the first time, SFF was profitable for the 2021 fiscal year. Despite the increasingly difficult environment, for the ten months ending July 31, 2022, operating profit was HTG 72.3 million ($628,000). In the adverse economy that is Haiti, this is a very strong performance.

And despite recent adversity, Fonkoze Financial Services received an official letter from the Central Bank on a great day of celebration in September 2021, granting SFF status as a licensed microcredit institution, the very first microfinance institution in Haiti to be licensed. The license represents the culmination of years of work from thousands of supporters, enabling SFF to grow deposits more aggressively, to provide direct access to the Central Bank's low-interest rate agricultural lending facility, and to gain advantages in handling US dollar remittances.

On November 18, 2021, SFF and Fonkoze were together awarded the European Microfinance Award for Inclusive Finance and Health Care. Forty-three applicants from 32 countries applied for the award. As the winner, Fonkoze received a Euro 100,000 prize.

Building Fonkoze – standing shoulder-to-shoulder with remarkable visionaries such as Father Joseph, our committed donors and investors, our global partners, and above all, the hardworking people of Haiti—is proof of that remarkable dynamic. The relationships formed with clients and partners opened up a world of upwardly spiraling opportunity. We positioned ourselves in Fonkoze to seize these opportunities. Father Joseph's vision of a democratic economy continues to grow and shine resiliently – all by saying *yes*.

Fonkoze Bank Branches Throughout Haiti

Anne H. Hastings with Fonkoze Clients

Anne H. Hastings' Leadership Story: Reflections

What Anne accomplished could be viewed as either miraculous or fortuitous; it was neither. Anne has a way of Being—what we refer to as part of her Signature Style—that called a Compelling Vision into existence. Over time, she chose to expand that vision in bold ways, bringing Mindset and Method to her leadership choices.

As friends and colleagues, to watch Anne H. Hastings' story unfold during her time in Haiti was often scary but always inspiring. In trying to understand how her leadership worked, what stood out for us was the way Anne became the mission. We saw her demonstrate that Leadership is a relentless, positive-energy enterprise marked by breakdowns that triggered surprise opportunities that lead to breakthroughs with extraordinary outcomes. Scary, inspiring, and exciting.

As we think about our own leadership stories, it would be easy to feel intimidated by Anne and Father Joseph's examples. It is unlikely that many of us are ready in mid-career to pursue a 17-year commitment to work in a field that we know nothing about, in a foreign land where we don't speak the language.

However, there are lessons in Anne's story that all of us can relate to. We see the origins of Anne's journey. Anne was seeking a change in purpose and direction. Leaders often launch their journey by encountering others in need. A vision emerges.

We have described a Compelling Vision as the intersection of the needs of others and our own circle of influence. In Anne's case, she was looking for a Compelling Vision she could embrace. She was ready to create new circles of influence to achieve it. Her meeting with Father Joseph gave her what she needed. In a sense, she adopted Father Joseph's vision and grew his circles of influence.

Once in Haiti, Anne's style propelled her and Fonkoze forward. The number of challenges Anne and her colleagues encountered every single day in Haiti extend far beyond what most of us experience in our own lives and careers. To deal with the onslaught of challenges – and the opportunities which were present but hidden within many of these obstacles – Anne adopted powerful, consistent ways of Being.

She chose to consistently accept problems as opportunities by saying *yes*. In doing so, she assumed accountability, trusting that existing and new partners could be tapped. This trusting in the flow is a powerful, courageous way of Being. She mastered being a source of Net Forward Energy and of being able to Flip Negative Energy.

Anne, in pursuit of the vision, frequently found herself in stressful situations. Without Resilience, this kind of stress can quickly wear us all down. Anne found the needed Resilience in her constant interactions with the women she was serving, and in the working relationships that gave her access to advice, guidance, and commitment. Purpose and partners—already present – can help each of us to counter stress with perspective, strength, possibilities, and support. Working with thoughtful and resourceful people like Father Joseph, Leigh Carter, Gordon McCormack, Georgette Jean Louis, Paul Farmer, Sir Fazle Hasan Abed, Rabeya Yasmin, and Julian Schroeder provided Anne with tremendous sources of personal and organizational Resilience.

An exciting lesson for all of us is how Anne accomplished extraordinary results by declaring she didn't know how to do it, but nevertheless, in the words of Father Joseph, she "figured it out." She engaged her network of partners by disclosing and asking. She approached partners with the challenges and barriers she confronted. She asked for their knowledge, guidance, and support. They became ready to say *yes*.

Anne's story can make it appear that the world was ready and willing to plug into Fonkoze with whatever it was that Fonkoze needed at the time. But as we look deeper, we see that others had to first become aware of Fonkoze, and then intrigued. Active engagement and many conversations were necessary to generate in others a sense of relatedness to the vision. We see there were significant resources that were needed, but hidden, and had to be surfaced. Leadership conversations were necessary to cause others to step forward with resources that were previously out of sight. Initiating conversations like these from a position of uncertainty and vulnerability, takes courage.

There is daunting professional, financial, and emotional risk, but the reward is worth it: access to an unimagined Abundance – life-saving and life-enhancing Abundance for those who need it the most.

Leadership and Choices in the Domain of Being

Being might not seem an obvious characteristic of leadership. The dictionary defines Being as 1) Existence; 2) The nature or essence of a person. Existence, our nature, and our essence cover a lot of ground and sound pretty important. Yet most of us don't often address them directly. How we are Being can feel like something that just happens.

In our work as leaders and with other leaders, we see Being as each of us actively choosing how we present ourselves as we engage with the world. There are often situations where we can choose to be a leader... or to be something else. Being is about choosing to be conscious and intentional about the way we react to the world and affect others.

But what does "choose to be a leader" really mean? The leadership stories in this book provide answers. In the domain of Being it means we choose to be a positive source of energy in our personal and professional lives. The Mindsets and Methods of fostering Net Forward Energy, Flip Negative Energy, and Resilience give all of us practical, actionable ways of Being leaders. We can consistently use these Mindsets and Methods to accomplish wonderful things, enriching our own lives and the lives of others.

Net Forward Energy is like having a superpower. We can choose to be a catalyst that helps ourselves and others become a source of positive energy. We can choose to turn on that power.

Flip Negative Energy is almost magical. Imagine being able to turn contentious, troubling situations into something positive – for you, for the source of the negative energy, and for others.

Resilience is a real and practical safety net. It's all about making ourselves ready and able to deal with the increased onslaught of problems that inevitably come our way when we choose to be leaders. As we gain greater mastery of Resilience, we can help others to do so as well. Drawing upon the sources of Resilience has the additional benefit of bringing us closer to our own humanity.

The examples of Bob and Barb Malizzo and of Loren and Monica Kersting show us that we can choose to be of service in ways that bring something good from terrible tragedies. These parents chose to bring their grievous losses to bear on national improvements in hospital safety and increased organ donation and transplantation.

Anne H. Hastings showed us powerful and uplifting ways of Being that brought about extraordinary change on an amazingly large scale. Hundreds of thousands of the most impoverished and challenged women and families in the Northern Hemisphere were helped onto effective pathways out of poverty.

We can learn from the ways of Being chosen by these and other leaders featured in upcoming sections by deliberately focusing on results, joy, positive energy, gratitude, celebration, respect for others, inclusiveness, resilience, appreciation of great work, and more. These ways of Being can lift us up in work and in life and help others to recognize the possibilities and opportunities of this vision. Join with us and each other. Choose to be an uplifting and effective leader by making good choices in the Domain of Being.

We Choose Our Leadership
LANGUAGE

Language is an exact reflection of the character and growth of its speakers.

CESAR CHAVEZ
American Labor Leader
Civil Rights Activist

LANGUAGE

Leadership Speech Acts

Leadership Stories

Access Abundance

Leaders sound different. They tell a unique kind of story, telling us what is possible and inviting us to generate a new future. What we say matters.

We do lots of things in life that do not require Language. We cook food, clean house, mow the lawn, drive to work and more. We can take many of these actions without uttering a word. However, in the case of leading others, Language is essential.

Leadership happens through Language.

Leaders set action in motion through Language, and those of us who lead know intuitively that how we communicate is vital. Through years of hands-on work, we have documented and employed key elements of the Language of leadership. Three leadership Mindsets and Methods are profiled in this segment on the domain of Language: *Speech Acts*, *Leadership Stories*, and *Access Abundance*. Mastery of Speech Acts allows us to craft, refine, and evolve our own Leadership Stories which create greater access to the natural Abundance that is available in the world.

Leaders Use Speech Acts to Produce Action and Results

Common wisdom encourages leaders to communicate clearly, to speak with inflection, and to show vulnerability in our communications. While all this strikes us as mostly good advice, in our work to make effective and joyous Choices in the domain of Language, we come at this from a much more basic and fundamental perspective. The real building blocks of Language are Speech Acts.

Ever heard this term? It is not commonly used. Some Speech Acts are Language that launches us and others into action by speaking it. Choosing to use certain Speech Acts with system and method is at the heart of mastering the Language of leadership. The use and power of Speech Acts was an important and unexpected insight for us.

While our framework on Leadership Speech Acts is primarily based on decades of use in the field and observation of leaders, it is also guided by significant literature on the topic. The writings of Fernando Flores, the Chilean Finance Minister under Salvador Allende and political prisoner during the regime of military general Augusto Pinochet, have been a significant touchstone. After being freed, Flores went on to found successful world-wide consulting practices, using *Speech Acts* to help executives and others to speak and act with intention. Our learning also takes inspiration from *Speech Acts* by John Searle, an expert in linguistics and the philosophy of Language, and from *Enlightened Leadership* by Doug Krug and Ed Oakley.

Leaders Tell Leadership Stories

Leaders stand out in a crowd with the types of stories they tell and the Language they employ. Leaders tell Leadership Stories. We have learned a lot about the impact of Leadership Stories by listening to former Treasury Secretary Paul O'Neill, Institute for Healthcare Improvement CEO Don Berwick MD, Fonkoze Executive Anne H. Hastings, and others whose Leadership Stories are featured throughout the book. We know from our own experience that it is possible to intentionally create our own Leadership Stories and to use them in powerful ways that increase effectiveness and joy. Each of us can also choose to help others on this same journey.

The development and use of Leadership Stories is a learnable discipline grounded in certain Speech Acts. Leadership Stories are one of the best ways to understand what it sounds like to make leadership Choices in the domain of Language.

Leaders Access Abundance Through Language

It's one thing to have a management assignment and the resources you need to achieve it. It's another to have a Compelling Vision or Bold Aim without those means. Leaders frequently dwell in this latter situation. As leaders, we can use Language to access the resources we need from the natural Abundance of the world. While the principle of Abundance can feel almost like magical thinking, it is in reality practical, disciplined work that can be used to produce real results.

Along with some of our own stories and those of other colleagues, the Leadership Story of Susan McVey Dillon at the end of this chapter provides an extraordinary example of how Speech Acts and Leadership Stories can be used to gain access to the natural Abundance of the world. Sue's leadership helped move an entire national community of practice to create a future where tens of thousands of lives were saved.

LANGUAGE

Leadership Speech Acts

Leadership Stories

Access Abundance

Choose to Use
Leadership Speech Acts

Speech Acts are Language expressions that frequently launch the speaker and others into action. Many will sound common and familiar:

"Can we meet next Monday?"

"Everyone in the room, please stand."

"Pass the salt."

Others are more epochal:

"I pronounce you man and wife."

"We hold these truths to be self-evident..."

Speech Acts are expressions we can master to establish our near and distant futures. It is Language, not just as a description of what is there, but as action that generates the future.

The type of Speech Acts we employ will influence the responses we receive from others and the impact we can wield in the world.

Understand and Use a Set of Eight Speech Acts to Practice Leadership

Certain Leadership Speech Acts precipitate action, forward motion, and results. Other Speech Acts, such as Commitments, actually create the future. Requests and Offers are the building blocks of Commitments. Non-leadership Speech Acts, such as gossip, complaints, blame, and insults, tend to stall action or to move us backwards.

A first step in mastering Speech Acts is to learn the difference between those that advance us and those that set us back. Next is practicing those that move us forward. Consistently choosing to apply these in our work and lives, while screening out retrograde Speech Acts, is a final step in gaining mastery of the Mindset and Methods associated with Leadership Speech Acts.

The following table outlines a series of eight Speech Acts we have adapted as part of our own leadership style. Take a moment and scan the list. Notice that just by name they have a positive energy about them. These expressions generate Net Forward Energy and action in ourselves and others.

The column on the right contrasts the Leadership Speech Acts with common alternative ways of speaking that often generate negative energy. Using Leadership Speech Acts requires us not to default into Language that moves us backwards.

Employing Leadership Speech Acts with system and method is the formation of a new habit for many of us. It isn't complicated, but it does have to be intentional and requires diligence, constant practice, and self-control.

Dysfunctional Speech Acts are prevalent, tempting, and often addictive. They can even feel like they are conferring benefit. For example, gossiping with co-workers is a way of establishing rapport and a sense of belonging. It can feel like fun and possibly even productive in the moment, but over the long-term it's ultimately destructive, just as the gossip between talking heads on TV who generate "angertainment" is destructive to the attitudes and conduct necessary to lead.

Understanding Speech Acts	
Leadership Speech Acts	**Non-Leadership Speech Acts**
Declarations	Wishing
Assertions	Gossip
Requests and Offers	Complaints
Commitments	Excuses
Acknowledgements	Blame
Assessments	Worries
"Yes, and …"	Insults
Effective Questions	Opinions

Resist the temptation of using and learning from those who use inherently destructive Speech Acts. They will invariably take us backwards, and then we will take others backwards along with us.

Speech Acts used effectively by leaders generate a special positive energy quality. Gaining mastery of the Language of leadership with Leadership Speech Acts is key to shifting ourselves and others into an uplifting state of leadership.

Incorporate Speech Acts into Our Own Personal Signature Style

Speech Acts can be used in the moment to enhance our effectiveness as leaders. They can also be called on to make our lives and the lives of others fuller and more joyous. Imagine using them at the family dinner table, in a social setting, in everyday work situations, and in conducting a large-scale conference. While the eight Speech Acts can be used to improve specific transactions and operations as individual methods, they are exceptionally powerful when tailored to our own overall approach to life. At the conclusion of this segment, we will discuss using these Acts to help you to establish your own personal Signature Style for using the Language of leadership.

Master the Eight Leadership Speech Acts

In this section we present the eight Leadership Speech Acts that have become part of our Signature Style and that of many of our colleagues. In the following chart, we list the eight Speech Acts that we frequently use, and describe how we see ourselves and other leaders using these Speech Acts.

As we review each and illustrate its use, keep in mind how these Speech Acts can become a way of Being in the world. More than a technique or task, each can become part of our leadership style. At the end of the section, we will consider how to help maintain them as practice habits.

Each Speech Act will be defined and then its use illustrated. A wide variety of situations and voices will be used to show the deep experience and the demonstrated power of Speech Acts. Before reading further, familiarize yourself with the table below—the list of eight, and their use in leadership.

Study each Speech Act with the following two questions in mind:

- *In what way is this Speech Act part of my own approach to Language?*

- *How might I use this Speech Act to create and expand my own more intentional use of Language?*

At the end of this segment, we create a space for you to perform a short exercise to capture how you use Language to lead yourself and others. Be prepared at the end to work with your own list as part of creating your Signature Style.

Mastering the Language of Leadership

Eight Defining Speech Acts

1. **DECLARATIONS**
   Leaders make declarations to define the world and its possibilities.

2. **ASSERTIONS**
   Leaders make assertions to show evidence of what's possible.

3. **REQUESTS & OFFERS**
   Leaders make requests and offers to generate commitments.

4. **COMMITMENTS**
   Leaders make and seek commitments to create the future.

5. **ACKNOWLEDGMENTS**
   Leaders acknowledge behavior and achievement to affirm others.

6. **ASSESSMENTS**
   Leaders control assessments to be interpersonally effective.

7. **SAY "YES, AND . . . "**
   Leaders say "Yes, and . . ." to team effectively and enable group action.

8. **EFFECTIVE QUESTIONS**
   Leaders use effective questions to create productive interactions & lead change.

1. DECLARATIONS Establish the New, Changing Reality

Declarations are statements that can change the state of the world. When spoken in the right context, Declarations are expressions of something inherently true:

> *"I pronounce you husband and wife."*
>
> *"I declare a mistrial."*
>
> *"I stand for universal health care."*

They are not statements to be argued or proven; they are neither right nor wrong. They reveal the personal or professional stand of the leader, and create a space for conversations, Commitments, and actions by others. Declarations can be liberating, self-defining expressions for the speaker.

Leaders make Declarations to define the world and its possibilities. Declarations can be used to express a future to which the speaker is in some way committed. The leader publicly stands for that future. The intent is for listeners to find that future compelling and to see ways to team with the speaker.

- Listeners hear a future state that appeals to them;
- Listeners hear a movement they are invited to join;
- Listeners can imagine how they might contribute;
- Listeners are moved to action within their own channels, networks, and other assets.

Declarations stand in stark contrast to softer language like wishing and hoping, or to harsher language like complaining, where the clarity of intent to pursue a better future is usually missing.

A colleague of ours, Mary Lou Andersen, described leaders as those who are "called to stand in that lonely place between the 'no longer' and the 'not yet,' and intentionally make decisions that will bind, forge, move, and create history." We can see in the examples above that both the 'no longer' and the 'not yet' in each statement are at the heart of the leadership Declaration.

> ### Declarations that Launched Great Movements
>
> *"We hold these truths to be self-evident, that all men are created equal."*
> —**Declaration of Independence**
>
> ---
>
> *"Before this decade is out, we will put a man on the moon and return him safely to earth."*
> —**President John F. Kennedy**

As leaders, what are we declaring? Where does Mary Lou's 'not yet' come from? From where do our Declarations originate? The Declaration may represent the leadership vision of our organization. Our Declarations can also emanate from our personal and professional vision. Experiences in life and work sometimes present us with Defining Moments. Our leadership Declarations can arise from those moments.

The Compelling Vision comes to us from the intersection of our circles of influence and the compelling needs of others. Living and working in the world, we accumulate a circle of influence. Our vision emerges as an insight about how things should be different and better for ourselves and others. Declarations are a powerful way to express that vision.

The needs that call for leadership will often be those beyond the reach of our initial circle of influence or that of our organizations. That circle will have to be expanded. Declarations can help make that happen by attracting others to our vision.

By making a Declaration, we create a new social understanding of the future we stand for. For example, Health and Human Services Secretary Tommy Thompson joined with other national leaders in 2003 to declare a Compelling Vision: "We commit to increasing the organ donation rate in the nation's largest hospitals from 46% to 75% of eligible donors." This leadership Declaration guided more than four years of intensive work in hospitals across the nation to achieve this result.

Leaders make Declarations that are compelling and create urgency. John Chessare MD, the President and CEO of the Greater Baltimore Medical Center, together with his Board of Directors, issued the Declaration that the hospital system he was leading "would provide the quality of care that we would want for our own loved ones." Don Berwick MD and his team at the Institute for Healthcare Improvement (IHI) declared that hospital safety could be improved in 18 months to save 100,000 lives. Sanjeev Arora MD, the founder and leader of Project ECHO, declared that the Hepatitis C patients in New Mexico would receive the necessary lifesaving care that they needed. Anne H. Hastings, the co-founder and Director of Fonkoze, declared that the rural poor in Haiti would have access to a bank that they owned themselves, and that it would help to move them out of poverty.

Each of us can learn to wield the powerful Speech Act of Declarations.

Make it a Habit to Use the Leadership Speech Act of Declarations

What is the most powerful Declaration I have encountered in my own life or work?

What is a Declaration I could make to address a compelling "need of others" that matters to me?

2. ASSERTIONS

Inspire the Confidence to Act

Leaders make Assertions to show what is possible. Assertions are powerful statements of what exists and how it works, backed up with evidence. Assertions open pathways to understanding and action. They give us a North Star to follow, a common direction and Language.

Having an evidence base makes Assertions powerful. We can visit the reality, review the documentation, study the data. Some examples:

> *Organ donation in the United States grew by nearly 9% a year, every year from 2018 through 2023. More and more patients are receiving lifesaving and life-enhancing transplants as a result of the generosity of organ donors.*

> *Fonkoze has successfully served 9,726 of Haiti's poorest women and their families, enabling them to emerge from ultra-poverty. There is a way to solve extreme poverty.*

Assertions can be useful in many situations, conveying the scale, depth, and urgency of needs. Assertions can highlight positive results that can be studied, adapted, tested, adopted, and spread to others. Assertions can call attention to inspiring work and showcase the people who produced it.

Assertions as Speech Acts are powerful ways of speaking about how the world works, enabling action. By contrast, dysfunctional Speech Acts of complaints, blame, opinions, and gossip, are not effective enablers of action.

In our leadership work, we have found two especially powerful ways to use Assertions:

- Naming a need that we are being called to address;
- Identifying situations that indicate how to address the need.

Using both is like a one-two punch for getting attention. We see that combination in Don Berwick MD's journey to improve hospital safety.

In late 1999, the Institute of Medicine issued a landmark report, *To Err is Human*. Don Berwick MD was one of the key leaders of the Committee who authored the seminal report. The report asserted that patient safety problems were rampant throughout US hospitals and estimated that as many as 98,000 people died each year as a result of medical errors in hospitals. These findings rocked the world of medicine.

The Assertions made in *To Err Is Human* changed the trajectory and practice of hospital medicine. The Assertions first led to a lot of denial, then blame, then hand-wringing – and then eventually, to concerted action.

In 2010, the federal government launched a $500 million campaign to reduce hospital-acquired conditions. The need was captured and expressed with the Assertion:

> *Care in US hospitals is not safe enough. The rate of harm in hospitals is unacceptably high, with 145 harms to patients for every 1000 discharges.*

This was a shockingly high rate of harm, with evidence drawn from well-designed studies of tens of thousands of hospital patient medical charts. Hospital-acquired conditions that were identified included adverse drug events, blood stream infections, surgical site infections, falls, and pressure ulcers among the many harms that patients can acquire from a stay in a hospital.

There are research-based approaches available for preventing each of these conditions. "Change Packages" were assembled to make this knowledge accessible and transferable. Change Packages, commonly used in action learning collaboratives, are Assertions that certain actions can produce measurable results. The strategies and practices contained in Change Packages are backed up by evidence, including other hospital sites that have put these into effect and successful practitioners who can show others the way forward.

The Assertions were put forward as a baseline against which to measure progress. A Bold Aim was established to produce a 40% reduction in the preventable national harm rate by the end of 2014. Assertions about the leading-edge practices in the field created confidence in our ability to move ahead. Even when there is no evidence base available, Assertions can still be built to inspire and guide action. Rapid cycle development and rapid cycle improvement can quickly generate insight and evidence, supported by data.

We can also turn to more well-developed fields with analogous or comparable situations. The best practices and experiences from other fields can be used as models of what is possible in our field.

The federal campaign that was launched in 2010 made tremendous progress. By the end of calendar year 2014, the harm rate had been dramatically reduced by 39 percent.

Assertions are evidence-based statements that can fuel, guide, and build confidence in our leadership work. They inspire ourselves and others to take action.

Make it a Habit to Use the Leadership Speech Act of Assertions

What is an evidence-based Assertion that has moved me to action in my life?

What evidence-based Assertions might I begin to use in my work or life to help myself and others to see ways we can take actions to address an important need?

3. REQUESTS AND OFFERS

Trigger Action Now to Create the Future

Requests and Offers are statements proposing that the speaker and others be in action to accept, decline, or negotiate with each other.

Leaders make Requests and Offers to generate Commitments that create the future. For example, if someone makes a Request of another person to speak at their conference and secures a *yes*, the requester and requestee co-create the future in that moment. Three weeks later, the Commitment is honored when the speaker shows up and speaks at the conference. We create the future in the present.

> *Dwell on this thought: We use the Language of Requests and Offers to generate the Commitments that create the future.*

Requests and Offers often lead to counter-Offers and counter-Requests, which can then be accepted. "**Yes**, *I will come to your event,* **and** *then will you agree to speak at mine?*" Acceptance becomes another agreement to create the future.

Not all Requests and Offers are accepted, but this is not a problem. A "no" can be the beginning of the next conversation. Over time, many other possibilities for responding positively to a Request or Offer can surface.

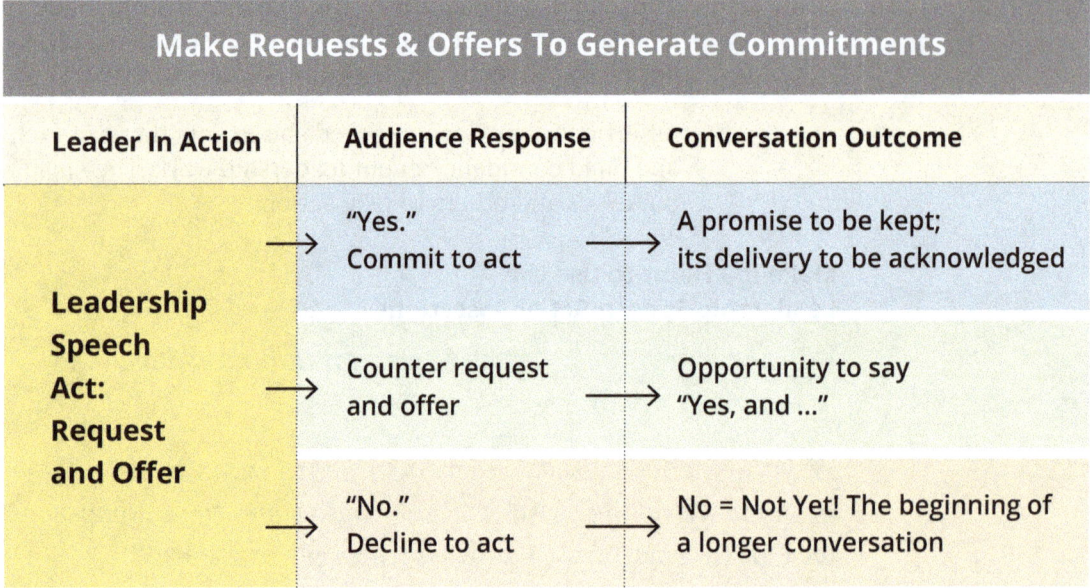

Requests and Offers are one of the most essential and versatile Speech Acts available to leaders in the domain of Language. Requests and Offers can be deployed to turn almost any encounter and event into a Commitment-generator. By generating Commitments, Requests and Offers open up the world of Abundance.

In Anne H. Hastings' Leadership Story, we learn how an exchange of Requests and Offers with a priest from Haiti turned into a Commitment to create Fonkoze, a bank for and by the poor. The Commitment by Anne H. Hastings resulted in a transformative 17-year working relationship with life-changing benefits for hundreds of thousands of Haitian women and families.

Within organizations, Requests and Offers can also be used to create a participatory culture promoting creativity and ownership. The intent is a less hierarchical and more collaborative way of generating action with colleagues and employees. The invitation that is present in a Request and Offer is very different from the command inherent in a direct order.

While organizations are commonly operated with command-and-control styles, Requests and Offers can be an appealing alternative way of teaming with employees and those who report to us.

The habit of making Requests and Offers in any situation can be an engine for accelerating progress to the future. Imagine a large conference with 3,000 people in the room. The speaker makes an action Request of the participants. When some or all of those 3,000 people say yes and agree to act on the Request, they have established potentially thousands of Commitments that accelerate action to the desired future state. Think of it! We have the ability with the strategic use of Requests and Offers to focus and amplify action.

We will see in other sections of this book that it is even possible to hear Requests and Offers that have not yet been spoken. They lie just below the surface of a conversation that is using energetic but non-leadership Language. Below the expression of complaints, worries, and criticism, Requests and Offers may be forming that can be surfaced as positive energy and Commitments. We can learn to name these underlying and unspoken Requests and Offers to Flip Negative Energy.

The systematic and intentional use of Requests and Offers is a powerful habit to form. Requests and Offers trigger action in ourselves and others, presenting an effective alternative to the passive information-sharing that we often encounter in run-of-the mill meetings and other professional exchanges and in the conduct of everyday life.

Make it a Habit to Use the Leadership Speech Acts of Requests and Offers

What is an important Request or Offer from my recent past that I made or that someone made to me?

What is a Request or an Offer I could make to a colleague to generate an important commitment?

Speech Act Practice
What Do We Do With *No*?

by **Tracy Washington-Enger**
Program Manager,
U.S. Environmental
Protection Agency

Get Comfortable Dealing with *No*

One of the biggest challenges to dealing with *no* is learning to recognize it. Sometimes people don't know how to say *no*, and sometimes people don't know how to hear it. Too often the fear of hearing *no* blocks our senses and blinds us to the opportunities that are actually present. That fear may even drive us to make others incapable of giving us a direct *no*. I maintain that *no* is nothing to fear since it really is more of a question or a Request for more information and assistance to get to *yes*. If we entertain the idea that *no* is not the end of the conversation but the beginning, a whole new world of possibilities opens up. Here's a case in point.

Using the Language of Leadership in Thailand

In the early 2000s, I had the opportunity to join colleagues from the Environmental Protection Agency on a mission to Thailand to train our Thai counterparts at their department of environment on the methods for running effective, results-focused Pacing Events, aimed squarely at generating energy and results. The training was a spectacular week of learning, sharing, and growing for both the trainers and our trainees. We were continually impressed by how eagerly and excitedly the trainees took to the powerful methods that we were sharing. The group of Thai government officials, ranging from senior managers to young junior employees, seemed delighted to step into modeling and practicing all the methods of transformative leadership and dramatic Speech Acts that were a part of our training repertoire.

An Ominous Warning

At the end of the week, we were eager to take our show on the road and showcase our trainees as lead facilitators for a series of three important events scheduled to occur the following week in communities across Thailand. At dinner the night before our first day of work in the field, Betina, the Australian volunteer who had been working with our Thai counterparts for about a year, issued an ominous warning to our US team. While expressing admiration for our training, she told us in no uncertain terms that it wasn't going to work: the Thais would never do it.

"What do you mean they're not going to do it?" we asked incredulously. "They've been great, they've done everything we've asked them to do."

Betina agreed with us that so far, our trainees had been completely compliant, but that was because Thais would never tell us no. It wasn't in the Thai culture to say *no* to our Requests. But it also wasn't in the Thai culture to behave in the fairly assertive and forceful ways that the training required them to act. "They won't say *no*," Betina said, "but they won't do it either."

While I was a little taken aback, I remained undaunted. I was accustomed to skepticism about the training methods, so I pretty much dismissed her concerns.

The next day Betina's warnings became reality. When the time came for our trainees to deliver the dynamic leadership statements we had prepared for introductions, they reverted to type. The first Thai official stood up and introduced themself in the traditional name, rank and serial number fashion. That set the tone for the rest of the day. Whenever it was time for a trainee to stand up and lead the session that they had volunteered to facilitate, they instead cast furtive looks at the American team and waited for us to take the stage —which we did in order for the event to continue. And so it went all day: instead of our trainees taking the lead and modelling, they deferred to us. At the end of the day, instead of having a course-correcting debrief, my co-trainer and I retreated quickly to our rooms, feeling defeated.

An Important Choice by a Thai Leader

Later that evening there was a knock at our door. I opened the door and there stood one of our trainees who was so quiet and reserved that her family nickname was "Little Mouse." Little Mouse proceeded to inform us with uncharacteristic directness that, if our goal was for the trainees to lead the training, we had failed. She wasn't being mean or sarcastic, she was just stating the obvious. What could we do but agree?

Then, Little Mouse made the most beautiful Offer I had ever experienced in my professional life. Little Mouse said that she wanted to lead the training the next day. She assured us that she would use all the training methods that she had learned, but that she needed to do it her way. Then she asked if we would help her. This was an example of Offers and Requests at its most magical.

Little Mouse took all the translated slides to her room to customize them to her own style. We met with her the next morning at 6 AM for a final coaching session. When Little Mouse took the stage that morning at 9 AM, she was ready to go and led the opening sessions with skill and confidence.

Mid-morning, a new participant who hadn't been present the day before, started to disrupt the training by injecting all the old-school problems and negativity that we were there to combat. Little Mouse successfully deflected him in the moment, and at the break took him by the arm, led him over to our flip charts, and basically gave him a primer on the methods he had missed by coming a day late. She dwelt on the Request to generate Net Forward Energy and explained that we were here to identify problems for the purpose of solving them, not to get stuck in them. The participant returned to the group appropriately schooled and ready to play by the new rules. Little Mouse saved the day for us and was lauded as a leader by her colleagues, who went on to follow her example in our final day of training.

Lessons Learned

So, what happened? What went wrong? In the years since this event, through lots of coaching and facilitation experience, I have learned a few things.

The first, and perhaps most important thing, is that there is a messy, liminal space between *yes* and *no* where a great deal of other behaviors and Speech Acts dwell. One of those messy Speech Acts is the *Corrupt Yes*. The Corrupt Yes happens when people don't feel fully empowered to say *no*. So they perform all of these yes behaviors but, in the end, they decline to follow through. The Corrupt Yes can happen for any number of reasons. Sometimes they happen as a result of outright coercion or force. But, most often they happen out of a desire on the part of the receiver to please the Requester. Usually, the Requester doesn't even realize they have prompted a Corrupt Yes until the fateful moment that no shows up.

There are methods to ensure that we are getting a clean and authentic *yes*. These methods involve creating a new default for people. This requires being aware of the power of default behaviors to attract people to return to what is safe and comfortable, and to develop techniques aimed at helping manage the natural human behavior of turning to a more comfortable default:

- **Actively secure complete Commitments.** Looking back, I realize that because people were parroting the behaviors that we were asking for during practice, I took that as consent and buy-in. I accepted that behavior as a *yes* without ever really securing an outright Commitment that they were going to adhere to the training methods when the time came. Be sure to secure a Commitment by making the complete Request of the specific things that we want people to do.

- **DNA Decide-Notice-Acknowledge.** Look for opportunities to recognize, notice, and acknowledge the behaviors that we are requesting of people when they happen organically, in their natural habitat. Trust people to craft their own personal Signature Style *yes*, knowing that it may not look exactly like what we are expecting. This will build confidence in people that they have the competency to do what we are asking them to do, using their existing abilities.

- **Model the behaviors we want to see.** Be the change and don't let the fear of *no* defeat us. I am ashamed to say that I failed to be a good servant-leader and model on that first day of training. When the trainees caved in, I imploded right along with them. Instead of modeling leadership and renegotiating with them in the moment, I followed their lead and accepted their initial *no* as a final answer. Fortunately, Little Mouse stepped into that space and worked with me to find her authentic *yes*.

The experience in Thailand taught me a lot about identifying *no*, dealing with *no*, and getting to an authentic, non-corrupt *yes*. I will be forever grateful for the courageous leadership Choice that Little Mouse made to step up and successfully try on the Language of leadership. We all have something we can learn from Little Mouse.

4. COMMITMENTS: Do the Real Work of Generating and Managing Meaningful Promises

A Commitment is a promise to do or deliver something by a specific time.

Leaders make and seek Commitments to create the future. An early morning breakfast seminar in Washington, DC on the topic of Real Work fundamentally expanded our view of the importance of the Speech Act of Commitment.

The Council for Excellence in Government invited one of their Principals named Robert Kohler, to share his insights about public and private sector productivity. Kohler knew how to get things done and attributed his success to the discipline of Real Work. He spoke from a track record of accomplishment, having served at the highest levels of the public and private sectors. Kohler was then serving as the Executive Vice-President of the defense contracting company TRW Corporation. He had just completed a major turnaround of the company's profitability. Prior to TRW, he had served as an Associate Director of the Central Intelligence Agency where his team was in charge of the hardware of intelligence: designing, producing, launching, and managing the nation's spy satellites.

In a 20-minute talk followed by 25 minutes of robust interaction, Robert Kohler taught us that Real Work was three things:

- Making Commitments;
- Delivering on Commitments We Have Made;
- Securing Commitments from Others.

Kohler boldly declared that everything else was mostly "talking about Commitments" and would have little or no impact. He was describing the approach he systematically spread across organizations where he had chosen to step into leadership Roles.

Kohler's guidance helped us to develop the art of making and securing Commitments as part of our Signature Style. Over two decades we've developed several key insights about the practice:

- Securing Commitments Takes Work;
- Requests and Offers Are the Key;
- Grow Your Network;
- Use Conversations for Action;
- Make a New Habit of All of the Above.

Guide: Focus on the Offer in Request & Offer
by Dennis Wagner

Many years ago, as a young Presidential Management Intern (PMI), I attended a training event on networking conducted by the US Office of Personnel Management that was organized for the 200 PMIs in the 1986-88 cohort. The agenda promised we would learn the #1 Secret to Effective Networking. It was an irresistible title for many of us young networkers.

The secret turned out to be:

Help others to succeed;

Focus on what you put into the network, not what you get from it;

Focus on giving, not taking.

I have used the #1 Secret over and over again throughout my life and career. This is powerful guidance and is a useful mindset for thinking about Offers and Requests. Offers and help to others are especially powerful in effective networking.

Securing Commitments Take Work

Commitments are promises. As leaders, we want to be generating and managing multiple meaningful promises.

Leaders, having committed to a vision, do this challenging work to accumulate the resources and actions needed to achieve our shared vision. Commitments form relationships; delivering on Commitments builds trust. As people make and deliver on Commitments, we move toward our shared future.

We approach people who have command of, or influence over, the kinds of actions and resources we need to get the job done. The Commitments sought can be wide-ranging and eclectic. The Commitments we seek can range from getting someone to come to a meeting, speak at an event, host a workshop, donate money, vote in an election, adopt a Bold Aim, join a collaborative, Offer communication channels, buy a product or service, accept a new job, and more.

Make Requests that Sound like Offers

In pursuing Commitments, all of us generally work to make attractive and thoughtful Offers or Requests so that people will find it easier to say yes. For example, we can ask a person to deliver something that the person is naturally inclined to deliver or would likely be excited to be asked to deliver.

Over time, we've learned that the best Requests are often actually experienced as Offers by the recipient. Maybe you have been asked to speak at an event about a topic you love to a group that you respect immensely? In this case, the Request to speak might actually sound more like an Offer, an opportunity, a reward!

Grow Your Network

Initially the work of generating Commitments can appear to be daunting and beyond our reach. However, there is a simple practice that each of us can learn in order to gain greater command of the task: start by talking to people you already know.

When we encounter successful leaders, it often seems like they are well connected. We may think, "Of course they are successful, they know everyone." What we don't see is that at some point, they did not have that network—they grew it. We can grow our own networks. Each of us, too, are connected to others. We all have a circle of influence to deploy and to build from.

We often start off knowing people who can help, but usually not the necessary and sufficient numbers of people to address our larger leadership needs. The challenge is to work with those we do know in order to meet and enroll the others we need to know. Doing this will have us in conversations with people who may join with us, but often in ways we don't yet know or understand. It is a process of courage, trying, asking, and working with the unknown.

Use Conversations for Action

As we organize our time to engage others, it helps to think about Commitments as not the first or the last conversation we will have with our colleagues. The Six Conversations for Action chart establishes Commitments as a special conversation within a sequence of conversations.

When we first meet people, we can think of ways to relate around mutual interest. Then we move to sharing world views and agendas. Together, we will start to see possibilities for action. As possibilities appear, we can look for events and situations that would have us in action together. Opportunities materialize. At this point, there is often enough context and relatedness to make Requests and Offers. As the resulting Commitments are made, relationships will flourish as those promises are kept and acknowledged.

Six Conversations Towards Action

1. **Relatedness** Mutual interests surface;

2. **Possibility** A new and positive future is seen;

3. **Opportunity** Options for working together emerge;

4. **Commitment** From Requests & Offers to a promise;

5. **Accountability** Delivery on the promise;

6. **Acknowledgement** Appreciation that the promise was kept and accounted for.

Form a New Habit

Securing Commitments is a Mindset that we can work to form into a deeply ingrained habit. We can use our meetings to make and secure Commitments. Here is a 90-second exercise that can help us as leaders prepare to be productive in our next encounter:

> *Daily Practice: Before walking into a meeting or signing on to a virtual event, stop for 90 seconds. Ask yourself: "Given who will be in this meeting and the topic to be discussed, what Commitments should I leave this meeting with, and how will I secure them?"*

This brief reflection from meeting to meeting can make a big difference in what we accomplish each day. It has helped us to use meetings and events in action-generating ways that go far beyond traditional information-sharing and dialogue. Keep a log for a period of time to record meeting-by-meeting the number of Commitments secured. If we are in meetings that are not generating Commitments, we may not be doing real leadership work. We are most likely doing something else.

In the end, we want to be making, securing, and managing a lot of meaningful commitments!

**Make it a Habit to Use the
Leadership Speech Act of Commitments**

What is a significant Commitment I have recently secured from others or made to others?

What is a Commitment that I need to make or secure from someone to advance an important aspect of my life or work?

5. ACKNOWLEDGMENT

Appreciate in a Memorable Way

Acknowledgment is recognizing and appreciating people for their behaviors, actions, and results.

Leaders Acknowledge behavior and achievement to affirm others. Acknowledging our friends, family, and colleagues for good things lifts all of us up. It is a building block for an appreciative and harmonious work culture and way of life. Acknowledgments help us to create upward spirals in our lives.

Over the years, we have become increasingly aware of the power of the simple act of acknowledging others. It is a joyous and exceptionally effective way to bring more of what we want into the world. We can apply Acknowledgment every day to many situations where we see something good happening.

It seems like such a small thing when we do this in everyday life. However, the systematic practice of acknowledging others is in fact a powerful form of influence in multiple ways. The act lifts up those acknowledged. In turn, they become role models whom others can emulate. Their importance and credibility are enhanced; they become more influential, triggering the interest of others.

The power of acknowledgment shows up in a number of ways:

- Acknowledgment to Express Intent;
- Acknowledgment to Generate and Sustain Commitments;
- Acknowledgment of Promises Kept;
- Acknowledgment of Promises Not Yet Kept;
- Acknowledgment Spread through Modeling;
- Acknowledgment as a Habit.

In the following section we highlight the power of Acknowledgment and present a case study to illustrate the power of Acknowledgment to influence and create role models.

Acknowledgment to Express Intent

Acknowledgment is an effective way to communicate Intent. The practice of Decide-Notice-Acknowledge (DNA) to bring more of what we want into the world is profiled in greater detail in the chapter on Intent. What we acknowledge communicates what we value, while also capturing the interest and attention of others.

We are all interested and often impressed when someone is singled out for praise. The act of Acknowledgment can guide and inspire others to contribute and to pursue shared Intent. A series of related Acknowledgments can establish a new standard of practice, a new normal.

As a Speech Act, Acknowledgment can be delivered in many ways. We can apply Acknowledgment in our everyday family, social, and work situations; we can build it into our transactions at work; we can organize events where Acknowledgments are made with clear design and Intent to send powerful messages. Each Acknowledgment we make is an expression of Intent.

Acknowledgment to Generate and Sustain Commitments

Leaders who use Acknowledgment with system and method can generate big impacts. We know from our own work and lives how effective this can be. As discussed earlier, a central element of the work of leadership is making and generating Commitments. Acknowledgments can be skillfully used by leaders to address at least three and possibly more facets of Commitments:

- Publicly acknowledging and generating more Commitments;
- Acknowledging Commitments that have been delivered;
- Acknowledging when Commitments are not yet realized.

Publicly Acknowledging and Generating More Commitments

We have learned that acknowledging and calling attention to a Commitment is a sure-fire way to build momentum for further Commitments, both by the person acknowledged and by others who witness the Acknowledgment. Momentum is generated whether in groups of two or three or in conferences with thousands of people.

Acknowledging Commitments That Are Kept

Acknowledgment of great work is also a powerful force for processing the outcomes of Commitments made and delivered on. Commitments have added impact when their outcomes are known and acknowledged. Without Acknowledgment, the results of Commitments may never become known and wither away. Appreciating great work is a key element in sustaining and expanding on it.

For Commitments fulfilled, there are many exciting and innovative ways to express gratitude and appreciation. We can do this with a single individual or by assembling others in events for awards and celebration. Doing this can have powerful effects on relationships.

- The relationships between leaders and partners are strengthened;
- The social capital and influence of the person delivering on the Commitment increases;
- An Acknowledgment can be broadcast as a message to inspire others;
- What can be done and how to do it becomes better understood.

Acknowledging Commitments Not Yet Kept

Sometimes, despite best efforts, Commitments are not realized. Acknowledgment can be a way to learn from the experience, appreciate the effort, and generate new Commitments with a higher likelihood of success. It's a way to avoid bad feelings and disappointment. With Commitments not yet kept, we acknowledge effort and also the challenge of a not-yet situation. Conversations continue to restore or re-make the Commitment, guided by what was experienced and learned.

Wednesday Morning Chat and Kudos
by **Dennis Wagner**

Good news is easy to take advantage of, but it's also easy to miss the opportunity. We have found it useful to intentionally set aside time for Acknowledgement to happen.

In a group that I led at the Centers for Medicare and Medicaid Services (CMS), we had a standard, fast-moving 30-minute All Hands meeting every Wednesday morning. We called it the Wednesday Morning Chat; everyone in the 100-person unit was invited to join, either in person or via phone conference.

I always looked forward to the meeting, in part because our final agenda item was always "Kudos." During the Kudos segment, anyone in the unit could recognize someone else for an accomplishment, an assist, a way of behaving, or some other thing that deserved attention and Acknowledgement by the larger group. My colleague and fellow senior executive, Jean Moody-Williams, was the leader who first established the Chat, together with the systematic use of Kudos. It was one of her thousands of effective and meaningful contributions to this Agency and its people. Some meetings had as many as a dozen Kudos expressed – usually within the space of only 5 or 6 minutes. The Kudos agenda item lifted all of us up. It was a great way to end the meeting and a great way to begin Wednesday morning at work.

Acknowledgment is Spread by Modeling

Modeling is known to be one of the most powerful forms of influence, and as leaders, our modeling of Acknowledgments has been particularly effective.

Stephen Covey, the author of the best-selling *7 Habits of Highly Effective People*, used a pyramid to describe the behaviors that we can use to influence others. He distinguished between training, relating, and modeling. These three forms of influence vary in their impact. The tip of the pyramid is persuading with teaching and explaining. The ability to influence is present, but it's less impactful compared to Relating or empathy or the most powerful form of influence, Modeling, which constitutes the base of the pyramid.

By Modeling leadership behaviors, we let others see what we want done. Actions speak louder than words. Systematic use of the leadership Mindsets and Methods in all four domains can be viewed as a form of Modeling. When we Acknowledge, we are modeling a leadership behavior that others can adopt and follow. Others can see the positive energy Acknowledgment creates and gain insight in how to practice it. Our modeling of Acknowledgments will be seen, heard, and replicated by others, and spread across an entire organization or network, creating a more joyous and uplifting experience for all.

Influencing Others

Adapted from
Principle Centered Leadership
by Stephen Covey

- **Training / Teaching** — Lower Influence
- **Relating to / Identifying with** — Moderate Influence
- **Modeling** — High Influence

Seize the Many Opportunities for Acknowledgment: Make it a Habit

Acknowledgment works in the smaller day-to-day things like appreciating a work colleague for running an uplifting and content-rich staff meeting. It also works with big spotlight occasions such as major professional awards.

There are a lot of competitive award programs in every field. There are hundreds of professional conferences held each year, and there are thousands of local civic and social events. Most colleges and universities have formal programs in place for acknowledging the contributions of their alumni. Leaders can choose to use these already-in-place platforms to acknowledge the contributions and performance of others.

We can make it a regular practice to nominate a colleague or a team for an award. We can make it a practice to call out colleagues for kudos at staff meetings. We can organize and convene special sessions at professional conferences and events to highlight the work of colleagues, team members, suppliers, customers and organizations. We can create our own new awards. We can think and act big in this arena!

Used effectively, the powerful leadership Speech Act of Acknowledgment can increase momentum, spotlight what's working, instill confidence, accelerate progress, showcase people, magnify positive energy, and motivate those who witness the Acknowledgments to pursue similar actions. The systematic, thoughtful use of Acknowledgments can not only increase our effectiveness as leaders, but can also make work and life richer, more joyful, and more meaningful for both the givers and the recipients.

**Make it a Habit to Use the
Leadership Speech Act of Acknowledgment**

What is a recent in-the-moment Acknowledgment I made of someone's performance or behavior -- and what message did it send?

What kind of action, behavior or result do I want to start making Acknowledgments about?

Speech Act Practice

Using Acknowledgment as a Strategic Force with Large-Scale Impact

by **Dennis Wagner**

Acknowledgments can be used strategically at large scale to recognize and generate further results. I was fortunate to experience the effects of being acknowledged when two of my fellow executives at the Centers for Medicare and Medicaid Services and I received a prestigious national award in 2016. Jean Moody-Williams, Paul McGann, and I were recognized as Federal Employees of the Year by the non-partisan, not-for-profit organization Partnership for Public Service.

The Partnership's Sammie Awards (named after entrepreneur Samuel J. Heyman, who advocated for more effective government) are known as the Oscars of Public Service. Sammie Award winners have been recognized for high-impact results such as developing the science used to create the COVID vaccine, rebooting the Mars Rover after it was damaged while landing, leading an international initiative to prevent and treat HIV-AIDS across the African continent, and more. Many Americans have no idea how big, exciting, and impactful it can be to work in the federal civil service. The Sammies call attention to this terrific work.

Our three-person team was nominated for a Sammie by the Administrator of the Centers for Medicare and Medicaid Services and the Secretary of Health and Human Services. We were nominated for successful work to achieve major improvements in hospital safety across all 5,000 US hospitals. Our team's work was estimated to have saved 87,000 lives and resulted in nearly $20 billion in cost savings.

The 60 or 70 public servants who were chosen from among nominees by the Partnership in 2016 were notified of our Finalist status and invited to a major breakfast event at an ornate Congressional Committee Room on Capitol Hill in Washington, DC. The event was attended by senators, congressmen and congresswomen, agency heads, and other dignitaries who systematically acknowledged the work of the Finalists. My own congressman from Northern Virginia, Representative Don Beyer, showed up and took a photo with me!

Federal Employees of the Year, 2016 Jean Moody-Williams, Dennis Wagner, and Paul McGann MD

The Washington Post covered the breakfast and featured a photo of the finalists. We all felt very acknowledged, for sure.

Award Finalists learned that the Partnership was only warming up with this initial breakfast event. Major national publications ran stories about our work. Finalists were interviewed on TV. President Barack Obama sent a letter of congratulations. We were invited to a baseball game of the Washington Nationals and called onto the field with our picture on the Stadium scoreboard. Wow!

Winners were to be announced at an over-the-top formal dinner for 1000 at the Andrew W. Mellon auditorium on Constitution Avenue in the nation's capital, with valet parking, red carpet photo shoots of the winners, and press interviews.

Videos featuring the work of award-winners were shown. Then Vice-President Joe Biden recognized the finalists and winners via video presentation. President Obama's Chief of Staff, Denis McDonough, joined on stage with Michael Kelly, the actor who played the Chief of Staff on the popular TV show House of Cards, to present the prestigious Federal Employee of the Year award.

Hearing my name called out along with Jean and Paul as Federal Employees of 2016, I never felt more acknowledged in my entire life. Whooftie. We were filled with overwhelming feelings of accomplishment, humility, and gratitude for the thousands of partners and colleagues who had teamed with us in this lifesaving work. The entire event was featured the next day in the Washington Post. Winning the 2016 Sammie was truly a major highlight of our careers with the United States government.

Strategically Extending Acknowledgment to Others Across the Nation

Jean, Paul, and I knew that we had been given something of high value that we could use to launch the hospital safety work into its next phase of extraordinary performance. The Sammie was first-class Acknowledgment by an organization that works to strategically and to publicly recognize the work of federal civil servants. Other aspiring federal employees pay a lot of attention to Sammie Awards and are inspired to do even better in their own work.

With such a high-profile award, we had a new asset to deploy. My fellow recipients and I resolved that the energy and sense of accomplishment we had gained would be spread and shared with thousands of our partners across the nation.

The Sammie Award came with a $10,000 cash prize. Jean, Paul, and I decided to use the prize money to Acknowledge nearly 400 organizations and thousands of individuals who played important and complex roles in the four-year effort to improve hospital safety nationally. We realized that nearly all these people would be among the participants at a previously scheduled national quality conference conducted by CMS each year. We decided to use the CMS event to recognize and acknowledge the extraordinary contributions of our partners.

Nearly 3,000 influential leaders in American healthcare convened in Baltimore for the three-day conference. Conference attendees included state and national hospital associations, quality improvement organizations, federal contractors, leaders from national hospital networks such as Ascension Health, other federal leaders from the Centers for Disease Control and the Agency for Healthcare Research and Quality, national associations such as the National Quality Forum and the American Nurses Association, and many others. This was an ideal professional audience for acknowledging the people responsible for creating the national transformation in hospital safety -- and to further institutionalize the emerging culture of hospital safety.

Ned Holland, a senior leader from the Partnership for Public Service and former Health and Human Services Assistant Secretary, gave remarks on behalf of the Partnership. He lauded the contributions of the folks in the audience. A special video commemorating our shared work to improve hospital patient safety was played to honor the award recipients.

Beautiful plaques purchased with our Sammie Award prize money were presented to 376 individuals and organizations (together, all at once!) in a moving plenary presentation. Each plaque was inscribed with the name of the recipient, the Partnership for Public Service Logo, and our shared, lifesaving national results:

- 2.1 Million Fewer Harms;
- 87,000 Lives Saved;
- 19.8 Billion in Cost-Savings.

Our Sammie prize money was also used to hire professional photographers to take red-carpet photos with award winners at the conference. Many of the receiving organizations issued press releases about their awards along with the photos. As a result, the awards were covered in major state and local news outlets across the nation. Professional provider associations also covered their own awards and those of their members in association newsletters, magazines and other publications.

Some Gifts Do Keep On Giving

When Max Stier, President and CEO of the Partnership for Public Service, learned of our extensive follow-on recognition of our own partners, he decided to feature the additional spread of the Partnership's Acknowledgments in their 2017 Annual Report.

The recognition, goodwill and positive energy resulting from this strategic use of Acknowledgment provided further momentum to the ongoing work to improve patient safety in hospitals across the nation. Our entire network of federal partners, private partners, contractors, patient advocates and others were bolstered by the decisions to acknowledge and publicly celebrate their hard work and results.

Most importantly, the renewed energy and Commitment to our shared purpose resulted in further major reductions in hospital harm in subsequent years – from 145 harms per thousand hospital discharges in our baseline year of 2010 to 86 harms per thousand discharges by the end of 2017. Thousands of lives and billions of dollars have been saved because of the energy, commitment, and actions of these leaders in hospital patient safety. Systematic Acknowledgment of the contributions of others is highly effective. It creates results and makes the work more joyous, for sure.

6. ASSESSMENTS

Be Civil, be Smart, Avoid Fights

An Assessment is a statement that conveys a judgment made by the speaker.

An Assessment is what it is; it cannot be proven right or wrong, but we often create justifications for them. Others can refute an Assessment and create justifications for their position. A lot of time can be spent on assessing or refuting an issue.

Leaders can choose to control Assessments to be interpersonally effective. As a leadership Speech Act, leaders choose to express judgments in ways that move the conversation from personal judgments to shared understanding of positions. Judgments emerge and become grounded in common standards and experience.

Assessments usually fall on some pro and con scale for a factor under review:

That is wrong ....**That is okay**

I don't like the product ....**I like your work**

I disagree with you ....**I agree with you**

We know from experience that critical Assessments are common phenomena and often cause trouble. When spoken, they have a good chance of a negative response. They occur naturally and happen spontaneously. They often show up in a raw form and with some emotional content. The statements can be positive or negative and the energy they produce can be positive or negative.

Here are several guides we have found helpful in dealing with the important and frequently used Speech Act of Assessment.

Monitor Our Own Assessments and How We Use Them

Assessments have to be dealt with because we are hard-wired to make them and they trigger often necessary engagements with others. They affect the moods and emotions of all parties involved.

A lot of time can be wasted arguing and fighting about Assessments. As Don Berwick MD advises: "Run from every fight. Don't ever waste time fighting someone. There is too much positive energy in the world for us to spend our limited time fighting anybody, especially our friends."

Find ways to use Assessments to trigger productive conversations that build relatedness, surface Intent and Assertions, and open the way for Requests and Offers.

Use I-Statements to Make Assessments Easy to Hear and Process

Assessments as Leadership Speech Acts call on us to recognize personal judgments as they show up, and to channel them in positive, informed, constructive, and uplifting ways. One effective method is to use I-statements and to avoid You-statements.

- **I-statement**: "I found the report difficult to follow and had to flow-chart the content."

- **You-statement**: "Your report was badly written and poorly organized."

An I-statement enables the speaker to raise an issue without accusing the listener, thereby reducing the chances that the Assessment will inspire defensiveness. It provides a strategy for giving constructive criticism and for having productive conversations. *Leadership Effectiveness Training* by Thomas Gordon provides great insight and guidance on these practices.

Relying on I-statements is a relatively easy habit to develop. As an emotional signal warns you that you are about to make a potentially critical Assessment, stop! Take 60 seconds and translate it into an I-statement. Work to consciously monitor the effect that speaking an I-statement has on you and on the listener. With the consistent use of I-statements, we will often experience immediate changes in mood, emotion, perspective and line of argument. What might have been undiscussable becomes discussable.

Distinguish Assessments from Assertions

Assertions can be proven through observation and measurement. Assessments are more a matter of informed judgment or opinion. Leaders can take advantage of Assessments to do sense-making. Assessments also help us to initiate engagement, pursue dialogue for clarification, carry out team-building, and more. By contrast, leaders rely more on Assertions to build shared confidence and drive action.

Distinguish Assessments From Opinions

Assessments are judgments on a matter; opinions are beliefs about something. Doctors make assessments of our health; teachers assess our understanding of a course subject. Most of us have a lot of experience in making and receiving Assessments. The same is true with opinions. However, anybody can have an opinion about anything. Recognize and work carefully with Assessments; avoid the use of casual, emotional opinions.

Remember, in using Assessments, be civil, be smart, and avoid fights!

Make it a Habit to Use the Leadership Speech Act of Assessments

What is a recent example of an Assessment I received or delivered that was done in an effective and productive way?

What is an Assessment I could make that might be helpful to a friend or colleague?

Speech Act Practice

Making Civil, Smart Assessments in Annual Performance Reviews

by **Dennis Wagner**

Leaders are often accountable for performance appraisals of those who report to them. These performance appraisals are a type of formal Assessment. The Assessments may often be linked to promotions, bonuses, annual compensation, awards, and more. Performance Assessments can feel high stakes, even when no additional compensation or incentive is attached to them.

We've learned to begin the performance appraisal process with a meeting where the employee performs their own self-Assessment to inform the subsequent Assessment to be conducted by the manager. As employees, we each have our own astute insights into what we do well, the accomplishments and behaviors that we value the most, and the areas where we know we need improvement. We generally know more about ourselves and how we think than anyone else.

As a boss, having a clear line of sight into how our employees see themselves is a powerful way to construct meaningful insights and feedback in conducting the formal performance review. We can affirm portions of the self-Assessment that we believe are on the mark. We may also identify areas that are blind spots to the employee. A self-Assessment also allows each employee to have a voice in the process of their own performance appraisal, and to know that their views are being factored into the formal performance Assessment.

Structuring Self-Assessments with Effective Questions

Effective Questions, another Speech Act detailed in the coming pages, is a useful tool for structuring a performance self-Assessment. Effective Questions for guiding self-Assessments can include the following:

What are your key accomplishments over the last year?

In considering your work over the course of the last year, what are you most proud of?

What aspects of your work matter the most to you?

What are some skill areas or work activities where you want to improve?

How would you like to grow in the coming year?

What assignments, training or other things could assist with your development?

Using our organization's rating scale, what is your own overall self-rating?

How can I be most helpful to you in the coming year?

The process of incorporating self-Assessments into the appraisal process is straightforward:

- Managers provide each employee with a set of Effective Questions like those outlined above;

- Employees are asked to write down their answers and bring them to a one-on-one meeting with their manager;

- Managers meet with each employee to learn their answers to the questions as the key driver for the employee's self-Assessment;

- Managers incorporate employee feedback into their own Assessments and share how this feedback was heard and acted on when they conduct their formal Performance Appraisal meeting and/or documentation with each employee.

Give it a shot. We've learned that these kinds of formal, organizational Assessments have the potential to take us from a process that must be endured to one that is uplifting and helpful for mutual learning and dialogue between the assessor and the assessed.

7. "YES, AND ..."

Accept and Build on the Contributions of Others

Yes, and ... is a statement that works to affirm and build on the ideas and actions of others. The key idea is to look for ways to say *yes* to others and then to use *and* to help bring the things we are affirming into greater alignment with shared purposes.

Leaders say *Yes, and ...* to team effectively and enable group action. *Yes, and...* brings together several ideas that in the moment may appear to have little or no obvious connection. The ideas can sometimes appear to be in competition for attention with whatever we are focused on ourselves.

Yes, and ... seeks to create synergy in work and connectedness among individuals and groups. This is a Speech Act that actively works to mitigate conflict while surfacing potential collaboration where there may have been no apparent possibilities to begin with.

Opportunities for *Yes, and . . .* Solutions are All Around Us

In leadership work, we are often in conversations where people are actively and sometimes aggressively sharing their unique perspectives, stories, recommendations, and more. Because the perspectives and desired ways forward are often quite different in style and focus, we risk being ships passing in the night, totally unaware of or comprehending the other. Our Declarations and Assertions are often met by counter Declarations and Assertions. Our Requests and Offers can be ignored or resisted. Even with a compelling Leadership Story and evidence-based strategies, it can be tough to be heard and to achieve constructive engagement.

Yes, and... as a Mindset has us actively listening for possible connections, with a bias toward agreement, and building on one another's perspectives and contributions. As leaders, when we hear people ready to go into action, but we are not sure how all the ideas, possibilities, and strongly held views mesh, we have learned, more often than not, to try and say *Yes, and ...* and then figure it out later. The "figure it out later" part is important. It is often quite doable—especially after sleeping on it. Insight and perspective can happen overnight!

Yes, and ... takes courage.

Improvisational Comedy is Built on Yes, and . . .

Saying *yes* to the Requests and Offers of others, to their ideas and vision, when they are starkly different from what we may have had in mind, can be uncomfortable or even terrifying. It's comparable to stepping on the stage to do improvisational comedy. It is from this arena of improv that we first gained tactical and strategic insights about the power of the *Yes, and...* Speech Act.

Most of us would not walk out on stage in front of a large audience without a script or preparation and attempt to make the audience laugh for an extended period of time. However, that is exactly what happens in improvisational comedy. Improv is a random, chaotic-looking high-wire act. It sounds like asking for trouble. But there are rules to follow to make this work. When they are not followed, the sketch loses energy and shuts down. The rule of engagement is especially important: have the characters accept everything that is advanced by others. The foundational rule of Improv is essentially to say *Yes, and ...*

It turns out that improvisational comedy has its own Mindset and Method. Malcolm Gladwell pointed this out in his book *Blink: Thinking without Thinking*. Gladwell quotes Keith Johnstone, a well-known teacher of improv: "Bad improvisers block action, often with a high degree of skill. As an example, if one player says something strange, another player may be tempted to negate it." For example, "Let's use your elephant to get to the wedding." Response: "I don't own an elephant." The negation suppresses action. Positive responses open up ways to keep the scene going. The first player has to start over. "Let's use your elephant to get to the wedding." Response: "He's in the back yard and full of gas." The first speaker now has a vivid scene and lots of options to work with.

Non-leaders block action, often with a high degree of skill. Good leaders – good improvisers—develop action.

Yes, *and* ... can move us into action with another person with very different perspectives or assets. Our experience is that there are almost always possibilities and opportunities available in union with others. As dialogue and communication occur, there is often opportunity to realize synergy with the ideas, offers, requests, and resources of others. Maintaining a bias towards *yes* and actively seeking to advance your own *and* provides the building blocks for teaming. The details of how often shows up in the "figure it out later" after we say Yes, *and* ....

The *Yes, and...* Speech Act not only surfaces the building blocks for synergy, it also provides a rewarding and uplifting way of engaging and teaming with others. It is a great tool for positive leadership in life and in work.

**Make it a Habit to Use the
Leadership Speech Act of *Yes, and* ...**

What is an example of a time in the past where I found a way to say Yes to something that I initially resisted –and it turned out well?

Who is requesting support/help from me that could potentially be aligned with something I care about?

Speech Act Practice

We Are Often in Violent Agreement

by **John Scanlon**

In a community setting, a local committee was meeting to complete an environmental action plan. I sat in as part of a visiting team from the U.S Environmental Protection Agency (EPA). At one point a committee person proposed a project. There was brief discussion. Then another person proposed a very different project. The first person apparently felt that this was a rejection and a criticism of his project. He objected to the second proposal and restated his proposal as preferable. The second person emotionally defended his project. They went back and forth, getting more and more agitated. Others joined in on one side or the other. An either/or debate had erupted. The full group was getting very uncomfortable.

The chair turned to the EPA team to ask us to share what we were hearing. I commented that I thought this was an exciting discussion ... and the two parties were in "violent agreement." I was hearing the two parties in agreement on goals and each was passionate about their proposed project or way of achieving the goals. It appeared that there was a lot of support for both projects in the committee. The projects were not competing, they were complementary. There was laughter about the "violent agreement" comment and after some discussion both proposals were added to the plan.

A *Yes, and...* solution emerged from an either/or debate.

8. EFFECTIVE QUESTIONS

Lead Change and Generate Energy, Insight, and Action

An Effective Question is a Speech Act that can help ourselves and others to invent our own constructive responses to situations in ways that align with shared purpose. Effective Questions can become a leader's most valuable tool.

They can be used to lead change, to deal with challenging problems, and to design and conduct meetings. Effective Questions are Speech Acts that produce insight and action. Effective Questions make us think.

Effective Questions are created by using *what* and *how* statements, rather than asking for *yes* or *no* type responses. See the table below for a straightforward guide.

Effective Questions look and sound generative:

- What's working?
- What's causing it to work?
- What can we do more of, better, or differently?

Creating Effective Questions

Start the question with *what* or *how*

- "What works?" "What is the objective?"
  "What are my best ideas for solving this problem?"
- "How can we get this done quickly?"
  "How can we be most helpful?"

Avoid *why* questions. Why tends to take us backwards and often generates justification and defensiveness:

- "Why did you do this?" can make the audience nervous.

**Avoid asking questions that can be answered *yes* or *no*.
These tend to surface opinions, instead of insights and action.**

- "Do you like the new boss?" simply produces an opinion.
- A more Effective Question would be:
  "What do you like about the new boss?"

Follow up by asking, "What else?"

Notice how these questions tend to put us in a positive mood and a creative, open frame of mind.

If there are Effective Questions, there must also be ineffective ones. Ineffective questions tend to focus us on problems, causes and blame. The typical questions can sound like a critical inquiry:

- Do I agree with this?
- Why won't this work?
- Why did they do that?
- Is their evidence solid?

One can argue that these so-called ineffective questions are actually another kind of critical inquiry. Critical inquiry can be useful in some situations, for example, in determining root cause analyses. However, it is the intentional use of Effective Questions that leads to creating insight, connection, shared action, and results. Perhaps most importantly, we can use Effective Questions to lead change in ourselves and others.

Use Effective Questions to Lead Change

Doug Krug, co-author of *Enlightened Leadership*, taught us and many of our colleagues about the power of Effective Questions. Doug points out that leadership is about leading change. We want others to change what they are doing, how they are doing it, with whom they are doing it, how fast they are doing it, and more. Leading change in today's complex and rapidly evolving environments often means helping skilled people to change when they know a whole lot more about their work and their situation than the leader does. Leaders don't have all the answers; they need others to step forward to help provide those answers.

Leaders face an additional challenge with change situations: it's been drummed into us, "people are resistant to change." Don't buy it. It's not true. **We change all the time.** We change our hairstyles, our clothes, our cars, our jobs, the foods we eat, our homes, the cities we live in and much more. People are not resistant to change. We are not resistant to our own good ideas. Think about it—what is the last great idea of your own that you were resistant to?

We are, however, resistant to being changed by others.

While we are creatures of constant change, we can be quite resistant to having changes imposed on us by others: our bosses, our parents, other family members, teachers, team leaders, peers at work, you name it.

What's a leader to do? If we are not resistant to changing ourselves, but are resistant to being changed by others, how do leaders deal with these seemingly contradictory realities? How do we use Language to lead changes for ourselves, our teams, our organizations, our families?

There is a way, an effective Mindset and Method: Use Effective Questions to help ourselves and others invent our own changes. Effective Questions provide a Speech Act proven to help leaders channel the frontline knowledge of others into productive actions, aligned with overarching purposes.

Inventing our own changes is an effective way of embracing the two truths that are in tension:

- Humans are change-friendly; and,
- Humans are resistant to being changed by others.

Effective Questions are the Speech Act that can be used to guide and support the invention of our own changes. When leaders learn to lead with Effective Questions, there is no resistance to overcome. We are not telling others what to do; we are not directing others. In fact, in many cases we will not know precisely what others will hear and do until they do it! How then do we as leaders use questions to move us all in similar directions to a common end?

As leaders, we get to lead in crafting the questions that will help people move in needed directions, in alignment with larger goals and purposes. For example, imagine a situation where we want to build support for a new CEO in our mission organization. We might use questions like the following:

- *What can we do to help the new CEO to succeed on the mission?*
- *What characteristics or qualities does each of us like the most about our new CEO?*
- *What are gaps in his/her skillset where he/she might need us to step in?*
- *What are his/her clear strengths that we can build on together?*

We can use questions like those in the prior page as a deliberate alternative to the common default questions that are often asked when a new leader is named. Examples of common default questions would be:

- *Do we like the new leader's style?*
- *Do we think the new leader has the ability and background to succeed here?*

Answers to questions like these will surface opinions, thoughts and actions that are neither constructive nor supportive.

We can also use Effective Questions to lead in one-on-one situations. Imagine a colleague, co-worker, or a direct report is unhappy about a project or responsibility. Maybe they don't like the task, or maybe they don't believe it will be effective, or maybe they don't want to team with certain people who are necessary colleagues in performing the work. As leaders, the kinds of Effective Questions that we might create to help could be any or all of the following:

- *What are the potential benefits to you and to the larger organization of doing this work well?*
- *What can I do to help make this task more rewarding for you?*
- *How might you reward yourself when this job is complete?*

Answers to any of these questions may be helpful to our colleague. As leaders, we are not neutral observers in the use of the questions; rather, we are actively creating the kinds of questions that will help others to move forward in needed ways and aligned with larger purposes.

Use Effective Questions in Meetings to Help Participants Invent Their Own Next Steps

All meetings are run on questions. Those questions are often unstated. We can lead our meetings and events far more effectively if we get clear on the questions that we want the meeting to be running on. Rather than have those questions surface randomly and unknowingly, we can articulate "the questions to run on" intentionally and proactively by drafting these questions in advance and using them to lead the meeting.

For example, a meeting to profile and spread the best practices of high performing organizations might run on the following kinds of questions:

- What best practices are being used to generate rapid, significant results in our field?
- What do we like about these practices?
- Which of these practices have the greatest applicability to our own organization?
- What actions might we take to adapt and test these practices in the coming week and month in each of our own organizations?
- What would each of us add or change to make the practice stronger?

Getting clear on the fact that these kinds of questions will be answered by both presenters and those in the audience is a powerful way to create a shared understanding of meeting purposes. It also helps to turn passive audiences into active participants as co-generators of answers, actions, and next steps. Responding to questions like those above opens up our participants by inviting them to invent their own solutions and answers to change and action.

Effective Questions enable us to turn a meeting of many people into a super idea-generating and processing machine. By using Effective Questions, we can help audience members to generate their own ideas about how to move forward. By sharing their answers, the audience gains further insight, perspective, and connection. The practice increases the power of the conversation and the degree of collaboration.

Just as Effective Questions can be used to turn meetings into powerful idea-generators, they can also be used to turn meetings into engines for action and progress. Straightforward questions like the following can be used to secure Commitments from participants that generate action and next steps:

- What am I taking from this meeting to apply to my own work by next Tuesday?
- What are the three Commitments for action on the Bold Aim that I can make as a result of what I learned here today?
- Who will I share this best practice with in my organization tomorrow?

There is a wide and exciting range of work that can be carried out in groups by using Effective Questions. Additional ideas and examples of how to systematically use Effective Questions in meetings are described in further detail as part of the leadership Mindset and Method of Pacing Events in the chapter on Roles.

Use Effective Questions to Invent Our Own Solutions and Positive Responses to Problems

Effective Questions are also highly effective ways to process negative or bad things in the moment. We can use them to flip our own perspectives and the perspectives of others when bad things happen to us.

When something unexpected or bad happens (and we know that these things happen all the time), we can ask the incredibly powerful McGann Effective Question: *What is good about this seemingly bad question?*

Paul McGann MD, a national physician-leader and fellow 2016 Sammie Award winner, is courageous, smart, bold, and hard-working. Dr. McGann teamed with us in applying the discipline of using Effective Questions while serving as the Deputy Chief Medical Officer of the Centers for Medicare and Medicaid Services (CMS), the large federal agency that pays for the healthcare of more than half the US population.

Speech Act Practice

The McGann Effective Question

"What is good about this seemingly bad situation?"

Paul McGann, MD

As a self-identified problem-solver with two scientific degrees from the Massachusetts Institute of Technology, Dr. McGann prided himself on being one of the Agency's go-to leaders for difficult and intractable problems. It was in this problem-solver Role that Dr. McGann invented one of the all-time best Effective Questions ever: *What is good about this seemingly bad situation?*

He observed that every day at work, bad things happened. Scary problems would emerge that drained the enthusiasm, energy and confidence of dedicated staff and managers. Dr. McGann equipped himself and our colleagues with the McGann Effective Question to use when one of these big, difficult problems showed up.

Although answers may not come immediately, we have found that if we stick with this question – what is good about this seemingly bad situation?—for five or ten minutes, especially as a group, we will begin to generate and invent answers that help us to shift our perspectives more quickly and to begin to see the potential for positive change. Together, we invent our own positive answers for finding the good things that are almost always present in bad situations.

Through constant, daily use of the powerful McGann Effective Question, we have learned that we need it the most when we believe that the situation is so bad that it won't be helpful. Try it. You'll be glad you did. Other examples of Effective Questions are detailed in the Flip Negative Energy section in the chapter on Being.

There Are Many Ways to Lead Change with Effective Questions

Effective Questions give us an unlimited number of ways to lead change in ways that generate and harness positive energy. We can use Effective Questions to design meetings and help participants to invent their own solutions and actions based on meeting content. We can use Effective Questions in performance appraisals to help those appraised to identify their own strengths, accomplishments, and areas for improvement. We can use them to flip negatives into positives, to generate Commitments and action, and more.

Make it a Habit to Use the Leadership Speech Act of Effective Questions

What is an example of an Effective Question I have encountered, possibly as part of a recent meeting?

What is an Effective Question that I could pose to increase positive energy and a sense of accomplishment as part of an upcoming meeting?

Speech Act Practice

Trying On the McGann Effective Question in a Seemingly Bad Situation

by **Jade Perdue**
Organ Donation
Breakthrough
Collaborative
Learning Session

Jade Perdue is a talented public servant who has always genuinely enjoyed and looked for opportunities to work with, to learn from, and to love children. She once led a major session with an audience of more than 2500 people where she interviewed young children about their organ transplants in front of everyone. Her years of dedicated work on pediatric and adult organ donation helped to make the gift of life possible for thousands of children and other transplant recipients.

It seemed right and fitting to many of her colleagues when Jade became the mother of twins: Benjamin and Indie.

One day, when Indie was about five years old, she decided to do something that she knew she wasn't supposed to do. She grabbed a big handful of Halloween candy, locked herself in the bathroom, and enjoyed a delightful little feast. Problem was, it turned out that Indie wasn't able to unlock the bathroom door.

This problem quickly went from bad to worse. The candy coverup would likely be discovered when Mom was called on to get Indie out of the bathroom. This became a secondary issue when it turned out that Mom was unable to coach Indie into how to unlock the door; she simply was not strong enough to turn the old lock. And, there was no help in sight—Dad would not be home for at least another hour. After 45 minutes of failed effort, Indie was sobbing hysterically.

This is when, out of near desperation, Jade decided to give the McGann Effective Question a try. She said, "Indie, I know you are scared and upset. We will find a way to get you out. While we do that, tell me, 'What's good about this seemingly bad situation?'"

Indie responded the way many of us do when we initially hear this question: "Nothing! Nothing is good about this!"

Mom persisted: "I can think of at least one good thing."

Sobbing abates a little and Indie says, "What?"

Mom: "You can go to the bathroom if you need to! Just think, it would be even worse if you were locked in another room and had to go to the bathroom."

Indie, tentatively: "Yes…that's right. And, if I need to, I can get a drink of water."

Mom: "Atta girl! What else?"

Indie: "I'll be really happy when I get out."

Mom: "Yes!! What else?"

Indie: "And, maybe you will be so glad to see me, all of the candy I ate won't be such a big deal."

After a long silence, Indie followed up with "Mommy, I love you," having come to her own conclusion that this situation, as bad as it was, was not so bad after all. Some good things were present in this seemingly bad situation. Soon after, things got much better—Dad arrived home and was able to climb a ladder into the second story window to free Indie from the bathroom.

This is how it feels to use the McGann Effective Question, *What's good about this seemingly bad situation?* It is often hard to start asking ourselves this question because the situation seems so hopeless. However, once we do, the actual situation begins to be broken down, the problem becomes not so overwhelming; this allows problem-solving to start and potential solutions to emerge. One potentially viable answer leads to greater confidence that there might be another answer. Creativity starts flowing. The answers start coming to us. We get onto the pathway of helping ourselves and others to invent the perspectives and the changes that are needed to work through the seemingly bad situation.

We Flip Negative Energy! Things get better. We get onto an upward spiral where one good thing leads to another.

Develop Our Own Distinctive Language of Leadership

Eight Speech Acts as Leadership Language Habits

The table below summarizes the Leadership Speech Acts that have evolved as a Signature Style for the authors over long careers. The use of action Language has made us far more effective in our chosen work as leaders.

We list in the first column the eight Speech Acts that we frequently use. The second column shows how we see ourselves and other leaders using these Speech Acts. The third column reminds us how to be in the leadership work we choose. These phrases are intended to capture our style in a concise way. They serve as mantras, as repeated phrases and prayers, to strengthen instinctive action that fosters effective habits.

Mastering the Language of Leadership		
Speech Acts	**Leaders Act Through Language**	**Way of Being**
Declarations	Leaders make Declarations to define the world and its possibilities.	Establish the new, changing reality
Assertions	Leaders make Assertions to show evidence of what's possible.	Inspire confidence to act
Requests and Offers	Leaders make Requests and Offers to generate commitments.	Trigger action now to create the future
Commitments	Leaders make and seek Commitments to create the future.	Generate, manage a lot of promises
Acknowledgements	Leaders Acknowledge behavior and achievement to affirm others.	Appreciate in a memorable way
Assessments	Leaders control Assessments to be interpersonally effective.	Be civil, be smart ... avoid fights
"Yes, and ..."	Leaders say *"Yes, and..."* to team effectively and enable group action.	Accept and build on contributions
Effective Questions	Leaders use Effective questions to create productive interactions and lead change.	Generate and harness energy, insight, change and action

Craft Our Own Language of Leadership

At the beginning of this segment, we suggested that you use the Leadership Speech Acts to consider development of your own Signature Style and approach to the Language of leadership. Use your answers to the summary questions provided after each Speech Act segment to inform this process. Use the following table to make an initial assessment of how frequently you use the eight Leadership Speech Acts, and to begin establishing goals for increased frequency—where appropriate and fitting with your own Signature Style.

Ramping Up Our Use of Leadership Speech Acts

Leadership Speech Act	Frequency Of Use: C = Constantly; O = Occasionally; R = Rarely	
To what degree do I currently use the eight Leadership Speech Acts in my Language with others? How frequently do I aspire to use each Speech Act in the near future?	Currently	Near Future
Declarations		
Assertions		
Requests and Offers		
Commitments		
Acknowledgements		
Assessments		
"Yes, and …"		
Effective Questions		

As a next step, we suggest you fill out the table in the adjacent page, using the Mastering the Language of Leadership table on the previous page as a model. Take some time to think about and create your own leadership style guide. And then play with it by asking Effective Questions:

- *What works for me already?*
- *What can I add or change to make it work better?*
- *To what degree do I actually follow the guide?*
- *What can I do in the next several days, weeks, and months to improve my use of Leadership Speech Acts?*
- *What am I intending to achieve in my chosen leadership Role?*

One quick suggested approach:

1. Scan the list of Speech Act types in the first table, Mastering the Language of Leadership. Eliminate those that do not resonate. Consider adding other Speech Acts that you find especially effective (apologies, invitations, greetings, thank yous, others). Use this info to fill in the first column of the following table.

2. Scan the middle column of the first table that defines the leadership actions and impacts. Keep the ones that resonate with you. Consult your answers to the questions following each Speech Act segment. Add other actions that strike you as key to your own unique style. Fill in the middle column in the following table.

3. Scan the last column of the first table. See which phrases capture your own style. Think of expressions you would use with others. Use this information to fill in the last column of the following table.

The Language I Choose to Use in My Own Uplifting Leadership		
Speech Act	Leaders Act Through Language	My Way of Being

This short, quick exercise can give you a quick sense of your own Signature Style and use of Language as a leader. After you set this book aside, continue to experiment with and develop with your own table. Keep revising it as you become more intentional and practiced in the development of your own Language of leadership. We will do more work on other aspects of Signature Style in the final chapter.

LANGUAGE

- Leadership Speech Acts
- **Leadership Stories**
- Access Abundance

Leadership Stories:
Language as a Narrative that Reaches and Engages Others

When we speak, we convey a story about who we are. In that moment we project an identity—our values, our style, our thought processes, the Role we are playing. The audience gets a message. We make an impression. The audience has a reaction, whether expressed or not.

Looking back on our own lives and careers, we now realize that we were often unaware of the identity stories we told about ourselves. Many of us naturally default to a simple set of descriptors when we introduce ourselves: where we grew up, where we went to school, our academic degrees, the organization we work for, and the title of our current position. We use variations of this list in different situations.

However, with intention, we can choose the story we tell in the moment to get the effects we want. Becoming more aware of our identity stories and projecting them with Intent can make us more effective in work and in life.

The Stories We Tell About Who We Are Have an Impact

Leaders tell special kinds of stories. This is an observation that came out of our long relationship with Mark Abramson and the Council for Excellence in Government (CEG). After listening to hundreds of conversations between public and private sector senior executives in Council events, it became clear that there was a countable variety of stories in play. The following table lists 16 types of stories that we identified.

When We Speak We Tell a Story About Who We Are Being			
Types of common identity stories that emerged over several years in hundreds of conversations between Council for Excellence in Government Principals and Fellows			
Organizational Story	**Skill Story**	**Social Story**	**Stress Story**
I am a leader	I am an analyst	I am informed	I am a complaint
I am a professional	I am a technician	I am smart	I am constrained
I am a manager	I am a specialist	I am friendly	I am beleaguered
I am a supervisor	I am a doer	I am a critic	I am a victim

The conversations were between CEG Principals—successful executives with private sector and public sector experience—and CEG Fellows, federal managers on a career executive path. It was common to hear a Principal tell a dramatic story of meeting a serious leadership challenge and then having a number of the federal managers explain why that kind of action was not possible in their situations. Stories of breakthroughs and transformation often triggered reactive stories of limits, such as "I'm a supervisor surrounded by constraints," and "I'm a manager beleaguered with insufficient resources." Initially, the CEG training exchanges were not generating much insight or growth on the public sector side.

People with strong leadership track records were telling what we came to call Leadership Stories. The Council shifted its training program to develop and test a fascinating concept—could people become leaders by learning how to tell Leadership Stories? Our experience with the Principals and the Fellows led us to believe that the prospects were promising. We sensed that some Fellows were already playing leadership Roles, a large number were open to and ready to step into leadership Roles, and others were not inclined to lead but were likely to play other valuable and satisfying Roles. By recognizing and understanding the nature of Leadership Stories, all the Fellows would be helped in their public service careers.

Leadership Stories Have a Structure to Them

We began by deconstructing the stories we were hearing to figure out what made the leadership version so different from other stories of identity or stress. Over time we found seven elements in common. First, the stories were nearly always grounded in a Compelling Vision of the future. That vision was expressed as "the future I stand for." That stand was brought to life by one or more of six other six elements: Defining Moments, Bold Aims, Visualizing the Future, Sticky Messages, Heroes and Heroines, and Moving into Action with Requests and Offers. The seven elements are presented in the following insert as brief scripts with short explanations.

The seven elements are used as a guide on story elements to listen for, but they do not represent a full story. True Leadership Stories are deeply personal and experiential, powerful narratives that emerge naturally in presentations and conversation.

Seven Expressions In Leadership Stories That Make Them Powerful

The power of a Leadership Story is its ability to cause listeners to create possibilities and opportunities for action.

A Leadership Story generates positive energy and net forward motion. It calls forward interest and commitments from those listening.

- **A STAND:** "The future I stand for is …" A leadership stand is a vision of a compelling future that is beyond the current drift of activity.

- **DEFINING MOMENTS:** "An event that made me see this future as an important mission for me is …." A defining moment is a personal experience where we have to make a conscious decision about what we are committed to. It is a Choice that defines me. The event makes the Choice clear.

- **BOLD AIM:** "I am committed to having ___(result) in place by __(date)." A Bold Aim makes it leadership work. The aim exceeds the reach of one person or organizational entity. Bold Aims create attractive campaigns that others want to join. Bold Aims establish places for accountability and create urgency.

- **VISUALIZING THE FUTURE:** "An exciting example of what I envision is …." Leaders share stories that show the future envisioned is possible. These "models that work" are vignettes of others in action producing the kind of results called for in the vision. They inspire and generate courage. Pathways for action appear.

- **STICKY MESSAGES:** "I want to tell you the story of Alexa, my teenage daughter who died last year waiting for her lung transplant that never came." Expressions and stories convey defining messages that stick in peoples' minds. Unforgettable. Easy to recall and pass along. They produce emotional commitment.

- **HEROES AND HEROINES:** "Let me tell you about a person you should talk to and work with." Leaders share the Leadership Stories of others. This happens naturally when "models that work" are presented. The stories are an asset that a leader accumulates and then deploys to build energy, confidence and courage in others. The stories trigger networking and action.

- **REQUESTS AND OFFERS:** "The request I am making is ____; the offer I am making is ___." The work of leadership is generating the future through requests, offers and commitments. Requests and offers produce commitments. In meetings, leaders are often speaking to generate commitments that propel the audience forward into action. Leaders model the request and offer behavior and encourage others to do same. The Leadership Story often has requests and offers embedded in it.

Leadership Stories Are Constructed with Speech Acts

It turns out that the seven story elements are versions of the Leadership Speech Acts. A Leadership Story can be seen as a strong narrative organized around Leadership Speech Acts to engage and enroll others.

One way to develop a Leadership Story is to link several Speech Acts together. An effective sequence is that of Declarations, Assertions, Requests and Offers, and Acknowledgment. These four Speech Acts can serve as the basic structure of a Leadership Story. Each carries engaging content: the vision of the storyteller, descriptions of relevant speaker experiences, evidence that the vision is possible, and actions that can be taken by others.

A Declaration states the future the leader stands for. Speaking the Declaration makes it so. It's what we stand for. To the degree that vision is compelling, it draws others to us. An effective Declaration gets people's attention.

Assertions in Leadership Stories are used to show that the driving situation behind the vision is real and that the vision is possible to attain. We bring forward comparable situations or leading-edge examples of the vision being achieved – somewhere, somehow, someone is often there to guide us. Assertions give the audience a path on which to move forward. They generate courage and confidence.

Building Blocks of Our Leadership Stories	
Leadership Speech Acts	**Leadership Story Elements**
Declarations	Compelling Visions, Bold Aims
Assertions	What works, leading practices
Requests and Offers	Make promises, gather commitments
Acknowledgements	Celebrate commitments, behaviors, results

Requests and Offers secure Commitments to deliver something tangible by a given date. This is the real work of leadership. A leader generates value by bringing others in and helping them to align their energy, assets and platforms with the leadership vision.

Acknowledgment enables us to create heroes and heroines as Commitments are kept. Celebration of those out in front making progress toward the vision is a remarkable source of energy. Their accomplishments can inspire and guide others.

A Leadership Story is a Declaration, backed by Assertions, and followed with the Requests and Offers that generate Commitments. As promises are kept, we Acknowledge how they helped us move toward the vision. The Leadership Story is a highly effective way of calling for action and results.

Four Examples of Leadership Stories in Action

Below are a few shining examples of Leadership Stories featuring Speech Acts that led to transformative change. More detailed analyses of these stories are provided in other chapters.

DON BERWICK MD, one of the principal leaders in crafting *To Err is Human* and the larger follow-on report, *Crossing the Quality Chasm*, delivered a powerful Leadership Story in December of 2004 in his keynote address at the 16th annual Institute for Healthcare Improvement Forum. Based on the Assertions and evidence amassed in these reports, the 100,000 Lives Campaign was born. In a recent leadership development session, Don remarked on his use of Requests and Offers:

"One of the key aspects of the 100,000 Lives Campaign was that we invited organizations to join us. You don't order someone to be in a campaign. You invite them to join you. And the response was electric. I've never seen a bigger outpouring of Abundance, of motivation, and interest as when we announced the start of the 100,000 Lives Campaign,"

SANJEEV ARORA MD, a medical school professor and practicing doctor, saw a way to bring lifesaving care to patients with Hepatitis C in New Mexico. To launch the effort, he spent his weekends and his own resources driving around the state sharing his Leadership Story with local primary care physician groups to enroll them as volunteers in his program.

He declared a Compelling Vision: "We can save your dying Hepatitis C patients." Dr. Arora delivered Assertions about successful treatment and access to knowledge. He made Requests and Offers and, after weeks and months of travel, began to secure Commitments and participation from local doctors. Together, Dr. Arora and participating doctors created Project ECHO, a successful movement that could treat all Hepatitis C patients in New Mexico.

Dr. Arora's story demonstrates that a Leadership Story is much more than a talk about a problem. A Leadership Story is the pursuit of a mission that the speaker is living. It's authentic. There is nothing rote about it.

PAUL O'NEILL was CEO of Alcoa (1987–1999). We encountered Paul in his Role as a Principal of the Council for Excellence in Government. He was well known for having brought Alcoa out of financial trouble by transforming its performance on workplace safety. For Paul O'Neill, workplace safety was not a one-time tactic, it was a lifelong mission.

Paul O'Neil
US Treasury Secretary
2001-2002

A client of ours, the Vice President of Strategic Planning at the US Postal Service, invited Paul O'Neill to speak to the USPS executive committee responsible for developing their nationwide strategic plan. At the time, USPS had nearly one million employees. About 20 people were in the room, with the Postmaster General at the head of the table. Mr. O'Neill was warmly introduced. They were interested in hearing of his experiences with Alcoa.

Paul began by thanking them for sending him their annual report. He held up a thick document and said it was impressive and very useful in preparing for the event. Then he commented:

"I looked through it and, in the appendix, I was pleased to find your occupational safety statistics. As I read them, I saw that the USPS is definitely not third rate in safety, but it is not yet first rate."

Paul O'Neill paused. There was silence for a very long 30 seconds as people tried to parse the last sentence. All of a sudden, the Postmaster General said:

"In the nicest way possible, Paul has just told us that our safety record is second rate."

He was smiling broadly. There was laughter and heads were nodding in the room about Paul's Assessment of the postal service safety record. A spirited discussion about safety broke out. Paul O'Neill discussed Alcoa's union relationships, their finances, worker productivity, and how these all were influenced through their safety campaign. Later that year, the USPS strategic planning exercise focused on workplace safety.

In 2001, Paul O'Neill was named Secretary of Treasury in the Bush administration. We had the opportunity to be in the audience when he gave a talk about the economy and tax cut proposals. In the middle of his talk, he addressed the issue of workplace safety at the Department of Treasury. Much to everyone's surprise, we learned that the Treasury Department had workplace safety problems! For example, workers at the US Mint suffered injuries from the constant and daily operation of equipment used to make coins.

We had first heard O'Neill speak about safety in a Council training session. We were surprised to see the topic show up the way it did in the USPS event and the Treasury presentations. Paul's Leadership Story on workplace safety was something he lived and pursued everywhere he went. His story on workplace safety was grounded in four tested principles: 1) focusing on workplace safety sends a clear and important message to everyone in the organization that you care about its people; 2) organizations that excel in safety practices and outcomes have to become very skilled and effective at the planning and execution of very challenging industrial processes; 3) this highly effective process management capability can be applied to the central business processes of the organization; and 4) sharing the transformation of Alcoa's safety acknowledged that Alcoa had become a recognized industry leader through these practices. Paul O'Neill's focus on workplace safety was central to his Leadership Stories and a highly effective approach to leading organizations throughout his entire career at the Office of Management and Budget, as CEO of Alcoa, and as Secretary of the Treasury.

ANNE H. HASTINGS' story in the chapter on Being relates her experience of starting with no resources or expertise and relying on the hidden Abundance in the world. She sought out and enrolled the many partners she needed to succeed. She found most institutional sources were not organized to help Haiti's rural poor. She became masterful at workarounds, at Flip Negative Energy, and saying *Yes, and* . . . Anne's personal story in Haiti is one of building and managing an ever-growing network of partners and advisors. Many of the important relationships took years to reach fruition. It was never hearing *no* to a Request; instead, it was hearing *not yet*, or the beginning of a longer conversation.

Testimonial to the Power of Leadership Stories
by Dennis Wagner

I first learned of the power of Leadership Stories from John Scanlon back in 1992 while participating in the Fellows training program of the Council for Excellence in Government.

The President and Founder of the Council, Mark Abramson, teamed with John to conduct a one-day event where ~130 Fellows were tasked with sharing our Leadership Stories in small groups. The strongest stories were advanced to larger groups of Fellows for further assessment and refinement. My own Leadership Story was eventually chosen as one of three finalist stories for sharing with the entire group.

Learning from John and others how to authentically share my own Leadership Story has made all the difference in my life and in my career. What we think, what we say, and what we spread to others – these are all leadership Choices. Our Leadership Stories help us to gain greater mastery of making, acting on, and extending these Choices.

Leadership Stories Make All the Difference in Work and in Life

Committed leaders like Don Berwick MD, Sanjeev Arora MD, Paul O'Neill, and Anne H. Hastings use Leadership Stories to generate tremendous benefit in the world. These kinds of stories are available to all of us. Declarations, Assertions, Requests and Offers, and Acknowledgments are powerful and effective building blocks for constructing our stories. Gaining command of the discipline of telling our Leadership Stories is at the heart of leading and living richer, more rewarding lives.

LANGUAGE

Leadership Speech Acts

Leadership Stories

Access Abundance

Choose to Access Abundance

Abundance is a leadership Mindset and Method that gives the domain of Language real power.

Abundance as a Mindset is the view that the resources needed to realize our Compelling Vision are out there in the world and available to us. Some are visible to us, most are initially invisible, some have yet to be made visible, and many are ready to be invented or called into the world. Abundance as a Method is the systematic use of certain Speech Acts and Leadership Stories to surface and secure needed resources. In the absence of an Abundance Mindset and Method, leadership can stall or wither away for lack of resources.

How do we unlock the natural Abundance of the world? How do we obtain the resources we need to achieve our shared vision? What do we need to do to make Abundance happen? The stories of Dr. Sanjeev Arora and Anne H. Hastings, touched on previously, are rich examples of leaders who reached into the invisible and discovered goldmines of Abundance.

Begin By Understanding the Nature of The World's Resources

Generating Abundance requires a basic understanding of the types of resources available to us in the world. At the most basic level, there are four types of resources:

1. Shared Resources that We Own Together With Others;
2. Resources that We Don't Own that are Owned by Others;
3. Resources that We Own Ourselves that are Not Owned by Others;
4. Resources that are not Owned by Others or Ourselves.

Figure A below shows and names the four types of resources and how they relate to each other.

FIGURE A. Understanding Resources
Leaders need to grow the "Shared Resources" needed to achieve the vision.

	Resources Owned by Me	Resources NOT Owned by Me
Resources Owned by Others	1. SHARED RESOURCES Arena of "Team"	2. RESOURCES OF OTHERS
Resources NOT Owned by Others	3. PRIVATE RESOURCES	4. EMERGENT UNKNOWN RECOURCES

1. SHARED RESOURCES include our time with one another in meetings, our relationships, funding we use together, our shared staff resources, partnerships, and more.

2. RESOURCES OF OTHERS are the almost infinite resources that exist in the world. Some of these resources are visible to us. For example, as described earlier in our segment on Intent, when Dr. Arora first began to implement Project ECHO in New Mexico, he realized that primary care doctors and nurse practitioners throughout the state were visible Resources of Others. Based on his own experience in becoming a liver specialist, he believed that he could potentially recruit these clinicians to learn how to provide hepatitis care to their patients.

It is important to also recognize that the world is a very big place—many of the Resources of Others are not initially visible and therefore unavailable to us. As we begin to practice the Speech Acts that unlock Abundance and to work together with others, more of these already existing Resources of Others become visible and available to our team. How this happens is an important insight and part of the method.

3. PRIVATE RESOURCES. A key Private Resource in creating project ECHO was Dr. Arora's own in-depth specialty care knowledge of how to treat patients with hepatitis. Another Private Resource was the time available to him in the second major part of his career—Dr. Arora had decided to allocate this time to giving back to others because he had been so richly blessed with success in the first half of his career.

4. EMERGENT UNKNOWN RESOURCES include things like relationships that are still to be formed, the connections and discoveries that remain to be made, and things that haven't been invented yet. When they emerge and become known, they will initially add resource possibilities to both Private Resources and Resources of Others. Quadrants 2 and 3 in the previous table will grow. Much of that growth will likely become Shared Resources through the on-going Requests and Offers process.

In the case of Dr. Arora's work with Project ECHO, his and his clinician team's successful actions throughout New Mexico paved the way for an organized worldwide network that is now on track to impact the health and well-being of a billion people. These results and the resources to achieve them—this Abundance—were never imagined or predicted when Dr. Arora first launched into action. The resources accessed from this quadrant of previously Emergent Unknown Resources gradually came into being because of new relationships, networks, funding, and technologies that grew out of the initial actions of those working in New Mexico. As specialty physicians in other disciplines became aware of how a liver specialist like Dr. Arora was solving access problems, they began to see possibilities for their own specialties.

A key Role for leaders is to grow the Shared Resources needed to achieve the vision and goals of ourselves and our colleagues. In Figure A, we want the box in the upper left corner to gain resources from the other boxes and grow. Returning to our key question of accessing the world's Abundance, *how do we make Abundance happen?*

Requests and Offers Expand the Pool of Shared Resources

The key to generating Abundance lies in the systematic practice of the two Speech Acts of Requests and Offers that link our own resources with the Resources of Others. Requests and Offers are the Method that helps us to expand the pool of Shared Resources needed to achieve our shared aims and vision.

Figure B shows how Requests and Offers expand the resources available in the Arena of Team where our shared work is performed. The intent of a leader is to grow Shared Resources.

FIGURE B. Requests & Offers Expand Shared Resources

	Resources Owned by Me	Resources NOT Owned by Me
Resources Owned by Others	SHARED RESOURCES Arena of "Team" ↑ Offers Requests →	RESOURCES OF OTHERS
Resources NOT Owned by Others	PRIVATE RESOURCES	EMERGENT UNKNOWN RECOURCES

We can Offer the resources we own, and we can Request the visible Resources of Others that we know. As Commitments are made in response to our Requests and Offers, the boundary of the upper left box moves to the right and the boundary on the bottom of this box moves down. Shared Resources grow because we add things from our Private Resources through Offers, and we add things from the Resources of Others that become available when they agree to our Requests.

As an example of this dynamic, consider how Dr. Arora traveled throughout New Mexico to Request that primary care physicians and nurse practitioners join with him to treat their patients with hepatitis. He simultaneously Offered to coach them in weekly case review sessions, using his time and specialized expertise as a practicing liver specialist. Ultimately 21 clinicians agreed to his Request and took him up on the Offer to train them in how to treat hepatitis patients. In this manner, Project ECHO was born in 2003, and tens of thousands of patients were successfully treated throughout New Mexico over the course of the next several years.

Generate Abundance from the Emergent Unknown Resources

Requests and Offers also unlock the relationships that are still to be formed, the connections and discoveries that remain to be made, the things that haven't been invented yet. Figure C shows the source of the Abundance that is realized from the previously invisible domain of Emergent Unknown Resources. Using Requests and Offers with system and method gives us the ability to surface resources from this invisible place and to access them in service to our shared vision.

FIGURE C. Abundance is the Bonus

	Resources Owned by Me	Resources NOT Owned by Me
Resources Owned by Others	SHARED RESOURCES Arena of "Team" ↑ Offers Requests →	RESOURCES OF OTHERS
Resources NOT Owned by Others	PRIVATE RESOURCES	The Source of Abundance EMERGENT UNKNOWN RECOURCES

How they all show up is often a surprise. But they can and do show up! What the resources will be cannot be precisely defined in advance, but we can discover and access them as they emerge. Knowing this, we can anticipate and be on the lookout for the additional benefits and Abundance bonuses that will naturally emerge from the domain of Emergent Unknown Resources. Our own experience and the experiences of others have taught us that the bonuses will show up in unusual forms that cannot be predicted in advance. Because of this, we need to maintain a mindset of watchful anticipation, flexibility, and action as new possibilities, new opportunities and new assets come into being.

Notice in Figure C how parts of the Emergent Unknown Resource area are now in Resources of Others and parts are in Private Resources. This is an awesome dynamic at work. We see it in the Leadership Stories presented in this book.

Let's return to our example with Dr. Sanjeev Arora and his initial team of 21 clinician volunteers. Over the course of several years, they achieved impressive results on their initial vision for the treatment of patients with hepatitis throughout the state of New Mexico. Dr. Arora documented their results in peer-reviewed articles in national medical journals. Other medical specialty leaders began to see that what was possible with hepatitis could be applied to HIV/AIDS, mental illness, and other forms of specialty care. The Robert Wood Johnson Foundation stepped forward with a grant to help expand Project ECHO in Washington state, and then nationally. Clinicians and governments across the world saw that Project ECHO could be adapted and spread in service to a larger, worldwide vision. Dr. Arora saw and then acted on these Emergent Unknown Resources as they became available to Project ECHO's Arena of Team. The result was a worldwide network that is now on track to impact the lives of one billion people worldwide by 2026.

This is akin to what happened when Dr. Paul Farmer approached Anne H. Hastings and the Fonkoze bank to team with him in co-locating health centers with bank branches. His vision was that Fonkoze would help patients in Haiti who were treated in the health centers to gain the economic footing needed to prevent relapse of their medical problems. Anne H. Hastings was in a constant state of watchful anticipation, flexibility, and readiness to act on this and many other new relationships and possibilities. She did this with nuns, with institutional investors, with other experts in micro-finance, and many others. Whenever new and Emergent Unknown Resources showed up as a result of her constant Requests and Offers to grow the scope and impact of Fonkoze's work to support their clients, Anne seized and acted on them – just as she did with Offers and Requests tendered by Dr. Farmer.

As the new resources spontaneously emerge, there are owners associated with them. These owners are now known and can be engaged in the Request and Offer process. The result is shown in the blue box in Figure C. We now have new Shared Resources in pursuit of the vision – resources that we never would have anticipated when we started out.

We access and generate these Abundance bonuses in the domain of Emergent Unknown Resources by engaging others to support our vision with Requests and Offers, and then by working to find ways to say *Yes, and . . .* to the unusual and unpredictable things that invariably surface as a byproduct of our Offers and Requests in the visible Private Resources and Resources of Others.

Four Ways to Realize the Miracle of Abundance

Making Requests and Offers and generating Commitments increases the resources available to achieve our shared vision. When we couple these Speech Acts with a clear line of sight on the four types of resources, we gain an incredible capability to tap into the natural Abundance of the world. Bring system and disciplined method to this joyous work in the following four key ways:

1. **Start by engaging your own personal circles of influence with your Leadership Story.** Couple this with the Leadership Speech Acts of Requests and Offers to generate Commitments from partners and colleagues who share our vision. Sharing our Leadership Stories can powerfully complement the behaviors of Requests and Offers. In presenting our Leadership Story, we create an identity that our colleagues can respond and link to. We model this behavior for other team members. We expand the shared resources needed to achieve our shared vision.

2. **Act as resources that have been hidden become visible.** As we engage and interact with Requests and Offers in pursuit of our shared vision, we get to know others better. Our network of relationships grows. Our partners bring new circles of influence into play. New circles of influence bring new resources into play. Resources of Others that were previously invisible now become visible and accessible. Our own reputation, influence and capabilities also grow in the domain of our Private Resources. Use Requests and Offers to sweep these newly visible assets into the Arena of Team where shared work occurs.

    Think of the new skills acquired by the 21 physicians and nurses in New Mexico who created the foundational initial success of Project ECHO. As these new resources become visible, we are better equipped to generate new Offers and new Requests.

3. **Spread the Mindset and Method of Abundance to produce exponential results.** Requests and Offers are a team sport. They can be made by every member, every organization that is part of the Arena of Team. Share the methodology of Requests and Offers together with the roadmap of the four types of Resources. Encourage colleagues to grow Shared Resources, and then create the space and time for organized deal-making among team members with each other and with their own networks. This will exponentially accelerate the progress toward our shared vision.

    For example, our team who organized the federal Organ Donation Breakthrough Collaborative profiled in the segment on Intent would frequently create organized deal-making sessions to facilitate Requests, Offers, and Commitments among the several thousand participants who came to national collaborative learning sessions. The Abundance generated by these sessions was truly extraordinary and fueled a tremendous number of actions to propel national increases in organ donation.

4. **Maintain watchful anticipation as a regular state of Being.** Know that unpredictable good things – bonuses – will show up as we engage with Requests and Offers. Coach yourself and others to be looking for these things. There is tremendous truth in the biblical adage of "seek and ye shall find." If you are not watching and anticipating these good things, you may miss them when they show up. We have learned that the opposite is also true: worry is a prayer for the unwanted – the bad things that could happen. Don't spend your time and the time of others worrying. Instead, focus on an approach of watchful waiting action on the many gifts that will come your way. The gifts will come to you—just as they came to Sanjeev Arora and Anne H. Hastings.

Leaders Have the Power to Generate Abundance

Think of it – leaders can choose to generate Abundance! Generating Abundance is a powerful discipline that can be learned, used by each of us to great effect, and deployed together with others to achieve exponential and joyous results. The prior series of graphics about this Mindset and Method, together with examples from the work of Sanjeev Arora MD and Anne H. Hastings, vividly show how leaders launch into action making Requests and Offers to grow the pool of resources available to achieve our shared goals. As we use these two straightforward behaviors to expand our Shared Resources from the visible world, we systematically gain access to resources we never imagined even existed.

"The more we do, the more we can do."

William Hazlitt
English Essayist and Philosopher

As we engage with this mindset and method of Abundance, we will see new ways to deploy our own assets. Our own reputation, influence, and capabilities as leaders will grow. We see how private resources that we control and had not previously offered can become essential and powerful assets to shared work. We see how our resources and knowledge can be combined with those of others in new and generative ways.

The abundant resources of the world can and will flow into our Arena of Team from all three of the other quadrants. Get into the joyous habit of using this incredible leadership Mindset and Method.

Learn About Abundance from Susan McVey Dillon

The following Leadership Story about the Requests and Offers of Susan McVey Dillon provides a compelling illustration of how this leadership Speech Act can generate expected lifesaving results from the visible resources of the world. Sue's story also shows how her initial actions helped produce an ever-expanding cascade of events and results that she could never have imagined, triggering the miracle of Abundance that ultimately helped save tens of thousands of lives over the last two decades. The dynamics of Language and Abundance can be seen in the actions and results flowing from Sue's encounter as a parent with the health care system, and then later as part of a large federal initiative.

LEADERSHIP STORY

Susan McVey Dillon's Leadership Story: Requests and Offers Generate Abundance

Lead with Abundance

Leadership often finds us looking out into a void, with limited or no apparent possibilities, facing tragedy, encountering daunting professional obstacles, or with no clear path in sight. As leaders, we will experience lonely times. Many of us tend to naturally default to a scarcity mindset in these difficult times.

In these stark moments, the Mindset to cultivate is one of Abundance. Abundance is grounded in knowing that the world and the large systems we navigate can behave to our advantage and to the advantage of others. Abundance is the unseen, unpredictable, and often unquantifiable good that can flow from our Requests and Offers.

Susan McVey Dillon, a mother of two children and a teacher, chose to act from a vision of how something good could come from the worst loss a parent can endure, generating an Abundance unforeseen and extraordinary with lasting effect.

Daunting Abundance of the Milky Way Galaxy

A Call from the Hospital

Sue served as a special education teacher in a high school in suburban Pennsylvania. She is a thoughtful, plain-spoken, firm, caring, and practical person. Students with special needs supported by Sue came to learn that she is a no-nonsense teacher with a big heart. Working late one afternoon to offer a few extra hours of tutoring in 1995, she received a phone call from the local hospital that would drastically change her life and that of her family.

Michael D. McVey

Her 14-year-old son Michael had fallen while climbing with a friend after school. She needed to come to the hospital immediately.

When Sue arrived at the hospital, a social worker met her at the door. Her heart sank; she knew that this was not a good sign. Over the course of that night and the next few agonizing days, Sue and her family would learn that Michael had suffered irreversible brain damage from his fall.

He would never wake again; he would never eat again without a feeding tube; he would never breathe without the support of a mechanical ventilator.

After heart-wrenching and prolonged medical discussions over several days, Sue, along with her husband, daughter, and Michael's father, made one of the most excruciating decisions a family will ever have to make. They decided to withdraw mechanical life support and allow Michael to die.

A Clear and Powerful Request

After making this painful decision, and in a moment of great clarity during this extraordinary hardship, Sue informed the medical team that Michael would have wanted to be an organ donor. Michael was an athletic, rambunctious, and deeply caring person. He took genuine pleasure in caring for his friend's baby brother and others. She knew he would want to save the lives of others.

The answer to her Request came back: "That's not possible."

Sue was astonished. "Why not? Except for his traumatic brain injury, Michael's a healthy 14-year-old—his organs could save the lives of others!"

The medical team explained that Michael's case was not a typical organ donation situation, and the hospital was not set up to handle this kind of special case.

In that moment, in a time of great personal pain, Susan McVey Dillon made a clear and powerful Request: "You need to figure out how to make this happen."

Sue knew that going home was not possible for Michael. But somewhere, she reasoned, another mother, in another hospital, would be able to take her son or daughter home if Michael's organs were donated. Sue and her family insisted that Michael's organs be Offered as a lifesaving gift to others.

To their credit, the hospital administrators eventually agreed to explore the possibility. They reached out to the Gift of Life Donor Program in Philadelphia. John Edwards, an experienced donation coordinator with Gift of Life, was sent to consult on an organ donation opportunity with the hospital and the family.

After an initial Assessment, Edwards and the Gift of Life team explained that Michael's case presented a special circumstance called Donation After Circulatory Determination of Death (DCDD). Organ donation typically occurs when a patient has experienced brain death. In Michael's case, death was anticipated to occur after life support was removed and his circulatory system ceased to function. Organ donation in these more specialized cases requires special protocols and more refined medical procedures.

Edwards and the Gift of Life leadership team huddled and made the decision to support Sue's family and the hospital team in enabling Michael to become a lifesaving DCDD donor. An emergency meeting of the hospital Ethics Committee was convened to review the existing policy and to augment it with the proven DCDD guidelines from other parts of the country. At that time, only two of 58 Organ Procurement Organizations in the nation were supporting donation from donors who died in circumstances like Michael's. The other two procurement organizations served hospitals throughout most of Wisconsin and in Pittsburgh. Special clinical protocols would need to be adapted from these models.

Sue, the hospital, and the Gift of Life team worked together to allow Michael to become an organ donor. His donation would go on to save multiple lives, just as Sue and her family had expected.

A completely unexpected Abundance manifested several years later when Susan McVey Dillon had the opportunity to meet Santos Felix, a father of young children. When Sue insisted that the hospital find a way for Michael to become an organ donor, she knew in her heart that Offering Michael's organs for transplant would allow other very sick people to go home to their loved ones.

Left to right:
Santos Felix,
Susan McVey Dillon,
John Edwards,
and Avi Shaked,
transplant surgeon

Santos, as a recipient of Michael's liver, was able to go home to his mother, his own sons, and to his extended family.

In the darkest days of their lives, dealing with the sudden loss of a vibrant loved one, Susan McVey Dillon and her family made Requests and Offers that would generate a tremendous Abundance for others, saving and enhancing five lives:

- Santos received a liver transplant;
- Two other patients received life-saving and enhancing kidney transplants;
- Two other patients received the gift of sight.

Abundance is Seen in the Ripple Effect of Requests and Offers

While Sue and her family had expected that Michael's gifts would save lives, they never imagined the unexpected and unpredictable ripple-effect that their Request and the Offer of Michael's organs would generate.

In addition to the unexpected joy of meeting Santos, Sue and her daughter became organ donation advocates and spokespersons for the Gift of Life Donor Program in Philadelphia. Additionally, inspired by the lifesaving results of Michael's case, Howard Nathan, President and CEO of Gift of Life, made the decision to proactively reach out to other hospitals in their service area throughout eastern Pennsylvania, Delaware and surrounding areas to establish the necessary procedures to enable Donation After Circulatory Determination of Death (DCDD) as a standard practice in their Organ Procurement Organization (OPO) and affiliated hospitals.

Howard M. Nathan
CEO, Gift of
Life Donor Program

Howard Nathan is a senior executive and leader who exudes personal warmth. He listens carefully, laughs easily, always has positive things to say of others, enjoys working through challenging situations, and is a walking history book of the people and progress of the global field of organ donation and transplantation. Howard also leads boldly. The Philadelphia-based Gift of Life Donor program became the third of 58 OPOs in the nation to standardize the practice of DCDD. Hundreds of lives would be saved because of the expanded organ donations enabled by Gift of Life.

All this, the result of a firm Request uttered by a mother determined to help others: *You need to figure out how to make this happen.*

The lifesaving leadership and actions of OPOs in Wisconsin, New England, and Pennsylvania caught the attention of the federal government's Department of Health, and Human Services. Virginia "Ginny" McBride, a forceful and dedicated Intensive Care nurse in the federal government's organ donation and transplantation division, had been working as an Improvement Advisor as a member of a small federal team.

Virginia "Ginny" McBride
Collaborative Improvement Advisor

The Health and Human Services team had initiated a large, national quality improvement initiative called the Organ Donation Breakthrough Collaborative (profiled in further detail in the Intent chapter) to generate rapid increases in organ donation, designed to spread the best practices of the highest performing OPOs and trauma centers in the nation. The Collaborative had become the centerpiece of a series of initiatives supported by Tommy Thompson, Secretary of Health and Human Services in Washington, DC. Secretary Thompson had come to his post in the nation's capital determined to increase organ donation, based on his successful experience as an organ donor advocate while Governor of Wisconsin.

Participating in this large, fast-moving federal initiative were 40 of the nation's 58 Organ Procurement Organizations and 136 of the largest trauma centers in the country. Ginny, with her deep experience and strong connections throughout the nation's organ donation and transplantation community of practice, saw an opportunity to use one of the Collaborative's big learning sessions to showcase the work of Howard Nathan's team at Gift of Life Donor Program.

The Collaborative provided a perfect venue for showcasing how making Donation after Circulatory Determination of Death more readily available would enable families like Sue's to save lives.

Ginny and her federal colleagues invited Howard and his team to fly to Dallas to present at a learning session where more than 1,000 clinicians and leaders from the OPOs and trauma centers would meet to share, study, and adapt the best practices of high performers. Collaborative Learning Sessions were organized as Pacing Events, where education and information transfer are always accompanied by deliberate work to secure Commitments for actions and next steps from participants.

Howard brought Susan McVey Dillon along as part of his team.

Tommy Thompson
Former Secretary of Health

A Call to Action

Sue's plenary keynote speech in January of 2004 before this group lasted only about seven minutes. She spoke of the phone call she received while tutoring after school that fateful afternoon. She told them about her rambunctious and loving Michael. She described the struggle with the hospital to enable Michael's gift of life. She described meeting Santos and how he had arranged for her to fly to Puerto Rico to meet his own mother. In the practical, thoughtful cadence of a teacher, she expressed her surprise and dismay to learn that most of the nation's largest trauma centers and their affiliated OPOs did not have the protocols and medical procedures in place necessary to enable lifesaving Donation after Circulatory Determination of Death for families like her own.

Sue ended her speech with a Request:

I'm a Special Education teacher. In my classroom, the words "I can't" and "I won't" are not allowed. I understand the miracles that flow through each of your hands every day, and **I expect no less from each of you.**

The Dallas hotel ballroom crackled with emotion and energy. The entire audience rose in extended applause, a resounding yes to Sue's Request for their increased action to make Donation after Circulatory Determination of Death part of their work on organ donation.

Organ Procurement Organizations and Hospitals Act

Following Sue's compelling presentation in Dallas, Donation After Circulatory Determination of Death increased dramatically in 2004 and subsequent years:

Year	DCDD Donors	Percent Increase
2003	270	
2004	393	46%
2005	564	44%
2006	642	14%
2007	781	22%

Each of the DCDD donors in the table above saved or enhanced as many as two or three different lives. And, once all the nation's OPOs and transplant centers developed capability and experience with DCDD donation and transplantation, the numbers continued to grow. Today, nearly one-third of all deceased organ donations in the United States come from DCDD donors. In 2022, there were 4,776 DCDD donors. Sue's leadership actions resulted in new, lifesaving policies in a hospital, spread across a region of the country, and ultimately impacted the entire national health care system.

The lifesaving Abundance flowing from Sue's Requests has helped save more than 46,000 lives through DCDD transplantation since Michael's gift of life in 1995 and Sue's plenary speech in 2004. She never imagined that the lifesaving bonus of Abundance from her actions on organ donation would help to save tens of thousands of lives.

Unexpected and Unpredictable Abundance

There is a comfort that eventually comes to bereaved families who choose to embrace organ donation for their deceased loved ones. Sue and her family were able to experience this comfort by knowing that Michael's donation gave the gift of life and sight to five others. The consequences of this life-giving action were predictable. But the Abundance of their decision did not stop there, and arrived in ways they would never have predicted.

Unexpected Abundance: A Leadership Calling

- Sue met Santos, the recipient of Michael's liver, personally seeing the lifesaving impact of her son's gift of life;
- Santos arranged for Sue to travel to his home in Puerto Rico so she could meet his Mom and family members. After learning more about the circumstances of the gift that saved his life, he wanted Sue to meet "the mom who got to take her son home." He even convinced the airline where he worked that because of the organ donation, Sue was now his "family" and was able to obtain steeply discounted first class tickets for her;
- Sue and her daughter added whole new dimensions to their lives as organ donor advocates and activists for the Gift of Life Donor Program;
- Sue was called on to serve as a national leader for Donation After Circulatory Determination of Death.

Unexpected Abundance: An Improved and Expanded National System

- Donation After Circulatory Determination of Death became a new standard practice across the nation for all Organ Procurement Organizations;
- Tens of thousands of lives have been saved as a result of this expansion;
- Lives continue to be saved today from the policies and practices that Sue's Requests and Offers helped to trigger.

Authors' Reflections on the Abundance Precipitated by Susan McVey Dillon

Abundance in The World is Accessed as Others Join Us in Response to Requests and Offers

Susan McVey Dillon's impact on that influential audience of organ procurement organization and large trauma center leaders and clinicians was transformative. Despite the thousands of medical and health system professionals in the organ donation and transplant field doing outstanding work every day, it took a mother and special education teacher to trigger the system into moving to a higher level of donation performance.

Her story shows how Abundance is accessed. She is seen moving through three levels of increasing leadership influence. At each level a larger circle of influence appears:

LEVEL 1. *Individual Defining Moment.*
Sue's Request and Offer on Michael's death creates a Compelling Vision for Donation After Circulatory Determination of Death (DCDD) that moves the local hospital and OPO into action;

LEVEL 2. *Organization Commitment.*
The experience with Sue moves the Gift of Life to join two other OPOs in practicing DCDD and becoming a champion for it across the OPO and donor hospital networks;

LEVEL 3. *National System Transformation.* The Organ Donation Breakthrough Collaborative provides a platform to move all OPOs and large donor hospitals to adopt the practice of DCDD. Sue's story energizes the national community.

As we read Sue's story, we see the dynamics that surface Abundance:

- Leadership circles of influence committed to DCDD expand;
- A Compelling Vision leads to rising action as more players make Requests and Offers;
- Necessary enabling technology and infrastructure are developed and become available.

LEVEL 1. ***Individual Defining Moment.*** Susan McVey Dillon made Choices around Michael's death that demonstrate the Language of leadership in action. Initially she was operating at an individual level. She asked herself an Effective Question: *What good could come out of this tragic situation?* Her answer created a Compelling Vision of her son as a donor, helping other mothers to take their children home from a hospital. This vision motivated Sue to stick with her initial Request. Sue used her circle of influence as Michael's mother to address the needs of other families. A Request was made to the hospital; when the initial response was *no*, Sue treated the answer as the beginning of a longer conversation.

Soon the hospital reached out for advice. The Gift of Life OPO was brought in and its coordinator, John Edwards, together with CEO Howard Nathan, came into action. Another organization was now engaged. Based on the example of two other organ procurement organizations, Howard and John made Assertions that it was possible for Michael to become an organ donor. They generated a positive strategy with the hospital. Together, the hospital and Gift of Life respond *yes* to Sue's Level 1 Request and Offer.

LEVEL 2. ***Organization Commitment.*** Operating at the Organization level, Howard Nathan then made the new protocol part of his organization's vision and standard operations. With Michael D. McVey as a defining case, Donation After Circulatory Determination of Death was installed in the Gift of Life's region throughout Eastern Pennsylvania and Delaware. Gift of Life was then able to Offer the opportunity to give the gift of life to more families.

LEVEL 3. ***National System Transformation.*** The practices and benefits flowing from work at Gift of Life attracted the attention of the Federal agency staff and the national Organ Donation Breakthrough Collaborative. Susan McVey Dillon found herself on a national stage, using Requests and Assertions to generate Commitments across a vast Network of trauma centers and organ procurement organizations, and became a leader and spokesperson for the adoption of Donation After Circulatory Determination of Death practices across the entire nation.

Leaders Can and Do Choose to Deliberately Access Abundance

Leadership does not always leave visible and lasting footprints. We can lose sight of how the changes happened. Those who come after the change see the result but not the cause. The lessons about how to create access to Abundance are lost. Many of us default into Mindsets of scarcity and limits.

The Abundance dynamic that created 20-year increases in DCDD involved hundreds of players stepping into leadership Roles at different times. Michael's death and Susan McVey Dillon's actions were important drivers. Googling the topic will not pull up the Pacing Events or Defining Moments that moved people into action on the national work to increase organ donation. Susan McVey Dillon and Gift of Life will not show up.

But having been there personally, we witnessed and now better understand the leadership Roles and forces that were in play. The journey began with a defining moment, a family decision rooted in tragedy that ultimately took the larger system off its current drift and onto a more hopeful trajectory for thousands of people awaiting organ donation. Howard Nathan's leadership on Donation after Circulatory Determination of Death, and Susan McVey Dillon's plenary speech in Dallas, both wielded an extraordinary impact on a gathering of the nation's top specialists in trauma and organ donation. Something extraordinary happened because everyone who needed to act showed up in the right place at the right time, hearing Sue's Request and making Commitments to create a new and better future for families and patients in their hospitals.

Sue's Leadership Story demonstrates how the systems in which we navigate can work naturally to extend our reach and impact. The leadership Mindsets and Methods profiled in this book show us how to manage and provoke systems to achieve great things.

Susan McVey Dillon and her family knew that Michael's gift of life could potentially save the lives of several other people. However, they had no way of knowing or anticipating the larger universe of unknown and unseen resources that their bold and selfless actions would unleash. They will never recover the loss of Michael, but they have helped save and enhance the lives of many thousands of other people.

The miracle of Abundance lies with the invisible, unseen resources that are unknown to us. Abundance lies with people we have not met, assets we have never heard about, things that haven't been invented yet, relationships that are still to be formed, the connections and discoveries that remain to be made. Our Requests and Offers trigger access to these unseen resources.

The natural Abundance of the universe is available and accessible. The ability of leaders to intentionally trigger the unseen Abundance through Requests and Offers may be one of the best secrets in life. We should let everyone in on this incredible secret.

Choose to Speak
the Language of Leadership

We can choose to use our Language to help ourselves and others to lead more effective, more harmonious, more joyous, more abundant lives.

We can choose to use powerful and uplifting Speech Acts like Declarations, Assertions, Acknowledgments, Requests, Offers and more. With attention and practice, we can screen out Speech Acts such as blame, insults, worries, complaints, and others that take ourselves and others downward. *Yes, and . . .* can become a natural habit for teaming and aligning with the ideas and contributions of others.

The examples of Susan McVey Dillon, Paul O'Neill, Anne H. Hastings, Sanjeev Arora MD, Don Berwick MD, Paul McGann MD, Jade Perdue, Tracy Washington-Enger and Little Mouse show us what's possible when we become practiced and effective in the use Leadership Stories. The Language of these leaders can help us grow our mastery and confidence in creating and evolving our own Leadership Stories.

Our Language can help us to access and deploy the natural Abundance of the universe. We can deliberately ramp up our use of Requests and Offers to access visible resources to trigger the invisible actions and contributions of many others. Resources that were previously invisible will become visible and available to us and others.

Our Choices in the domain of Language can lift up ourselves and those we touch in our work and our lives. Choose to use Speech Acts and Leadership Stories and to intentionally access the natural Abundance of the world.

Help thy brother's boat across, and lo!
Thine own has reached the shore.

Hindu Proverb

We Choose Our Leadership
ROLES

Organizational effectiveness requires us to perform the leadership role— and other roles. Leaders have to get good at switching.

KEVIN O'CONNOR
President and CEO
LifeCenter NorthWest
2010-2022

ROLES

Role Switching

5 Dimensions of Action

Pacing Events

The Role of Leader, by definition and out of necessity, requires a special agility in a cooperative effort. Choosing to lead requires knowing how to navigate and switch among several other essential Roles. It calls for boldly leading across multiple dimensions of action. And it challenges us to be present with our Compelling Vision throughout every engagement opportunity, creating a format and a pace to generate the commitments that will lay the groundwork for extraordinary results.

Each of these characteristics of leadership gives us a Mindset and Method to work within the Roles Domain. We refer to these Mindsets and Methods as Role Switching, 5 Dimensions of Action, and Pacing Events.

Role Switching: At least four distinct Roles are present in most cooperative efforts: Observer, Administrator, Manager, and Leader. Each of these Roles is essential, and each calls for different levels of accountability and responsibility at different junctures. Very often the Role of Leader turns out to be lacking, leaving us in disharmony and frustration. The status quo prevails. As Leaders, it is critical to discern which of the Roles is called for and then to switch among them depending on the constantly evolving demands of any cooperative enterprise.

5 Dimensions of Action allow us to embrace accountability across well-established Role boundaries which we define as *Subordinate, Hierarchical, Collegial, Process,* and *Public*. Our leadership Intent will expose us to a potentially daunting field of bosses, employees, internal departments, external partners, suppliers, customers, auditors, and other stakeholders whose assigned Roles will influence our work in ways that extend beyond our formal responsibilities. This clear and powerful Mindset and Method can help us reach beyond the one or two dimensions of action we are typically drawn to or that may be formally embedded into our job descriptions, while helping us to understand and function within leadership accountabilities we may find less attractive.

Pacing Events: Many of us lament how much of our time is wasted in meetings. One-on-ones, working sessions, task forces, staff meetings, large-scale professional conferences in-person or virtual, are a just few of the many ways we strive to get the work done. Pacing Events are an approach to organizing our meetings with the use of several straightforward tactics that generate positive energy, voluntary commitments, uplifting progress, and results.

Leadership Stories that Highlight Choices in the Domain of Roles

Three Leadership Stories in this chapter demonstrate the practical application of Role Switching, 5 Dimensions of Action, and Pacing Events in the Roles Domain.

Dennis Wagner recounts how traditional professional education and management training can end up blocking the path to leadership Roles. We will see how Dennis undergoes an innovative professional development program and emerges with a transformative set of leadership tools. Organizations tend to silo leadership potential into narrowly defined Roles such as administration or management. An Intent of this book is to release that tamped-down talent through the method of Role Switching.

In our feature Leadership Story, John Chessare relates how as CEO of a large healthcare enterprise, he engaged his Board, his executive team, and thousands of employees in organizational transformation. Ultimately, this transformation was recognized with the Malcolm Baldrige Award, a prestigious national achievement for performance excellence. We follow how Dr. Chessare made use of Role Switching and the 5 Dimensions of Action, creating responsibility for quality and excellence throughout the workforce while generating extraordinary and sustainable results.

The use of Pacing Events is highlighted in Dennis's case study of transforming a straightforward national meeting into a far more comprehensive and ambitious healthcare initiative to improve the health and safety of newborns. This case study demonstrates how effective leadership work revolves around securing voluntary commitments while also illustrating a powerful way to exercise discretion.

The international applicability of Pacing Events is shared in the case study featuring Brenda Doroski and John Mitchell of the US Environmental Protection Agency and their campaign to increase global use of improved cookstoves in the world's poorest households. Steven Chen of the University of Southern California School of Pharmacy recounts how adopting the practice of Pacing Events has become foundational to his own Signature Style.

Attending to the Domain of Roles helps us to see and act on the unique nature of leadership while interacting with and inhabiting other critical Roles of a cooperative enterprise. The lens of Role Switching gives us a powerful tool for assessing the overall design of the enterprise in place and for ensuring accountability. 5 Dimensions of Action and Pacing Events enable us to grow the accountability we need by effectively partnering with larger systems around us and by organizing cooperative enterprises that produce meaningful shared results.

ROLES

Role Switching

5 Dimensions of Action

Pacing Events

Switching Among Four Roles
For Different Results

Defining A Cooperative Effort

Cooperative enterprises provide us the opportunity to perform in four distinct and valuable Roles: Observer, Administrator, Manager, and Leader. The four are defined in this chapter as personal Choices, not positions conferred by hierarchy, job title, or authority. Each Role brings with it specific intents, skill sets, and outcomes—*insight, process, results, and commitments*—outlined in the chart below. Each is usually time-limited and transitory, requiring us to master performing in one Role for a limited amount of time before switching to another as the need arises.

Four Key Roles, Four Different Outcomes, and Ways of Being in Action	
Observer	*Insight*. The Observer looks at a situation to understand and gain insight. Work is sense-making. The Observer's challenge is to be descriptive, accurate, reliable, and insightful.
Administrator	*Process*. The Administrator operates in a known world with control over resources being deployed, carrying out procedures and activity through reliable and efficient process.
Manager	*Results*. The Manager orchestrates a set of resources to create the time-bound, high-value outcome or results, controlling the uncertainty of how the resources come together.
Leader	*Commitments*. The Leader begins with the transformative end in mind but without all the means to achieve that end. The leader's vision guides the generation of commitments—relationships, resources and solutions—needed to achieve the end.

Our education, training, temperament, and the demands of our work can result in our being thrown into a Role without any intention on our part. However, as we become more conscious of the distinct Roles and our inherent skill sets, we can purposefully choose the Role we most naturally align with. And as we learn to appreciate the Roles that others choose, we can become more agile in switching to different Roles for maximum results.

Successful collaborative efforts require that the overall effort be driven by the right Role at the right time. When a misaligned Role is driving a situation or a key Role is missing, the effort falters. A large conference with thousands of attendees, travel arrangements, and breakout sessions calls for administrative skills. An organizational Bold Aim in need of resources and partners calls for a person with leadership skills. Ideally, the assets of an insightful Observer, an efficient Administrator, an effective Manager, and a generative Leader would be available in all of our cooperative endeavors.

Hierarchy or bureaucracy is one way to assign these Roles in a coherent, thoughtful manner. Establishing diverse teams of members with multiple perspectives and skill sets is another way to make sure the ideal assets are in place. Learning to master all four Roles and to switch at critical junctures is still another way to ensure that our cooperative enterprises and initiatives thrive.

We can understand key distinctions among the Roles of Observer, Administrator, Manager, and Leader from three points of view: each Role represents different combinations of *accountability* and *responsibility*; each Role is driven by different correlations of *what we know* and *what we don't know*; and each Role represents *different kinds of results we can commit to*.

In the following sections, we examine each of these distinctions to illustrate the defining differences and how they can integrate to create successful leadership enterprises. We end by noting how we can continuously assess the situations we are in to make the Role structure stronger and more effective.

Four Ways To Deploy Accountability and Responsibility

Accountability and *responsibility* are often used interchangeably. However, in an executive training session conducted several years ago by the Council for Excellence in Government, we encountered private sector executives who drew powerful distinctions between accountability and responsibility in describing their own Roles.

Accountability was defined as committing to deliver a result. Responsibility was defined as control over certain resources. As we listened to these senior executives detailing their experiences, a pattern emerged that helped distinguish the varying level of accountability and responsibility between the four Roles.

Four Roles With Differing Accountability and Resources

	Accountable For An Outcome	Responsible For Resources
Observation		
Administration		●
Management	●	●
Leadership	●	

The Observer delivers insight. In this Role there is little or no accountability for results and little or no responsibility for resources. The Observer's value is in generating insight that can be applied in the work of the other Roles. Like a fan in a stadium studying his or her team on the field, the Observer will have opinions and emotions about what is happening on the field. They may be vocal and may sound accountable and responsible, but they are only observing, not playing or even coaching. In organizations, Observers often show up as professional evaluators, auditors, and consultants.

The Administrator delivers efficiency and reliability, deploying resources he or she is responsible for, but is generally not accountable for producing a larger outcome. Consider the different Roles in building a home. An electrician or a plumber is responsible for installing the appropriate system according to the design and local codes, but they are not accountable for the finished saleable house. The Administrator goes by the book. The plumber and electrician follow protocols and rules, meet standards, and adhere to schedules. In larger organizations, Administrators often have titles such as budget comptrollers, chief operating officers, and human resources specialists.

The Manager delivers defined results with given resources. Management is accountability joined with responsibility. The Manager has the resources needed to deliver the agreed-upon outcome on time. The outcome is something valued beyond the activities involved. The general contractor of a home-building project is accountable for delivering a finished house that is compliant with building codes, using a blueprint, subcontractors, and budget. The Manager is responsible for dealing with all the uncertainty of managing a large number of independent pieces to come together on schedule, meeting requirements to create the intended outcome.

Management is an intensely studied field and a well-defined profession. Colleges and universities offer degrees in fields such as Management and Business Administration. Managers are expected to deliver the promised results. As Managers, we are often advised that if we take on a new accountability, we need to make sure we have the budget, staff, and authority that are needed to deliver on the accountability. The rule is to under-promise and over-deliver. Put differently, a management mentor would counsel, "Don't take the job unless they give you the staff and the budget to get the job done."

The result of management is value-added: the delivery of an expected product that has value beyond the resources that were used to produce it. Not surprisingly, most line and project managers in organizations are performing in traditional management Roles.

Leaders deliver on Bold Aims through Commitments. Leadership is accountability without the sufficient responsibility. Leaders assume accountability for Bold Aims such as "putting a man on the moon and returning him safely before the decade is out." Leaders commit to and deliver on challenging outcomes, often in the absence of a blueprint or resources to achieve them.

It is fair to ask: How can anyone do that? Why would anyone take that on? The Role of Leader challenges the traditionally taught rules of management and administration that most of us have been steeped in. Understanding this amorphous, risky, and challenging dimension of leadership is a powerful initial step in consciously and intentionally getting comfortable with what is often an uncomfortable accountability. Naming it is one of the first steps in taming it.

By choosing a Bold Aim, a Leader creates a need for accountability and responsibility that does not yet exist. The work of leadership is to fill in that empty field of necessary accountability and responsibility by securing Commitments from others. As the Leadership Stories in this book attest, partners can and will emerge, committing to the leadership enterprise and contributing by performing in one or more of the four Roles.

Four Ways To Work With Knowledge

Professionally, we are assigned Roles based on our knowledge and experience. The Role of Administrator requires a very specialized knowledge, but the Roles of Observer, Manager, and Leader have less to do with specialized knowledge and more to do with knowing how to secure and deliver it.

Within each Role, there are different levels of awareness of our own knowledge and the knowledge of others:

- **Don't Know** what we **Know (DKK)**
- **Know** what we **Know (KK)**
- **Know** what we **Don't Know (KDK)**
- **Don't Know** what we **Don't know (DKDK)**

Four Roles, Four Different Relationships with Knowledge

Observation ....Don't know what we know (DKK)

Administration .....Know what we know (KK)

Management..........Know what we don't know (KDK)

Leadership..............Don't know what we don't know (DKDK)

Don't Know what we Know (DKK) is associated with the Role of Observer. DKK is to realize we know something when we see it. Observation brings it into view. Something that was out-of-sight is now in-sight. It often shows up first as our "gut feeling" or intuition about something. As we observe carefully, intuition and recall kick in. When we want to know what is going on and make sense of it, we become an Observer. Just go look—conduct a site visit, do research, sit in the stadium, observe the construction site. DKK is about attention, description, and accuracy.

Know what we Know (KK) is associated with the Role of Administrator. KK means we know what we need to know to do the job. We have command of the steps, protocols, and rules. The knowledge is present and at hand. There are no fundamental unknowns. The focus is on execution. In the home-building example, the electrician and the plumber administer a set of standard processes. One knows electricity, the other plumbing. They are each licensed to operate in their trade by knowing and following very defined sets of protocols. KK is about reliability and efficiency of process.

Know what we Don't Know (KDK) is associated with the Role of Manager. KDK is about orchestrating the parts to create value. KDK means we know what must be done, but there are parts of the undertaking that we don't know how to perform. All the necessary steps can be identified. But there is significant uncertainty in how the undertaking comes together. The general contractor knows that electricity and plumbing are necessary but is often not able to perform these functions themselves or to properly evaluate their execution. The Manager hires specialists to perform all these known unknowns, and then hires inspectors to make sure they are properly executed. The Manager is working with all the elements known to be necessary to achieve a successful home-building enterprise. The finished product is worth more than the resources used to create it.

Don't Know what we Don't Know (DKDK) falls within the Role of Leader. Leadership begins with a vision of a compelling future, but without knowledge of how to achieve that future. It is unknown who will join the effort or precisely what resources will be necessary and available or how best to achieve the vision. The Leader must operate in the arenas of discovery, innovation, and transformation. Leaders figure out how to do by doing. In home-building, a developer looks at a piece of land and imagines building a community with dozens of homes. At that moment, the developer typically does not know what is underground or in the immediate area to confound or support the vision. The developer does not know who will step forward with the financing, purchase agreements, approvals, design, or execution. Knowledge surfaces by moving forward toward the vision. Roadblocks and breakdowns that surface simply define the new and emerging job that needs to be performed. DKDK is about systematically encountering the unknown, and then creating new possibilities and opportunities to deal with the emerging, unpredictable realities.

Four Ways to Choose Purpose and Results

Every Role in a cooperative effort has a different purpose and delivers a different result. The table below summaries the distinctions. The Role distinctions enable us to understand how and when to choose leadership and how leadership creates situations that call for the other three Roles. Switching among Roles as a leadership Mindset and Method captures the true transformative nature of leadership work. The cooperative enterprise often requires all four Roles to be in play over time.

By choosing to deploy a specific Role, we are committing to pursue an intended future. The following series of charts visually illustrates the Choices the four Roles offer us about the future.

Four Roles with Different Purpose and Outcome Characteristics		
Roles	**Purpose**	**Outcome Characteristics**
Observation	Insight	Possibility, Opportunity
Administration	Process	Efficiency, Reliability
Management	Results	Realistic, Predictable
Leadership	Commitments	Transformative

The graph below to the left sets up defining factors that go into Choices we make about the future we want. The horizontal axis is time, from today out into the future. The vertical axis represents the value we deliver into the world, with the red box at **Today** representing the value we can deliver in the present moment. Value is established by those who in some way want, live with, and use the result produced to address the compelling needs of others.

Today we are ready to make a Choice about the future we want to see. What is the nature and degree of value we want to realize in the future?

A common yet important Choice can be to see the future simply as a continuation of the present, or "business as usual," as depicted in the graph to the right. The Administrator Role delivers business as usual. The value delivered in the future will be much the same as today by administering the resources that the Administrator currently commands. The result is reliable and efficient, and we can commit to it with great certainty by Knowing what we Know **(KK)**.

Note that good administration is essential for most enterprises. A goal of many leadership efforts is ultimately to establish a new higher-value, better-performing production system that is well-administered.

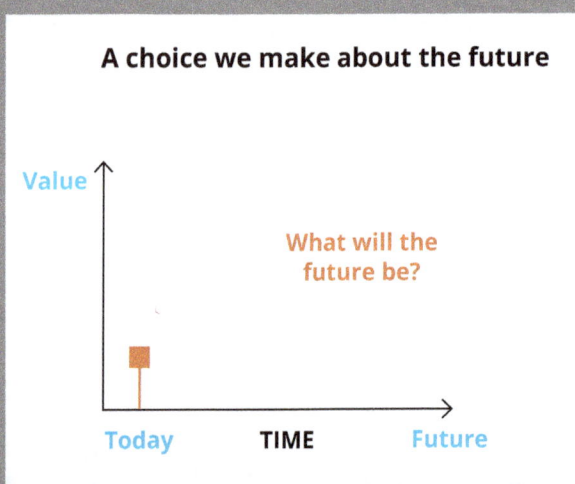

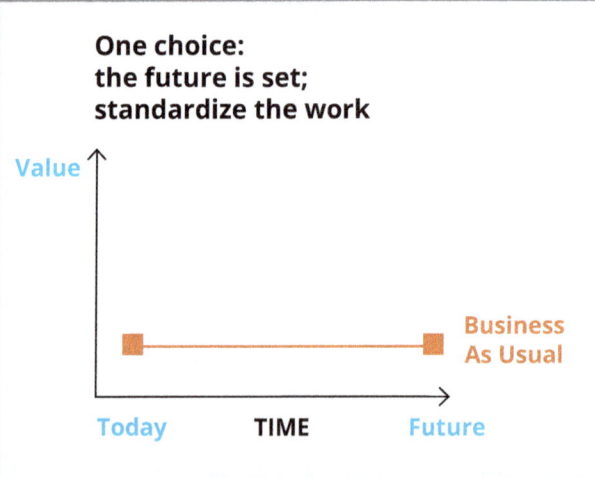

Another Choice is to have a better version of results we already know how to produce. A Manager would choose to manage the resources they control to produce results that are increasingly valued by the consumer of those results. Knowing what we don't know (**KDK**) gives Managers the tools to commit to and deliver high value and improved outcomes. The rising dashed line in the following figure illustrates managing the resources at hand to produce a high-value result in the future.

The result in the Manager Domain of Roles is labeled realistic. A Manager commits to value-added outcomes that are realistic to achieve. It is part of the management culture to under-promise and over-deliver. There is continuous improvement, a "doing more with less." Managers are expected to deliver what they commit to if not more. Therefore, a lot of effort goes into making sure Managers have access to and control of the resources needed.

Together the effort of the Manager and Administrator produces the ever-increasing standards of living that are common to human progress over time.

The Role of Leader offers a third Choice of purpose and result. The chart below on the right shows a future being envisioned **Today** that transcends business as usual or realistic outcomes. The blue star represents the high-value outcome of the Leader's **Future I Stand For**. It is a future envisioned as the Leader encounters the needs of others from within their circle of influence. It's a compelling future to be invented.

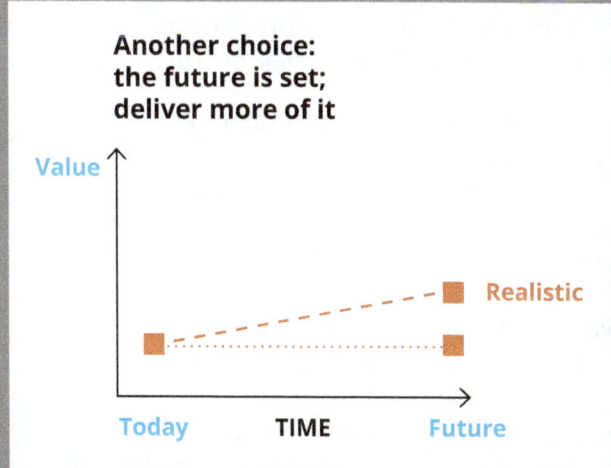

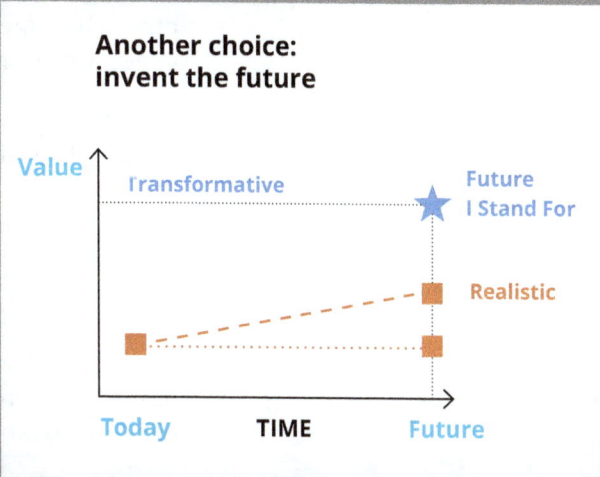

This kind of result represents the transformative result. It is far beyond the incremental performance of what we can deliver with our current resources and predictable practices. To achieve it, the current situation at hand has to be transformed.

This raises the question: How do we get there from here? We cannot do it solely by administration or management.

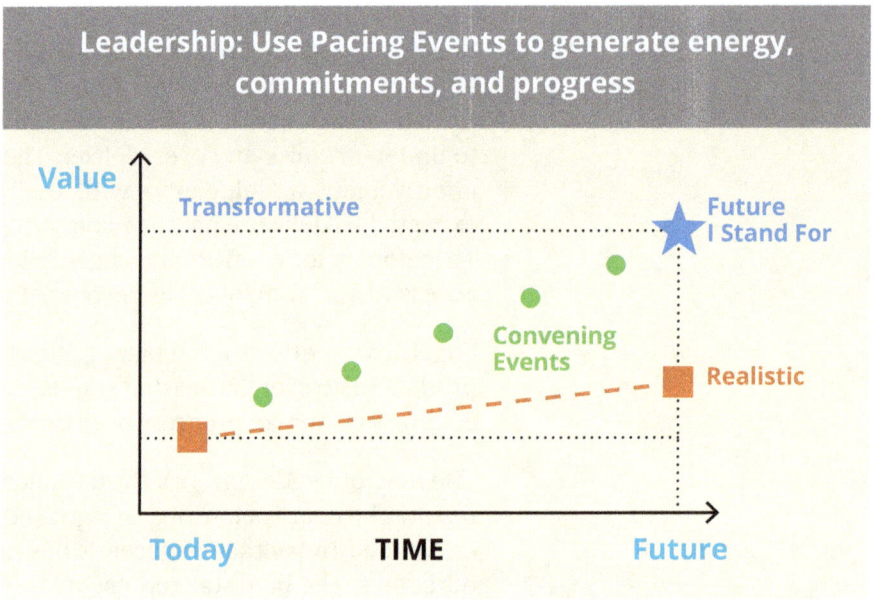

If we do not have command of the resources needed to achieve the desired future, we must generate Commitments by recruiting partners with those resources. To aim for the Transformative future, we can use events to convene people with a stake in the vision and the means to contribute to its achievement. Events of our own or others become a platform for sharing, action, dealmaking, generating Commitments, and celebrating their delivery.

The chart above shows events moving us in a smooth line toward the vision. However, the actual path is always more like a series of broken lines with frequent breakdowns where we fall back, followed by breakthroughs where we leap ahead. As shown in the following chart, events can become a special Mindset and Method to constantly move us forward to the vision in the face of disruptions. This special Mindset and Method is called Pacing Events and is discussed more fully later in this chapter.
Leadership faces a special challenge here with its

relationship to knowledge. Since as Leaders we don't know what we don't know (DKDK), we may not yet be sure who to convene with or what to ask for. Observation becomes a valuable Role in this case. By deploying observational methods and resources, it is possible to map out the relevant environment and begin to identify the best practices, innovations, and assets—often owned or controlled by others—that create possibilities and opportunities.

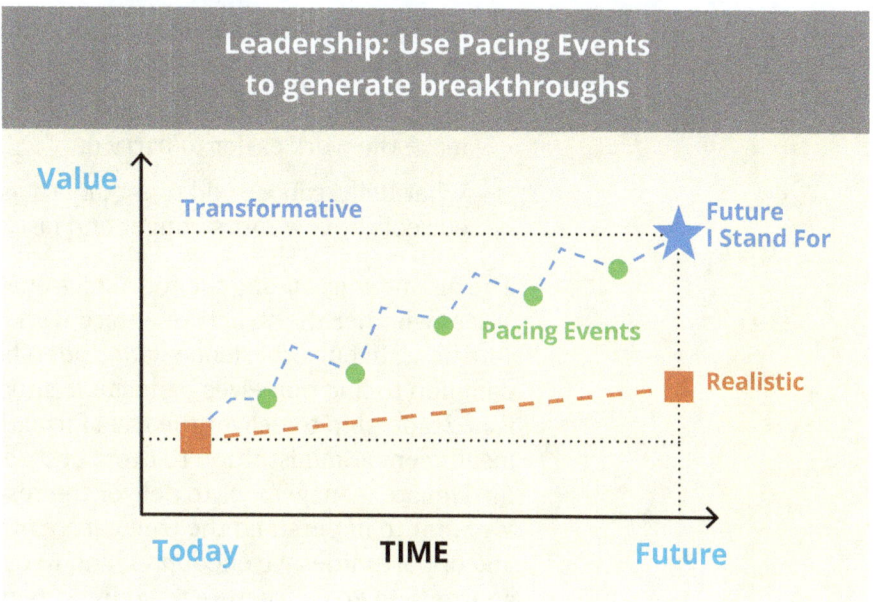

Fortunately, there are Mindsets and Methods described in the pages of this book for Leaders to pursue those possibilities and opportunities. We can consciously choose to cultivate Net Forward Energy in ourselves and request it in others. We can use the power of DNA to call more of what we want into the world. We can become more aware of our own circles of influence and the needs of others to establish the Compelling Vision and Bold Aims that will attract others. We can cultivate Resilience in ourselves and our partners to persist through the inevitable breakthroughs and breakdowns we will encounter in pursuing Bold Aims.

Forming and Deploying the Necessary Roles

With distinctions among the Roles of Observer, Administrator, Manager, and Leader in hand, we now have access to a powerful diagnostic and design tool as we work to achieve the Future we Stand For. We can analyze the situations we encounter and ask:

- In what way are the necessary Leadership and Management accountabilities in place?
- Do we have the Observation underway necessary to provide the insights we need?
- In what way are Administrators helping to make the work easier to carry out?
- What Roles can we add or modify to make our collective effort stronger and faster?

The distinctions among the four Roles enable us to assess whether the structure we are working with is sufficient. In our experience with leadership work, it is common to find ourselves in unstable situations. There is no leadership to deliver the transformation we seek, insufficient administration to avoid costs and delay, and inadequate management to deliver the results we expect. We want to understand the true nature of the problems and opportunities we encounter, and to establish the appropriate Role structure to address them.

Disruptive forces and performance breakdowns may require the executives and employees of an enterprise to assume new accountability Roles. There are two accountability Roles to look for in an organization: management and leadership. When a major turnaround is needed, the common and natural course of action would be to establish a change process and aggressively manage it to new, predictable target outcomes. However, in some cases it may be better to carry out the change through leadership approaches. The current resources and relationships may not be sufficient to affect a turnaround through management alone. Consider the two following insights about executive level accountability from Principals of the Council for Excellence in Government (CEG). These two leaders shared their experiences and solutions with federal Managers in leadership seminars.

Michael Walsh had a track record of turning around large corporations in financial trouble. He accomplished a major turnaround during his tenure as CEO of Tenneco, which at one point was one of the nation's largest companies. He achieved similar results with the Union Pacific Railroad Company. Trained as a lawyer, Walsh advised and supported company Boards and executives on challenging situations.

At a Council event for federal government Managers, Mike shared a key insight about a pattern that he often observed in his work: "When I encounter an organization in trouble, I almost always find that some of the executives are operating at one or more levels below their actual accountability. Certain Roles critical to success are not being carried out." He described a CFO performing the comptroller's job, a COO acting like a division head, and a CEO acting like a COO. Necessary domains of leadership and management action were not in play.

A second Council Principal, Robert Kohler, described how upon assuming an executive position with a large defense contractor, he found himself in charge of a multi-million-dollar contract with a foreign country. His company was locked into a series of deliverables that were beyond what Kohler could produce with the budget and authorities available to him. The financial terms were not negotiable. He described this stressful situation as "having the accountability without the sufficient responsibility." This was the first time we heard these two words, accountability and responsibility, used as two distinct concepts. He described how in his situation "managing better" was not the solution. Kohler dealt with the dilemma by creating a leadership breakthrough and developing new relationships with new partners. He re-imagined the project within the contract terms that were already in place and transformed the overall effort. In the end, his organization was able to deliver on the contract.

Michael Walsh and Robert Kohler were offering the Council for Excellence in Government Fellows a way to use accountability as a tool for assessing and helping organizations in trouble.

Understanding Accountability Informs Effective Role Switching

The Mindset and Method of Role Switching provides us with access to a powerful diagnostic and design tool as we work to achieve the future we intend. Role Switching enables us to understand the nature of accountability and how to surface and deploy the accountability needed – for ourselves, or for other team members who complement our own strengths. The following table provides examples that illustrate common problems when Roles are not being properly filled or performed. With greater understanding of the four key Roles, we can better track how the Roles are and should be in play.

Organizational Breakdown: A Necessary Accountability & Responsibility is Missing		
Role Called For By The Situation	**The Accountability and Responsibility Expected**	**Example of Default Role Triggering Breakdown**
Observer	Describe what is; provide insight, evidence	Describe study methods; provide opinion, gossip
Administrator	Operate a reliable, efficient process	Respond to demand with ad hoc transactions
Manager	Set expectations, deliver results on budget	Request extensions of budget and schedule
Leader	Embrace needed new levels of accountability; partner to deliver results	Focus on bottom line, cut budgets

The first column are the Roles expected in most organizational situations. The middle column shows the accountability or responsibility needed from the Role. The column on the right shows the effect Michael Walsh encountered in troubled organizations. He found missing critical accountabilities and responsibilities, with the Leader defaulting to a Manager Role, the Manager to an Administrator Role, and so on.

Note that the functions in the column on the right are useful in certain situations; however, they are not the required Role needed for the situation at hand. As we engage with people who have chosen or been assigned to the Roles in the first column, we can surface the actual accountability they have assumed. This exercise of observation enables us to see how much of the middle column is missing, making it possible to fill the gaps.

Role Switching is a Unique and Accessible Leadership Choice

Successful collaborative efforts call for performance and interaction among the Roles of Observer, Administrator, Manager, and Leader. All of us need to have the ability to perform at some basic level of competence in each of these four Roles. Understanding the differences between these Roles is a critical asset and key to the practice of effectively switching Roles or teaming with others as we navigate breakdowns and breakthroughs towards extraordinary results.

In the following section, we will see how the Role of Leader is the Role most often absent or tepid in its delivery. This happens in part because conventional academic and on-the-job training often only teach us how to administer or manage. This instruction, while useful and important, can also be limiting when it comes to the exercise of leadership.

Practicing effective leadership sometimes involves unlearning key principles taught to us as Administrators and Managers. In the next section, Dennis relates how he came to understand the distinction among Roles, ultimately empowering him to switch to the right Role at the right time, and to carry out the consistent and transformative practice of leadership over the course of three decades of work in the federal civil service.

Role Switching

A Transformative Introduction to Role Switching and the Real Work of Leadership

by **Dennis Wagner**

A New Window into Leadership: the Council for Excellence in Government

The trajectory of my career in the federal civil service changed dramatically when I encountered Mark Abramson and the Council for Excellence in Government (CEG) in 1991. Mark Abramson is an energetic, committed, and outgoing leader who left a GS 14 position in the federal Department of Health and Human Services to establish the CEG, a national not-for-profit organization committed to improving the performance and effectiveness of the federal government. During the Clinton Administration, Mark and the Council worked closely with Vice President Gore on the Administration's Reinventing Government initiative.

Vice President Al Gore and Mark Abramson at the Council for Excellence in Government

I was fortunate to be nominated by my organization, the US Environmental Protection Agency (EPA), and then ultimately to be selected as one of 120 members of the second annual class of the CEG Fellows program. This one-year government-wide training program would provide a tremendous and exhilarating boost to my career and to my understanding of leadership.

As Fellows, we were routinely brought into leadership development sessions with Council Principals, extraordinary leaders in the private sector, with prior service as senior leaders in federal government from both Republican and Democratic administrations.

The Council was supported by close to 850 Principals recruited by Mark Abramson who were committed to seeing improvement in government management and leadership, with executives such as Paul O'Neill, then-chairman of Alcoa, who had previously served as Deputy Director of the Office of Management and Budget, and later Treasury Secretary in the administration of President George W. Bush. Other Principals included William Ruckelshaus, the President and CEO of Weyerhaeuser, who had previously served as the first Administrator of the US Environmental Protection Agency under President Nixon. Ruckelshaus was regarded as a federal leader of great integrity who resigned from his Role as US Deputy Attorney General in the Justice Department, taking his place in the infamous Saturday Night Massacre alongside other senior Justice officials protesting President Nixon's firing of the independent Watergate prosecutor, Archibald Cox. He later returned as EPA Administrator in the Reagan Administration to help when its credibility came under attack.

The experience, guidance, and proven leadership practices provided by Ruckelshaus, O'Neill, and other accomplished Council Principals stood in stark contrast to the coaching on administration and management I had received through my formal education and extensive federal training up to that point.

Breaking Free of One-Dimensional Training into Role Switching

After completing a Master of Public Administration (MPA) degree at Montana State University, I joined federal civil service as one of approximately 200 members of the 1986 class of Presidential Management Interns, PMIs for short. PMIs (now called Presidential Management Fellows or PMFs) were hired into a wide variety of GS 9 federal jobs. The internship extended over a two-year period and included quarterly management training sessions conducted by the Office of Personnel Management. PMIs also completed one or more three-to-six-month rotations in other federal agencies and on Capitol Hill.

Serving as a PMI provided a comprehensive big-picture introduction into the worlds of civil service, executive and legislative branch operations, and the discipline of federal management. Every PMI was required to secure and learn under one or more management mentors in our respective agencies.

As a PMI, I was introduced to a very specific culture. We learned to never put anything in writing that we would not want to see printed in the Washington Post. We learned to under-promise and over-deliver. We learned to never accept a new project unless it came with the requisite budget and staffing. We learned to stick to the official policy and to clear any public statement. We learned that career advancement was judged by the size of our program budgets and the number of people who reported to us. In short, we were systematically exposed to the standard tenets associated with the discipline of public sector administration and management. The PMI program provided in-depth training into the exciting and diverse world of the federal civil service. It was like networking on steroids, and it was exciting.

It was also deeply constraining.

In hindsight, I realize now that the message routinely drilled into us as PMIs was essentially, "Go forth and do great Administration." As a CEG Fellow, I encountered a completely different performance culture, one of seizing leadership. This distinction would fundamentally reshape my approach to making a difference by learning to switch in and out of the essential Roles of Observer, Administrator, and Manager, and to seize the Role of Leader when commitments, deals, and action were called for.

The Real Work of Leadership and Debunking "They"

Council Principals took administration and management skills as a given. But to make a truly significant contribution, we learned that they had chosen to advance beyond administration and management by accepting accountability for leadership Roles. The Principals shared with CEG Fellows the Mindsets and Methods that enabled them to assume these Roles.

As noted in an earlier section on the Domain of Language and the Speech Act of Commitment, CEG Principal Robert Kohler, a former Associate Director of the Central Intelligence Agency and successful private sector executive, knew how to get things done. An accomplished leader and Role model, Kohler attributed his success to understanding, spreading, and acting on the discipline of what he called "the Real Work." He taught us that the *real* work of leadership was:

- Making Commitments;
- Delivering on Commitments, and;
- Securing Commitments from Others.

Kohler boldly asserted that most everything other than commitments was "talk." Kohler also poignantly shared with us how the Signers of the Declaration of Independence committed "their lives, their fortunes and their sacred honor" to independence from Great Britain. Victory was by no means a given, and the signers knew full well that to sign such a radical document could cost them everything they held dear in the event of defeat. Kohler's potent example illustrated how the signers' collective Commitment, one which they made, delivered on, and secured from others, was born of tremendous risk-taking and courage. It rang unmistakably clear for us Fellows sitting at that breakfast seminar over 30 years ago that the much more modest risks we were called on to take as public sector leaders were quite reasonable by comparison. I am forever indebted to Robert Kohler for his indelible introduction to the concept of Real Work and his instruction on the fact that leadership often requires us to take real risks.

Another CEG Principal, Dennis Bakke, a highly successful entrepreneur who started out in the Federal Energy Administration, gave each of us Fellows a coffee mug emblazoned with the words, *Who are '**They**' Anyway?* Bakke described how he would engage Managers and staff in the utility plants acquired by his company, Applied Energy Services (AES), on what was lacking or in need of improvement. He would often hear back, "They won't let us do that." Bakke would ask these folks, "Who are *'They'*?" *"They"* were often excuses for inaction, grounded in a prior organizational hierarchy and culture that had stifled individual initiative from folks on the ground doing the work. The mug was a pointed reminder that as leaders, we don't get to blame an invisible *"They"* for our own lack of action and accountability.

Bakke coached his employees into assuming leadership Roles. They were empowered to own and champion the ideas and solutions that they had previously been trained to tamp down. In one dramatic example, staff began showing up at company board events requesting AES to plant millions of trees in equatorial countries to offset the emissions from construction of a coal-fired plant. Teams at the plant level were also assuming strategic Roles such as securing financing. Prior to AES acquisition of these utility plants, this kind of work had been solely the domain of a distant corporate staff.

Hearing the stories of leaders like Bakke, Kohler, O'Neill, and others during my one-year CEG tenure was jarring, shocking, and revelatory. Above all, it was inspiring. I resolved to follow their leadership examples.

I began to sense that the disciplines of administration, management, and leadership were quite distinct. My year as a CEG Fellow catalyzed what would become a life-long working relationship with my CEG Fellows Coach, John Scanlon, to assemble, test, use, adapt, and spread the leadership Mindsets and Methods documented in this book.

A Career of Leadership Campaigns inspired by Real Work and Role Switching

CEG leadership lessons became powerful tools in my career. Teams I supported and led over the last three decades have actively spread Kohler's straightforward model of the Real Work—making, delivering, and securing commitments—to employees, partners, contractors, bosses, and national and international communities of practice. In partnership with thousands of others, I have adapted and spread the use of Real Work and Mindsets and Methods such as Role Switching to great effect on a wide variety of national and international campaigns, as detailed in the baker's dozen listed below.

	Agency	Campaign	Year(s)
1	US EPA	Reducing the health risks of indoor radon gas	1987-97
2	US EPA	Improving indoor air quality in homes, schools, and workplaces	1992-98
3	US EPA	Making secondhand smoke socially unacceptable	1992-98
4	US HRSA	Increasing access to healthcare and reducing disparities for underserved populations	1998-02
5	US EPA	Cleaning up the outdoor air in Bangkok, Thailand	1998-02
6	US EPA	Helping the Pollution Control Department in Thailand with air quality, landfills, river and estuary restoration, and more	1998-02
7	US HRSA	Increasing organ donation and transplantation	2002-07
8	US HRSA	Integrating clinical pharmacy services into primary healthcare	2007-10
9	US EPA	Improving the cookstoves of the poorest families on the planet	2006-10
10	CMS	Increasing hospital patient safety	2010-20
11	CMS	Improving healthcare quality in tens of thousands of nursing homes, hospitals, dialysis facilities and clinical practices	2010-20
12	CMS	Implementing the Affordable Care Act	2010-20
13	CMS	Reducing early elective deliveries of newborn babies	2011-14

It is a tribute to Mark Abramson that the Excellence in Government Fellows program continues to support senior federal civil servants in their leadership journeys, more than 30 years since its establishment. Now housed with the Partnership for Public Service, the Excellence in Government leadership development program boasts more than 500 Fellows who complete a dynamic and inspiring program of leadership development every year.

My federal service has given me many joyous and rewarding opportunities to improve the world, as inspired by the Principals of the CEG Fellows program. 27 years after my own graduation, it was an extraordinary honor to serve as the graduation speaker for the 2019 class of Fellows. I am confident that the Fellows experience will provide them and many future Fellows with comparable joy and reward in their own careers of service and leadership.

ROLES
Role Switching
5 Dimensions of Action
Pacing Events

Exercising Accountability Through 5 Dimensions of Action

At one time or another, most of us will either choose or be assigned to different Roles in our professional lives. Trained to respond to those above and below us in an organizational hierarchy, we behave accordingly and adhere to a traditional chain of command in which we must either obtain approval or give orders. We often adopt a one or two-dimensional mindset, with little perceived room for discretionary action. This default mindset is primarily defined as *Subordinate and Hierarchical* dimensions of accountability. But there are in fact multiple dimensions for action: not only *Subordinate and Hierarchical*, but also *Collegial, Process, and Public*.

5 Dimensions of Action in Pursuit of Our Accountabilities

1. **Subordinate action:** upward with those in authority over us;
2. **Hierarchical action:** downward with those who report to us;
3. **Collegial action:** with peers in our unit or related units;
4. **Process action:** with procedures and systems;
5. **Public action:** with relevant stakeholders in the environment.

In the Subordinate dimension, we report up and are given assignments and guidance by those above us in authority. Hierarchical refers to the people below us in the chain of command over whom we have authority. They report to us and we give them assignments. The Collegial dimension is composed of co-workers, either equals in our unit or people in other parallel independent units; in this dimension, we collaborate and cooperate. The dimension of Process involves the work to create and tend the operational and administrative systems that are in place to support the organization.

Process accountabilities are intended to make work easy, efficient, and high quality. They can also impact some of the external organizations and individuals who interact with our own organization. And finally, the Public dimension consists of those who work outside our organization and may include our customers, suppliers, competitors, regulators, and other stakeholders.

Understanding the Directionality of Accountability and Action

The 5 Dimensions of Action make clear the wide discretion we have for action from any organizational position and for the multiple ways we can choose to make ourselves accountable. As seen in the following diagram, each Dimension of Action can be thought of directionally: upward with our bosses, downward with our direct reports, sideways with our peers, inward with our organizational processes, and outward towards our external customers, suppliers, and other public entities.

5 Dimensions of Accountability and Action
LEADERSHIP CHOICES

Insight: Leadership can be exercised from any position in an organizational setting by taking actions in up to five organizational dimensions defined by that position

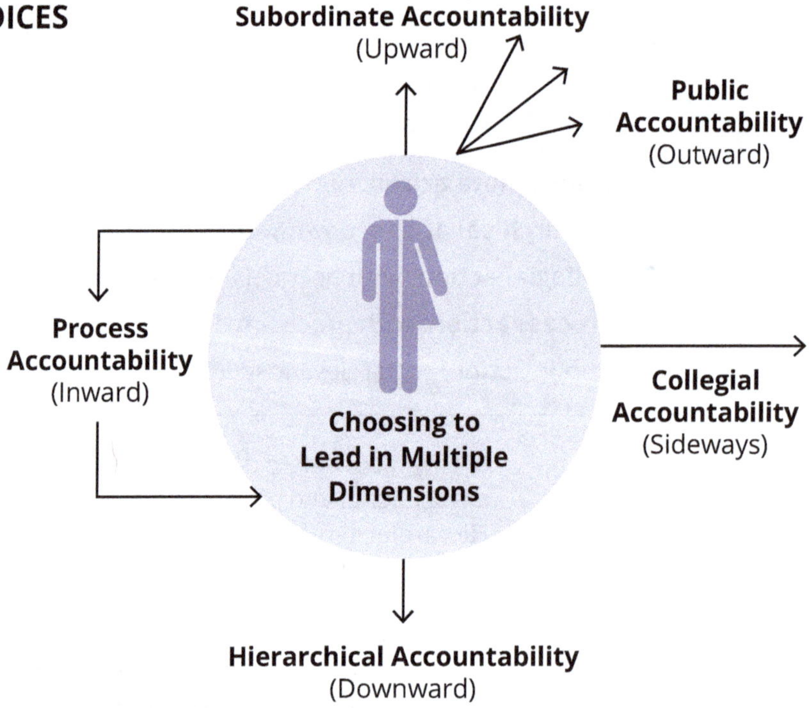

- Subordinate Accountability (Upward)
- Public Accountability (Outward)
- Collegial Accountability (Sideways)
- Hierarchical Accountability (Downward)
- Process Accountability (Inward)

Choosing to Lead in Multiple Dimensions

Mark Abramson
Founding President and CEO, Council for Excellence in Government

Correcting a Common Misconception of Accountability in Government

Mark Abramson advanced this view of accountability for action (originally known as the 5 Dimensions of Leadership) in a paper co-authored with John Scanlon. The experiences and achievements of Principals highlighted in the CEG program provided hard evidence of leaders who routinely embraced accountability across all 5 Dimensions of Action.

The CEG team observed that many of the federal Managers who participated in the Council's developmental programs initially held narrow definitions of their own accountabilities, often characterizing them either as Subordinate accountability to their supervisors or Hierarchical accountability towards their direct reports. Many Fellows initially did not view themselves as accountable for action and results across the Collegial, Process, or Public dimensions. Their concept of accountability was largely one or two-dimensional—and inherently limited.

For example, if a collegial peer in a different office failed to adequately perform a function that was essential to the work of the Manager and their organizational unit, this was frequently viewed as the fault of the larger organization and beyond the control of the Manager. Those managers who did embrace the accountability for a peer's performance often did so in the traditional and cumbersome bureaucratic way, with the manager going up the chain of command to his or her supervisors. Those supervisors would then go over to the peer's supervisors, who in turn have to go down their chain of command to engage the non-performing unit. Up, over, and down is often an ineffective way of getting a peer in another organization to perform the needed work. Council Fellows did not routinely embrace accountability for securing the cooperation and needed actions of peers and others who did not directly report to them. Conflicts or poor performance in other organizational units had to go up and down the chain of command to be resolved.

Similar mindsets prevailed with regard to perceived accountability for creating, improving, or eliminating processes such as organization of staff meetings, performance reviews, hiring, contracting, budgeting, approaching customers, responding to complaints, and more. Many Fellows saw these processes as "something to put up with" because they were mandated and implemented by others beyond their supervision.

Likewise, many of CEG Fellows did not initially assume accountability for how their actions and programs were perceived by external partners and customers. Fellows often viewed public reactions to their programs, whether positive or negative, primarily as a response to the laws passed by Congress rather than a product of their own accountability for action, influence, or implementation.

Multi-dimensional Contributions and Skills for more Effective Government

Extraordinary results and highly effective organizations require far more than the traditional management models. Effective organizations need their people to act across multiple dimensions, regardless of where they serve in the organizational hierarchy. Mark and John's CEG paper on the 5 Dimensions of Leadership called for an expansion of the accountability mindset and the actions of federal Managers across all dimensions. As a member of the 1991-92 Fellows class, Dennis attests to the profound impact of the 5 Dimensions of Action on his own effectiveness, his career, and the thousands of others he has encouraged to adopt this Mindset.

Opportunities for Contribution in 5 Dimensions

Dimension	Opportunity
Subordinate	**Mission Driven:** Equip and support your boss to succeed on the organization's mission
Hierarchical	**Support Your Staff:** Remove barriers, empower, and obtain extraordinary results from people and resources who report to you
Collegial	**Collaborate:** Team with peers to enable and support interdependent work across the organization
Process	**Improve the Structure:** Ensure that processes to support supervisors, employees, and others are efficient, reliable and value-added
Public	**Engage Stakeholders:** Involve the organization effectively with external audiences to support results on mission

The dramatic leadership contributions of CEG Principals show the way to embracing an expanded accountability in ways both smart and acceptable. Whether in the private, not-for-profit, or public sectors, the 5 Dimensions of Action reveal that each of us has discretion to make Choices that expand our ability to contribute far more. See the table on Opportunities for Contributions in 5 Dimensions arising from effective action in each of the Dimensions.

When we choose to assume leadership accountability for action and results across the 5 Dimensions, we not only open pathways for formidable contributions—we become more adept at building teams that are proficient in the different skill sets associated with each dimension. Working across the 5 Dimensions of Action can open new pathways for tremendous personal and professional growth. The following table outlines the top skills needed to prosper in each Dimension of Action.

Top Skills Needed to Be Effective in 5 Dimensions

Dimension	Skills Needed
Subordinate	**Manage Up:** Ability to fill gaps in the capability of your boss; courage to prevent and correct missteps; loyalty
Hierarchical	**Show Why:** Goal-setting, unrelenting focus on mission and purpose; managerial skills; clarity on the behaviors and actions to achieve results
Collegial	**Teamwork:** Understanding of the inter-relatedness of organizational units; ability to cajole, team with and support others without line authority over peers
Process	**Quality Improvement:** Ability to establish and improve needed processes, and to eliminate those that are ineffective or unnecessary
Public	**Networking:** Effective listening, writing, and speaking

Embrace and Act on the 5 Dimensions of Action

Having adopted and taught these 5 Dimensions of Action as a Mindset and Method for more than 30 years, we have identified three key elements that contribute to the "special sauce" of this powerful leadership model:

Expanded Circles of Influence: The Dimensions of Action dramatically expand the scope of our accountability and our influence. Consistently choosing to hold ourselves accountable for working across these dimensions dramatically expands our circles of influence and our effectiveness.

Leadership Opportunity: Line staff without management accountabilities can still gain new opportunities for leadership action. There are opportunities for action and results for each of us across multiple dimensions.

Growth: Spreading the leadership Choice to exercise accountability through action and results across all 5 Dimensions is incredibly empowering for staff who discover new ways to lead and grow.

To embrace the 5 Dimensions of Action is a leadership Choice. As the Leadership Stories in this chapter and throughout the book demonstrate, choosing to act across all 5 Dimensions opens up incredible opportunities for increased contribution, personal and professional growth, and the joy that accompanies the development of new skills in ourselves and others.

The following pages present Dr. John Chessare's Leadership Story focusing on the transformation of a large regional hospital system. Watch for the natural way Role Switching and the 5 Dimensions of Action can come into play within and across organizations.

Encountering John Chessare as a Leader in a National Quality Improvement Program

We first encountered John Chessare MD, MPH in 2002 when he was serving as Chief Medical Officer of the Boston Medical Center. Our team was creating the Organ Donation Breakthrough Collaborative (ODBC), a national quality improvement initiative to achieve rapid and dramatic increases in organ donation rates in the nation's largest trauma centers, and we were in search of effective practitioners to help lead the nation in this effort. These faculty leaders would serve as the living embodiment of "best in class" practices in organ donation. Two particularly effective faculty members would be invited to serve as Co-Chairs of the national initiative.

In the wake of several site visits to high-performing trauma centers in Boston, our colleague Dr. Frank Zampiello enthusiastically shared that he had a line-of-sight on a potential co-chair. John Chessare was not only a highly qualified, personable doctor: he had also been directly involved in creating the improvement system and overseeing the work that resulted in high donation rates at the Boston Medical Center. Dr. Chessare was an expert in quality improvement and had worked with the Institute for Healthcare Improvement (IHI), counting IHI CEO and President, Don Berwick, MD, whose leadership is featured elsewhere in this book, as his mentor.

During the Boston Medical Center site visit, Dr. Chessare showed Frank a stack of quality improvement run-charts on organ donation at Boston Medical Center. That stack clinched the deal in convincing Frank and the rest of us that Dr. Chessare was the perfect candidate for this important leadership Role.

Dr. Chessare ultimately agreed to serve as one of the national co-chairs of the U.S. Department of Health and Human Services ODBC from 2003 to 2005. He stepped into this influential Role and became a key leader in making the Collaborative a national engine for innovation, action, and life-saving results.

Dr. Chessare continued his career as a hospital executive. In 2010, he became CEO of the Greater Baltimore Medical Center (GBMC) and its associated healthcare system. The Leadership Story presented here describes a ten-year journey (2010 - 2020) to make GBMC a national award-winning model of excellence in quality. You will follow Dr. Chessare as he introduces leadership Roles and accountability into the management and administrative structures of the healthcare system. This is a striking story of a bold leader who masterfully switches among Roles and routinely assumes accountability across multiple dimensions of action. He does this in a large health care institution with hundreds of operational units and several thousand employees to create a sustainable model of care-giving that all of us would want for our own loved ones.

LEADERSHIP STORY

Leadership Choices in a Journey to Excellence

by **John Chessare MD, MPH**

Leadership Vision Grounded in Career Defining Moments

Early in my medical career, I learned of the work of W. Edwards Deming, a highly regarded management consultant, statistician and engineer. Deming explained that poor quality was not the result of people-failure, but of system failure—good people stuck in bad systems. Deming asserted that a key role of management was to get down to where the work was done and to engineer the systems that would enable workers to produce quality.

I had graduated from medical school some years prior with the intent of becoming an academic pediatrician. However, I soon began encountering visionaries committed to improving organizational quality.

In a fellowship program, I had the good fortune of having Don Berwick MD, as my mentor who guided me in writing my first published paper. Don then was the Vice President of Quality at the Harvard Community Health Plan, and later became one of the world's foremost leaders in healthcare quality improvement. Later, in pursuing a master's degree in Medical Care Organization at the University of Michigan, I took a course on the history of quality improvement taught by Avedis Donabedian MD, a founder of the healthcare quality movement. I learned of the work of John Wennberg MD, who was studying variation in healthcare services, and who would go on to become the editor of *The Dartmouth Atlas of Health Care*, which examines the patterns of medical resource utilization in the United States.

As I migrated into executive roles in hospitals, this particular focus on organizational quality attracted me. I came out of these formative years with my eyes opened: executives in health care were simply not focused on quality improvement in a disciplined way. I felt strongly that had to change.

I went on to the Albany Medical Center, and then in 1998 to the Boston Medical Center, where I encountered Dennis Wagner, John Scanlon, and the Organ Donation Breakthrough Collaborative, becoming co-chair of this major, national quality improvement initiative. The Institute for Healthcare Improvement's (IHI) breakthrough collaborative methodology taught me methods and tools to spread best practices and achieve dramatic results across many organizations in very short periods of time. My work with the ODBC and IHI also inspired me to understand what constituted compelling and effective leadership, and to develop my own personal style in fostering this kind of leadership.

Throughout all these experiences, I was learning not only how to create systems, but how to gauge quality. I learned of the national Baldrige Award, introduced by the federal government to recognize organizations with exceptional quality. I had never encountered a Baldrige-achieving organization, yet the approach made perfect sense to me. I began to learn more about the Baldrige criteria and the kinds of systems and results that Baldrige reviewers expected of the highest performing organizations in the nation. I was intrigued.

My first shot at leading a hospital came about in 2005. My hospital was part of a larger Catholic health system in the Boston area. When the CEO got into difficulty,

John Chessare MD, MPH
Career Journey in Quality

1979	Graduated from Medical School
1983-94	Medical College of Ohio
1987	Introduction to Baldrige Award
1994-98	Albany Medical Center
1998-05	Boston Medical Center
2005-08	President, Caritas Norwood Hospital
2009	Interview with Hospital in Vermont
2010	CEO of GBMC HealthCare System
2020	GBMC Achieves Baldrige Designation

I was tapped to become the interim president of the entire system of hospitals. In 2008, the Archdiocese of Boston chose a permanent Chief Executive Officer and decided to divest the system, and I went looking for a new job.

Throughout my job search, quality improvement preyed on my mind. One of the most vivid memories from my search occurred in 2009. I was interviewing for the CEO position at a Vermont hospital with one of the board members who presented himself as a management expert. Over a private lunch, he asked me, "What's your career goal in health care?" I replied, "To lead an organization in providing better health and better care and do it at lower cost." And before I could even think twice, I spontaneously added, "And I'd like to lead a hospital that has what it takes to achieve the Malcolm Baldrige Award." The board member was completely taken aback, as if I had voiced an irresponsible and overwhelming undertaking. "You'll never ever win a Baldrige Award with a hospital!" he stated emphatically.

I never forgot that statement. This was a job interview, so I smiled and stayed calm, but it was hard for me. My mind was already teeming with the challenge from this board member, and I resolved in that moment that, indeed, someday I would lead a hospital in providing better value for the patients, providers, and community at lower cost, while at a level of excellence that met Baldrige standards.

Leadership Choices Set the Stage for Transformation

My job search ultimately culminated with my appointment as Chief Executive Officer of the Greater Baltimore Medical Center in 2010. And from the very outset, I began implementing a number of leadership Choices designed to transform the Center's delivery of health care.

GBMC was a nearly 50-year-old institution with three major areas of work: hospital, physician practices, and hospice. We have sites throughout northern Maryland in the counties of Baltimore, Harford, and Howard. We employ more than 3,900 people, clinical and non-clinical. GBMC is a critical provider of healthcare for the Greater Baltimore community.

The owners of GBMC are the people in the community and are represented by the Board of Directors. When I arrived, there was a sense of pride in the good work that was being performed by GBMC, and a well-earned confidence in the solid financial performance of the organization. The Board was business-oriented and managed the enterprise to the bottom line.

Our challenge in 2010 was to move beyond being a good community hospital and hospice with excellent staff to becoming a true system of care for the local population. The Board and I were mindful that healthcare organizations everywhere were facing serious challenges to improve performance and control costs. We found ourselves drawn to the "Triple Aim" of the Institute for Healthcare Improvement (IHI), an approach to optimizing health system performance by simultaneously pursuing three dimensions of quality:

- Improving the patient's experience of care;
- Improving the health of the population;
- Reducing the per capita cost of health care.

A difficult conversation. Within weeks of my arrival as the new CEO, the Board and I convened a two-day visioning retreat. At the retreat, the Board zeroed in on the status quo and clearly saw there was serious work ahead. In that era, GBMC had focused on selling healthcare "widgets" – procedures which were financially covered transactions rather than results—to ensure that we could cover all expenses on an annual basis. We realized the need to adopt a new mindset that would focus our performance more intently on the true healthcare needs of the community.

The retreat was a challenging and stressful event, and conversations were not easy. I can still picture the looks of concern on the faces of Board members and the common refrains of, "What are we talking about? "What does this mean?" and, "What are we doing?"

We examined our Intent. We adopted the radical perspective that, unless a person was coming to the hospital to have a baby, we should consider most hospitalizations as defects in the larger healthcare system. We should ask, "Was there a way we could have prevented this event?" After all, who wants their loved ones to require hospitalization?

It was only natural for that conversation to jump to, "What will happen if there are fewer patients in the hospital?" It made the Board very nervous to hear me say things like, "The financial bottom line is no longer the sole bottom line." The bottom line had to be expanded to include clinical outcomes, the care experience, and the reduction of waste.

The Board members had valid concerns. "What if we spend too much money as revenues fall? What if we can't control spending? We might go bankrupt!"

A Bold Aim emerges. As we considered changes in direction, we also began to share stories of our patients' experiences, including those of friends and family members of our executive team and board members. Many of the stories made us proud. And then there were stories of all-too-common glitches in the process. We heard of patients falling between the cracks of the hospital and their doctor, between primary care and specialty care. We heard of safety errors like adverse drug events and infections acquired by patients from the hospital. These kinds of preventable medical errors had to end.

Out of this very intense series of conversations, we landed on a unifying vision. We crafted a four-paragraph vision statement to capture our commitment.

Our Vision Statement 2011-2021, Co-Authored by CEO & Board In 2010

GBMC ... as a provider of the highest quality medical care to our community ... we must transform our philosophy and organizational structure and develop a model system for delivering patient-centered care.

Our professional staff will be able to say with confidence that the guidance and medical care they are providing mirrors what they would want for their own family.

This new organization will be defined by collaboration and continuous improvement. Physicians will lead teams that will manage patient care.

We welcome all those who share our vision of health care .... both community-based and employed physicians will form the foundation of the Greater Baltimore Health Alliance

To guide our everyday decision-making, we reduced the vision to one ringing declaration:

To every patient, every time, we will provide the care that we would want for our own loved ones.

This declaration would enable each of us to stay on-point with the vision. We would call on the statement whenever decisions were being made and actions taken. For example:

"Beds are being stored in the hall outside my unit. Should I have them moved right away? They could be a hazard in the event of a fire and we had to move our patients quickly. If my parents were in that unit today, would I have the beds removed? ... Yes!"

When everyone starts thinking in this way, the results are stunning. People suddenly know what to do; solutions are implemented quickly. This resonated with me, having worked in organizations that had no idea of mission or vision. In the absence of this kind of clarity, the default driver almost always becomes money and profits.

Our Board and leadership team collectively chose to embrace this new direction. The retreat conversation enabled us to realize that this was the vision of the perfection we wanted to seek. We knew we might never arrive at perfection, yet all of us were committed to moving GBMC toward this Compelling Vision.

A "Yes, and . . ." commitment to excellence and joy. We didn't want our vision statement to be a platitude, etc ...We wanted people throughout the organization to have a meaningful stake in what we were about to undertake.

First, we all agreed that if our loved ones were in the hospital, we would want the very best possible healthcare outcome for them; we would desperately want them restored to their previous good health. Our colleagues at the Gilchrist Hospice wanted to see pain and suffering mitigated during their patients' final days. We saw good health outcomes as the highest possible aim. But that wasn't all we wanted:

We wanted to see our loved ones treated with respect and kindness;

We wanted a clean environment;

We wanted better use of time (health care is full of wasted time);

We wanted patients to experience efficiency, not inordinate waiting.

At some point, we collectively began to realize that we were fashioning our own version of IHI's Triple Aim (better care, better health, at lower cost). We changed the wording on the cost aim to "eliminate waste" because we understood that achieving great health outcomes might not always permit us to do so at the lowest cost. At the same time, we all knew that there was tremendous waste in the system. The United States spends 40% more per capita on health care than anywhere else in the world, and yet much of that spending does not generate value. These were the costs we wanted to eliminate.

As we worked with our refined version of the Triple Aim, it became clear that the Board wanted something that actually surpassed the Triple Aim: we wanted our loved ones to know that we considered it a gift to serve them in their most vulnerable times, that it was joyful to serve them.

All my GBMC colleagues got it: *there is joy in service*. When we have a bad day, calling to mind one person we helped can bring a smile to our faces and joy to our hearts. This is not a giddy type of joy; it's the power of purpose —knowing that we've served another in their time of need.

We emerged from the retreat with the **GBMC Quadruple Aim** underlining our vision:

- The best **health** outcomes;
- The best **care** experience;
- The least **waste**; and
- The most **joy** for those providing the care.

We collectively decided to move from being simply a very good medical center to becoming an organization that would *provide our patients the quality care we would want for our own families*, **with joy.** Achieving this vision meant that we would have to change our philosophy, our organizational structure, and culture. We would have to create a model system for delivering patient-centered care.

We resolved to constantly strive to live out two key behaviors: continuous improvement and intentional collaboration with one another. We would not only live out these behaviors, we would embody them.

Our delivery of care would also need to change. We realized our physicians could not be patient-centered on their own; team-based care would be needed. Instead of functioning as Lone Rangers, GBMC physicians would now need to become adept at managing teams that would consistently and reliably improve patient care.

We also created a new company, the Greater Baltimore Health Alliance, to welcome private practice doctors into helping us achieve our goal of serving the community. Their engagement would be needed to provide more primary care, more preventative care, and to avoid unnecessary hospital care.

The Board and I left the retreat recommitted to being financially sound, with a new commitment to achieving the Quadruple Aim for our patients, providers, and payers. *We were actively choosing to move towards managing the health of an entire community, while ensuring that the organization remained financially sound.*

Looking back, the key steps in transforming our organization were:

- Identifying our Quadruple Aim;
- Reducing our vision to a straightforward, actionable statement;
- Repeating the statement at every juncture;
- And, when challenges arose, using the statement to guide decisions and act.

From 2010 on, everything flowed from the leadership Choices we made together in that two-day retreat.

The Baldrige Award Program, a way to spread a Bold Aim. With this newly defined vision, we would need a system to move the organization into action. How would we get there? How would we systematically orient ourselves to something as complex as healthcare to excellence?

Our employees were fabulous people – talented, dedicated, and well-intentioned. But channeling the wisdom of W. Edwards Deming, good intentions were not enough. If we wanted to change behavior, we would need systems to guide our staff in adopting the Quadruple Aims.

My years of experience in health care had made it clear that my field suffered from a lack of deliberate and intentional system design. Staff showed up and performed their obligations by rote. It was a day-to-day fire drill, with no overarching system to support or lead staff.

At GBMC, there was a cadre of people schooled in the financial mindset: "*If I hit my budget, I'm a good leader.*" We had to change that way of thinking. We had highly trained, committed, caring clinicians, but the larger institution lacked an overarching design to enable efficient and smart coordination. The leadership challenge was to introduce this design element into health care: we had to ingrain systems-thinking into our managers.

I've always subscribed to the adage that "*it's easier to act our way into a new way of thinking than to think our way into a new way of acting.*" We needed our staff to act in ways that focused them on improvement and excellence. We shifted to teaching system design and began building an institution-wide quality improvement infrastructure.

As we undertook this shift, initially there was no mention made of Baldrige performance criteria or the possibility of achieving this designation. But in the third year of our endeavor, we decided to implement these criteria to organize people into action. We embraced the Baldrige criteria as a powerful way to help us all in designing systems of excellence, and in doing it quickly.

Baldrige is not prescriptive. Instead, in seven critical areas, it asks the "how" question. For example, "How do you get all your executives to follow a plan?" Baldrige evaluators want to see workflow charts put into action and to see the results. They look for a leadership system as one of their criteria. They expect to see excellence and score it accordingly.

Not entirely sure of what we were doing, we took the Baldrige plunge. The whole movement was at first a fuzzy idea. However, it became clear that meeting Baldrige criteria was essential to achieving our ultimate goal of providing the quality care for our patients that we would want for our loved ones. To achieve that standard would require a concerted rigor far beyond what was in place those early years.

Our approach was to create a model system for delivering patient-centered care. The Board's four-paragraph vision statement from our 2010 retreat called for us to implement a new economic and organizational infrastructure to respond to the healthcare needs of a population and to continually improve. Adopting a patient-centered medical home model enabled us to do that. We became a medical care transformation site under an agreement with the federal government and the state of Maryland called the "Maryland Primary Care Model." This agreement helped us to build greater accountability for using primary care as a means to improve health and reduce avoidable hospitalizations.

Installing Leadership Across GBMC with Enabling Systems

Having agreed on our vision of quality care, we needed to operationalize it with employees in a way that moved the organization toward the vision. How would we activate almost four thousand employees to transform GBMC together? We had dozens of executives, several hundred managers and supervisors, all working with thousands of clinicians and non-clinicians; how would we enable them all to embrace the GBMC vision and assume Leadership Roles?

Throughout my career as I would hear other leaders give great speeches, I would often think, "If I could only give a speech like that … everything would move forward." But the ten-year process of committing GBMC to quality care made me realize that speeches are not enough. People may be inspired, but they quickly get caught up in the problems of the moment and inspiration vanishes. We're all good and well-intentioned people, but we still need systems to support and reinforce us in our daily actions.

At GBMC, we came to understand that we needed to implement universal organizational systems to give employees the tools they needed in order to lead, and to model behavior that was universal. Leadership would be made a vital part of management and supervision.

We defined a leader as anyone who was managing at least one other person. Supervisors were called on to play an expanded leadership Role in realizing our shared vision. Over time, we established well-defined systems to provide the necessary support to employees who were stepping into leadership accountabilities.

The Malcolm Baldrige National Quality Award

The Baldrige is the nation's highest presidential honor for performance excellence. Established by the U.S. Congress in 1987 to raise awareness of quality management, and to recognize high-performing U.S. companies that have implemented successful quality management systems. Organizations are judged by an independent board of examiners on achievement and improvement in seven areas.

Baldrige Criteria Categories for Performance Excellence

1. Leadership
2. Strategy
3. Customers
4. Measurement analysis, knowledge management
5. Workforce
6. Operations
7. Results

Five system elements stand out: *strategic planning, performance review, daily executive rounds, leadership as a system of practice,* and *an integrated management system.*

Strategic Planning. The GBMC strategic planning process set goals in a systematic process for all units, with our Board relying on an environmental scan and discussions with an advisory council to update three-year goals. These goals defined what it means to be achieving our Quadruple Aims.

The goals were presented as an expectation – not a request or suggestion—that unit managers would meet. Managers of operational units were held responsible and accountable for performance on these goals. This came with a second accountability, a leadership accountability for improving performance across units. We introduced a formal Leadership System.

Performance Review. GBMC implemented two formal systems of review to help us secure the results we sought:

1. *The Organizational Performance Review System* was implemented as a formal process and method to gauge results in each unit at regular intervals. It became a means of answering the question, "How do we know we're achieving our goals and realizing our vision?" Each organizational unit used the review process to re-set goals and track performance. Executives with oversight were able to assure accountability for goals and acknowledge results.

2. *The Staff Performance Review System* centered on individual employees, with managers meeting with direct reports to engage and coach them. Employees learned how they were performing as individuals and as part of their team. We reviewed, rewarded, and mentored in one-on-one conversations. This was important because, in the end, employees are the true source of performance.

Daily Executive Rounds. For a number of years, rounds were undertaken daily, seven days a week, with the original method driven by a set of Effective Questions: "What are you working on? What are you learning? What is the next test of change?" Each organizational unit was expected to share their ongoing improvement work.

The executive team would meet every morning and walk to each of the major units of the hospital to observe and engage directly with frontline clinicians and staff on the real work of the organization. We would participate in a five-to-seven-minute huddle with the managers and team members in each unit: surgery, labor and delivery, Emergency Department, the intensive care unit, and other key parts of the hospital. Leadership was expected at the unit level, with staff empowered to make changes and share the status, results, and anticipated next steps on their improvement work using a Plan-Do-Study-Act (PDSA) model of improvement. The system of rounds made all this visible and reinforced on a regular, frequent basis. The executive team benefited immensely from our constant and close observation of what was really happening on the front lines, where the real work was being performed.

But now, with our new focus on integrating leadership system-wide, we altered the Executive Rounds to focus on a more strategic approach. We had discovered that improvement and beneficial changes were occurring but were difficult to maintain over time. The teams needed help with strategic design and sustainability. We added six specialists in process design to our quality department. The six began working with units to help build accountability and sustainability into the regular rhythms of improvement, with rounds conducted several times a week, slightly longer and more complex.

On the new system of rounds, staff were routinely recognized and acknowledged. The process encouraged and supported leadership activity and created Net Forward Energy. Frontline employees could see that the senior leadership team was engaged, knowledgeable, and supportive of their daily work.

Leadership Practice as a System. The Baldrige criteria were of immense value in guiding us in establishing an integrated system needed to make leadership universal throughout GBMC, a system of which I'm particularly proud. The system was designed to support leadership behavior across the entire organization. GBMC adapted this leadership system from one used by another high-performing hospital that had received a Baldrige award prior to us in 2002. We taught the system to staff and applied it vigorously.

As mentioned, a leader was defined as anyone at GBMC who managed at least one other person. In addition to their more traditional management responsibilities, every leader was held accountable for seeing the vision come alive in the work of their teams. How managers assumed their leadership Role is described by the GBMC Leadership System in the diagram on the following page.

The system involves four levels representing a set of methods, skills and practices that reinforce each other. At the center, the first level, GBMC vision and aims are used by leaders to capture the stakeholder requirements (the blue and green circle in the center of the diagram). Reviewing how the work at hand aligned with our vision and the Quadruple Aim helped each leader to understand the requirements of our stakeholders.

For example, teams worked hard to improve patient flow among units. To improve patient flow out of the Emergency Department required that the leader of a Medical unit had to understand the requirements of the Emergency Department, as well as the needs of the patient. We recognized that we were all part of the system that the patient moves through, and the parts had to work together.

GBMC Leadership System

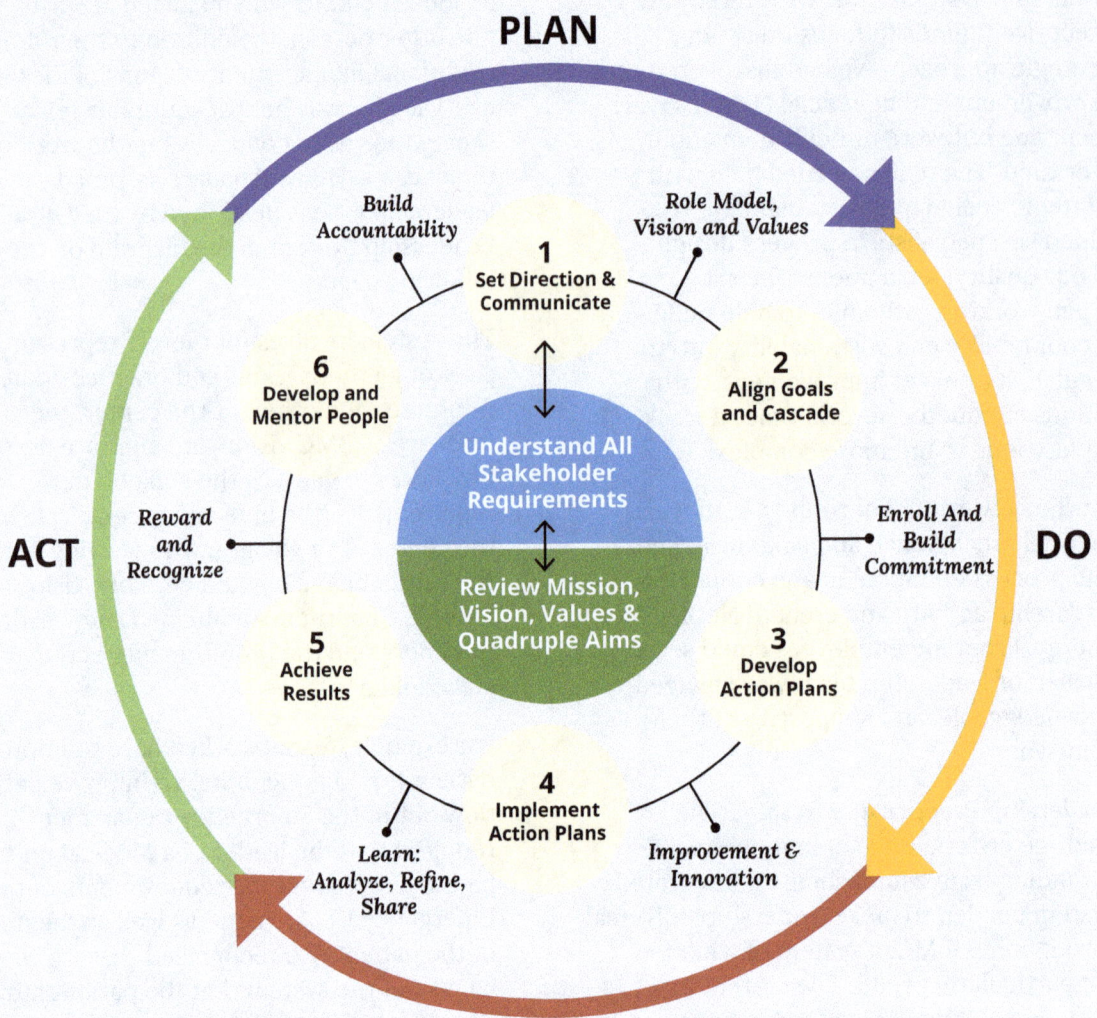

Once the team understood the stakeholder requirements for any given day or task, they followed the six-step action process (the beige circles in level two) in the Leadership System. By following these steps, our leaders and their teams were able to implement the infrastructure and practices needed to serve the patient. The unit level leaders designed the operations they manage by deciding how to meet stakeholder requirements:

"If this is what our stakeholders are telling us, in what ways are we meeting their needs or not meeting their needs? What works? What can we do differently? How will we implement what needs to be done?"

The staff worked through these questions as a team. Leaders then moved to align their team requirements with organization-wide goals. Without alignment, things were not likely to go well. As the goals took shape, the leader cascaded them down to his or her people. Leaders verified that alignment and that the cascading goals were owned by the relevant members of the team. The final three steps were aimed at assuring that action plans were developed, implemented, and that expected results were achieved, all while developing and mentoring people. Each unit leader had a method for designing effective operations.

The leadership work generated a set of six leadership behaviors for which the staff assumed accountability. As named in level three of the figure, the behaviors are intended to reflect unit's Signature Style:

- Role-modeling the vision and values;
- Enrolling and building commitments;
- Driving innovation and improvement by looking for ideas;
- Becoming students of improvement, always learning and sharing;
- Recognizing and rewarding excellent performance;
- Building accountability for results as a habit.

The behaviors create positive energy and strong performance in each unit. These value-driven behaviors help build the Signature Style of each team. They are a proven and effective way of doing work.

The final level of the leadership system was a straightforward and widely used tool mentioned earlier, our Plan-Do-Study-Act (PDSA) model of improvement. At every point in the cycle, and with every behavior, we wanted leaders to know that they can and should always be open to improvement, and that we had an organized method for achieving the improvements. PDSA became a way to help ingrain leadership as a daily habit: to be in action, to test changes, to study their impacts, to learn, refine, improve, and repeat.

The intent of the Leadership System was to make leadership universal. In addition to responsibility for organizational goals, managers were also asked to assume leadership accountability. They were expected to lead by finding ways to model leadership behavior and improve performance across units. They were asked to know where the entire organization was headed at any given moment, and to determine what their units could do to contribute.

The GBMC leadership system required that managers and staff be proactive as leaders. We would reap the tremendous value of this in 2022 when the onslaught of COVID filled Emergency Department waiting rooms to capacity. At first, the strategic goal of reducing throughput time for the Emergency Department (ED) started to crash, with examination times causing an ever-increasing backlog—not what we wanted for our loved ones. Yet on their own initiative, the ED team devised, tested, and refined a triage solution. Doctors were sent out to conduct triage in the waiting room, sending some patients home, and moving others quickly into the ED for examination, treatment, and potential admission. In this manner, our managers were able to relieve pressure on the ED throughput.

Well beyond our ten-year implementation period, GBMC leadership improvement efforts continue to be concrete and visible. One year, we had a six-person hospital-wide team address CAUTI (Catheter Associated Urinary Tract Infection) issues. The team studied hospital performance and designed an evidence-based intervention. The intervention was tested in one surgery unit, refined, and demonstrated to be effective, shared with executive and board leadership, and then proliferated throughout the entire organization, with the CAUTI team ultimately publishing the results.

In summary, every single GBMC manager was charged with a leadership responsibility. They came to expect and accept self-accountability for action: to test, refine and spread solutions, while modeling the behaviors known to engender the culture and the quality care we sought to provide.

Integrated Management System. Students of quality improvement understand that one of the most powerful ideas in Baldrige is the integration of systems that are put in place for planning, managing, evaluation, and administration. As part of the Baldrige criteria, we were expected to integrate a set of organizational systems to grow and deliver excellence. The systems gave us a platform from which to deliver excellence. We designed an organization-wide system to carry out a function in an effective way, learning how that system impacted other systems and how it was impacted in turn by those systems.

As shown in the below figure, the GBMC Integrated Management System was a way to integrate all the operating systems in GBMC. The Strategic Planning system generated three-year targets on our Quadruple Aim. The Daily Executive Rounds connected the senior leadership with the frontline staff on the constant, regular work of improvement. The Organizational Performance Review assured that we produced the results we promised. The Staff Performance Review assured that our workforce was aligned with the commitments we needed to deliver results.

GBMC Integrated Management System

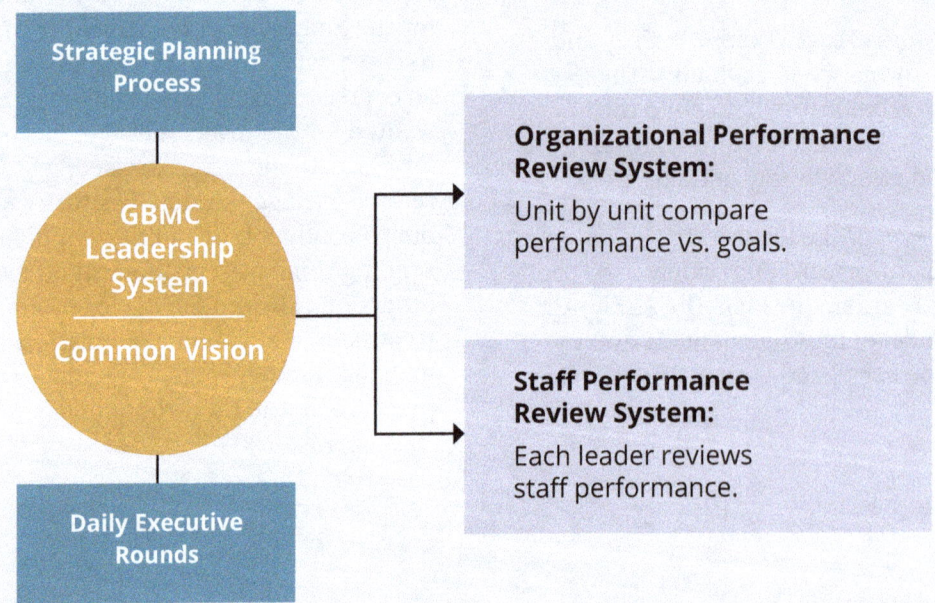

Reaching Out into the Community by Changing Our Business Model

In the past, hospital investment decision-making was driven by covering costs. GBMC couldn't assume initiatives that didn't at least break even financially. But the vision we forged at the retreat back in 2010 required us to take into consideration the genuine needs of the community, and switching to engage in the leadership Role of securing the resources to provide for those needs. We committed to a different business model. We committed to finding others who would bring new and necessary resources to the table.

Several years earlier, the Baltimore Sun had published an article highlighting the troubling lack of healthcare in certain poor neighborhoods, an overwhelming problem that many assumed was too costly to solve. But GBMC leadership chose not to let ourselves off the hook. By asking ourselves that defining question—what access to care would we want for our loved ones?—the answer resulted in an initiative to establish clinics in poor neighborhoods to provide primary and end of life care, and then to add elder care in the home for those who were too frail to be transported to the primary care office. By increasing our philanthropy efforts and partnering with community organizations and local government, GBMC learned how to take on and assume essential projects that would otherwise never be considered because they would not break even. For example, a small hospice program approached us several years ago with a request for help.

They were providing end-of-life care for 25 indigent people, but the program was facing bankruptcy and would be forced to put their dying clients out on the street. With our commitment to quality care at top-of-mind, we agreed to take over the hospice, keep the providers on staff, and care for the patients. Because the original facility was in very poor shape and too costly to repair, GBMC wound up asking the city for help with the building, raising $15 million dollars for the new facility. Through a community development program, the city ceded land to us. Today we are running this hospice in a brand-new, state-of-the-art facility that is part of a larger city "campus" of needed services for poor and vulnerable populations.

This experience helped our team realize that there were many other community organizations eager to connect to a stable, influential, mission-driven healthcare provider like GBMC. From food banks to sport clubs, literally hundreds of charitable social services organizations wanted to team with GBMC. We seized opportunities to better organize community-wide systems of care with many of our partners, such as the one that originally approached us for help on the hospice front. GBMC provided the heavy-weight organizational support needed to integrate these resources into systems of care. As a result, we were able to demonstrate to Baldrige examiners how we were actively and systematically caring for the region's population.

Adopting a Signature Style to Transcend Problems

Effective systems enable us to work productively, lower transaction costs, increase reliability, become efficient, and be creative. Good systems are about people working together. As a person who had worked in a lot of different systems (and non-systems), I learned that leaders can develop a *personal style* that generates positive energy and produces remarkable results.

While at the Boston Medical Center, I became co-chair of the Organ Donation Breakthrough Collaborative (ODBC) of hospitals committed to increasing organ donation rates in their trauma centers. Thousands of participants from hundreds of the nation's largest hospitals would meet in "All Teach, All Learn" events for several days every three or four months. As I participated in these events, I saw approaches used that consistently generated action and caused me to adjust my own leadership practices.

For example, each event began with a profound example of the overarching vision, reminding us why we had joined the collaborative. It was usually a presentation by an organ donor family or a transplant recipient. These were emotional family stories, as the death of one family's loved one leads to the life-saving transplant for another family's loved one. We would ask event participants "What resonated with you about the story of these people? What insight does this give you about the urgency and importance of this work?" This meeting style always created great energy and productive collaboration.

In our work, we naturally process with our brains. But at GBMC we wanted to involve the heart as well as the brain; the story of "why" gets to our heart, triggering the motivation to improve and take action. Attention to the "why" in leadership work is how we generate the will to meet the requirements we set. On assuming my role of GMBC CEO, I was determined to carry over the method continually asking the "why" of leadership and staff and engaging the heart as well as the brain.

Another GBMC leadership approach I carried over from the organ donation events involved a powerful and effective alternative to the traditional problem-solving method.

From early on in my career I was a determined problem-solver: I would step forward, take the problem apart, find out what was broken, figure out who and what was at the source, and then fix it. This was the traditional and widespread approach that I learned and practiced in academic medicine. It's analytical, diagnostic, and it can work. But it can also be time-consuming, painful, blame-centered, and ineffective in many situations.

Looking back on my prior experience in other organizations, I saw that we spent many hours in meetings where we debated and assessed why things were broken and who was responsible. Rarely did we land on effective solutions. For example, in one hospital where I had leadership accountability, we discovered we had over one thousand delinquent patient discharge summaries (clinical reports prepared by physicians outlining the details of the patient's hospitalization).

Lack of discharge details, diagnosis information, and patient health status make it difficult for subsequent primary care doctors and other providers to determine appropriate post-hospital care for their patients. 1000 delinquent discharge summaries posed a serious quality problem and operational breakdown. We had to act. I convened the clinical chiefs to solve our problem. Hour-long meetings would inevitably result in intense discussion on all the reasons why there was a problem . . . and why no one in the room was accountable for the mess. We got no closer to a solution or accountable actions. We even tried surfacing rules as solutions: "If your discharge summaries are not in within five days, your privileges will be suspended," but obviously this wasn't an approach that engendered quality or a constructive, positive environment. There had to be a better way.

During my tenure as Co-Chair of the national collaborative, I learned many simple alternatives to this problem-oriented approach. When a breakdown occurred, we didn't define it as a problem. Instead, we focused on the results we wanted. An influential author and thought leader, Doug Krug, taught us that "we move toward what we focus on." Focus on the problems and you get closer to the problems; focus on your desired results and you move closer to your desired results.

To move closer to the results we wanted, we learned to start by asking effective questions:

- What is already working?
- What are others doing to effectively get the results we want?
- What is our objective?
- What has worked in the past?
- Based on the experience of others, what actions can we take to make things better?

We learned to pull in evidence-based ideas, and then to start testing promising changes quickly. With this approach, I saw the organ donation collaborative teams move quickly into action and systematically make progress toward our goals.

So when I arrived at GBMC, I knew these approaches – asking "why," engaging the heart as well as the mind, moving toward the solution rather than the problem, running on effective questions—would be keys to achieving our vision of quality care. And once that occurred, solutions quickly emerged. I saw my leadership generating positive energy. We shifted the focus from problems to possibilities and opportunities.

As we pursued the Baldrige Award, we ran into problems all the time, as might be expected. We had begun by submitting applications for the award every year; it was not only a way of keeping us accountable to our goal of quality health care, but also placing our endeavor on the radar of the Baldrige selection committee. In 2019, we again submitted an application, thinking we were finally ready, but were disappointed to be passed over.

As we worked to recover from this setback, and learned from our feedback report, we needed a way to take on the inevitable issues that would continue to arise and the breakdowns that would occur. Carolyn Candiello, our Vice President of Quality and Patient Safety, steered us through the process by posing a powerful question:

"Given this situation, what process do we need to redesign to get closer to our vision, and what measures do we have that demonstrate excellence?"

Asking questions like this help to make a setback a learning situation. It represents a dramatic shift in approach – from problem-solving to solution-finding. Carolyn helped us all avoid flipping into the victim box, fumbling around with complaints, and getting lost in answering ineffective questions.

The discipline of Carolyn's question kept us centered and in action in productive ways, and most importantly, kept returning us to our vision: *to provide the quality of care we would want for our loved ones.* That was the vision, our commitment, and our goal. The Baldrige was simply the means to ensuring we would achieve it. And even though we didn't achieve the award in 2019, we did receive "best practice" recognition in Leadership, one of the criteria categories, which let us know we were on the right track.

Carolyn Candiello
Vice President
Quality & Patient Safety, GBMC

Excellence is Embodied Throughout the Entire Institution

We began to realize it would require a solid ten years to effectively integrate systems using Baldrige standards. We kept learning and improving, submitting again in 2020 and earning another site visit. This time, a team of examiners met with several hundred of us virtually. They wanted to understand how we used continuous improvement to provide value.

Baldrige examiners reported excellence throughout the organization. At every level, every one of the hundreds of employees they encountered spoke and lived the mission, which the evaluators found impressive. They saw exceptional performance visibly documented with actionable data across each of the seven Baldrige criteria areas. Two of the many facets of excellence they witnessed stood out: a mission-driven community approach, and health care managed for results.

A *mission-driven community approach* to investment and financial management.
We featured a number of strategic initiatives that brought us closer and deeper into meeting the needs of the community.

- **Population Management & Delivery System Design:** delivery system components that intentionally match the needs of the population in the region – we make the right care available at the right time;

- **Investment In Primary Care:** comprehensive primary care to advance prevention and reduce avoidable hospital utilization, thus reducing the demand for expensive—and profitable—hospital-based services;

- **Joint Ventures to Meet Community Needs:** GBMC launched desperately needed programs that had been avoided in the past on financial grounds. We subsidized them and teamed with community partners to make them sustainable;

- **Pursue Waste Reduction:** the total cost of care is managed under global budgets in order to extract inefficiencies and wasteful practices.

We showed the examiners our Service Pyramid (below), an organized system of care designed to meet the needs of our total population. Level 1 primary care medical homes are at the base. They take care of the many problems that show up day to day. Level 2 is the medical neighborhood. As people age, they develop chronic conditions and need the on-going help of specialists. GBMC integrates primary and specialty care for them to form a medical neighborhood. Level 3 is complex care. We manage the care transitions. With age and more complex illness, our patients may require service in post-acute care and hospital care. At Level 4 we provide in-home elder care and, for those too frail to stay in the home or access the medical home, we provide facility-based care. Level 5 is Hospice care at the top of the pyramid for end-of-life. Gilchrest, which is part of the GBMC system, is the largest hospice on the east coast, with 1,000 patients.

GBMC's Systematic Approach to Caring for a Population of Patients

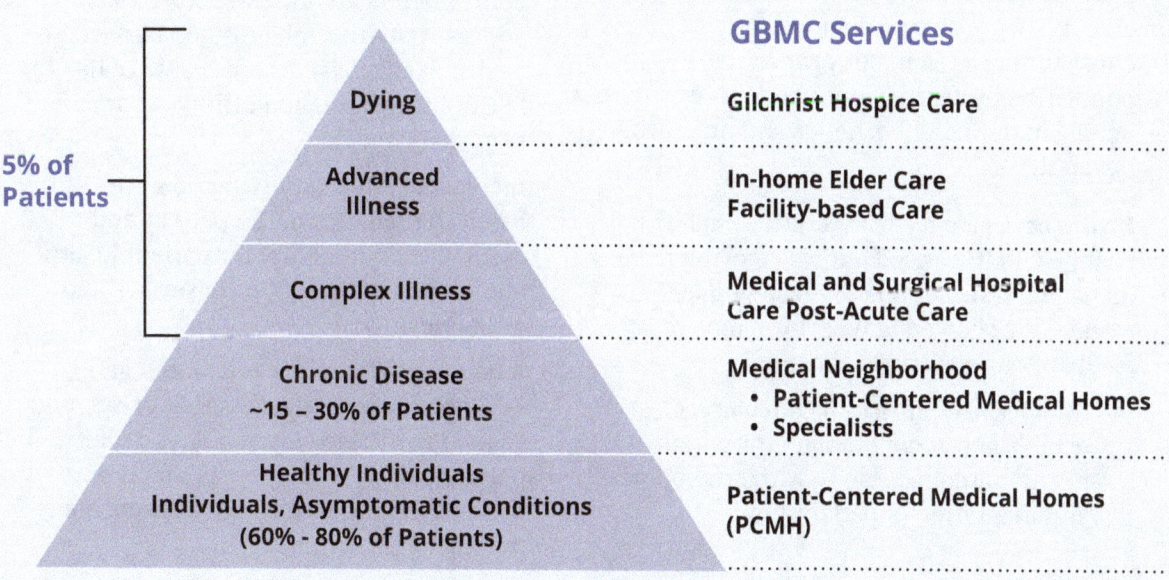

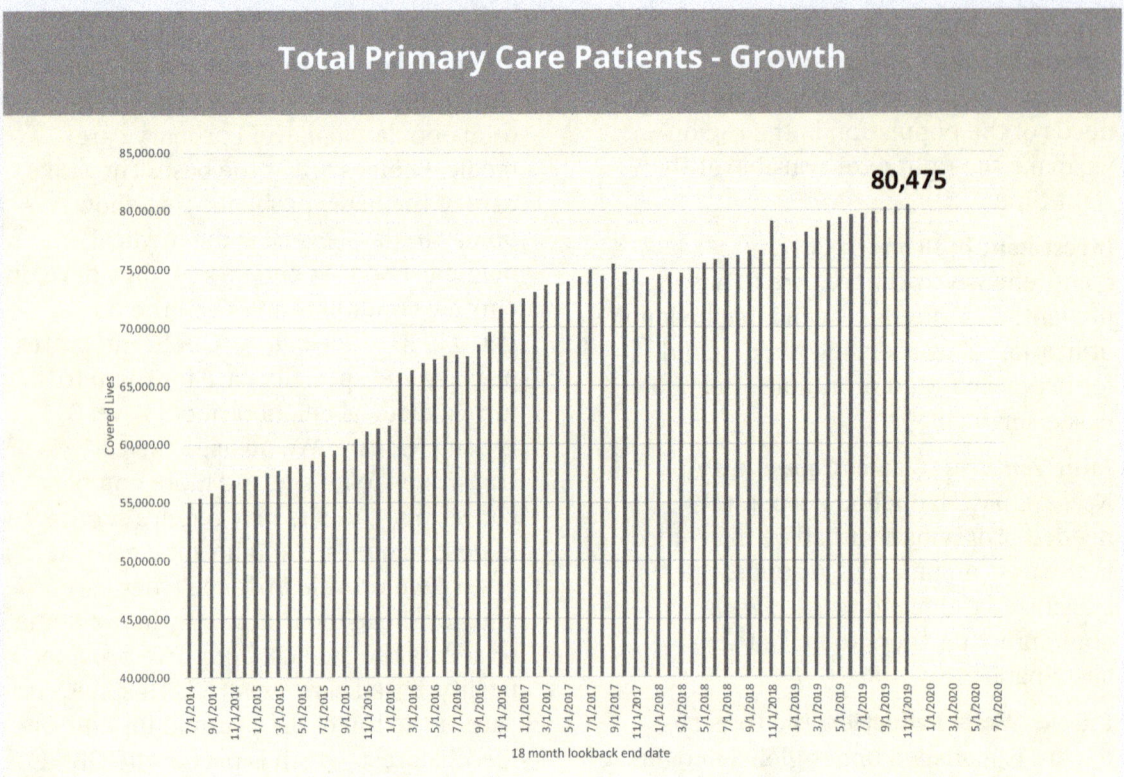

Significantly, GBMC committed to avoiding expanding profitable hospital services to increase revenue. Our approach was to emphasize primary care in order to prevent avoidable hospitalization, and to keep patients at home and out of institutional care. We were able to demonstrate consistent growth in our primary care population by serving more and more people in our neighborhoods and not at the hospital.

Health care managed for results. A major change GBMC carried out was moving from managing transactions to managing for results. We showed real performance on all facets of our quadruple aims:

- *Management of Health Outcomes*: clearly established accountability for patient health outcomes, along with streamlined administration of patient flow.

- *Management of Preventative Services*: systems that assure patients are using and benefiting from preventative care.

- *Addressing the Social Determinants of Health*: regular assessments and coordinated care infrastructure that address patient problems and barriers to health from social determinants of health like housing, food and other essential services.

- *Increasing Patient Satisfaction*: we listen to the voice of the patient and assume accountability for patient health and patient satisfaction via service and outcomes.

- *Advancing Workplace Joy*: watch and advance the many factors that create and sustain workplace joy: employee safety, patient safety, employee satisfaction, patient satisfaction, career advancement, mentoring, and more.

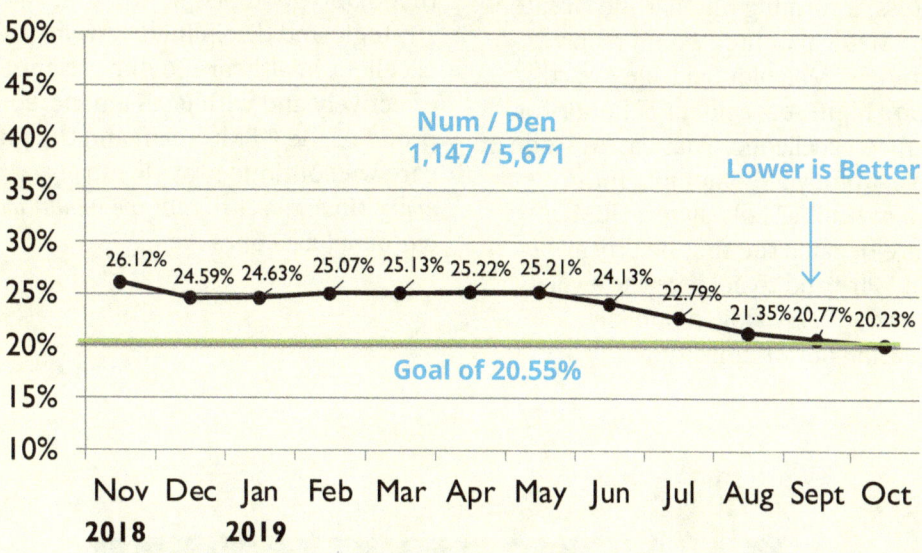

Back in 2010 when we focused on the bottom line and widget care, we didn't know how many patients had which chronic conditions. Now we perform population management of chronic conditions. We can set targets and track performance for the patients we serve. We now know we have 5,600 patients with diabetes out of 80,000. We know we have 1,100 of the 5,600 still lacking in good glycemic control. We can manage care to the population. Primary care practices are now accountable for improvement.

The Baldrige examiners saw and heard how our Quadruple Aim – better health, better care, least waste, and most joy for care providers—was truly being realized, and how our commitment to the community was being met. As the examiners continued to interview staff and review our operations and performance, our scores kept going up and up.

The Phone Rings and GBMC is Acknowledged for Excellence

On November 18, 2020, I got the call. It came from U.S. Commerce Secretary Wilbur Ross, informing me that the Greater Baltimore Medical Center would receive the prestigious Malcolm Baldrige Award, the nation's highest presidential honor for performance excellence. That day was one of the happiest of my life – not just for myself, but for all my GBMC colleagues. GBMC HealthCare became the first healthcare system in Maryland to achieve the award, with Governor Larry Hogan publicly congratulating our organization.

Achieving the Baldrige meant that we had attained a level of system and improvement worthy of national recognition. But far more important, the Award acknowledged that 3,900 good people were engaged in a strategic and disciplined system, providing excellent healthcare to our patients effectively and with joy. I am incredibly proud of the GBMC team and the quality care we continue provide—*to every patient, every time, the care that we would want for our own loved ones.*

Reflections on John Chessare Leadership Story

When Dr. Chessare came to GBMC in 2010, he brought with him a passion for managing large health care systems and a career-long commitment to quality improvement. His early career track caused him to see that hospital system health care could be so much better in an era when most executives were not focused on quality. On arrival at GBMC, he made a series of leadership Choices with the Board that resulted in a powerful shared vision, placing the hospital system on the road to becoming a recognized national leader for excellence in quality.

Dr. Chessare and the Board were committed to a Compelling Vision and to a way of Being: *For every patient, every time, we will provide the care that we would want for our own loved ones.* They set bold quadruple aims to manage. In moving forward, Dr. Chessare and his leadership team had challenging Choices to make within the Domain of Roles.

Choices Guided by Role Switching and Dimensions of Action

One of GBMC's key challenges was establishing the embrace of leadership Roles throughout the organization.

"We had dozens of executives, several hundred managers and supervisors, all working with thousands of clinicians and non-clinicians; how would we enable them all to embrace the GBMC vision and assume leadership Roles?"

Notice that in other Leadership Stories, the challenge is to obtain voluntary commitment to the vision from independent parties. In the Berwick story of the 100,000 Lives Campaign, the vision was to engage several thousand hospitals. In the Sanjeev Arora story, the vision was to enlist independent physicians, first throughout the State of New Mexico, and eventually across the world. GBMC had 3,900 employees to enlist in the vision. They were not independent players, but the leadership vision was not the kind of goal that could be issued as a directive through the organization structure. Employees had to choose to voluntarily commit, own the vision, and step into leadership Roles. Dr. Chessare and the team had to introduce leadership as practice throughout the workforce and align it with compatible management and administrative Roles.

Pursuing the Baldrige designation turned out to be an effective way to mobilize action and build leadership and other enabling systems at GBMC. To achieve the Baldrige Award, the entire organization had to engage and commit. The process was very public, involving outside examiners doing deep reviews. There was no hiding.

The Baldrige program is not about implementing a checklist and it is not about compliance. Instead, the criteria require generative, thoughtful leadership in action and building systems. Rather than adopt specific practices and follow a set of rules, the organization had to create their own culture and performance systems. Dr. Chessare used the Baldrige Award process to move the entire GBMC healthcare system into action on the vision and to achieve the GBMC Quadruple Aim.

Over the course of ten years, GBMC was remade internally on four of the 5 Dimensions of Action: hierarchical, subordinate, peer, and process. The GBMC vision also resulted in new work on the public dimension of action: the external community served by the hospital. GBMC changed its business model to enable it to work with the community by assuming greater accountability and new partnerships for expanded local delivery systems, such as the struggling hospice program with 25 indigent patients.

"The vision we forged at the retreat back in 2010 required us to take into consideration the genuine needs of the community, and to locate the resources to provide for those needs."

GBMC moved from investing in profitable, but not necessarily the most needed, hospital service lines ("widgets") to developing partnerships and financing that meets serious community needs in primary care, clinics in low-income areas, and hospice care. Without the commitment to a Compelling Vision, these external partnerships would have been considered too risky and would not have happened.

A Story of Employee Leadership, Workforce Joy, and Signature Style

Dr. Chessare's Leadership Story illustrates many of the Mindsets and Methods presented in this book. Three unique lessons of Dr. Chessare's story stand out for us: the focus on employee leadership development; the experience of workforce joy in providing service; and the refinement of a Signature Style of leadership.

The first lesson is the universal spread of employee leadership development throughout the organization.

"We defined a leader as anyone who was managing at least one other person. Supervisors were called on to play an expanded leadership Role in realizing our shared vision. Over time, we established well-defined systems to provide the necessary support to employees who were stepping into leadership accountabilities."

This was a courageous step and a long-term commitment. Leadership behavior was requested and investment in a robust leadership development campaign and a formal leadership system supported the Role. The entire workforce was mobilized.

The second lesson concerns the addition of workforce joy to the IHI's Triple Aim, a telling and effective leadership action by Dr. Chessare and the GBMC board of directors. It sent a vitally important message to the entire workforce that their well-being mattered, and it anchored them in the compelling and rewarding purpose of "providing care that they would want for their own loved ones."

"All my GBMC colleagues got it: there is joy in service. When we have a bad day, calling to mind one person we helped can bring a smile to our faces and joy to our hearts. This is not a giddy type of joy; it's the power of purpose—knowing that we've served another in their time of need."

This is an example of creating Net Forward Energy. It also illustrates the creative and energizing use of Bold Aims.

The third lesson lies in Dr. Chessare's development of his own unique leadership Signature Style. Over a 40-year career, Dr. Chessare worked at developing his personal vision while incorporating the Mindsets and Methods of Role Switching and working across the 5 Dimensions of Action.

"As a person who had worked in a lot of different systems (and non-systems), I learned that leaders can develop a personal style that generates positive energy and produces remarkable results."

It was exciting and personally rewarding for us to learn how Dr. Chessare was able to further develop a number of leadership tools he acquired during his work in the Organ Donation Breakthrough Collaborative and then apply them at GBMC.

"Another GBMC leadership approach I carried over from ODBC events involved a powerful and effective alternative to the traditional problem-solving method . . . So when I arrived at GBMC, I knew this approach – asking 'why,' engaging the heart as well as the mind, moving toward the solution rather than the problem, asking effective questions to lead change— would be key to achieving our vision of quality care. And once that occurred, solutions quickly emerged. I saw my leadership generating positive energy. We shifted the focus from problems to possibilities and opportunities."

We saw Dr. Chessare's effectiveness in mastering the ability to switch among each of the key Roles of Observer, Administrator, Manager, and Leader. He developed and used his ability in each of these Roles to help make GBMC an exceptional Baldrige-achieving enterprise. In particular, he intentionally chose to develop the skills needed to establish the organizational systems necessary to help clinicians and others to thrive in hospital and healthcare environments.

Observer	Leads executive team in Morning Rounds - everyday— in all major hospital departments in huddles with teams
Administrator	Keeps GBMC in sound financial standing through disciplined budgetary and payment processes, while focusing on investments in population health
Manager	Delivers exceptional results on multiple dimensions of care quality by establishing the necessary systems to support patients and caregivers
Leader	Establishes, models and effectively spreads a Mission/Vision, Net Forward Energy and the necessary systems, which ultimately results in achieving the prestigious Malcolm Baldrige Designation in 2020

National Leadership Recognition

The Baldrige campaign required ten years of disciplined action, testing, and systems-building. This was a long-term effort that touched everyone in the organization—all 3,900 employees in clinical and non-clinical areas. When the Baldrige examiners visited GBMC in 2020, they encountered excellence and the discipline of leadership throughout the organization. Every one of the hundreds of employees they met with spoke and lived the mission. The examiners saw exceptional performance documented and displayed with actionable data and results. There was both leadership and management accountability for results and for positive, productive, uplifting, and empowering ways of Being.

In April 2022, two years after GBMC achieved the Baldrige Award, the Baldrige Foundation honored Dr. Chessare more personally with its prestigious Harry S. Hertz Leadership Award which recognizes role model leaders who challenge, encourage, and empower others to achieve performance excellence. Al Faber, President and CEO of the Foundation for the Malcolm Baldrige National Quality Award, Inc., called Dr. Chessare "a role model leader deeply committed to the Baldrige framework and who embodies the Baldrige leadership principles."

We would also call him a role model for demonstrating the joy and "the power of purpose" in choosing to deliver transformative results while serving the needs of others. All of us have much to learn and to gain from the compelling leadership example of John Chessare.

ROLES

Role Switching

5 Dimensions of Action

Pacing Events

Leaders Thrive on Pacing Events

Pacing Events Move Us into Action on our Compelling Vision

Former CIA executive and business leader Robert Kohler reminds us that a critical element of leadership work is the making, securing, and delivering of commitments. Idle talk about commitments, which dominates the agenda of many conferences and meetings, will not change the world. Meetings and events in which participants make, secure, and deliver commitments are one of the key pathways to action, change, and results. Meetings that generate uplifting and transformative leadership work are what we refer to as Pacing Events.

Pacing Events bring together people with a stake in a Compelling Vision and the means to contribute to its achievement. For this highly impactful Mindset and Method, the term *pacing* conveys movement, action, and results. The movement and action are often preparatory or incremental rather than defining or complete. The event becomes a platform for sharing, learning, action, and dealmaking. Pacing Events, by design, generate commitments and celebrate their delivery. They transform regular meetings into engines for results. Think of that—meetings as result engines!

Any ordinary meeting can be turned into a Pacing Event, whether we own the event or have been invited by someone else to participate in their event. Size can range from two attendees to tens to hundreds and even thousands, and can take the form of staff meetings, campaign events, professional conferences, working sessions, education programs, virtual meetings, conference calls, or myriad other possibilities.

But design is required. The vision needs to be communicated in a way that the audience finds relevant and compelling. Shared understanding and Net Forward Energy need to be generated.

Uncertainties, ambiguities, competing priorities and negative energy will naturally make an appearance. They need to be acknowledged and worked with. Requests and Offers and deals are made. Commitments are sought, and because commitments are personal, new relationships are formed. Time and space are needed for serious conversations, with each person provided ample opportunities to express themselves.

There are multiple approaches for designing and conducting Pacing Events that represent a marked and often joyous departure from the conventional and unproductive formats that are frequently a fixture of our professional lives. Pacing Events are also an outstanding way to rapidly develop and refine our own Signature Style of leadership. The sections that follow provide the methods and examples of Pacing Events that will equip and support leaders in proactively designing and conducting your meetings and events to bring the transformative future you want into the world.

If Pacing Events are the Solution, What is the Problem?

How many times have we heard ourselves or our colleagues lament the hours wasted in meetings? Meetings should be time well-invested, useful, and uplifting. As leaders of multiple major initiatives over the last three decades, we have participated in or guided thousands of meetings and events ranging from small to enormous, from less than an hour to covering several days. We found ourselves constantly confronted by the same three challenges: participant mindsets, passive design, and lack of clear Intent.

The challenge of participant mindsets

One of the main challenges in our virtual and in-person meetings is participant mindset. In particular, we encounter three major barriers which can affect participant behavior and event outcome: short attention spans, unique controlling concerns, and pent-up information processing power:

- *Short attention spans.* People are easily distracted. Presentations of 45 minutes or longer and multiple back-to-back presentations cause audiences to tune out. Smart phones and other devices create hard-to-resist distractions. We need our participants to remain present, listening, and engaged.

- *Unique controlling concerns.* Each person in the room brings in their own agendas, perspectives, and personal circumstances that can substantially impact their listening and their focus. Competing logistical or personal topics silently intrude: "How am I going to get caught up on that project back at the office?" "Am I going to need to reschedule my afternoon meetings?" "My daughter's home sick. I wonder how she's doing?" We need our participants to own and remain anchored in the meeting purpose, not the myriad other issues which, while important, distract from the needs of the present moment.

- *Pent-up information processing power*: Participants can become resistant when listening to speaker after speaker, often eventually leading to a spiral of critical and frequently negative assessments about what can't be done, why that won't work, how others stand in the way, how their situation is different, etc. We need our participants to hold these critical assessments in check and instead to connect with the content through relatedness, possibilities, and opportunities for potential action.

The challenge of traditional passive meeting design

Traditional meeting design is based on the default structure of a relatively passive exchange of information. Consider the format of a professional conference:

- Opening, with topic and speaker introduction;
- Presentation by speaker;
- Questions & Answers.

One or more speakers, their Intent often unclear, present for 45-60 minutes. A handful of participants pose random questions. Others observe, listen or not, drifting in and out. Decisions about what action to take based on the presentation content, if any, are left to each participant, and those decisions are not made visible.

For leadership work we saw the need for shorter presentations followed by participants rapidly processing the information, fully engaged and interacting, committing to mutual action with each other. We realized that participants themselves had much to contribute. They could become co-generators of the content, not just passive receptacles for the wisdom of a few chosen speakers. The answers to the most pressing questions are often in the room but are unintentionally suppressed by traditional event design.

The challenge of establishing Intent

It is important to link the Intent of the event to the interests and needs of our participants. But these interests and needs can vary depending on differences in participant organizations, professions, and work cultures. We came to see that we needed to clearly demonstrate how the activities and purposes of the event were tailored to the needs and interests of its participants.

Clear Intent is at the heart of the design of Pacing Events. The design of a Pacing Event, large or small, is driven by our goals for whatever meeting, webinar, or conference we are conducting. Consider just a few examples of the diverse intentions we might establish for a Pacing Event:

- *Securing commitments for action and next steps on our Compelling Vision;*
- *Tapping into the Abundance of knowledge and experience of all participants;*
- *Creating a renewed sense of energy and momentum;*
- *Pausing to celebrate progress and those responsible;*
- *Creating a breakthrough—altogether new ways of thinking to get beyond a plateau;*
- *Generating a flurry of innovations for achieving our goals*
- *Understanding and spreading best practices of ; high performers.*

Depending on which of the above Intents we are seeking to achieve, the content, presenters, and questions to run on would be quite different.

Addressing Pacing Event Challenges with 10 Principles of Design

Early on as event leaders, we found that our meetings were constantly falling short of what was possible due to the challenges of audience mindset, passive design, and lack of clear Intent. We learned that we needed the full attention of the room and an ability to have participants talking to each other on a common agenda. We learned that generating commitment, action, energy, joy, and results on vision required a far more dynamic format than we were using. And we learned that once our Intent was established and challenges addressed, we could successfully gain mutual ownership and action towards shared goals.

Systematically working on these challenges spurred us to identify features of effective meetings and events. Over the course of years and with thousands of our colleagues, we have developed, tested, and established a handy list of ten overlapping design principles for Pacing Events:

1. **Establish a Common Mindset:** Frame the event with key, shared purposes; request that participants be present as a source of Net Forward Energy for these purposes;

2. **Run On Effective Questions:** Craft one or a few questions that enable participants to quickly understand and easily contribute to the shared purpose of the event;

3. **Intentional Use of Speech Acts:** Use powerful Speech Acts such as Declarations, Assertions, Requests, Offers, Commitments, and Acknowledgements to create participant insight and action;

4. **Short Presentations:** Segment content for presentation; follow each presentation with participant processing to mine the wisdom of the group; sustain high levels of participant presence and energy;

5. **Participant Interaction:** Have participants in small groups respond to Effective Questions throughout; have participants engage with and benefit from the processing power in the room;

6. **Participation Acknowledged:** Reflect on and celebrate the level of interaction in the event and the energy it creates;

7. **Variation In Process:** Use variation in methods of presentation and interaction to keep attention and engagement high;

8. **The Answers are in the Room:** Surface the knowledge, capabilities, interests of participants; replace standard meeting Q & A format with participants responding to Effective Questions;

9. **All Teach, All Learn:** Provide all participants with opportunities to contribute;

10. **Captured:** Acknowledge and document in some manner the insights and commitments by those in the room – publicly appreciate these contributions.

Over time, we incorporated these design features into a straightforward template for planning and designing Pacing Events. The following three-part template on Pacing Events enables each of us to deploy the essential features listed above and to continuously test and add new features.

A Three-Part Template for Pacing Events

Imagine: a results-oriented meeting driven by audience engagement, dynamic design, and clear Intent. Such a meeting—a Pacing Event—follows a very specific and active structure:

A. Event Framing: Establish the purposes, mindset, and tone of the meeting; don't just let these critical factors evolve on their own;

B. Powerful Cycles: A few short presentations with immediate processing of the content;

C. Moving Into Action Together: Create spaces for participants to engage with one another in order to generate insights, foster relationships, and make and share commitments.

The figure below shows the logic structure of Pacing Events as significantly different from the logic structure of Traditional Events. The Pacing Event template represents a group process for effective learning, engagement, and action. Both templates are effective, but each serves a markedly different purpose.

Traditional Event	Pacing Event
Objective Share well-developed, timely topic information; create opportunity for networking	**Objective** Secure interest in and commitments to action on a Compelling Vision
Core Agenda **A. Opening** Introduce speaker and topic **B. Formal Presentation** Speaker shares subject matter information in formal presentation style **C. Question and Answer** Questions or observations from several participants with speaker response	**Core Agenda** **A. Event Framing** Establish the shared purposes, Net Forward Energy, and type of listening needed for this particular event **B. Powerful Cycles** Short content presentations, with rapid information processing in small groups **C. Moving Into Action Together** Group processes enable participants to work together through the six conversations for action

The Pacing Event structure can work for groups of any size, ranging from small team meetings to international conferences with thousands of participants. The possibilities are infinite.

A. Event Framing: create readiness for shared work

Framing the Event is a short conversational presentation between the moderator and the participants. For example, a 60- or 90-minute session may have an opening 5-minute framing. The moderator engages directly with the participants and establishes the conditions that will enable the moderator, presenters, and participants to work effectively together. Presenters and participants are asked to engage with a "How-to-Be" mindset, and to process the content and experience accordingly.

Framing creates a common mindset in the room. It transforms participants from a roomful of individuals to a group poised to work together toward a common purpose. The framing elements used to create this readiness are:

- *Leadership Intent articulated through Declarations and Assertions;*
- *Effective Questions that will drive the event;*
- *Requests that call for certain ways of Being, linked to event purpose;*
- *Participant acknowledgement of the framing.*

Leadership Intent articulated through Declarations and Assertions.

Intent can be expressed in terms of the leadership vision and, depending on how aligned or unaligned the audience may be with that vision, in terms of immediate desired outcomes. The statement of Intent should be expressed memorably and in under one minute. A visually striking picture or slide can serve as a graphic reinforcement. Use Leadership Speech Acts such as Declarations and Assertions to express what the leadership team stands for. (Note: Do not waste precious high-attention minutes at the beginning of your event with administrative details like where the bathrooms are located and when lunch will be served.)

Offer the Effective Questions that will drive the event

In framing, we ask participants to listen throughout the meeting with one or more Effective Questions they will be asked to answer. Consider the following examples of common event purposes framed as Effective Questions:

Event Purpose	Questions to Drive Event
Gain information and insights about new and emerging practices in our profession.	*What are cutting-edge practices that my organization should be made aware of?*
Become more effective and current in the ways we perform our work.	*What actions will I take to put these new information and insights to work in my job?*
Deeper engagement with colleagues to transform performance of our organizations.	*What Requests and Offers can I make today to colleagues to significantly expand our impact?*

Launching an event by explicitly stating the questions the meeting seeks to answer is a highly effective way to begin creating a shared mindset for those present. The Effective Questions draw us in and make crystal clear the nature of the work that will take place in the event. The common mindset is a powerful way to enhance shared learning and action. We start thinking about our own answers and wondering what answers we may hear from presenters and other participants.

Requests on How to Be.

For Pacing Events, we want to proactively establish a specific mood or state of Being. Get clear on the states of Being needed to achieve the goals of your event, and then call for these states of Being among participants, e.g., to be celebratory; to be analytical; to be engaging with experts and others to make deals and commitments. Above all, Pacing Events need people to be present and positive, to be engaged with one another, and to be in action.

- *Be present and positive*: To answer the Effective Questions driving the event, audience members need to pay attention and share with others. The leaders of the event need to describe the fast pace and exciting dynamics that participants are about to encounter. Coach them quickly on the nature of Net Forward Energy and request that they join with each other in fostering it.
- *Be engaged.* Prepare the audience for the interactive nature of the event. They will be asked to process what they are hearing in small groups and the insights they are gaining. Request that people be prepared and open to volunteering answers to Effective Questions.
- *Be in action.* Coaching presenters and participants to make Requests and Offers to each other will instantly transform events from a state of information sharing to a state of commitment and future action.

Participant acknowledgement of the framing.

Coming out of the event Framing, take a moment to have participants acknowledge the Requests and Offers being made. Create an engaging way to get a reply with a show of hands, a head nod of affirmation or a Word Cloud. Consider using a quick poll to jump-start the interactive nature of the event. Perform these actions with the Intent of affirming the answers from the audience – make any answer a good answer. Having ways to affirm and acknowledge participation throughout is a powerful way to build energy and momentum.

The goal is to create a positive and shared listening mindset that opens participants to achieving the central purposes of the event.

B. Powerful Cycles: short presentations with rapid processing by all participants

Most Pacing Events feature several speakers delivering short but impactful presentations. Each of these presentations is part of a process called the Powerful Cycle.

The Powerful Cycle is a five-step moderated process that begins with framing the cycle and ends with participants understanding how they and their colleagues are processing and using the presentation content.

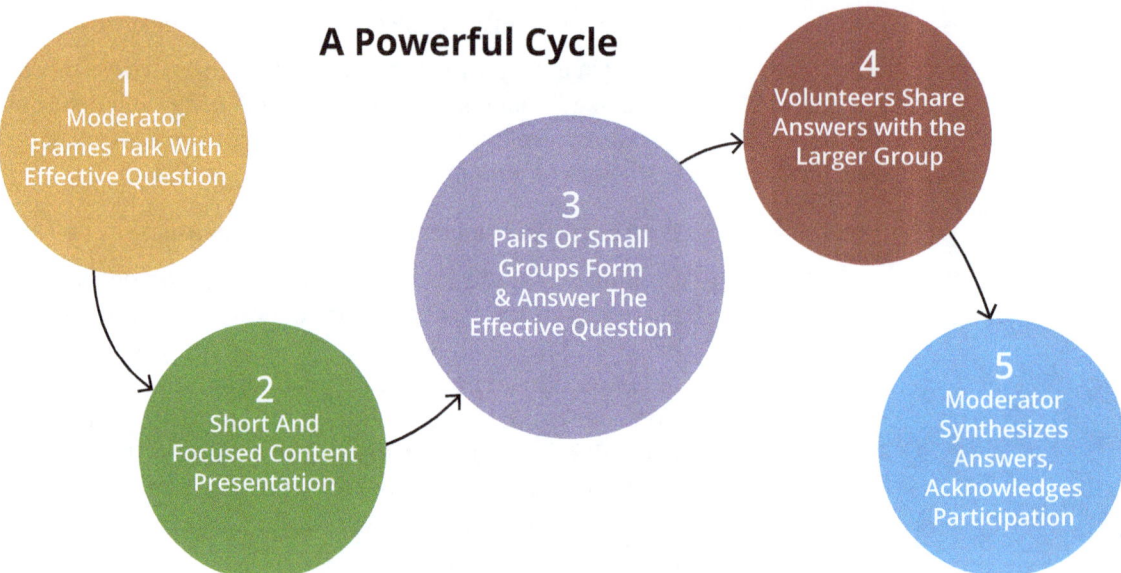

A five-step Powerful Cycle might take no more than 20 to 30 minutes total. As always in this format, the participants answer questions rather than the speaker!

Step 1: Framing with an Effective Question

Format: The moderator takes 1-3 minutes to frame the presentation by articulating the purpose of the meeting segment and giving the audience an Effective Question to consider as they listen such as: "What resonates with me the most as I listen to this presentation?" or "What action am I likely to take based on what I am hearing?"

Benefit: The Moderator establishes a common mindset and way of listening to the content for every person present in the room. All of those present will be in small groups answering the same generative question. Groups will surface a variety of answers which will enrich the conversation.

Step 2: Short Focused Presentation

Format: The presentation might take 7-12 minutes.

Benefit: Requires the presenter to condense content into the most relevant and actionable information. The natural short attention spans of adult learners are honored.

Step 3: Processing in Pairs or Small Groups

Format: Following the presentation, the moderator gives participants 3-5 minutes to pair with one other person and discuss their answers to the framing question.

Benefit: Every single person in the audience has an opportunity to express themselves. This keeps individual energy from becoming suppressed, as frequently happens with lengthy presentations and limited opportunities to engage with others. The interactive discussion enables every participant to process the content of the speaker with at least one other person, which supports positive energy and engagement.

Step 4: Volunteers Share Content and Ideas

Format: following the paired discussions, the presenter or moderator takes another 5-7 minutes to ask several participants to share their answer with the full group. The moderator should select volunteers in a way that makes evident the full range of answers in the room.

Benefit: Enables the larger group to see, appreciate, and possibly to act on the diversity and richness of ideas expressed by others. We tap into the wisdom of the group. We see a wider range of responses to the presentation.

Powerful Cycle

is a term coined by Simon McNabb, a former senior analyst at the US Environmental Protection Agency. Simon named this method as our team was working on the design of Pacing Events to be held with senior leaders in Thailand and Vietnam as part of the EPA's Office of International Activities effort to assist other nations with their pressing environmental challenges.

Step 5: Acknowledgement and Synthesis of Responses

Format: As responses are collected, the presenter should look for ways to affirm and acknowledge the insights and planned actions of those who volunteered answers. We often have small gifts or books to present to those who share answers as a way of physically and more viscerally conveying appreciation for the engagement of active participants.

Benefit: Active listening by the moderator helps to affirm the answers for the full group, showing that insights and actions of participants are valuable. This rewards energy and engagement, which helps to sustain continued energy and engagement for subsequent cycles and sessions. Energy skyrockets.

While the Powerful Cycle is a straightforward and relatively easy to implement process, the implications are immense. More than two decades of experience with the Powerful Cycle have taught us and thousands of others that this simple but structured method of conducting meetings is highly effective. We not only use the Powerful Cycle in meetings that we design and conduct, we also use it when we are invited to participate in the meetings and events of others. For example, if invited to give a 45-minute keynote presentation at a conference, we would construct the keynote with two or three Powerful Cycles so that the audience is actively engaged in the content of the presentation. The energy, commitments, and actions generated by the systematic use of this one method are truly transformative.

What Makes The Powerful Cycle Powerful

Powerful Cycle Element	Benefits Realized
Framing The Cycle	All are present and "running on" the same question.
Short Focused Presentations	Information packets easy to process quickly.
Processing in Pairs or Small Groups	Everyone in audience is actively participating.
Volunteers Called on to Share Content	Tap into the collective wisdom of the crowd.
Answers Synthesized, Participation Affirmed	Communication verified. Energy skyrockets.

C. Moving Into Action: Effective questions guide conversations for action

In designing Pacing Events and selecting the Effective Questions for audience processing, it is helpful to remember the dynamic stages that people move through in contemplating relationships, change, and action. These six stages, described in an earlier segment on Language and Speech Acts, are presented in the Table on the following page.

When we first meet people, we can think of ways to get related around mutual interest. Then we move to sharing world views and agendas. Together, we will start to see possibilities for joint action. Opportunities present themselves. By this point, there is often enough context and relatedness to make Requests and Offers. As the resulting Commitments are made, relationships will flourish as those promises are kept and acknowledged. Knowledge of these stages can help us plan the sequence of Effective Questions that will keep our participants moving quickly through these stages towards united action.

Throughout the Pacing Event, group processes can be used to foster conversations, or in a series of Powerful Cycles, or 15-30 minute table conversations, or full group polling sequences. We have had good experience with other similar well-established meeting management methods such as Open Space and Peer Assist.

In our experience, the use of Effective Questions to guide conversations is essential. For example, following presentations by several high performers, we might ask the following question to precipitate insight and understanding:

"What were the greatest insights that each of us got from this set of presentations?"

We might follow this with another question to generate action:

"What did each of us hear in these presentations that we could adapt and test back home in our own organizations?"

If we study these two very straightforward Effective Questions, we can see that almost every answer we can imagine could potentially move us forward. The answers are about insight and action, generated by the people answering the question. Crafting and using these kinds of Effective Questions is at the heart of leading change; we use the questions to help ourselves and others to invent our own changes. When we do this publicly in front of others, we also tap into the wisdom of the group and exponentially expand the scope of answers provided to participants.

The sharing of answers across the full audience also creates new insights and additional action possibilities for others. These questions are also sequenced in accordance with what we know about the natural order of Conversations Towards Action described in the figure below.

Six Conversations Towards Action

1. **Relatedness** Mutual interests surface;
2. **Possibility** A new and positive future is seen;
3. **Opportunity** Options for working together emerge;
4. **Commitment** From Requests & Offers to a promise;
5. **Accountability** Delivery on the promise;
6. **Acknowledgement** Appreciation that the promise was kept and accounted for.

Pacing Events Are Dynamic and Generative Experiences

Leaders can benefit immensely from gaining the ability to produce effective Pacing Events. There are a lot of techniques and tools to play with in designing Pacing Event. Mastering them takes time and experience. It helps to keep in mind and prepare for several features: Pacing Events must be managed; Pacing Events will deliver dramatic results; and Pacing Events are likely to present new challenges. It's important and exciting work with big payoffs.

Pacing Events must be managed.

Pacing Events are not a rote method or a cookbook recipe – use of these methods require thought, planning, and a tailored approach to each event. There are infinite ways to configure and use the methods detailed here in the design and management of your own events. Additionally, the insight, deals, and commitments produced by the event are unpredictable, but in a good way. Event design needs to allow room for these to surface, with capture and follow-through on the results.

The figure below illustrates a sample design for management of a two-hour Pacing Event by a team of one or more moderators with 25-50 participants. After Event Framing, a series of three Powerful Cycles is followed by group conversations for action.

A Pacing Event Model: 2 hour meeting, 25 – 50 participants

Team Preparation

Event Framing: creating a listening mindset
- Declarations & Assertions express intent
- Request on how-to-be: Net Forward Energy, Requests & Offers
- Effective Questions to drive the meeting
- Acknowledge audience acceptance

2 Hour Event Agenda

Framing (10 minutes)

Dialogue (75 minutes)
- Power Cycle #1
- Power Cycle #2
- Power Cycle #3

Small & Full Group Exercises (35 minutes)
- Share Commitments
- Leaving In Action

Follow Through

Power Cycles: Short talks, rapid processing
- Effective Questions
- Leadership Stories
- Small group processing
- Use of Scripts for reporting out

Moving Into Action Together
- Group processes for insight and deals
- Requests and offers
- Commitment sharing

The nature of Powerful Cycles and group processes make Pacing Events dynamic, generative, and full of surprises. Many of the most exciting results of a Pacing Event are unexpected. Consider these examples from the Organ Donation Breakthrough Collaborative work that was profiled in an earlier chapter:

- Clinical triggers for potential donors were surfaced at an event in response to physician resistance to early notification of organ procurement organizations;
- Donation after cardiac death (DCD) became a national movement in the Collaborative after a presentation and call-to-action Leadership Story by a parent whose son was a DCD donor.

These are the kind of transformative insights and actions that we seek, and they are precipitated by well-managed Conversations Towards Action among participants. Leadership Stories can be used with great effect as presentations in Powerful Cycles.

Powerful Cycles and group processes in the above design will surface possibilities, opportunities, and Commitments. Leaders must be prepared to see and hear these assets as they surface and respond in ways that embrace them. Event managers should be ready to adjust the design to take advantage of the energy and emerging possibilities, to acknowledge Commitments being offered, to use Speech Acts such as Requests and Offers, DNA, *Yes, and* ..., and to Flip Negative Energy.

Yes, Pacing Events can be unpredictable. The good news is that they are manageable. And when well-managed, the result is Abundance – of energy, ideas, offers, requests, commitments, action and results!

Pacing Events deliver dramatic results.

Pacing Events are a radical and surprising departure from the conventional meeting format we have been trained to expect. The remarkable differences are shown in the table below.

The dramatic results referred to are participants in action toward achievement of shared goals. Participants gain insight and energy as they move through some version of the Six Conversations Towards Action. Results can range from greater insight, stronger relatedness on to significant commitments and new partnerships.

It's useful to view Pacing Events as a practice that takes time to master and a skill set that is worth continually refining. Look for ways to introduce Pacing Events into your current work and to introduce the Powerful Cycle and other Pacing Event methods as you participate in the events of others.

Traditional Event vs. Pacing Events: Distinctions In Approach		
Meeting Design Factor	**Traditional Events**	**Pacing Event**
Purpose	Information share, learning	Leave in action on vision
Agenda	Topics to be covered	Possibilities, opportunities
Participant Mindset	Unique to each participant	Common, tied to vision
Presentations	Lengthy talks, heavy slides	Short talks; few, simple slides
Audience Involvement	Asks the speaker questions	Answers Effective Questions
Processing Content	Weak; solo or with colleague	Powerful, by all participants
Networking	Informal during breaks	Organized dealmaking
Participant Interaction	Few opportunities	Major time commitment
Energy	Left to chance, dissipates	Re-energized systematically

Pacing Events present opportunities for further development.

Mastering effective use of Pacing Events is a never-ending opportunity for change and improvement. There are always thorny new issues to address and interesting methods and technologies to try. While we have surfaced methods that enable us to navigate known challenges with relative ease, there is still room for improvement. Four areas that we would give special attention to in the future are:

- Making virtual convenings as powerful as in-person events;
- Helping participants learn to engage in the moment;
- Providing access to the leadership Signature Style in play; and,
- Acknowledging in-the-moment the participation of individuals.

In-person vs. virtual conferencing. Much of our work has taken place with in-person events. Here size made a difference. Different approaches are needed for the ten-person event and the 1,000-person event. Over the last few years, virtual events (Zoom, Microsoft Teams, etc.) have become much more common, and they present special challenges. Technology limits personal interaction; at the same time, additional features are constantly being added to improve and enhance the technology.

In-person events are in some ways the ideal setting for advancing leadership work. It is easier to monitor and manage energy and to play with different group processes. A learning we had here was to keep changing and refreshing the methods we were using to support participants in processing content. Once the agenda becomes formulaic, attention can begin to fall off. It is important to keep changing things up to keep folks fresh, interested, and engaged.

Also, the kinetic motion of an in-person event keeps energy high. We have learned to have people pair off with different partners through Powerful Cycles. We often switch up small group size and membership. We set up exercises where people walk to the whiteboards to review and contribute to evolving content. The challenge is to figure out how to perform some of these kinds of kinetic effects in a virtual meeting environment.

Virtual meeting technology makes convening easy and inexpensive. It has its own set of tools: chat, polling, whiteboards, small group breakouts, and more. While in-person events can be day-long or several days, our experience with web-based events is that they need to be kept to usually one to two hours. Leaders and event planners need to figure out how to make the best use of the web tools available in applying the Pacing Event template. Given our many excellent experiences in conducting both in-person and virtual Pacing Events, both present exciting arenas for further development.

Help participants learn to engage in the moment. Participants are usually not ready to jump into group process exercises and perform well. As event designers, we can help. Two areas that we watch for opportunities are: giving easy instructions for group exercises, and providing Scripts for reporting out to the full group.

Large groups frequently have trouble hearing and processing instructions for group exercises. And they generally cannot handle multiple instructions all at once. The sense we get is that one third of the group is listening and processing, one-third is listening but not processing, and one-third is distracted. As we instruct participants on exercises, we have learned to state the instructions only for the next step, to keep the instructions simple and on a slide, and to repeat them. We also check-in on small groups to make sure they are on task.

There are also challenges at the end of group exercises. Volunteers who report out on a group answer or their own answer to a question often lose their focus and can get out of control. Although we ask for the most important insight expressed in a few sentences, people are not used to summarizing or being concise. Many will ramble, not answer the question, and keep talking. A very effective tool turns out to be the use of Scripts. A Script can help participants consolidate and organize their learning, potential actions, and next steps. For example, following a presentation, or possibly to sum up action at the conclusion of a Pacing Event, we provide participants several minutes to work quietly on a Script, such as the example provided here. When asked to share with others, participants are instructed to read their completed Script. With the systematic use of Scripts, the full group can absorb and process the volunteer report-outs.

Script for Relatedness, Possibility and Potential Action

The thing that resonated with me the most in this presentation was _____

The possibility I see for putting this content to work in my own situation is _____

One potential action I could take next week to get started on this possibility is _____
_____

Signature Style and coaching. Pacing Events are part of a leadership Signature Style, and the leader's Signature Style is in evidence throughout a Pacing Event. The event is an opportunity to model and spread the practice of leadership. Leadership is so often the missing Role in collective work. Consider building time into your Pacing Events to enable participants to recognize and learn the leadership Mindsets and Methods that make the Pacing Event successful. We find that most participants are intrigued by the methods and interested in applying them in their work. The necessary coaching can be built into the framing and exercises. Name the leadership Mindset and Method you are using in real-time as you apply it.

Appreciate participation. Use the leadership Mindset and Method of DNA (Decide-Notice-Acknowledge) in Pacing Events to call higher attention and energy into the event. Affirm participation, interaction, ideas, actions, and other contributions by participants. Give small gifts to participants who volunteer to share their insights, reactions, and planned actions based on presentations. Encourage participants to try these methods in their own meetings and to watch the energy soar.

Pacing Events Travel Well

Whether it's your own event or one in which you are a guest, the Pacing Event approach moves people into collective action. We have discovered that Pacing Events work in other nations and cultures, and can apply to almost any problem, no matter how technical or contentious.

As one example, our team from the US Environmental Protection Agency (EPA) used the Pacing Event Mindset and Method with senior leaders in the government of Thailand. We helped senior Thai leaders conduct a series of Powerful Cycles throughout a two-day Pacing Event to help the Electrical Generating Authority of Thailand (EGAT) work through the sensitive issue of financial reparations for residents harmed by accidental sulfur dioxide emissions in Mae Moh, Thailand. Leading experts from the US Environmental Protection Agency teamed with our counterparts in Thailand's Pollution Control Department.

The workshop was judged by all to be highly successful, resulting in a series of planned actions and commitments by key leaders and village residents. The Deputy Director of Thailand's Pollution Control Department characterized the meeting involving his department, Mae Moh villagers, and the Electrical Generating Authority of Thailand, as their single most productive gathering in decades on the issue of financial reparations. Pacing Event methods travel well and translate to leadership work around the world.

Dennis Wagner coaches Thai Pollution Control Department team during a tense moment in Pacing Event on financial reparations from the Electrical Generating Authority of Thailand to residents of Mae Moh.

Mae Moh Powerplant, Thailand

In the sections that follow, two examples showcase the versatility and applicability of Pacing Events. The first is a case study of how Dennis and his co-lead, Paul McGann MD, effectively flipped a large-scale working session with thirty federal contracting teams representing 4,000 hospitals into a Pacing Event to take on an eleventh-hour unfunded national healthcare initiative. The result provides a vivid example of how a single Pacing Event can wield a profound impact.

The second leadership vignette demonstrates the applicability of the Pacing Event model in an international setting, with Brenda Doroski and John Mitchell of the EPA conducting a major six-day Pacing Event in Uganda. This Pacing Event involved 249 representatives from 42 different countries who were working and teaming to help hundreds of millions of the poorest households across the globe adopt the use of improved cookstoves.

For leaders seeking transformative results, Pacing Events are a revolutionary and essential tool.

Pacing Events

Launching a National Initiative on Early Elective Deliveries

by **Dennis Wagner**

Installing a National Hospital Safety Program

During my ten years as a member of the Senior Executive Service at the Centers for Medicare and Medicaid Services (CMS), I was asked by Administrator Don Berwick MD early in 2011 to serve as Co-Director of the Partnership for Patients. The Partnership was a massive national quality improvement campaign aimed at achieving a 40% reduction in preventable hospital harm over a four-year period. Hospitals would be asked to address the top ten hospital-induced harms. Although many in the broader public are not aware that patients are frequently harmed in hospitals, the Agency for Healthcare Research on Quality (AHRQ) with other federal health authorities had determined that there were an estimated 145 harms to patients for every thousand patients discharged from US hospitals. And some of these harms result in deaths to patients.

Achieving the Bold Aim of a 40% reduction in harm would be a monumental undertaking, and if successful, it would result in tens of thousands of lives saved and billions in cost savings. The new initiative was an important element of work to demonstrate the impact and results possible through effective implementation of the new Affordable Care Act. A leadership strategy was needed to enroll as many of the nation's 5000 hospitals as possible and move them into effective action in pursuit of quantitative, time-limited Bold Aims. Fortunately, this accountability came with a sizeable federal budget of $500 million (sizable on the face of it, but inexpensive at roughly $25,000 per hospital per year).

The Partnership's leadership and management strategies were straightforward. We contracted with roughly 30 organizations with expertise in systematic quality improvement. Our new contractors were also connected to and trusted by the nation's 5000 hospitals—organizations such as state and national hospital associations as well as quality improvement organizations. Our CMS team supplied these contractors with materials, evidence-based practices, quality improvement change packages, and other tools to implement known best practices to address the ten biggest forms of hospital harm. The contractors enrolled their hospital partners into the program and then worked with their affiliated hospitals for the best practices to be applied with system and method. The top ten hospital-induced harms included adverse drug events, pressure ulcers, and hospital-acquired infections.

To convince thousands of hospitals to voluntarily transform their practice models to eliminate ten very different safety issues was a daunting communication, enrollment, and implementation challenge. Our 30 contracting organizations went about securing commitments from hospitals and making commitments to help them succeed. This was Real Work, for sure. But given the $500 million investment and an extensive knowledge base, it was also manageable. By the end of 2011, the Roles of Observation, Administration, Management, Leadership that were needed for success were in fully in place, and we had awarded hundreds of millions of dollars of contracts through competitive and complex federal procurement processes.

An Eleventh Harm Emerges at the Eleventh Hour: Early Elective Deliveries

Shortly after awarding the contracts and beginning our juggernaut implementation of the national initiative, Rick Gilfillan MD, the gifted and influential Director of the newly formed federal Healthcare Innovation Center, called me into his office to explain that Health and Human Services Secretary Kathleen Sebelius wanted us to add an eleventh harm to our program of work. The Secretary had recently been presented with clear evidence that 17 percent of childbirths across the nation (about 3.5 million/year) were being performed as early elective deliveries (EEDs). New research findings were showing that these elective deliveries were harmful to babies, increasing the incidence of cesarean section and risks for the mothers and increasing overall costs to the system. In some states such as Georgia, the rate of early elective deliveries was more than 60%. The Secretary saw this as a preventable health problem with a clear solution. She was determined to address it.

In my Role as a seasoned federal Manager, I calmly explained to Dr. Gilfillan that adding early elective deliveries as an 11th harm was not possible. We had already committed our funding to highly competitive four-year contracts that clearly stipulated the ten harms targeted for improvement. Ten harms, not eleven. Ten. Adding early elective deliveries as an additional harm to be addressed would simply not be possible without additional resources, along with additional time for a lot more contracting work. As a good Manager I was holding the line for the necessary authority, resources, and time.

In our initial conversations, Dr. Gilfillan made clear that these additional needs were not in the cards. There were no additional resources, and we both knew that there was no way to change our contracts at a moment's notice. And the Secretary wanted action, now.

After several days of intense wrangling with Dr. Gilfillan and other senior political leaders at the Centers for Medicare and Medicaid Services and at the larger Department, the request was made abundantly clear. They wanted us to address the harms of Early Elective Deliveries regardless of the numerous constraints we had identified. We needed to accept leadership accountability for a rapid national decrease in early elective deliveries—without additional resources, time, or authority. This Defining Moment was an example of the stark difference between management responsibility and leadership accountability. Fortunately, my earlier training on the differences between leadership and management helped my team and me to understand and ultimately embrace the needed changes in mindset and action. When we accepted this new accountability, I knew that a leadership approach would be necessary to address the 11th harm.

My multi-talented and bold co-director, Paul McGann MD, and I chose to start running on a new Effective Question: "What could we do to get our 30 contractors and their thousands of hospital partners to embrace accountability for reducing early elective deliveries without any new resources?" We didn't know the answer to this question. We didn't know how our contractors would respond to the question. It was truly a DKDK situation—Didn't Know what we Didn't Know. However, as we started looking, probing, and listening in our Observer Roles, we discovered some compelling answers to the new question:

- *A real solution at hand.* The alarming national rate of early elective deliveries was a big problem with a very clear solution: get hospitals to implement what was called a "hard stop policy" to refuse to allow OB/GYN doctors to perform early elective deliveries in the hospital. A single voluntary action by the hospital to implement a hard stop policy would prevent early elective deliveries in that hospital across many private practice providers.

- *Contractors could shine.* Actions by thousands of hospitals could generate rapid improvements and allow the 30 contractors to show the Secretary and our entire federal hierarchy that they could deliver results quickly. Thinking in this way, the early elective deliveries (EED) work wasn't so much an extra cost, but really more of a benefit to the contractors.

- *To the hospitals' advantage.* A "quick win" with substantial early progress on this harm area would help our hundreds of thousands of participating hospital clinicians and leaders see and know that they could generate rapid national improvements to reduce harm. With rapid early progress, we might also be able to obtain additional resources down the road to continue work on this 11th harm area.

- *Consequential results.* The medical benefits to both mothers and babies were clear and incontrovertible. Generating results in this area would both improve health and lower costs, two key goals of the Affordable Care Act.

We were going after two levels of new voluntary commitments—first with our contractors, and next with their affiliated hospitals. The contractors would need to ask hospitals to do the right thing, right away. This meant thousands of requests and offers for hospitals and their leaders to commit and take on a new accountability. We had our requests. Now we needed a way to act on them.

A Work Session is Transformed Overnight into a Pacing Event on Early Elective Deliveries

As fate would have it, Dr. McGann and I already had a two-day national working session scheduled for the following week in Chicago with teams from all our contractors. We went into high gear to fundamentally change the agenda for this meeting. We decided to use the working session to share the new accountability with our contractor teams, and work to get them to embrace the tremendous benefits that would flow to them, their hospital partners, and the patients we all served. On our flight to Chicago, Dr. McGann and I reconstructed the agenda to run on Effective Questions like:

- *What are the benefits of adding reductions of Early Elective Deliveries to our current program of work?*

- *How can we achieve this in ways that will not increase costs?*

- *What are our best ideas for getting hospitals to implement the hard stop policy?*

Powerful Cycles were used to introduce the hardstop policy solution. Group processes were improvised for processing the effective questions over two days.

It worked! Although our new contractor partners were initially surprised at the sudden turn of events, they gradually warmed up to the new accountability. By the end of the two-day meeting, we had constructed 30 contractor-specific plans and high-energy commitments to generate rapid reductions in Early Elective Deliveries through the end of 2014. Every single contractor signed onto the new accountability and used our working session to devise the plans and strategies for implementing the work with their partnering hospitals.

A Series of Small Pacing Events with Big Payoffs

We also mobilized our national and federal partners to join in this effort. Organizations such as the American Academy of Pediatrics, the March of Dimes, the Leapfrog Group, and many others used their influential organizational platforms to mount aggressive efforts to complement the federal work. Christine Hunter MD, the Chief Medical Officer of the federal Office of Personnel Management, convinced the dozens of companies that provide insurance to federal employees to urge hospitals who participated in their plans (thousands of them) to put "Hard Stop" policies in place. Dr. Hunter shared with us that there were thousands of childbirths every month among the families of federal employees. Who knew!? The Abundance of solutions and actions to address this harm area was quite extraordinary.

Visible, Dramatic, Rapid Results

Early elective deliveries in the United States dropped precipitously over the next several years. from 17 percent in our 2010 baseline year to approximately 3 percent by the time our initiative formally ended in 2014.

Based on our success in the first year, we were even successful in securing modest additional resources for a formal amendment to our 30 contracts. Several years later, Secretary Sebelius recognized our federal team for the rapid results with the prestigious Hubert H. Humphrey Service to America award in 2014.

Our successful work to reduce early elective deliveries was incredibly rewarding and joyous for all involved: the federal team, our contractors, our private partners, hospital leaders, private practice clinicians, and thousands of others. And most importantly, as the run chart shows, the results that ultimately flowed from a meeting transformed into a Pacing Event provided many life-enhancing benefits for millions of babies and their families.

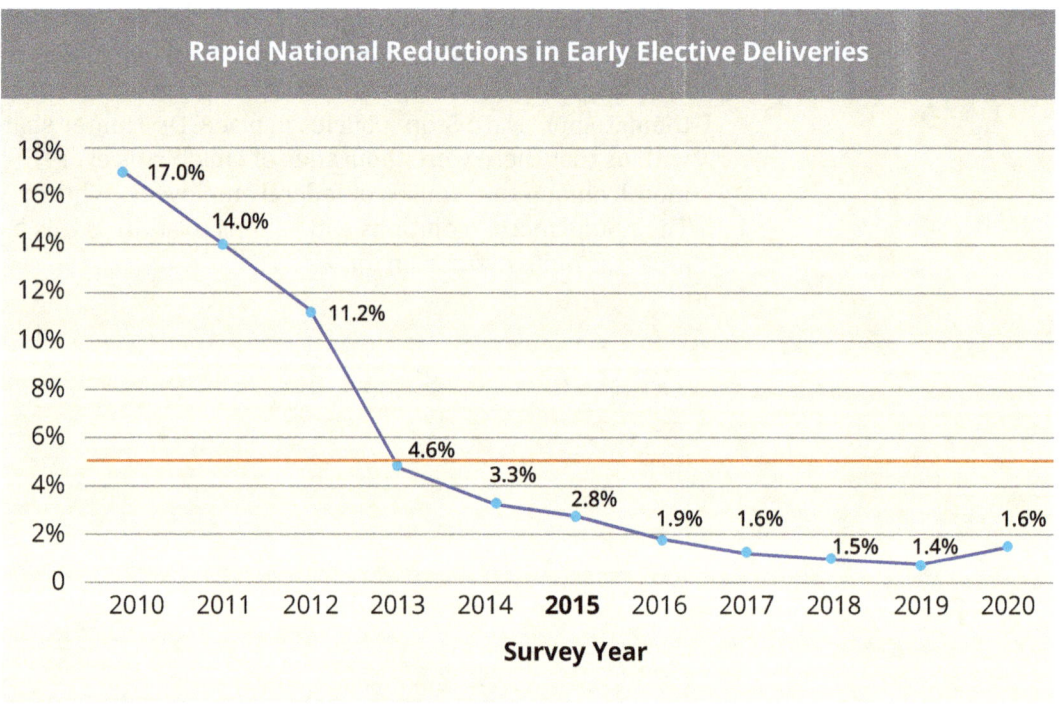

Source: *Healthy Moms, Healthy Babies: 2020 Leapfrog Hospital Survey*, courtesy of the Leapfrog Group

Pacing Events

A Leadership Vignette on Improved Cookstoves

Pacing Events have been successfully used throughout the United States and worldwide. In addition to the earlier example of reparation work in Thailand, two colleagues of ours, Brenda Doroski and John Mitchell of the US Environmental Protection Agency (EPA), have made extensive use of this method in their leadership of the Partnership for Clean Indoor Air. Between 2002-2012, 590 Partner organizations joined together through the Partnership to contribute their resources and expertise to reduce smoke exposure from cooking and heating practices in households around the world (for more information on this work, go to the legacy website at *PCIAonline.org*). John and Brenda have designed and conducted major international Pacing Events in India, Uganda, Peru, and other nations throughout the world.

An International Partnership on Clean Indoor Air

The mission of the EPA Partnership was to rapidly increase the sustained use of affordable, clean, reliable, safe, and durable cooking and heating stoves to help hundreds of millions of the poorest households around the world. Using basic technology, these cookstoves improve indoor air quality for millions of families by reducing emissions; reduce fuel use through increased efficiency which reduces land degradation, deforestation, desertification, and habitat loss; reduce climate emissions of CO_2 and black carbon; and more. An improved cookstove is a simple apparatus that can cost as little as $12 to $30. Some parts of the world even use low-cost solar cookstoves.

Another advantage of using more efficient cookstoves is that families – usually the female head of household – can substantially reduce the amount of time spent each day foraging for fuel. When mothers spend less time gathering fuel, they typically invest the timesavings in activities that benefit the education, health, and well-being of their children. Research shows that the social benefits associated with improved cookstoves are immense.

U.S. Environmental Protection Agency Partnership for Clean Indoor Air
4th Biennial Forum in Kampala, Uganda

Above: 249 leaders from 42 different countries who participated in a 6-day high-energy and content-rich global Pacing Event led by the EPA team in Kampala, Uganda in March, 2009.

Below: low-cost solar cookstoves

Clear Intent

As part of their leadership of the worldwide initiative, John and Brenda started convening global Pacing Events for their network to achieve multiple, overlapping Intents, including:

- Tracking global progress on the numbers of improved cookstoves sold;
- Bringing together diverse sectors to comprehensively address this challenge;
- Increasing the confidence and engagement of national leaders performing this work;
- Identifying and spreading best practices in stove effectiveness, stove marketing, stove manufacturing, and fuel efficiency;
- Recognizing and celebrating the accomplishments of governments, local and international organizations, and people taking action to achieve results;
- Establishing, refining, and pursuing Bold Aims for the global network.

Effective Questions, Commitments, Powerful Cycles, Scripts, Net Forward Energy

The EPA team used Effective Questions in engaging participants to foster worldwide learning, deal-making, commitment, and action in each of their biennial forums, including the 4th Biennial Forum in Uganda previously shown. Effective Questions were used to frame the entire event and to help participants process content and invent their own ways of using the content on returning to their home countries after the conferences. Effective Questions used to frame the worldwide conference in Uganda included:

- *What can each of us do to rapidly increase the use of cleaner, more efficient cook stoves?*
- *What is working around the world?*
- *What is causing it to work?*
- *What are our shared worldwide results so far?*
- *What can each of us do more of, better, or differently?*
- *What will be our ambitious Bold Aim as we go forward from here?*

The Uganda global conference included national experts from around the world who delivered presentations with various solutions and answers to these questions. The EPA team used the Powerful Cycle repeatedly over the 6-day event. Following case study presentations on specific projects, participants worked in pairs and small groups to develop their own answers to questions such as the following:

- "*What resonates the most with me about how families in Nepal are recycling newspapers to create more efficient and cleaner burning fuel briquettes?*"
- "*What possibilities do I see for introducing the use of solar cookstoves in my country, such as those used in other African nations?*"
- "*What actions might my organization take to foster self-sustaining businesses to manufacture and build small efficient stoves as they are doing in India?*"

The EPA team used Effective Questions to help their partners learn from the best practices of their peers and to act on them. A key goal of the conference was to scale up and replicate these best practices to rapidly "make best practices the common practice." Effective Questions were used to create positive energy in situations where hesitancy to share what is working because of competition for scarce resources, and perhaps even negative energy, were anticipated. Scripts were employed to help participants rapidly grasp key learnings, and then to quickly translate the learnings into actions they planned to take back home.

Bold Aims

The shared learning, commitment, actions, and results of the Partnership for Clean Indoor Air produced dramatic and lasting impacts on the health and well-being of millions of people worldwide. This chart was used in the Uganda Pacing Event to show the rapid progress of the EPA team and their worldwide partners. Based on their success, participants at the Uganda forum established a new Bold Aim to **double the number of improved cookstoves used worldwide every two years.**

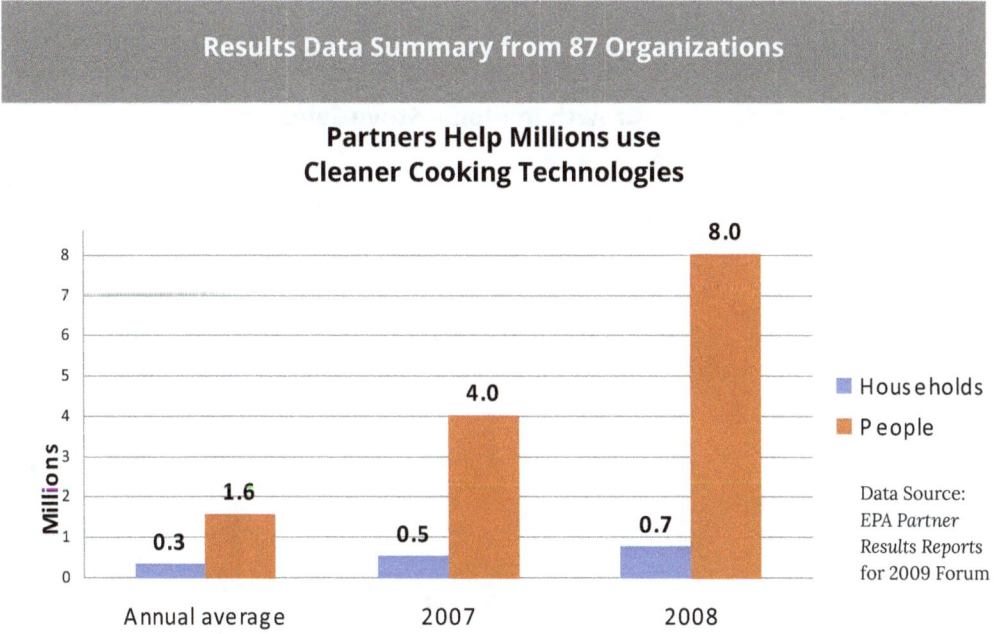

Results

This new Bold Aim propelled major global progress among partners in the EPA initiative, more than doubling the number of households with improved cookstoves, from reporting 1.5 million sold as documented in Uganda in 2009, to 3.6 million cookstoves sold as documented in Peru in 2011. This impressive track record caught the attention of the United Nations Foundation, which then teamed with EPA and the other parts of the U.S. government to help establish a new Global Alliance for Clean Cookstoves.

The Global Alliance joined with the EPA Partnership for Clean Indoor Air to continue and expand on the Bold Aim of generating major environmental and public health improvements with improved cookstove technology. Millions of families around the world have benefitted from the Pacing Events, Bold Aims, and ground-breaking work of the Partnership for Clean Indoor Air and its partners.

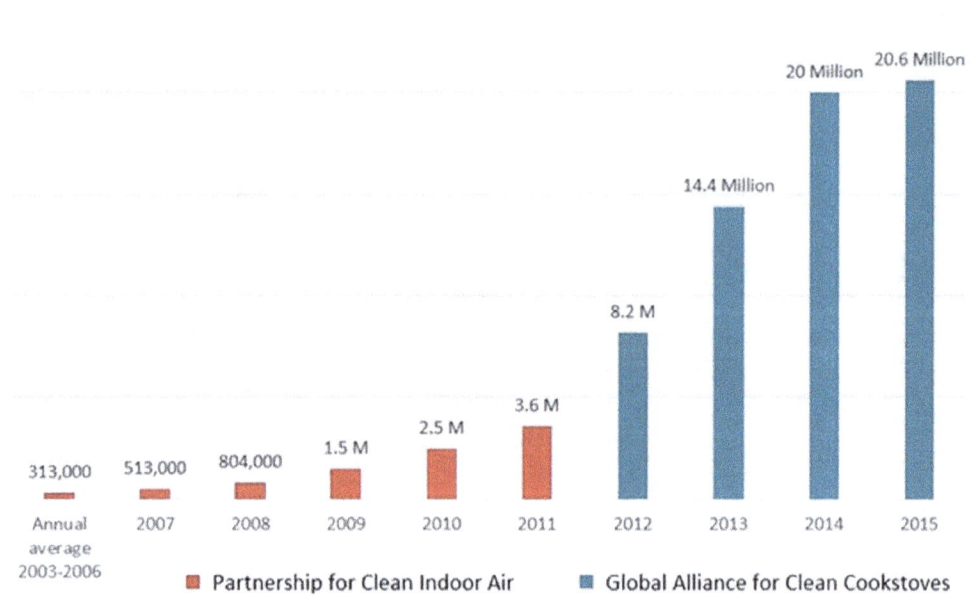

Bold Aim in Uganda Propels Major Worldwide Results

Growth in Global Stove Sales

Partnership for Public Service Medal Finalists

Brenda Doroski and **John Mitchell**
Program Managers, U.S. Environmental Protection Agency

The U.S. Environmental Protection Agency nominated Brenda Doroski and John Mitchell for the prestigious Samuel J. Heyman Service to America Medal (or SAMMIE, the Oscar Award for Public Service), awarded by the Partnership for Public Service. They were honored as one of three SAMMIE finalists for their foundational work in leading the Partnership for Clean Indoor Air in 2007.

Eight years later, John and Brenda's close partner and colleague at EPA, Jacob Moss, was nominated for and won a SAMMIE in 2015 for his leadership in transitioning the Partnership for Clean Indoor Air into the Global Alliance for Clean Cookstoves in partnership with the United Nations Foundation.

Pacing Events Can Change the World (and each of us too)

Pacing Events are a tremendous leadership opportunity to create extraordinary and joyous change in the world. We can employ Pacing Events to transform our conferences, webinars, and staff and team meetings, and in doing so, generate positive energy, showcase inspirational Leadership Stories, surface insights and contributions from participants, foster commitments, and generate results on our Bold Aims and Compelling Visions.

When we step into the leadership work of designing and conducting Pacing Events, we also create an endless stream of opportunities to experiment, test, and refine our Signature Style of leadership. In the next leadership vignette, Dr. Steven Chen describes his journey from skeptic to convert. Dr. Chen is now a highly effective practitioner of Pacing Events and other Mindsets and Methods and has actively used them in the evolution of his own unique Signature Style.

Pacing Events

From Skeptic to Expert Practitioner

by **Steven Chen**
Associate Dean for Clinical Affairs,
University of Southern California
Mann School of Pharmacy and
Director, California Right Meds Collaborative

In 2007, I was invited by Dennis, John, and their federal colleagues to share our work with underserved communities at a national meeting. I was honored and asked, "How long do I have to present?", thinking I would hear the usual 30 to 45 minutes.

"You have five minutes. And you're presenting with two other speakers for a total of 15 minutes." My excitement turned to confusion, and I began to suspect that these federal partners really weren't that interested in our work after all.

At the start of the meeting, I expected a quick introduction, agenda overview, and a launch of multiple presentations, followed by question-and-answer periods. Instead, the meeting started out with event framing, *declarations* and *assertions*, an explanation of how the participants should "Be" including being prepared to make Requests, Offers, and Commitments, and the difference between Net Forward and Net Backward Energy. The pace was fast, with no time dedicated for the audience to ask questions of the speaker. Instead, we were being asked to respond to reflective questions! I didn't quite know what to make of it.

Then I heard leaders in the room engaging with others, sharing key insights in response to reflective questions, making bold *requests*, *offers*, and *commitments*. The energy in the room was like nothing I had ever experienced. People were in action, engaging with one another, actively learning, and applying the content of the meeting to their own work. Many of them were making deals and commitments with one another for things they would do when they returned home. I was sold on this new way of running meetings!

However, it wasn't until I spent several years as part of the federal government's Patient Safety and Clinical Pharmacy Services Collaborative that I developed a more in-depth understanding of how the Pacing Event I experienced in 2007 along with other Mindsets and Methods on display would come to shape my own Signature Style of leadership. I began adapting Pacing Events and other Mindsets and Methods to our practice and healthcare payment initiatives, and they have transformed our work here in California.

The best example of how we've used Pacing Events and related methods comes from our California Right Meds Collaborative. An Abundance of evidence demonstrates that embedding pharmacists in medical practices has a profound impact on important outcomes for patients. Bringing pharmacists more directly into medical care increases patient safety, reduces healthcare costs, improves medication adherence, and increases patient and provider satisfaction. Pharmacists know how to provide much-needed services, such as Comprehensive Medication Management (CMM), to patients.

However, the business case for hiring a pharmacist to provide clinical services is challenging. Pharmacists are not federally recognized as healthcare providers. This means they have limited opportunities to be reimbursed by insurance companies and other payers for these vital services to patients, except only in a few states.

This is unfortunate for many reasons. Community pharmacies are ideal community-based extensions of our healthcare system. They have widespread, regular access to patients (90% of the US population lives within five miles of a pharmacy), a high level of public trust, and there is frequently strong cultural and linguistic alignment between pharmacy staff (pharmacists, technicians, interns, or clerks) and the local populations they serve. Many attempts have been made to provide needed medication therapy optimization services through community pharmacies, but most have not been successful, scalable, or sustainable.

The California Right Meds Collaborative is working to change this picture. Our goal is daunting: to establish partnerships with health plans to provide payment for these comprehensive medication management services, targeting the highest-risk patients through local community pharmacies. That sentence alone is an invitation for backward energy: fear, doubt, problems, what can't be done, judgment!

Steven Chen, PharmD with a Patient

We have leveraged the lessons of Pacing Events, and I have leveraged my own evolving Signature Style of leadership to introduce and team with hundreds of pharmacists throughout southern California on our challenging and important goal. In our conferences and working sessions:

- We provide clear Event Framing for our purpose;
- We make Assertions about much-needed services, grounded in data and evidence that we know our participants value;
- We explain the Offers, Requests, Commitments and actions that are needed from all of us involved, both during and after our events;
- We establish, together with them, how we will generate Positive Energy, for all of us.

Many other ideas flow from my initial experience with these Mindsets and Methods. We often "plant" responders in the audience to help encourage others to share their own insights and actions. We keep the audience focused by emphasizing the need to "keep the main thing the main thing." We bring in the voice of the patient and other major stakeholders to show the benefits of providing lifesaving and life-changing services needed by those we serve.

We apply rapid iterative change cycles (using the established quality improvement model of Plan-Do-Study-Act) during action periods for efficient refinement of processes. One of my favorite lessons developed by John and Dennis addressed the distinctions between the Roles of Manager and Leader. While no one likes to hear that leading often means being accountable for results while having no resources, it allows us to shift the conversation towards potential opportunities or partnerships that are often overlooked.

So how have Pacing Events impacted the California Right Meds Collaborative? Despite our launch at the beginning of the COVID-19 pandemic, our initiative has grown to four health plan partners covering eight million lives! Vulnerable patients are getting better care. Dozens of pharmacies are receiving value-based payments for providing medication management services to high-risk patients, both in-person and via telehealth. Pacing Events and their companion Mindsets and Methods have been instrumental in the growth and development of our work, keeping participants focused, working together and learning from each other, and excited about the journey!

The Domain of Roles: Choices that Make Us Architects of Leadership Work

Choices in the Domain of Roles give us access to methods for organizing ourselves and others in practically any situation imaginable. Under the Domain of Roles, we have offered three Mindsets and Methods that can be used to organize the collective effort of people and organizations in pursuit of a Compelling Vision. Role Switching, 5 Dimensions of Action, and Pacing Events enable us to generate joy and growth, and at the same time organize ourselves and essential partners for contribution and impact. These Mindsets and Methods make us creative architects of collaborative work!

Role Switching Helps Us Assume the Right Roles at the Right Time

Understanding the four defining organizational Roles of Observer, Administrator, Manager, and Leader, and gaining mastery of the practice of switching among them, is a tremendous asset. It opens the possibility of never feeling stuck, or, if we do feel stuck, understanding that it's only for a short period.

To step into a leadership Role, we sometimes must unlearn some otherwise effective management practices.
Switching mastery is especially important when the situation calls for a Leader to step in. To hear the call and act upon it, we frequently need to unlearn or transcend some of the central practices associated with the disciplines of the other Roles of Observer, Administrator, and Manager. Managers are taught to under-promise and over-deliver in matching resources to task. Leaders, by contrast, must learn to commit to accountabilities in the absence of the necessary resources for achieving them. Understanding and acting on this counter-intuitive truth gets easier when equipped with the method of Role Switching.

Build a team; at some point more Roles will be needed than one person has the time or skills for.
Access to the Mindset and Method of Role Switching helps us to better discern which of the four Roles is necessary in which situations. Armed with this knowledge, we can choose to step into the right Role at the right time or choose to deploy others to perform the Role as needed.

Some Roles we enjoy and have mastered; there are always other Roles we can learn and master.
The practice of switching is not only necessary and important, it can also be a tremendous source of personal growth. Most of us are naturally drawn to one of the four Roles and often appropriately focus on performing our touchstone Role. However, access to the Mindset and Method of Role Switching can equip us to deliberately and consciously expand our repertoire to gain greater capabilities with other Roles.

The 5 Dimensions of Action Open Up the World to Us

The 5 Dimensions of Action enable us to go far beyond the traditional two-dimensional approach of managing up and managing down. The world is bigger than that!

- Choosing to act across all 5 Dimensions will rapidly expand our circles of influence and ultimately our impact;

- Spreading the use of the 5 Dimensions is a way to empower and tap into the leadership of others in the organization, including non-managers;

- Assuming accountability across all 5 Dimensions is a rich source of personal and professional growth as we learn to deal effectively with the new and the unexpected.

Pacing Events Generate Horsepower

Knowing how to transform a meeting into a Pacing Event is like the difference between composing with a typewriter and composing with a laptop computer. Our leadership horsepower exponentially increases with the systematic use of Pacing Events methods.

- Effective Framing will unite people into clear and intentional ways of Being together in the event;
- The Powerful Cycle will engage the capabilities of all participants, tap into the strengths inherent in diverse audiences, and unleash joyous energy;
- Framing, Effective Questions, and Requests and Offers are straightforward and highly effective practices for moving participants to action.

Pacing Event methods are surprisingly simple, readily available, and can be implemented with relative ease.

Leadership Stories Help Us See the Transformative Power of Choices in the Roles Domain

When leadership is successful, the world is better off. We see it in the Leadership Stories and vignettes throughout the book. Homes and families are made safe from radon gas. The rural poor in Haiti gain access to banking services and entrepreneurship that lift families out of poverty. Hospitals provide safer care to patients. Organ transplants increase and save lives. Mothers and newborns are healthier and safe from high-risk early elective deliveries.

Behind each of these changes are transformed systems with new standards, accountabilities, and responsibilities. Behind the transformed system is the leadership work that enabled the transformation to occur. The Leadership Stories and case studies profiled in this chapter give us confidence that we can choose to lead when the opportunity arises. We see how switching among the Roles of Observer, Administrator, Manager, and Leader enables us to organize activity and grow infrastructure. We see people assuming accountability and adding responsibility across the 5 Dimensions of Action. We see the potential for growth, impact, and joy in the conduct of Pacing Events.

Choose to Lead in the Domain of Roles

The Domain of Roles is the last of the four domains that support effective and joyous leadership Choices. As we become architects of our own leadership work, we are deploying the necessary combinations of accountability and responsibility to make extraordinary things happen. We are putting a field of action into play that is big enough to contain the vision. We are using events to surface what is knowable and to generate new relationships that can help form and realize the vision.

Choose to lead in the domain of Roles. The Choices we make across the domain of Roles help to form our own unique Signature Style.

Choices across all four domains of Intent, Being, Language and Roles come together to create transformative collective action. As we develop our Signature Style, we can apply it to make the Choices that help us become more effective, more involved, and more satisfied with life. The next chapter is designed to help each of us consider our own Signature Style in making leadership Choices. We will present several leadership vignettes, exercises, and a final Leadership Story to illustrate the development of leadership Signature Styles. Our goal is to help readers to examine and further develop each of our own unique leadership Signature Styles.

SIGNATURE STYLE
We Craft our Own Signature Style of Leadership

Watch your thoughts,
they become your words

Watch your words,
they become your actions

Watch your actions,
they become your habits

Watch your habits,
they become your character

Watch your character,
it becomes your destiny.

ANONYMOUS

All of Us Have a Signature Style

Each of us has a Signature Style of leadership. Although many of us may not be consciously aware of our own Signature Style, it most definitely already exists inside us, waiting to be further grown, shaped and refined.

Style refers to how we carry out our activities and responsibilities in various situations. Signature indicates the certain behaviors that define us to ourselves and others. A Signature Style of Leadership is how we conduct ourselves and interact with others in situations that call for leadership. Our leadership Signature Style can become a set of skilled habits that we can learn to name, practice intentionally, and share with others.

Our Signature Style is always evolving as we continue to gain experience and insight, increasing both our own effectiveness and the effectiveness of others as leaders. The twelve leadership Mindsets and Methods profiled in this book are key tools for further developing and refining our own Signature Style as we make Choices to lead and contribute across the four domains of Intent, Being, Language, and Roles.

Authors Signature Style: Twelve Mindsets and Methods

INTENT	BEING
Compelling Vision	Net Forward Energy
Bold Aims	Flip Negative Energy
Decide-Notice-Acknowledge	Resilience

CHOOSING TO LEAD

LANGUAGE	ROLES
Leadership Speech Acts	Role Switching
Leadership Stories	5 Dimensions of Action
Access Abundance	Pacing Events

We Develop and Share Our Signature Style

In this final chapter we have invited two of our colleagues, Karen Minyard and Zandra Glenn, to share how the concept of Signature Style has shaped their own way of Being, not only professionally but also in their personal lives. These vignettes illuminate how two highly effective leaders have adapted, tailored, and used some of the leadership Mindsets and Methods to craft their own unique Signature Styles for making productive, joyful Choices every day in common situations.

Building on these examples, we offer a series of four exercises to guide you in crafting a version of your own Leadership Signature Style. The exercises will help you to process and make use of one or more of the many Leadership Stories in the book, and to pin down and add to the Mindsets and Methods that can work best for you. We share three tips for learning how to more consciously spot and act on the leadership Choices that are constantly thrown our way.

We present a final Leadership Story as told by Dennis, selected to illustrate how a Signature Style enables leadership to surface and thrive in the wake of a challenging and disheartening career setback that he experienced in 2002. John uses this final Leadership Story to reflect on and illustrate how multiple Mindsets and Methods can be used across all four domains of leadership Choice.

Each of these final examples and stories vividly demonstrate how living our Signature Style is the way we resist the temptation to opt-out, to give up, to self-disqualify. We can avoid giving in to the mistaken belief that leaders are different from the rest of us, when in fact the principal difference is that in choosing to lead, they have chosen joy over the current drift, chosen extraordinary results over business-as-usual. The lived experiences of leaders profiled in this book show how each of us has access to the leadership Choices that can make our lives more productive and joyful.

Living a Leadership Signature Style

Signature Style is a series of habits to be nurtured. These habits have tremendous payoffs, not only in dealing with the bigger Defining Moments, but mostly in the many everyday moments.

Over several decades and dozens of initiatives, we have worked with many extraordinary people who have developed exceptional leadership Signature Styles. It was clear that they were something special. You could feel it just by being in a meeting with them. Good things were noticed and amplified. Bad things got better. They were living a leadership style.

Two of these special leaders are Karen Minyard and Zandra Glenn. We asked them to share their own unique applications of the Mindsets and Methods profiled in this book, and how these became part of their individual Signature Styles. Karen Minyard actually coined the term Signature Style many years ago as she was reflecting on and describing our mutual development and use of the Pacing Event and Speech Acts Mindsets and Methods profiled in this book!

Karen Minyard Ph.D, RN

Karen is a research professor in the Department of Public Management and Policy at Georgia State University and CEO of the Georgia Health Policy Center (GHPC). She assumed leadership of the newly formed Policy Center in 2001 and grew it into a major national research and development institution specializing in health policy and the transformation of community-based health care systems.

We first met Karen back in 1998 when she brought GHPC into the HRSA 100% Access and 0 Health Disparities Campaign as one of our key partners. That campaign lives on today in the national non-profit Communities Joined in Action, housed in the Center. Karen's passion is enabling communities to develop a strong political voice that shifts power among sectors —causing population health and equity to improve, community by community.

As we worked with Karen, we discovered that she had a knack for enabling the groups she was working with to develop coalitions and build the organizational structures they needed to accomplish their goals. Moreover, she was acutely aware of and constantly helping to shape the mindsets and methods that were in play and were impeding or helping communities to generate progress. We teamed with Karen in developing and testing methods for conducting national and community meetings that generated action, progress, and results. This work ultimately resulted in the codification of the Pacing Event methodologies profiled in the Roles chapter. We are indebted to Karen for helping us to name the concept of Signature Style and for helping so many of us to learn how to live it.

"LeadersSpeak"

Karen Minyard,
PhD, RN, CEO
Georgia Health Policy Center

I carry with me multiple copies of a card that lists seven powerful leadership expressions on one side and a list of powerful Speech Acts on the other.

Georgia Health Policy Center

Speech Act	Powerful Expression
Declaration	"The future I stand for is …"
Assertion	"A model that works is …"
Accountable	"By next June I will have …"
Calling Together	"Our pacing event will be on …"
Framing.	"In this talk listen for …"
Mission Empathy	"A person whose life is about …"
Request & Offer	"Would you do __ by Friday?"
Acknowledge	"Thank you for …"
Say "Yes"	"I'll find a way to support that."
Effective Questions	"What worked? What to add?"
Active Listening	"What I hear you say is …"
"And" not "or".	"We can do both"

Georgia Health Policy Center
Georgia State University
404.413.0314 • ghpc.gsu.edu

Seven Powerful Expressions in Leadership Stories

1. **A Stand**
   "The future I stand for is …"
2. **Defining Moments**
   "An event that made me see this future as an important mission for me is …"
3. **Bold Goal**
   "I am committed to having __ in place by (date)."
4. **Painting the Future**
   "An exciting example of what I envision is …"
5. **Sticky Messages**
   "I want to tell you the story of a community that went from worst to first in health by changing the local culture."
6. **Heroes and Heroines**
   "Let me tell you about a person you should talk to and work with."
7. **Requests and Offers**
   "The request I am making is __; the offer I am making is __."

These two sides lay out what I consider the Language of leadership. I call the Signature Style represented by the card, "LeadersSpeak." If there is a magic bullet to be effective in leading change, this is it. It guides my work in many situations.

I have three uses for the cards. First is in workshops on leadership. I spend half a day or longer with participants on the idea that leadership is a Choice they can make, a skill they can develop. With the card I have them work on their Leadership Stories. Draft the story, share it, and process the feedback. Learn to express the story in the most powerful way. These workshops are with client groups, like several hundred rural grantees of the Health Resources and Services Administration, and state public health teams from across the nation, or by invitation from a convening organization.

The second use is in coaching individuals. People often ask me for advice or assistance on a matter. I will respond with an abbreviated form of the workshop. I will walk the person through the steps in forming his or her Leadership Story. Given the outcomes they are after, we discuss how to deploy powerful expressions in their work.

The third use is in my own practice. As I encounter difficult situations, I will use the card to plan my course of action. I will focus on the offers and requests I can make to secure outcomes that are useful to me. Rather than be in conflict or at odds with someone I ask myself, "What requests and offers can I make to change this situation I find myself in?"

"LeadersSpeak" is around me all the time. As a complicated meeting approaches, I prepare with the card. I choose five expressions from my card and craft a brief Leadership Story statement to express at the beginning of the meeting. I attend ready to use the Speech Acts. I have had incredible success with this practice in difficult meetings. And difficult meetings are common.

Several years ago, a high-level government official contracted with GHPC for assistance on policy questions. The partnership was going well. Then, at some point we learned the official had contracted with an administrative services organization that had no experience in this field to advise on several policy matters that we were experts in. Quickly the administrative services organization found itself unable to deliver. We learned about it when that organization came to GHPC for help. They offered us a very small subcontract to develop the product for them. I found myself upset with the situation and angry with our client, the official. I wanted to express my criticism of the awkward and dysfunctional situation he had created.

I wanted to confront our client. Instead, I followed my rule—when upset, stop. Take out the "LeadersSpeak" card, and craft a leadership response. In my next meeting with the official, I began with a Leadership Story and statement. That meeting ended with the official requesting a multi-year relationship with GHPC at a level of effort that enabled us to address significant issues. There is a magic bullet!

People are drawn to the method. I was on a Zoom webinar with public health staff across the country. I was teaching "LeadersSpeak" showing participants how to craft their Leadership Stories for a difficult situation. I gave an example of a situation I was in. I showed the Leadership Story I was crafting to deal with it. To my surprise, audience members began to offer me advice. They suggested adjusting the offers I was making; they suggested alternatives to the requests I was considering. In the moment, the audience was demonstrating it understood and could do this Leadership Story work! Later, when I ran into people who were on the Zoom call, they introduced themselves and asked how my difficult meeting worked out. They remembered "LeadersSpeak" and were interested in the outcome of my case. Apparently, many of us are looking for ways to deal with difficult situations.

My career has been about building strong communities in urban and rural areas. We work to increase the power of communities to improve health. We advocate for the importance of community in national, state, and local health policy. We know that policy decisions affect how markets function. Unchecked markets can create inequity and, in health care, severe disparities. Health care needs practitioners at all levels to play leadership Roles in crafting the nation's health related markets. We need effective markets to support thriving communities that are vibrant and economically strong. A mission I have as Director of the Georgia Health Policy Center is to help payers, providers, and consumers of health care to develop and practice their leadership Signature Styles in pursuit of a nation with great health. We do much of this work in meetings.

I am always using the "LeadersSpeak" card. It's not a now-and-then thing. When I am facing important conversations I stop, get out the card, and begin to ask, "What do I want, what am I willing to do?" My tendency is to always create requests and offers to break through a difficult situation. Given the situation, "What request am I making? what offers can I make?" Every time someone makes a request to me, I seek ways to say *yes*. I ask, "what part of this request can I say *yes* to?" In some way, it always works!

Zandra Glenn, PharmD, RPh

Zandra is a practicing pharmacist, an expert in the management of government change programs in healthcare, and a nationally recognized leader in the design and conduct of action learning collaboratives. We first met Zandra when we invited her to serve as a Faculty leader in the Patient Safety and Clinical Pharmacy Services Collaborative (PSPC), sponsored by the Health Resources and Services Administration (HRSA). The PSPC Collaborative was about moving pharmacists into roles in healthcare organizations where they could provide hands-on clinical pharmacy services to vulnerable patients with complex, high-risk medication regimens.

Zandra is an authentic leader and wonderful human being who literally lights up a room when she enters. We quickly learned that Zandra's presence always meant exciting, high-energy meetings that caused good things to happen. Over time, Zandra became a key leader in the development and support of a new national advocacy organization, The Alliance For Medication Management (AIMM), which was created to carry on the work of the collaborative. Zandra is also a parent who enjoys sharing stories of her husband's and children's experience in conveying the power of Signature Style Mindsets and Methods.

The Signature Style Way of Being

Zandra Glenn PharmD, RPh
Pharmacist and National Leader in Quality Improvement

Let me start with the Signature Style.

I am very grateful for having been exposed to it. It's a way of Being. It is not didactic ... not a method you follow. It's the way you react to things, the way you manage yourself, the way you do your work.

I had a discussion with a colleague of mine who has a fair amount of experience with the leadership Mindsets and Methods of the Signature Style profiled in this book. She described the Signature Style as a checklist of activities to be followed.

I said, No! It's how you think and respond.

It changes who you are. Adopting a Signature Style is not work. It's the way you are.

My greatest satisfaction is when I hear my children speaking it back to me. Recently my daughter was complaining about something. She concluded by saying, "*I know that I always have a Choice. Now I have to make it.*" Another time she described a good experience she had. "*Today, I used the DNA method (Decide-Notice-Acknowledge) on my boyfriend.*"

I love talking about the Signature Style. I am about spreading the gospel if we can call it that. It's who I am. It's part of the way I live my life.

I am always looking for ways to teach it. For example, in my work with the College of Pharmacy I was recently asked to run a Board meeting. I pulled in concepts like Effective Questions from the Signature Style. We used statements like "let's focus on what is working."

The Signature Style changed my life. I believe the more we can get people to live life this way the better it is for everyone.

Crafting and Practicing Your Own Signature Style of Leadership

The authors selected the Leadership Stories and vignettes in this book to expose and support readers in choosing to expand your embrace of leadership. These examples illustrate the rich diversity and wide range of leadership styles. Our Intent is that readers become conscious of each of our own unique leadership Signature Styles, and then actively share and refine them with colleagues. Intentionally sharing our Signature Style with others both gives us greater command of the Style and generates the feedback that helps us to strengthen it.

Take some time to map out your leadership Signature Style. We provide here four easy exercises you can use to get started. As your personal leadership Signature Style takes shape, you face the prospect of considering action in four domains with at least a dozen Mindsets and Methods to draw on. That's a lot of material to master and work with. To help this along, we conclude this segment by offering three everyday tips on how to put your Signature Style into active practice. Make what works for you a habit.

Craft your Signature Style by drawing on insights from the stories you read here and your own experience. The first exercise will help you capture the insights you gained from the Leadership Stories in the book. The second and third have each of us reflecting on our own leadership experiences. With the fourth exercise, you bring it all together: the first cut at summarizing our own unique Signature Style of leadership for presentation and use with others.

EXERCISE 1 **Walk through several Leadership Stories presented in this book to understand and contrast different leadership Signature Styles in action.**

The set of stories presented here, most of them told in the voice of the leader, are an opportunity to study a wide range of Signature Styles and defining moment situations. Use Exhibit A to revisit the five stories identified below; choose three more that especially resonate with you. To advance your own style, begin to highlight Mindsets and Methods that you want to develop and refine. Note the most striking Mindsets and Methods that stand out for you. Note the defining moments that represent leadership being chosen.

EXHIBIT A.	Signature Style Elements From Key Leadership Stories	
Leadership Story	**A Defining Moment**	**Most Interesting Mindset & Method**
Project ECHO, Democratization of Expert Knowledge: Sanjeev Arora MD		
A National Campaign to Save "100,000 Lives": Don Berwick MD		
A Nationwide Bank In Haiti For and By The Rural Poor: Anne H. Hastings		
Requests and Offers Generate Abundance: Sue Dillon		
Leadership Choices in a Journey to Excellence: John Chessare MD		

EXERCISE 2 **Recall and reflect on what worked in a successful leadership enterprise you experienced.**

Become aware of the leadership that is always occurring around you. Identify a leadership situation that you encountered or were involved in. Pick one that had some degree of success. Using Exhibit B, recall the experience and write down a brief characterization of the effort. Then for each of the four leadership Choice domains try to recall any Mindset and Method that stood out and proved to be effective.

EXHIBIT B. Mindsets and Methods Deployed In A Successful Leadership Enterprise I Encountered

Overview of the Enterprise:
....
....

Highlights of My Role and The Contribution of Others:
....
....

Exciting and Effective Mindsets and Methods Deployed:

Choosing INTENT
1. ....
2. ....

Choosing BEING
3. ....
4. ....

Choosing LANGUAGE
5. ....
6. ....

Choosing ROLES
7. ....
8. ....

EXERCISE 3 **What might have worked to make an ambitious but less effective effort a successful initiative?**

Similar to Exercise 2, identify a situation you were involved in, but one that was not especially effective. Using Exhibit C, recall the experience and write down a brief characterization of the effort. Then, for each of the four leadership Choice domains, indicate what you now see as the Mindsets and Methods that might have made the effort more successful.

EXHIBIT C. **Mindsets and Methods That Could Have Been Deployed To Address A Difficult Situation That Was Never Resolved**

Overview of the Difficult Situation:
....
....

Most Serious Barrier or Constraint That Was Encountered:
....
....

Mindsets and Methods That Could Have Been Used to Improve the Situation:

Choosing INTENT

1. ....
2. ....

Choosing BEING

3. ....
4. ....

Choosing LANGUAGE

5. ....
6. ....

Choosing ROLES

7. ....
8. ....

EXERCISE 4   **Map out your current leadership Signature Style for presentation with your Leadership Story.**

Each of us can develop and express a working version of our own Signature Style. Exercises 1, 2, and 3 provide each of us with examples and insight to help us see what makes up our own unique leadership Signature Style. The four Choice domains of INTENT, BEING, LANGUAGE, and ROLES can serve as a framework for understanding, developing, and sharing the dynamics of your style.

Take a few minutes to summarize your current leadership style for potential presentation to others. Do it quickly and map it out at a high level. Be guided by Exhibit D on the next page an example and summary of the authors' Signature Styles. Draft your own version of Exhibit D.

Your domains of Choice may be different from the authors'. And your Mindsets and Methods may be different in content and number. The point is to begin to characterize your own style and to have greater command of it. You want to be able to apply it and share it with others. You want colleagues, mentors, and others to use it with you, and to help contribute to the constant and evolving development of your own unique Signature Style.

EXHIBIT D.	Authors' Signature Style, Methods and Mindsets
INTENT	
Compelling Vision	The future we stand for as shaped by our circle of influence and the needs of others
Bold Aim	A breakthrough outcome that we voluntarily assume accountability for achieving
DNA	Decide what we intend to get more of in the world and acknowledge it when it shows up
BEING	
Net Forward Energy	Positive energy in individuals and groups that moves us forward toward the vision
Flip Negative Energy	Expecting negative energy situations to occur and readiness to channel them into positive action
Resilience	Drawing on purpose, partners, and other sources to sustain ourselves during breakdowns
LANGUAGE	
Speech Acts	Expressions that move ourselves and others forward on leadership visions and aims
Leadership Stories	Personal stories that convey our Vision and ways of Being that draw others to contribute
Access Abundance	Opportunities that surface through systematic use of Requests, Offers, and Commitments
ROLES	
Role Switching	Learning to switch and team with others on four key Roles, especially the Leadership Role
5 Dimensions of Action	Embracing accountability for action across 5 Dimensions: up, down, sideways, process, and public
Pacing Events	Using events in deliberate ways to generate positive energy, shared learning, action, and results

As shown throughout this book, the Mindsets and Methods come alive in the personal Leadership Stories that feature them. The Leadership Story is part theory-of-practice and part how-to. You will want to gain control of your own Leadership Stories, and possibly the Leadership Stories of your partners and colleagues. We recommend that you develop a 7-to-15-minute presentation of your Leadership Story and experiment with sharing it with colleagues.

We also recommend that you prepare to teach your style. One of the best possible ways to learn and master a subject is to make ourselves accountable for teaching others. This is at the heart of the highly effective All Teach, All Learn philosophy that is frequently encountered in leadership work. Expect to train others in the overall style and, depending on the situation, in the art of specific Mindsets and Methods. Over time, work to develop presentations, stories, and group exercises for each critical domain of your Signature Style.

We urge you to start now on the work of planning and modeling the leadership development program you offer to others – we know from our own experience that this is deeply personal, joyous, and effective work.

Straightforward Tips for Remembering and Using the Mindsets and Methods

You can practice your Signature Style by responding to everyday signals telling us there are real Choices. We know from many years of experience and work with many people that it will often appear daunting to have control over and use of the diverse array of twelve Mindsets and Methods in making good leadership Choices. How can we be in action in different domains? How can we get our minds around a dozen tools?

Three straightforward practices can help, as laid out on the following page.

Gain conscious awareness of the many Choices available to each of us every single day. Job #1 is to recognize the signals that Choices are there to be made. Rely on your feelings for those signals.

If we are feeling buoyant, happy, and in the zone, this can be a signal that we have opportunities to amplify the good, using a Mindset and Method like DNA. Conversely, if we're feeling negative, challenged, angry, this can be a signal that we have opportunities to use the Flip Negative Energy toolkit. Our feelings can help us gain greater awareness of the need to make leadership Choices. This awareness can trigger our use of the Mindsets and Methods we can use to make these Choices.

As you engage the world, ask yourself *"What would be the Leadership Choice for the situation I am in?"* This is a way to bring the Mindsets and Methods into play as part of routine situations that frequently present themselves to each of us. Some examples of what this might look like include:

- If you're invited to make a presentation at a meeting, conference, or other event, think about the powerful cycles or other Pacing Event tools you can apply to your part of the agenda. Break your 60-minute presentation into two or three highly interactive cycles that will generate energy and action among participants;

- As you enter a staff meeting, team meeting or other gathering, ask yourself, *"What Requests, Offers, Assertions might I make at this event to drive action and progress towards shared goals?"*

- If you are leading an important interaction or series of interactions with a group of people, give conscious thought to how you might both project and call for Net Forward Energy or other ways of Being that are tailored to the work at hand;

- If you or your colleagues are suffering through some difficult and unexpected challenges, consciously work to call up and apply the Sources of Resilience that you and your team can draw on to persist through the breakdown on your way to the next breakthrough.

At the end of the day, look at your version of Exhibit D and ask " *What did I learn? What worked? What would I change to make it better?*" Take a few minutes to reflect on the feelings you had during the day and the situations you found yourself in as you encountered others. Review how you responded. Notice the Choices you made and could have made. Consider your leadership Signature Style to always be a work in progress. Refine and add to it as you use it.

Constant practice of these three straightforward tips and the resulting regular use of the Mindsets and Methods that work best for you will soon become second nature – a series of powerful leadership habits. These habits will ultimately be your Signature Style of leadership. We encounter former colleagues all the time who jubilantly share with us how their own exposure to Bold Aims, Requests and Offers, Pacing Events and other Mindsets and Methods – sometimes learned decades ago—have now been burned into the very culture of their organizations. Recall how John Chessare MD learned about the deliberate use of Effective Questions, Net Forward Energy and other Mindsets and Methods from his experience with the Organ Donation Breakthrough Collaborative, and then applied these methods to his leadership work with the Greater Baltimore Medical Center. This can be your experience as well.

Give the Mindsets and Methods featured here a shot. Use them to develop and refine your own leadership Signature Style. Using these Mindsets and Methods will increase your self-discipline, your character, and your integrity. The final Leadership Story that follows helps to show how even very painful experiences can somehow turn out to be wonderful sources of contribution, growth and joy.

LEADERSHIP STORY

Choosing to Lead Through a Demotion

by **Dennis Wagner**

An Appealing but Risky Opportunity

I made a tough career Choice in 1997. I left a fulfilling management job at the US EPA where I was responsible for a smart, exceptionally talented, and diverse team of 27 folks who I had recruited and worked with for eight years. Although I aspired to one day join the ranks of the federal government's Senior Executive Service (SES), I relinquished my EPA job to become a non-management Senior Advisor to Rear Admiral (RADM) Marilyn Gaston MD, the Director of the Bureau of Primary Health Care in the Health Resources and Services Administration (HRSA). What enticed me to this new agency was the challenge of a bigger, bolder mission with a larger platform for society-wide change.

But moving from a management position to a staff position was not generally considered a good career move in government service. This was a concern to me.

My longtime mentor, colleague, and now co-author, John Scanlon, had introduced me to Rear Admiral Marilyn Gaston MD, her Senior Executive Service deputy Mary Lou Andersen, and a host of other hard-charging government leaders who were committed to a bold vision: 100% Access to Healthcare for All and 0 (Zero!) Health Disparities. I was drawn to this Bold Aim and believed that my skillset was ideally suited to the challenge facing Dr. Gaston and Mary Lou, as well as Regan Crump, Jim Macrae, Donald Coleman, Chuck Van Anden, and other members of this talented team of leaders. Although Dr. Gaston's Bureau of Primary Healthcare had extensive federal platforms through the Community Health Center program and the National Health Service Corps, the Bureau had no formal statutory authority, no appropriation, and no designated staff for realizing the much larger Compelling Vision of 100% Access and 0 Health Disparities. The next five years of hard work and teaming on 100% Access and 0 Health Disparities (100%/0 for short) would turn out to be both challenging and rewarding.

The 100%/0 vision took root in discretionary staff work. And at first, it seemed that this untraditional and inadvisable career move was working out for the best. Our team made tremendous gains in increasing healthcare access and began to systematically identify and spread community based "Models That Worked" to reduce and eliminate healthcare disparities. Our work caught the attention of HRSA Administrator Claude Earl Fox MD, Health and Human Services Secretary Donna Shalala, US Senator Patty Murray (WA-D), and others. These senior policymakers worked successfully to secure statutory authority and funding for what became the institutionalized version of our campaign, the Healthy Communities Access Program (HCAP).

So just a few years after making that risky career Choice, I was suddenly leading the HCAP program with $100 million in annual funding and a brand new, talented staff. We worked to create integrated, connected, and collaborative community healthcare systems. The coalitions that we funded were expanding healthcare access and quality for uninsured, vulnerable people throughout the nation. The modest federal investments were leveraging major increases in healthcare access, while reducing overall costs to the system. Our bottom-line results were impressive and growing. It was impactful, meaningful work.

New Administration, New Policy Agenda

Less encouraging were glaring indications that the new HRSA Administrator, Elizabeth "Betty" Duke, PhD, who joined the Agency when the Bush Administration arrived in 2001, was determined to end what the new Administration viewed as the "Shalala HCAP initiative." Elizabeth Duke was a talented, high-ranking career civil servant; she had served as the Assistant Secretary for Administration in the Department of Health and Human Services and had mastery of personnel functions, budget planning and execution, grant-making process management, and more. My colleagues and I rapidly learned that she was also decisive, steely, and comfortable in her own skin. Administrator Duke knew what she wanted and was highly effective in using the administrative processes of government to achieve her goals and those of the new Administration.

Elizabeth "Betty" Duke
HRSA Administrator
2002-2009

My federal colleagues and I worked hard to get the substantive, quantitative results of the HCAP work in front of Dr. Duke. We reasoned that the compelling results of this program would be highly persuasive to a no-nonsense leader like her.

It didn't take long for us to be proven wrong. Despite my persistent and detailed efforts to share the program's significant impacts with Administrator Duke and political leaders in the Department, it soon became clear that the new team was determined to zero out HCAP's budget. In plain English: they wanted to end the program. But because the program now had a statutory mandate, with more than 100 grant recipients across the nation and a sizeable budget, ending it was not going to be an easy task. And it gradually began to dawn on me that my committed stewardship of the program was not viewed as an asset by the new Administration.

A Unilateral Reassignment to a Staff Position in A Remote HRSA Unit

The hammer fell several months into Dr. Duke's tenure, in early 2002, when my new boss called me into his office to tell me that Administrator Duke was reassigning me to a staff position in HRSA's Division of Transplantation, effective in three weeks. My new job would be to recruit 1000 organizations into the new Secretary Tommy Thompson's Workplace Partnership for Life initiative. Secretary Thompson's program was aimed at getting businesses, churches, universities, utilities, and other organizations to promote organ donation to their employees and customers.

I was shocked and disheartened by the reassignment. Despite a track record as a results-oriented federal manager with 15 consecutive years of outstanding performance ratings, I was being unilaterally reassigned by Administrator Duke. Although federal civil service rules prevented a reduction in my salary, it was clear that I was being demoted to a staff job. The decision had been made, and I was informed of it after the fact, without any inkling that this action was even being contemplated.

My new role came with zero staff and zero budget resources. What's more, my new assignment, the Workplace Partnership for Life, came with a dismal history. The straightforward vision for the program was to enroll businesses, churches, schools, healthcare organizations, and others into the Partnership and to help them encourage their employees and customers to become card-carrying organ donors. Despite major airplay by senior departmental leaders and eight months of concentrated effort, fewer than one hundred organizations of the targeted 1000 partners had been enrolled, and there was no effective management strategy or function in place to attain the 900 Partners to go in the remaining months of the first year.

An Attempt at Win/Win

I still had three weeks in my job as the Healthy Communities Access Program Director. I decided to take that narrow sliver of time and use it to prove that my management position in the Healthy Communities Access Program could achieve the Administration's goal for the Workplace Partnership. I was scheduled to deliver two keynote speeches at upcoming national and regional meetings with some of my grantees and their extensive networks of community partners. I decided to explore using my current circle of influence to recruit Workplace Partners by devoting several minutes of each keynote presentation to enroll CEOs and organizational leaders in the audience into the Secretary's languishing program.

It worked. After only two speeches in two weeks, I had enrolled nearly 120 additional organizations into the Partnership, more than doubling the total number of participants in the Secretary's initiative. Jubilant, I returned to the Agency and proposed that I continue in my current HCAP Director accountability, and that I could also confidently commit to recruiting the remaining 700-some Workplace Partners within Secretary Thompson's one-year deadline. I would offer to take on both Roles. To me, this felt like a win/win solution.

An Offer is Made and Firmly Rejected

I soon discovered that this ambitious plan did not fully consider the policy agenda of the new Administration, and that I was naïve to think it would be embraced. Shortly after proposing my win/win scheme, I was called into a meeting with Administrator Duke, my soon-to-be new Bureau Director, and the Administrator's Senior Advisor. It became immediately clear that Administrator Duke had called the meeting and that she would lead it. Sitting directly across from me at the conference room table and looking me straight in the eye, she said in her most no-nonsense voice:

"*I have three messages for you, Dennis.*

One—you no longer will report to the Bureau of Primary Healthcare. You will instead report to the Director of the Bureau of Special Programs.

Two—you will no longer serve as Director of the Healthy Communities Access Program and will have no further association with that program whatsoever.

And three—you will have sole accountability for recruiting 1000 Workplace Partners into the Secretary's initiative by the end of April.

Have I made myself clear?"

The Administrator repeated variations of the above throughout what was a short meeting. She requested confirmation of my understanding of her directives, multiple times. She made my reassignment crystal clear. I left the meeting privately resolving to achieve two new goals:

1. I would not only meet, I would also exceed Secretary Thompson's target of enrolling a total of 1000 Workplace Partners over the next several months;
2. I would get new job offers outside of HRSA as fast as possible.

Circle of Influence, to the Rescue

I achieved both goals.

Although demoralized, I energetically drew upon my networks and circle of influence from over 16 years of government service at EPA and HRSA. Several months into the new accountability, I achieved Secretary Thompson's target of 1000 Workplace Partners. The Secretary promptly convened a press event during the April Donate Life Month in which he not only declared success, but also announced the even more ambitious goal of enrolling 5000 Workplace Partners over the coming 12 months. This new accountability was news to me. Once again, I was not informed in advance nor given any opportunity for buy-in.

Almost at the same time, two appealing job offers from former bosses at the US Environmental Protection Agency rolled in. It was an incredible boost to my Resilience to be told by one of these exceptional leaders, "*Dennis, I'll always have a place for you in any organization that I lead.*" Both offers were for influential management positions. One was located at Research Triangle Park in North Carolina, reporting to the Director of the Office of Air Quality, Planning and Standards. The other was in Ann Arbor, reporting to a senior executive at the National Vehicle and Fuel Emissions Laboratory.

My wife and I traveled to these two delightful communities, met with realtors, explored neighborhoods and schools, and assessed the pros and cons of these two excellent career opportunities. I felt a genuine sense of connection with the vibrant and committed staff in each location.

Although we loved living in the nation's capital region, Diane and I were open to broadening our horizons to other areas of the country. We especially liked the idea of living in less rushed, less congested urban areas where we would have more time for our young children, friends, and neighbors. Teaming with bosses who respected my capabilities and wanted me as a valued member of their leadership teams was another critically important benefit.

A Compelling Vision Emerges

But in the midst of these exciting opportunities, something completely unforeseen happened. I discovered that I had developed a very real commitment to the mission of increasing organ donation and transplantation.

My work on the Workplace Partnership had brought me into direct contact with patients who had received life-saving transplants, as well as the smart, caring, committed medical professionals in organ procurement organizations and transplant centers. My work with the Division of Transplantation also helped me to see more clearly how I might contribute to the mission of increased, lifesaving and life-enhancing organ donation and transplantation.

Based on my experience with large-scale change management, it was abundantly clear that the Workplace Partnership activity was not likely to result in marked national increases in organ donation, even with 5000 new Workplace Partners. However, I could also see the tremendous need for improvement. Lives were at stake. Further, I knew that my skills in social marketing and with leading systematic quality improvement at national scale would be powerful assets for generating dramatic increases in organ donation and transplants. It was also clear to me that Secretary Thompson expected Administrator Duke and the Division of Transplantation to perform on his agenda of increasing organ donation and transplantation.

The convergence of these needs with my own circle of influence and skillsets, even as a solitary GS 15 staff person, had produced for me a clear and Compelling Vision for change and improvement. I had come to believe that a bold quality improvement initiative, targeted to the nation's largest hospitals, was a potentially viable pathway to dramatic increases in life-saving organ donation.

Compelling Vision Emerges as We Choose to Bring Together Two Forces in Our Lives

Graphic is adapted from Covey Institute training materials

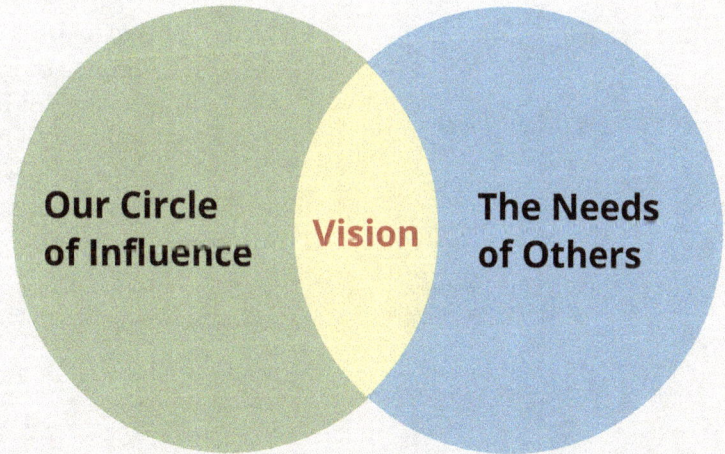

A Defining Moment Crystallizes a Commitment

I was on the horns of a dilemma. Should I stick with my ignominious staff level demotion in the Division of Transplantation, or seize one of the attractive EPA job offers? Reclaim my former status and career pathway to the Senior Executive Service in an influential management job, or pursue a Bold Aim to increase organ donation and transplantation on a national level? Pursue a long-standing career goal as a senior federal executive, or opt for uncertainty and resistance in an agency that was trying quietly but resolutely to disappear me?

There was no guarantee that I could convince HRSA to agree to the dramatically more intense level of work necessary to achieve bold organ donation goals. Generating substantial and lasting increases in organ donation was clearly much more than a management job – it was a leadership challenge that would involve uncertainty, risk, and requiring me and my new colleagues in the Division of Transplantation to overcome significant barriers to progress. It was one thing to enroll Workplace Partners, but quite another to actually generate increases in the number of grieving families willing to consent to their loved ones' becoming organ donors.

Enlisting Workplace Partners was a relatively simple task of asking organizations to help educate their employees and customers about organ donation. It was an entirely other thing to recruit hundreds of the nation's largest trauma centers to rapidly and effectively improve their implementation of heart-wrenching, carefully orchestrated, time-sensitive processes in the wake of fresh, unexpected family loss. Organ donation is not what grieving family members want to discuss at the time of the death of a loved one.

This decision was a defining moment for me. I remember it vividly. I was at Dulles airport, scheduled to leave on a lengthy flight to Thailand to assist an EPA team with two weeks of intensive work aimed at helping the Thai government develop their social marketing strategy to improve air quality in Bangkok. My new HRSA bosses had agreed to let me join the EPA team when they had reached out to request my help.

My deadline for accepting one of the two EPA job offers was at hand. My wife, Diane, had given me the greenlight to accept either of the two EPA offers. As a strong-willed leader and experienced senior Congressional staffer, Diane's support for a move from the nation's capital to Michigan or North Carolina was a big deal. There was no Congress for her to work at in North Carolina or Michigan. This was a major decision for both of us and for our young family. Both of us were already anticipating —in a good way—an exciting change in our lives and careers.

Ann Arbor or Chapel Hill? From my seat on the airplane, sitting on the tarmac, I made the first call and accepted the formal offer in Ann Arbor. I made the second call and ended the process of securing a formal offer from the EPA personnel folks in North Carolina. I felt that a momentous personal Choice had been made. We were moving to Michigan.

After the two calls, I immediately began to internalize the decision. Prior to making the decision, I was mainly focused on implementing my plan of finding and choosing a new position. As I reflected on the impending change, I began to seriously consider the missed opportunity to impact the lives of thousands of people who needed a transplant to save their lives. These included people like Amy Luxner, a graduate student and young professional in Washington, DC who I recently met who had received a heart transplant that saved her life.

I knew in my heart that leadership, boldness, courage, and expertise with large-scale quality improvement would be necessary to achieve significant increases in life-saving organ donation. And I knew that these were things that I was ideally equipped to supply at this moment in time and at this particular place in the federal government. I felt a strong sense of duty to do the job that the world, through no deliberate Intent or actions on my part, had thrown my way.

An agonizing five minutes later, I called Ann Arbor back and reversed my acceptance. The airplane doors closed, cell phone use was discontinued, and the flight took off for Thailand. For good or bad, I had made a completely unexpected and potentially unwise career decision to stick with the organ donation work.

A leadership Role is sometimes launched with a defining moment. In that moment, I left behind the certainty of a secure and appealing management job and stepped into a leadership Role, with the Compelling Vision of increasing life-saving organ donation and transplants across the nation.

Choosing to Lead: Managing Workplace Partners to Success

By choosing to remain in the Division of Transplantation, I assumed accountability for two commitments: an assigned professional job with responsibility for enrolling 5000 workplace partners, and a personal vision to generate significant increases in national organ donation and transplantation.

Hitting the new 5000 Workplace Partners target seemed like the best way to make further progress on our way to a bigger, more meaningful program of work. Now fully committed to the organ donation mission, I resolved to expand my circle of influence with Administrator Duke and with Secretary Thompson's office. I was already off to a good start by quickly hitting the 1000 Workplace Partners target in just a few months.

Building on my track record in recruiting the first 1000 partners, I was able to secure $40,000 in funding to hire a savvy, connected contractor to help me hit the 5000 Workplace Partners goal. Having previously managed an annual budget of more than $100 million, that meager victory of $40,000 in additional funding served as a glaring reminder of my newly diminished status in the Agency.

Enrolling workplaces was essentially a management and networking accountability. The new contractor I had located was a determined, energetic, social, retired executive named Jim Low. Jim was the former President and CEO of the American Society of Association Executives (ASAE), and brought with him over 20 years of leadership of the national "association of associations." Think of it, an association of association executives!

These association execs were connected to big membership networks that were literally brimming with future, potential Workplace Partners. As might be expected, Jim, my new colleague and federal contractor, was highly connected, respected by practically every person of influence in the association world. Jim had circles upon circles of influence. As an accomplished beltway insider, Jim was also skilled in appealing to political appointees like Secretary Thompson. Although it wasn't in his contract, Jim coached me constantly on how to perform this part of my job better.

Jim lined up meetings, often the two of us with a transplant recipient, to talk with leading association executives across the capital region. For example:

- Jim arranged for us to meet with his good friend, Tom Kuhn, President of the Edison Electric Institute, the association of investor-owned electric utilities. Tom agreed to promote the Workplace Partnership to all his members. His members, in turn, agreed to do things like include messages on tens of millions of their monthly utility bills to encourage their customers to become card-carrying organ donors. Wow.

- Larry Minnix, the CEO of Leading Age, the association of the nation's not-for-profit nursing homes met with Jim and me. Larry agreed to promote Workplace Partnership membership to thousands of leaders of nursing homes when they convened at his annual meeting. He enrolled 900+ nursing homes, in a single conference! He wrapped the stack of enrollment papers in a red ribbon and presented it to Secretary Thompson at a photo op we convened at the Department of Health and Human Services.

Larry Minnix, Nursing Home Association Leader Presents New Workplace Partner Enrollments to Secretary Thompson

We met with association executive after association executive and leveraged their platforms and influence to enroll thousands of new Workplace Partners. Camille Haney, Secretary Thompson's Special Assistant and our new key partner, was ecstatic with our progress. Camille had served as a key confidante and assistant to Thompson when he was Governor of Wisconsin and continued to support him when he transitioned to his new role as Secretary of Health and Human Services. She was excited to be teaming with someone at HRSA who was committed to hitting the Secretary's ambitious Workplace Partnership goals.

Multiple opportunities kept presenting themselves. Jim learned that a Cabinet Secretary slated to speak at a big conference of association executives had canceled only a few days before the big event. We reached out to Camille, who worked to rearrange Secretary Thompson's calendar so that he could step in as the new Keynote Speaker at a conference banquet at the National Building Museum in Washington, DC. We used the Secretary's speech before more than a thousand association leaders to recognize the work of association executives who were already leveraging their networks to promote organ donation. Plaques were given. Photos were taken. More association executives stepped forward to support the Workplace Partnership.

Secretary Thompson Recognizes Association Workplace Partners at Their Annual Conference

Jim Low, far left
Camille Haney, 3rd from left
Secretary Thompson, middle rear
heart transplant recipient Amy Luxner, front center

Four months ahead of schedule, we hit the 5000 Workplace Partners goal in January 2003. The number of partners continued to grow. Our track record on Workplace Partnership recruitment (thank you Jim Low!) is detailed in the chart below. Administrator Duke, Special Assistant Camille Haney, and Secretary Thompson were all delighted with our shared progress on the Workplace Partnership.

Shifting Focus to the Ultimate Outcome – More Patients Receiving Transplants

While we had made tremendous progress in recruiting and supporting our cadre of Workplace Partners, the nation was seeing no significant gains in terms of the actual numbers of organ donors and transplants – donation increased a mere 1% in 2002. Having studied the data, this was not surprising to me.

While national surveys showed extensive public support for organ donation, that support was not impacting consent rates in hospitals where it really mattered. In 2002, fewer than half the families of those who died in the unusual circumstances that permit donation to occur actually consented to allow the donation to proceed. These deaths usually result from accidents involving traumatic head injuries of some kind. The consent rate in the nation's largest trauma hospitals was only 46%.

Patients who can become donors experience brain death from the injuries and are typically on ventilators in large trauma centers. Family members are shocked at the sudden death of their loved one, and donation is not something many are prepared to talk about in these painful and unexpected circumstances. I knew that our Workplace Partnership initiative would not have much impact on the situation encountered with stunned families in these hospitals.

However, we also knew that there were nearly 30 large trauma centers in the United States that had organ donation consent rates greater than 70%, even though the national average was only 46%. Medical professionals and staff in these hospitals and their affiliated procurement organizations knew how to care for these families and to secure consent for organ donation. Their knowledge and skills were the key to increasing organ donation.

Several key colleagues in the Division of Transplantation and I believed that we could codify and spread the donation best practices of these large trauma centers and their affiliated organ procurement organizations. Doing this would make it possible to generate dramatic, rapid improvements in organ donation rates in other major trauma centers and hospitals. And approximately 90% of the potential organ donors originated in the nation's 500 largest trauma centers. Our little federal team crafted a plan of action.

A Bold Aim:
500 Hospitals, 75% Donation Rate

Camille Haney, the Secretary's Special Assistant, liked our plan. So, too, did Joyce Somsak, the new Acting Director of the Division of Transplantation. Our federal Team ran the numbers. If we could help the 500 large trauma centers to move from a 46% national average donation consent rate to that of the highest performers in the nation, we could increase organ donation by nearly 2000 more donors per year, equating to nearly 6000 additional lifesaving and life-enhancing transplants annually.

We knew we had to act. We settled on putting forward a Bold Aim for the nation of hitting a 75% organ donation rate in the nation's largest hospitals.

Frank Zampiello, MD
Former HRSA Quality Improvement Expert

Together with John Scanlon, Frank Zampiello MD (1936-2011), a former federal Public Health Service Officer, was instrumental in coaching and supporting our team in these analyses and in formulating the Bold Aim of a 75% donation rate in the nation's largest hospitals. John and I had met and teamed with Frank as part of shared work on 100% Access/0 Health Disparities. Dr. Zampiello was an expert at using the Institute for Healthcare Improvement (IHI) Breakthrough Series methodology to achieve large scale improvement. By adopting the IHI methodology, we could establish a platform to move hundreds of hospitals to the 75% target. In an ironic twist of fate, years later Frank would suffer an unexpected injury that led to him requiring and receiving a lifesaving liver transplant.

With No Authority or Resources, We Have a Leadership Challenge

Now we had a true leadership challenge, and at three levels: How to introduce the Bold Aim to officials in the Department and team with them to adopt it? How to invite and enroll the national professional organizations in organ donation and transplant field to stand for and act on the Aim? And how to convince Organ Procurement Organizations and hundreds of independent hospitals to voluntarily take this on? What could we do to support these key policymakers, advocates, and implementers in publicly announcing the aim and truly owning it?

Engaging the Department to Adopt the Bold Aim

Federal agencies do not casually issue Bold Aims. If we pursued a strategy of 'business as usual," we would have to take the proposal up through multiple levels of review and approval. Our request to target 500 hospitals for an organ donation rate of 76% was not likely to get very far through that gauntlet, and it would take months or possibly as long as a year to navigate the traditional clearances. Plus, we knew that an Aim this bold would look challenging if not impossible to many of the evaluators, budget analysts and others. And they would be correct. Significantly impacting the culture and practices of dozens of OPOs and hundreds of independent trauma centers was daunting. Our proposal was likely to die in review.

Our little HRSA team in the Division of Transplantation decided to pursue a much more direct route. Secretary Thompson had been invited by the United Network for Organ Sharing (UNOS), the government contractor who operated the organ allocation system, to participate in a ground-breaking ceremony for their new building in Richmond, Virginia. Camille and Secretary Thompson reached out to the HRSA, who then tasked its Division of Transplantation with drafting the speech for the ceremony. We put an announcement of the new collaborative initiative and the 75% organ donation aim into the speech. HRSA Communications cleared our version of the speech (amazing) and sent it on to the Department and the Secretary. Camille briefed the Secretary on the proposed plan. He approved it! We were off to the races.

Engaging National Professional Organizations to Support the Campaign

Camille and our team went to work to launch the new initiative. Acting Division of Transplantation Director Joyce Somsak secured and redirected modest funds of ~$4 million to fund the initial year of work. Ginny McBride, Jade Perdue, and other federal colleagues teamed with Camille and myself to get key national executives from the Association of Organ Procurement Organizations, UNOS, the Coalition on Donation, the Institute for Healthcare Improvement, the North American Transplant Coordinators Organization and others to join with the Secretary in committing to our Bold Aim. We reasoned, who in this esteemed community of practice would say "no" to an invitation to join with the HHS Secretary in a bold commitment to increase life-saving organ donation? We reasoned correctly. Everyone invited said "yes."

It all came off seamlessly. Secretary Thompson signed a Contract for Results that our HRSA team created, committing to achieve a 75% donation rate in the nation's largest hospitals. Leaders from each of the participating national organizations joined with the Secretary in signing the Contract at the groundbreaking ceremony. Donald Coleman, the talented Director of HRSA Media Services, captured the entire event on video, and interviewed many of the participating leaders to get their commitments on tape for further distribution and use. We used the momentum and excitement generated by the announcement to begin to recruit improvement teams from OPOs and their affiliated large trauma centers.

The President of the Association of Organ Procurement Officials at that time, Helen (Leslie) Bottenfield, also signed the Secretary's Contract for Results in her role. Helen Bottenfield is an extroverted, candid, passionate, and incredibly effective nurse executive with decades of experience in the intricacies of organ procurement and transplantation. She is deeply committed to the well-being of donor families, patients, and transplant recipients.

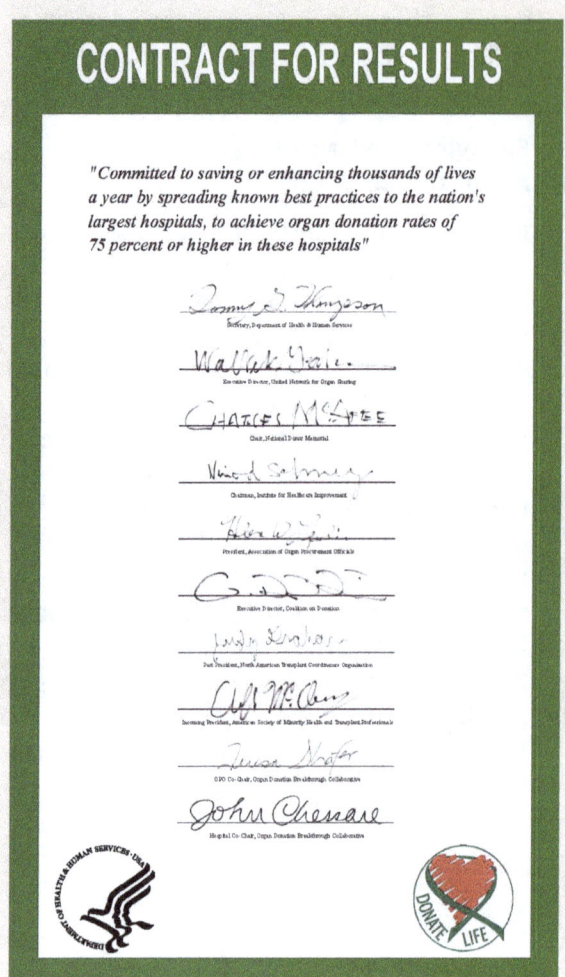

Bottenfield would later confide that when she joined with Thompson in committing to the Aim, she did so because he asked. Based on her many years of experience with organ donation, she privately had doubts at the time about whether the Bold Aim could be achieved. It would be a heavy lift. Yet she was drawn to the challenge. Helen's doubts were soon replaced by genuine enthusiasm and commitment to the Aim as she encountered the best practices and the leaders who delivered them. Helen Bottenfield would later join the federal core team, implementing the Secretary's Organ Donation Breakthrough Collaborative and devoting her full-time efforts, expertise and infectious energy to the juggernaut national quality improvement initiative.

Organ donation leader and expert Helen Bottenfield with Rose, a young transplant recipient at a collaborative event in Little Rock, Arkansas

Enrolling Hospitals and OPOs in the National Initiative

The Department now had a new and nationwide Bold Aim to pursue. The Secretary's adoption and articulation of the new goal was a major asset. The resources of the Division of Transplantation could now be organized to support a national campaign to engage the OPOs and trauma centers. The Secretary's public commitment to the Bold Aim provided a clear performance management path to follow. Administrator Duke used the full force of her influence as Administrator to support the new Organ Donation Breakthrough Collaborative, visibly supporting and speaking at Collaborative Learning Sessions. She used her mastery of federal budgeting to ensure that the annual resources were in place to support the juggernaut national improvement initiative.

Our federal team worked with John Scanlon, Frank Zampiello, and the Lewin Group, an accomplished federal contractor, to codify the best practices of the highest-performing hospitals and organ procurement organizations.

We convened our first learning session of the Secretary's Organ Donation Breakthrough Collaborative in September of 2003 in Washington, DC. Nearly 800 people joined us at the Learning Session, in teams from 95 of the nation's largest trauma centers and their OPOs. The following month, October of 2003, the nation set a new record for the most organ donors per month.

Achieving National Results

Following our first event, we organized and conducted large national learning sessions of 1000 to 3000 people every four to six months over the course of the next three years. The learning sessions were convened as Pacing Events, with vibrant, content-rich, positive agendas where we systematically secured commitments from participants to test out and implement the changes in practice that were shown to be associated with higher organ donation rates. In the months following the first and subsequent learning sessions of the Collaborative, the number of US organ donors increased compared to the same month of the prior year over 35 of the next 39 months, as captured in the adjacent chart.

Organ donation increased dramatically over the next several years as the Collaborative continued. We convened the first-ever National Learning Congress in May of 2005, where we would present the Secretary's Organ Donation Medal of Honor to teams from 184 of the 500 largest trauma hospitals and their OPOs who had achieved the 75% donation rate.

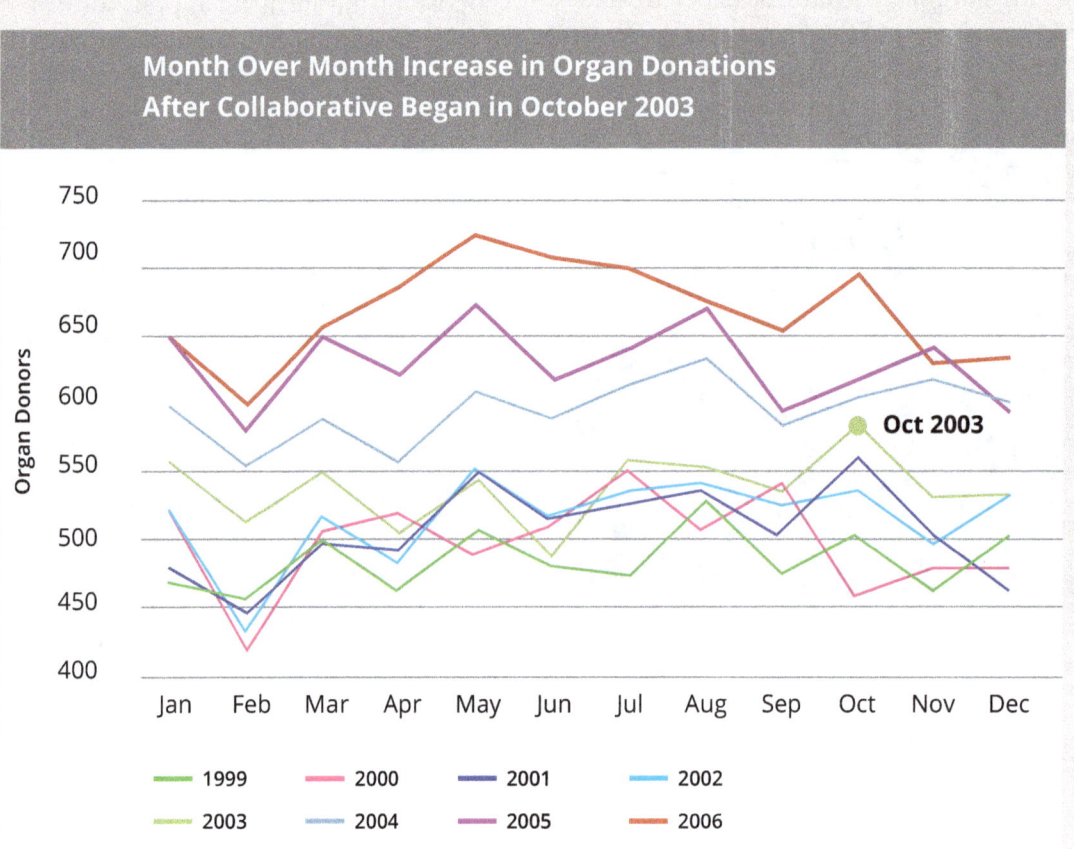

World Class Acknowledgement

With the first Medals of Honor to be awarded in Pittsburgh at the National Learning Congress on Organ Donation and Transplantation in May of 2005, the Collaborative Faculty members faced a challenge: how do you meaningfully award medals to over 1000 healthcare providers in 184 teams at a single event? We didn't want to ask 1000 people to walk across a stage. This would turn a meaningful award into a tedious ceremony.

So, when it was time for the awards to be conferred, Dr. Elizabeth Duke, the Administrator of the Health Resources and Services Administration, called on all who were designated to receive a Medal to please stand.

In a jampacked room of over 2500, about 1000 people rose to their feet.

From the sides of the room emerged men, women, and children of all ages and ethnicities, every one of them beneficiaries of organ donation. Each of them held 20 or 30 Medals of Honor dangling on thick ribbons from their arms. They fanned out throughout the banquet hall placing ribbons around the necks of the standing awardees. As they made the awards, the transplant recipients would say things like:

"I'm a 41-year-old mother of three. I got a heart transplant last year. Thank you."

"Thank you for making it possible for me to spend time with my grandkids."

"My lungs have given me a new shot at life. I can run again! Thank you."

Department of Health and Human Services Organ Donation Medal of Honor

The doctors, nurses, social workers, chaplains, procurement coordinators and others who were receiving the medal would often burst into tears and hug the award-giving transplant recipient. It was one of the most impactful and heartfelt events anyone could possibly imagine—20 minutes of organized chaos and emotion, transplant recipients posing with medal-winning team members in hundreds of spontaneous celebrations and photos on the floor of the convention center.

Partners in the hospitals where donors originated could now see the life-saving results of their work. We closed the loop on this important process.

HRSA and the Department recognized 371 of the 500 hospitals that had achieved this rate in 2006, and we recognized 392 hospitals in 2007. In the years following the Collaborative, the nation's organ procurement organizations have continued to successfully pursue year-after-year increases in lifesaving and life-enhancing organ donation. Organ donation was up by over 50% cumulatively for the most recent 5-year period of 2018 to 2023.

Administrator Duke Nominates Organ Donation Team for SAMMIE Award

In 2005, Administrator Duke supported the nomination of our federal Team for a prestigious SAMMIE Medal, known as the "Oscars of American Government," granted by the Partnership for Public Service, a non-partisan, not-for-profit organization that is dedicated to improving and calling attention to exceptional government performance. Every year the Partnership recognizes approximately 10 federal individuals or teams in an over-the-top awards ceremony of 1000 people at an impressive venue in the nation's capital. The SAMMIEs are covered by the Atlantic, the Washington Post and other influential media outlets. Thanks to Administrator Duke's support, our team was one of three finalists for the Citizen Services Medal, a very great honor. Although we didn't win the Medal, the occasion was a beautiful capstone to what had begun as a very rocky relationship between Administrator Duke and me.

Dramatic, rapid increases in organ donation results were also a key element of Administrator Duke's own recognition from President George W. Bush as a 2006 recipient of the Presidential Rank Award as Distinguished Executive. Dr. Duke and I parted on very good terms in 2009 when the Administration changed again and she exited the Agency.

Prior to her departure, Administrator Duke and a member of her senior team, Michelle Snyder, supported me in becoming one of three Agency professionals selected to participate in the Department's Senior Executive Service (SES) candidate program. This helped to pave the way for my entry into this elite cadre of senior federal executives. In the end, Dr. Duke's support as Administrator turned out to be a key aspect of achieving the federal SES position that I thought had been jeopardized by my move from EPA to HRSA. In 2023, Dr. Duke would be elevated to the Government Hall of Fame, a prestigious honor bestowed on very few Americans, joining the ranks of distinguished public servants such as Thurgood Marshall and Theodore Roosevelt.

SAMMIE Award Finalists with Administrator Duke: (l-r) Ginny McBride, Donald Coleman (seated), and Jade Purdue, with Administrator Duke and Dennis Wagner.

Choosing to Lead is About Lessons Learned—and There are Always Lessons to Learn

My reassignment lecture and demotion to a staff position at HRSA, removing me from work that I loved and had nurtured over several years of intense labor, was a disruptive and disheartening experience. The reassignment was a serious blow to my self-image of accomplishment, strategic leadership, and positive attitude. Coping with my new reality as a staff person in a job I did not choose was painful and hard work. But through it, I gained greater humility in dealing with others, and useful insights about what disruption means and how to handle it.

Humility came with learning to see apparent adversaries as fellow humans with their own visions and difficulties. The disruptors were not my enemies. We were pursuing different goals in the moment but still had vital things in common. With the effort and the forgiveness that come with time and perspective, I found ways to collaborate and team on meaningful work.

Even more important, this disruptive experience has become a source of compassion I have for others when they fall on hard times. Experiencing a major setback has made me much more conscious and empathetic with others who suffer similar setbacks of their own. This matters because so much of leadership work is about helping others sustain their own Resilience. The humility and compassion resulting from this experience have made me a better leader, and I hope a better person.

Insights from my HRSA experience have been key in forming my Signature Style of leadership as well as codifying the Mindsets and Method detailed in this book to help others determine and develop their own Signature Styles. I became aware that negative energy is often self-generated by how we choose to respond to any given situation or other stimulus. An important attribute of leadership is recognizing our ability to choose positive responses to seemingly negative stimuli, and learning to deal with the negative energy that is inevitable throughout our work and professional lives.

I also learned the value of asking for help. The support of mentors and partners made all the difference for me and were a source of great Resilience. My wife Diane, my mentor John Scanlon, prior bosses like Mary Lou Andersen, federal colleagues and peers like Regan Crump, partners in the field like Karen Minyard of the Georgia Health Policy Institute – all played key roles in helping me to weather the storm of my reassignment. When I later encountered Don Berwick's advice to "never worry alone," it immediately clicked with me. Talking to others makes it difficult for us to justify a conspiratorial view of what's happening. Talking to others helps us to look forward, not backward. Talking to others opens up possibilities and opportunities.

I came away from this challenging series of events with a much better sense of how to flip the negative energy in a situation. As I experienced the new staff Role with the Division of Transplantation, I was effectively asking myself questions that have now become an organized part of my leadership toolkit: *"What is something good that could come out of this seemingly bad situation? Why is this happening for me?"*

There turned out to be many positive answers to these questions. Working through the resentment and disruption I initially felt at the demotion resulted in the forgiveness of others. Over time, I learned that the seemingly bad things we encounter in work and in life's transactions can actually turn out to be good things for us in the long run. The most surprising insight is that in almost every situation we are thrown into by fate, there are usually opportunities for doing positive, impactful things. The reassignment to the Division of Transplantation initially felt like a punishment. One of the lessons I learned was to stop, step back, and look at what was really going on in any given situation. John Scanlon and other mentors and friends helped me to do this, and much to my surprise, I found a needed and rewarding leadership campaign waiting to be embraced and acted on, a once-in-a-lifetime opportunity to contribute to work that has saved tens of thousands of lives.

Overcoming these psychologically jarring problems is not a passive act. Leadership involves Choice. And my experience taught me that this is not just a one-time big Choice, to "get over it." Growing through the difficulties was mainly achieved in the constant, every day, in-the-moment Choices. This meant learning to sit across the table from and actively team and collaborate with people who I held responsible for forcing me into a work situation that I had not chosen. I had to deal with and ultimately learn to transcend the bitterness and anger that their actions had triggered in me. This was hard to do.

In leadership work I have now come to expect disruptions as natural reactions of a complex world, not as personal failures or rejections, and not as attacks by others. In my best moments, I have even come to see disruptions as sources of energy and opportunities for breakthroughs. Looking back, the demotion turned out to be an extraordinary opportunity to make a difference by consciously and wholeheartedly choosing to lead.

Tracking A Signature Style of Leadership In Action

by **John Scanlon**

The situations that each of us encounters in work and in life – including, especially, the difficult ones—can help us to evolve our own unique Signature Style. Our Signature Style can become a series of intentional, positive Choices in multiple domains that increase our effectiveness and joy, and that of others who are in our orbits.

The challenges Dennis encountered during his time at HRSA ultimately helped him to expand and hone his own unique Signature Style of leadership. The leadership Choices he made were informed and assisted by multiple leadership Mindsets and Methods.

How does a person handle a negative situation like this? We see how in Dennis' career his leadership Signature Style was both challenged and further forged in dealing with painful situations, triggered by powerful external forces.

We are all challenged like Dennis in at least two major ways:

- By the leadership opportunities present in almost every situation; and,
- By the need to flip the negative energy that naturally arises in the course of our professional and personal lives.

We can mine Dennis' experience for insight about leadership Mindsets and Methods. When push comes to shove, what kind of Choices do we make? In each section of the story, Dennis is choosing to lead in some way. Think of a difficult situation that has come up in your own life. Reflect on the challenge and the learning it has generated for you. What are the Mindsets and Methods that worked for you and have now become part of your own Signature Style? Make your own assessment of the dynamics Dennis is encountering and the Mindsets and Methods he chooses to use in his own Signature Style of leadership. These insights can help us build out and further refine our own Signature Style.

The story of two leadership undertakings in a federal department—the 100%/0 Campaign and the Organ Donation Breakthrough Collaborative—pivoted around a change in presidential administrations. The first leadership undertaking is abruptly shut down. This action turned out to be very disruptive to Dennis' role, position, and career. Forces outside his sphere of influence created a psychologically distressing situation.

Then we saw how a seemingly negative situation could generate new leadership possibilities and opportunities. What makes that possible is having a productive way of handling the negative energy so that we can see and act on the ever-present opportunities. In the end, the disruptive forces became supportive, celebratory and a source of personal growth and shared accomplishment for an entire national community of practice.

Ultimately, Dennis was able to overcome psychologically jarring problems and disheartening disruptions. As each of us crafts our own Signature Style, we can identify insights from Dennis' story. The seemingly bad things we encounter in work and life transactions can actually turn out to be good things for us in the long run. It's all in the Choices we make. In the following section, walk with me through the story again and develop your own assessment of key insights from this case study. Use the insights to further clarify and develop your own Signature Style and Leadership Story.

A Walk Through the Author's Signature Style in Action

INTENT
Compelling Vision
Bold Aims
Decide-Notice-Acknowledge

INTENT

There are two career Choices in Dennis' story. In one he steps into an active leadership effort; in the other he creates one. In the beginning of the story, Dennis switches agencies to join a team effort with a robust leadership vision: every community would have 100% Access to Healthcare and 0 Health Disparities. He chooses to play a leadership Role in a situation with "no legislative authority, no budget, no designated staff." This is not a career move to be taken lightly. However, there was a clear way forward.

Using the circles of influence associated with the HRSA health center program, the team was able to make the Vision compelling to others. Following the DNA method, community best practices were surfaced and celebrated. Funding sources and partners were slowly but systematically secured. The vision was being realized.

Abruptly, with a new administration, the whole effort is shut down! Dennis finds himself in an unfamiliar part of the agency, the Division of Transplantation. He is responsible for a completely different and much lower-level staff job of recruiting organizations to promote organ donation with their employees and customers. Losing the 100%/0 campaign that was generating commitment and results, and effectively being demoted, was negative and devastating.

His style was to try to flip the negative energy in all that by coming up with win-win solutions for the incoming executives. Often a "no" to a request and offer can be taken as "not yet." However, in this case a key meeting with Administrator Duke made clear that the "no" was a firm "no." Dennis found himself transferred to a small program with a management objective that would not meaningfully affect the Division's larger mission of increasing organs available for transplant.

Rather quickly and naturally, he looks for the compelling need of others that lies behind this unit's mission. People are dying because they do not have access to donated organs. The mission to increase transplantation becomes compelling as Dennis and his colleagues meet donor families and donor recipients and see the large scale of the transplant wait list. Observation of what is in place surfaces outlier trauma centers and OPOs with high organ donation conversion rates. This finding suggests that increases in donor rates across trauma centers is possible.

Dennis describes a defining moment in his life: sitting on an airplane about to take off, he turns down two attractive management job opportunities and chooses to stay in the Division. He makes a career Choice to stay in the unit and stand for a Compelling Vision: life-saving organ donation rates in the nation's trauma centers would increase dramatically.

Again, Dennis puts himself in a situation with "no authority, no budget and no designated staff." However, prior experience gave him a path to follow. Living the principle of DNA (Decide-Notice-Acknowledge) had the team looking for and noticing the OPOs and trauma centers who already knew how to deliver what was high end performance, i.e. organ donation rates greater than 70 percent. These outliers enabled the team to assert that dramatic increases in performance were possible. The team set a Bold Aim: organ donation conversion rates in the nation's largest trauma centers would be increased from an average of 46% to 75%. The outliers provided faculty to both inspire and coach their peers. Rather than try to tell organizations they must hit 75%, the federal team encouraged their voluntary commitment by showing how their peers get those life-saving results.

Observation guided by a DNA style enabled Dennis and the Division team to develop a Compelling Vision and put forward a Bold Aim. By choosing this Intent it became necessary for them to step into a leadership Role.

BEING

Net Forward Energy

Flip Negative Energy

Resilience

BEING Dennis was in an unusual job situation. "Generating substantial and lasting increases in organ donation was clearly much more than a management job—it was a leadership challenge." The work of leadership was getting others to publicly commit to the Bold Aim. The team had to create Net Forward Energy by enrolling others. However, business as usual was ready to greet the effort with skepticism, indifference, resistance.

Dennis and the team began by taking advantage of the federal Health Secretary's commitment to increasing organ donation and transplantation. This turned out to be a high-level source of energy. It got the attention of other important circles of influence.

We saw how the Bold Aim was inserted into the Secretary's planned speech to the donation and transplant community. The Secretary's commitment to the Bold Aim captured the attention of national associations and organizations in the field. The Division team created Net Forward Energy by inviting the executives of multiple organizations to sign a contract committing publicly and dramatically to the Bold Aim. They said "yes!" to an attractive opportunity to join with a Cabinet Secretary on important work.

The executives from leading edge OPO's and donor hospitals added energy by being co-chairs of the initiative and faculty to their peers in the campaign. The regular convening of all participants in action learning sessions keep the energy positive and high.

In a personal way, Dennis managed to Flip Negative Energy by turning frustration with the workplace partner enrollment program into a high performing success that got the attention of the Department's administrative structure. As the goal was expanded from enrolling 1000 workplace partners to 5000 partners, Dennis assumed management accountability for embracing and surpassing the new targets. By being results-focused, Dennis and his team in the Division increased its influence in the Department. Their work and their successes got the attention of staff in the Office of the Secretary.

There is a certain way of Being that generates Net Forward Energy for a leadership campaign. That way is to always be looking for sources of energy and then using Intent and Language to turn that on in the form of productive relationships and action. It's living in a cycle of interest, enrollment, commitment, and partnership. Rather than tell and direct, the leadership team notices and celebrates.

This way of Being brings a Resilience needed to overcome natural breakdowns. Throughout Dennis' story we see disruptive events being turned into new relatedness, possibility, and opportunity. Partners in a shared mission become an important source of Resilience for each other. Additionally, focusing on an important purpose, pursuing Net Forward Energy, and working to Flip Negative Energy all help make Resilience a way of Being, a habit.

LANGUAGE

Leadership Speech Acts

Leadership Stories

Access Abundance

LANGUAGE Dennis and the immediate federal team had a Compelling Vision and Bold Aim, but it was not yet known or owned by Federal officials and organ transplant professional organizations.

The Division team engaged others in conversations where they made Declarations and Assertions, and followed with Requests and Offers. Leadership Speech Acts gave them the tools they needed to get the attention of others and to secure Commitments. The Bold Aim was a Declaration that attracted others. Best practices provided fertile ground for assertions that trauma centers and OPOs could achieve the Bold Aim. Request and Offer conversations resulted in Commitments from others.

Leadership Stories from the field were deployed to inspire and enroll others. Field studies surfaced high performing OPOs and trauma centers. The executives of these units had Leadership Stories that the Division team celebrated. Executives and staff from best practice sites were asked to be faculty for a national action learning collaborative. Conversations with leaders in the field and partners inside and outside the Department of Health and Human Services were a source of Abundance for the team and its growing network of influence.

What began as a daunting undertaking was now gaining national traction by the systematic use of Leadership Speech Acts and Leadership Stories. Leadership Language helped the team to access an Abundance of content and willingness to participate that was hidden below the surface.

ROLES

Role Switching

5 Dimensions of Action

Pacing Events

ROLES

The roles of Observer, Administrator, Manager, and Leader are needed to operate successful enterprises. Role Switching allows for different roles to be performed at different times as enterprises mature and unique challenges arise. Understanding the distinctions between these four Roles can equip us with the mindset necessary to "switch" among these Roles, depending on the needs of any given situation. All may be in play, but at a point in time, one will be the driver. We can follow how switching happens in Dennis Wagner's experience with organ donation and transplantation.

Dennis initially stepped into a formal Management Role with the Workplace Partnership program. He was made responsible for enrolling 1000 and then 5000 Workplace Partners over specified periods of time. As organizations signed up to become partners, Administrative processes were established to follow up on their pledges. With Workplace Partnerships, the HRSA Division of Transplantation was implementing a successfully managed program, but even so, a significant increase in actual donors and transplantation was highly unlikely. The Workplace Partnership program was not designed to address the key factors that would achieve the federal Intent of rapid increases in organ donation and more transplants. The Division's challenge was for their team to recognize and act on the leadership opportunities that would make this Intent achievable.

Team Observation of what was actually happening in the larger donation and transplant system generated high impact possibilities. Observation showed that although the national average donation rate in large trauma centers was 46%, there were some large trauma centers with rates of 70% and higher – and leaders and staff in these organizations knew what practices generated the high rates. Impact could be realized by working more directly with OPOs and trauma centers to increase hospital organ donation rates to those already proven possible by the highest performers. Higher rates would deliver more organs for transplant.

Dennis and his team began with "no goal, no authority and no resources." They stepped from observation into a Leadership Role by (1) committing to move organ donation rates across the nation's largest hospitals from 46% to 75%, (2) establishing ownership of the 75% Bold Aim among Department officials and stakeholder organizations, and (3) securing the resources needed to run a national action learning collaborative to achieve the Bold Aim.

Once these commitments were in place, Dennis and the HRSA Team assumed major Management Roles in addition to their defining Leadership Role. Over four years they managed a large-scale national quality improvement initiative with OPOs and donor hospitals to deliver the well-defined outcome now agreed to: a 75% organ donation rate among the nation's largest trauma centers. The Leadership Role was critical in moving the Division to set up a managed program; the managed program was critical to realize the aim and save thousands of lives.

As the best practices that increased organ donation rates became widely understood and accepted, those practices came to be administered as evidence-based standards. Administration steps were taken to codify the proven practices to gain greater reliability and efficiency. Over time all four Roles came into play. For large scale change to happen, timely and effective Switching among the four Roles is a necessary requirement.

The HRSA stories shows that the leadership Role, while daunting, isn't "build something out of nothing." It is more like "build something out of many things you initially do not have access to or influence over." Leadership is unique from Management and Administration because it is about assuming accountability for transformative results in the face of many unknowns, in the absence of resources, and then partnering effectively with others to gain shared commitments to the Bold Aim and the resources necessary for achieving it.

As we learned from Mark Abramson at the Council for Excellence in Government, both HRSA leadership teams (organ donation and 100%/0) worked across all 5 Dimension of Action. With organ donation, Dennis and his colleagues demonstrated Subordinate leadership in working up the Agency's organizational structure with their supervisors and then several levels beyond to engage more directly with the Office of the Secretary in the larger Department.

Dennis's team demonstrates Public leadership in reaching out to OPOs and trauma centers that are high performance outliers. Then they reach out even further to engage and team with a wide variety of professional associations who have influence and impact on hospitals, quality improvement, organ donation, and transplantation. Hierarchical, Process Improvement, and Collegial leadership were constantly in play as part of the management of Action Learning Collaborative. Similar multi-dimensional reach is seen in the 100% Access and 0 Disparities Campaign. The Secretary and HRSA Administrator are engaged. Members of Congress come forward to establish the Healthy Communities Access Program that helped to institutionalize the 100%/0 Campaign. This goes considerably beyond traditional work in organization silos. The leadership style in play was action across all 5 Dimensions.

In this style of work, convenings are acted on as Pacing Events – opportunities to engage participants and secure commitments to help achieve the Compelling Vision. Secretary Thompson's UNOS speech is an example of an already-planned event that was turned into a campaign Pacing Event. Suddenly a Secretary's speech at a traditional ground-breaking ceremony becomes an opportunity to announce a bold new national goal and to secure commitments from influential organizations to make themselves accountable for the Bold Aim. The National Learning Congress award ceremonies are Pacing Events intentionally designed to Acknowledge increases in organ donation and generate large scale Net Forward Energy. In both HRSA campaigns, an event structure called "action learning collaboratives" was established where in-person, multi-day Pacing Events are used to generate the energy, Requests, Offers, and Commitments necessary to move together toward the Bold Aims and Compelling Vision.

Seeing meetings as potential Pacing Events enables each of us to turn management, administration and observation platforms into leadership forums that impact the multiple dimensions of system transformation. Observation, Administration, Management and Leadership, acted on across the 5 Dimensions of Action, together in vibrant Pacing Events, become an integrated force for change, action and transformation.

Reassuring Insights from Experience with a Signature Style in Action

The leadership Signature Style conveyed in this book grew out of the work of the authors with many people over 30 years. As each of us crafts our own Signature Style, we can identify insights from Dennis' story. The work to increase national organ donation and transplantation covers an especially formative and creative time in our shared work together. Many of the Mindsets and Methods profiled in this book were surfaced and shaped in this period.

The following items illustrate some of the powerful insights present in Dennis' story:

- *Robust leadership attracts talent and resources.* The executive team in HRSA's Bureau of Primary Health Care was able to recruit Dennis Wagner from EPA to lead the 100%/0 campaign. In a similar way, Secretary Thompson's leadership on the 75% organ donation goal attracted other influential leaders to this goal. Performance outliers inspired voluntary performance commitments from their peers;

- *Some of life's most difficult situations often contain opportunities for assuming leadership Roles.* Even a bleak personal situation such as a shut down, demotion, and transfer offers leadership opportunities. The organ donation collaborative itself is organized around family tragedies that result in life-giving opportunities for others;

- *Defining Moments can emerge during periods of transition.* The churning and reorientation of a transition enabled Dennis to see and act on a new Compelling Vision. A defining moment is a profound convergence of insight and clarity. If seized, it can be life changing. We observed a similar pattern in Anne Hastings' Leadership Story;

- *Flip Negative Energy is a teachable skill and learnable habit.* By gradually setting aside anger, resentment, and negative judgments, Dennis was eventually able to ask Effective Questions about his situation: "What good can come out of this seemingly bad situation?" Flip Negative Energy is a remarkable exercise in Choice. It is an instant way to make the world a better place—and it's available to all of us.

- **Leadership Roles and Management Roles require personal commitment.** The Workplace Partners program required Dennis to be accountable to enroll first 1000, then 5000 partners. The organ donation and transplant vision required Dennis and his team to invent and become accountable for achieving a much Bolder Aim. Both leadership and management call for accountability;

- **Leadership action can start with "no authority, no legislation, no budget."** Both the 100%/0 campaign and the organ donation collaborative began with a staff team using limited to no discretionary resources. Over time they built the authority and infrastructure needed to pursue Bold Aims. This turns out to be exhilarating work!

- **Acknowledgement of commitments met builds valuable social capital.** By showcasing and celebrating performance in the Workplace Partners program, Dennis and his colleagues expanded their circle of influence in their Agency and the larger Department. By inventing and awarding Medals of Honor to high-performing OPOs and trauma centers, Dennis and his colleagues expanded their circles of influence across the nation's health care system.

Ultimately, Dennis was able to overcome psychologically jarring problems and disheartening disruptions. His leadership Signature Style has evolved to deliberately and intentionally cultivate and draw on the sources of Resilience that are available to all of us. The seemingly bad things we encounter in work and life transactions can actually turn out to be good things for us in the long run. It's all in the Choices we make.

In a quiet moment, walk through the story again and develop your own assessment of key insights from this case study. Use the insights to further clarify and develop your own Signature Style and Leadership Story.

The World Needs More Leadership

The temptation and tendency to self-disqualify is one of the greatest inhibitors to the unique and special leadership that resides in all of us.

Reading any of the Leadership Stories in this book, including Dennis's journey from being sidelined to spearheading a national life-saving effort, it would be easy to tell ourselves, "No way could I ever achieve results like that. Those were extraordinary people in extraordinary circumstances. My situation is different."

It's not about Being extraordinary . . .

Yet without exception, we know that every single person featured in these stories would want you to know: extraordinary starts with you. Just as it started with a middle-aged woman who set out on mountainous dirt roads to help impoverished women start their own businesses without speaking a single word of the Haitian language. Just as it started with a lone doctor in the state of New Mexico who meditated on the preventable death of his patient—a young mother—and thought, *I can get in a car on my weekends and recruit other doctors to help.* Just as it started with grief-stricken parents who resolved to turn the loss of their child into an opportunity to save another family's loved one. Just as it started with a demoted government manager who makes the choice to stay where he isn't wanted because he's fallen in love with the mission of saving lives through organ donation.

It's not about the awards . . .

These are all every-day, ordinary people. Not one of them would have told you they were extraordinary. Few of them would have considered themselves leadership material. But in a defining moment or series of everyday actions, they began to step out of their comfort zones and into what felt like a daunting Bold Aim. They said yes to a Compelling Vision of an extraordinary future. Every one of them risked failure, and yet to their minds the worst outcome was not to have failed but to not have tried. They chose to use Net Forward Energy, Effective Questions, Pacing Events and more to generate problem-solving, commitments, and solutions. And even when some of these individuals were ultimately lauded for their contribution, it was never about the award. Even in the case of Dr. Chessare, the Baldrige Award had nothing to do with winning and everything to do with transforming an entire workforce of nearly 4000 employees into a mindset of accountability and responsibility for delivering the patient-centered care that we would all want for our own loved ones.

. . . It's about having purpose

Every one of these ordinary people chose to lead. This is what we are asking of you: to discover and embrace the extraordinary future you stand for.

Discover it by speaking the vision and purpose that come to you today. Share and discuss your purpose with those in your circle of influence. Listen to how they respond, form your next steps. Choose to expand your circle of influence. Pick someone you'd like to know. Read their stuff, give them a call. Have a conversation. Listen to how they respond; form your next steps.

Practice the current version of your Signature Style. Get better at trying out key Mindsets and Methods. Increase your self-discipline, your character, and your integrity. As you do this, add new Mindsets and Methods as the circumstances may call for. Your unique Signature Style will evolve and strengthen.

. . . It's about Joy

Throughout this book, we have made frequent reference to joy.

It's the joy of expecting, looking for, and discovering the natural Abundance surfaced by Requests and Offers.

It's the joy a team experiences when working shoulder-to-shoulder across all 5 Dimensions of Action.

It's the joy a team experiences when discovering the agility to Role Switch from Observer to Administrator to Manager to Leader as needed.

It's the joy a team experiences when adopting a listening mindset in an attentive, respectful atmosphere where they are confident that the answers are in the room.

This concept of joy is one you will seldom if ever encounter in other management or business school case studies or workshops. But it is real, it is contagious, and it spurs results and connections never imagined. In a world that can feel dark and hopeless at times, this joy fosters an Upward Spiral of collaboration, generating possibility and opportunity, and helping all involved to experience the power of purpose.

Join with us and others in making ourselves accountable for the transformation work that the world cries out for. Use the Mindsets and Methods to develop and refine your own leadership Signature Style, ideally in team with trusted colleagues and mentors. Help others to develop their own leadership Signature Styles. Pursue the Compelling Visions and Bold Aims that will make things better for all of us.

Choose to
    create the work and life experiences
    that others will always remember.

Choose to
    get onto an Upward Spiral
    of purpose and joy.

Choose to

LEAD

About the Authors

DENNIS WAGNER

Dennis Wagner believes in committing to and delivering on Bold Aims in work and in life. He is a nationally and internationally recognized leader in the arenas of public service, social marketing, healthcare quality improvement, and large-scale change management.

Dennis has worked for more than 30 years as a federal leader serving the United States at the Environmental Protection Agency, the Health Resources and Services Administration, and the Centers for Medicare and Medicaid Services. He has led and has supported other leaders in conducting successful, joyous, results-driven national and international initiatives to increase organ donation, to improve air quality, to increase healthcare access for the underserved, and more.

Dennis served as a member of the federal Senior Executive Service for ten years. He and two executive team colleagues were recognized for their successful national work to improve hospital patient safety in 2016 as Federal Employees of the Year by the non-partisan Partnership for Public Service.

Dennis grew up in rural Montana where he attended Fertile Prairie, a one-room country school, followed by high school in Baker, Montana, and then undergraduate and graduate degrees from Montana State University in Bozeman. He now lives in Alexandria, Virginia with his wife, Diane Hill, whose determination, compassion, and authenticity inspire him daily. Dennis and Diane have three children: Tess, Grant, and Margo.

JOHN SCANLON

John Scanlon is a lifelong student of how to achieve maximum effectiveness in organizations and people. Trained in chemical engineering and applied mathematics, John sees organizations as dynamic, complex systems that can bring individuals together to create extraordinary results for themselves and for the communities and markets they serve.

After graduating from Northeastern University (1963) and Rensselaer Polytechnic Institute (1967), John spent 1968 in a VISTA community organizing project in Omaha's Near North Side. He experienced the power of community organizing and the potential for collaboration between neighborhood advocates and government. In 1969, he joined the Urban Institute, a newly formed think tank founded by President Lyndon Johnson, as an analyst in its Program Evaluation Group. He co-authored the Federal Evaluation Policy report, with recommendations on how the Federal government should establish and manage program evaluation offices to support program management and federal policy making. As staff and later Director of the unit, John championed the development of innovative evaluation methods as essential to public sector management in a democratic society.

From 1980 to present-day, John has been a strategic advisor and designer for leadership coalitions pursuing large-scale transformational change in governmental program systems. He worked in public and private initiatives such as the Bureau of Primary Health Care's 100% Access/Zero Disparities campaign; Mark Abramson's development of the Council for Excellence in Government; the EPA's Indoor Air programs; the Health Resources and Services Administration's Organ Donation Breakthrough Collaborative; and, the Patient Safety and Clinical Pharmacy Services Collaborative, as well as several Centers for Medicare and Medicaid Services national improvement programs, including the Community-Based Care Transition Program and Partnership for Patients. Throughout, John has worked with teams who were successful in assuming leadership accountability and running leadership campaigns. He has also worked with a network of colleagues from these efforts to capture how this type of personal leadership constitutes what he calls Signature Style leadership, which is the crux of this book.

What DENNIS Says About JOHN

Meeting John in 1991 dramatically impacted my life and career. John was serving as a strategic consultant and coach at the Council for Excellence in Government where I was enrolled as one of 140 participants in the Excellence in Government one-year leadership training fellowship. John was a smart and challenging coach, with deep expertise in leadership. We learned that John's mission was to serve others as an Executive Architect. He believed that government managers like those of us in the Fellows program needed to embrace the accountability for delivering significant, needed results at national scale in the federal programs we served. He challenged us to add "leadership" to our management and administrative repertoire. John helped us learn to interpret and follow the powerful leadership examples of Council Principals like EPA Administrator Bill Ruckelshaus, Alcoa CEO and Treasury Secretary Paul O'Neill, and many others. I made a key decision during my year as a 1991-92 Fellow to pursue mentorship from John Scanlon, even after the Fellowship ended.

John has been coaching and teaming with me ever since, as well as with many highly accomplished leaders in a wide variety of disciplines. When John coaches and mentors, he doesn't just advise and recommend; he serves as a trusted partner and a co-leader, joining with his mentees in delivering on Bold Aims. John provides thoughtful, discerning, collaborative guidance that challenges the executives he serves to learn, grow, and achieve extraordinary results.

Many of the leadership Mindsets and Methods profiled in this book are the result of John's discerning observations and approaches to addressing the challenges confronted by me and other leaders he has supported over the years. John is not only a transformative Executive Architect, but also a national and international leadership treasure.

What JOHN Says About DENNIS

In the late 1980s and early 1990s, I had the opportunity to support a large number of exceptional public and private sector leaders —people who transformed organizations and generated extraordinary results. With Mark Abramson, the founder of the Council for Excellence in Government (CEG), and the team he assembled, we worked to understand what distinguished such leaders from the more common effective manager or administrator.

That work surfaced Dennis Wagner, one of 140 Fellows in a CEG leadership development program for mid-level federal managers (GS 14, 15). Dennis stood out as having one of the most impressive Leadership stories stemming from his work at EPA in monitoring and remediating residential radon gas levels. Dennis's exercise of leadership has become a blueprint for how one can actively step into and perform a leadership role. As we studied Dennis's approach, we realized he followed very simple but consistent methods, and that he had cultivated a very disciplined mindset. Without titular authority or the necessary resources, he was nonetheless able to secure commitments and move others into action and generate extraordinary results.

I had the opportunity to work with Dennis off and on over the next 20 years as he assumed assignments with bigger and bigger missions. I saw Dennis move into a number of federal agencies, always finding the opportunities hidden below the surface. In every agency, he chose to step into leadership roles and produced major program transformations.

Dennis' career demonstrates there is a method to leadership. No matter where you put him, he creates a leadership campaign. In a dozen situations, I've seen him seek out the performance outliers who generate possibilities. He forms teams by bringing together people with talent and energy and has them work as a force towards a bold, shared vision. He uses the resources at hand and leverages the influence and resources of others. He makes connections up and down the larger organization and enrolls and aligns with outside players. It can be disheartening to encounter the negativity that Bold Aims can surface, but Dennis always finds a way to flip the negative to the positive and to move forward on a constructive path.

This remarkable leadership style is a personal Choice by Dennis to be a positive force in the world. Dennis creates situations where everyone involved can find joy in the collaborative work that brings us together. Dennis has made leadership a habit!

Sources, Permissions and Photo Credits

Page	Description	Source	Permission/Credit
6	Image of Maya Angelou	Wikipedia	Public Domain
11	Image of Viktor Frankl	Wikipedia	Prof. Dr. Franz Vesely
34, 49, 51	Images of Sanjeev Arora MD	Project Echo	Reprinted by permission of Project ECHO, University of New Mexico Health Sciences Center, Albuquerque, NM
34, 79	Images of Don Berwick MD, MPP	Don Berwick	Images courtesy of Donald Berwick MD, MPP
35, 160	Image of Bob & Barb Malizzo speaking	Barbara Malizzo	Image courtesy of Barbara Malizzo
35	Image of Anne H. Hastings	Anne Hastings	Image courtesy of Anne H. Hastings
36	Image of Susan McVey Dillon	Susan McVey Dillon	Image courtesy of Susan McVey Dillon
36, 346	Image of John Chessare MD	John Chessare	Photo courtesy of Dr. John Chessare, President, CEO, Greater Baltimore Medical Center
40, 94	Image of Joe McCannon	Joe McCannon	Reprinted by permission of Joe McCannon
40, 98	Image of Tom Evans MD	Tom Evans	Photo courtesy of Dr. Tom Evans
40, 140	Image of Alan McKenzie	Alan McKenzie	Photo by Susan S. McKenzie
41, 164	Image of Doug Krug	Doug Krug	Photo courtesy of Doug Krug
41, 180	Image of Marie Schall	Marie Schall	Photo courtesy of Marie Schall
41, 238	Image of Tracy Enger	Tracy Enger	Photo courtesy of Tracy Washington Enger
42, 407	Image of Brenda Doroski and John Mitchell	Partnership for Public Service	Courtesy of the Partnership for Public Service
42, 408	Image of Steven Chen	Michelle Keller	Photo by Ed Carreon/USC Mann
43, 420	Image of Karen Minyard	Karen Minyard	Photo courtesy of Karen Minyard
43, 424	Image of Zandra Glenn	Zandra Glenn	Courtesy of Zandra Glenn
45	Painting of Johann Wolfgang Von Goethe	Wikipedia	Public Domain photograph of original artwork by Joseph Karl Stieler (1781-1858)
58	Map Graphic: Global Footprint of Project ECHO	Project ECHO	Reprinted by permission of Project ECHO, University of New Mexico Health Sciences Center, Albuquerque, NM
58	Image of Project ECHO Team	Project ECHO	Reprinted by permission of Project ECHO, University of New Mexico Health Sciences Center, Albuquerque, NM
62	Image of Dennis Wagner	Author	Photo provided by Dennis Wagner
66	Image of C. Everett Koop MD	United States Department of Health and Human Services	Public Domain
66	Image of Lee Thomas	Wikipedia	GNU Free Documentation License
69	Front page of New York Times, September 13, 1988	New York Times	From The New York Times ©1988. The New York Times Company. All rights reserved.

82	Image of Don Berwick	Author	Photo provided by Dennis Wagner
85	Image of 100,000 Lives campaign leaders in front of bus	Don Berwick	Photo reprinted by permission of Don Berwick MD, MPP
86	Map illustrating hospitals that participated in 100,000 Lives Campaign	Don Berwick	Map reprinted by permission of Don Berwick MD, MPP
86	Image of hospital leaders in stadium with yellow balloons	Don Berwick	Photo reprinted by permission of Don Berwick MD, MPP
89, 163	Graphic of AHRQ National Score Card results	Agency for Health Care Research on Quality	Agency for Healthcare Research and Quality (AHRQ) Online report: https://www.ahrq.gov/sites/default/files/wysiwyg/professionals/quality-patient-safety/pfp/hacreport-2019.pdf , page 21
93	54-word quote: "Healers are called to heal..."	Don Berwick	The Moral Determinants of Health, Journal of the American Medical Association by Donald M. Berwick MD, MPP, July 21, 2020 Volume 324, Number 3
103	Graphic showing Partnership for Patients earns rare Geppetto Checkmark	Noel Eldridge	Pinocchio graphic courtesy Steve McCraken
109, 448	Image of Contract for Results	Author	Photo provided by Dennis Wagner
109	Image of Tommy Thompson speaking at United Network for Organ Sharing	Donald Coleman	Public Domain photo courtesy of the Health Resources and Services Administration, photographer Donald Coleman
114, 451	Image of the Department of Health and Human Services Organ Donation Medal of Honor	Donald Coleman	Public Domain photo courtesy of the Health Resources and Services Administration, photographer Donald Coleman
134	Image of Marilyn Gaston	National Institutes of Health	Public Domain
134	Image of Mary Lou Andersen	Donald Coleman	Photo provided by Dennis Wagner
153	Image of Mahatma Gandhi	Wikipedia	Public Domain studio photograph of Mahatma Gandhi taken in London, 1931
160	Image of Bob and Barb Malizzo at their daughter's grave	Chicago Tribune	Photo by Heather Charles, Chicago Tribune
175	Image of sailors harnessing wind energy	iStock	Mbbirdy via iStock
178, 270	Image of Paul McGann MD	Author	Photo provided by Dennis Wagner
179	Image of former Congressman Elijah Cummings	Maryland State Archives	Fair Use © May 4, 2020, Maryland State Archives
179, 362	Image of Carolyn Candiello	Carolyn Candiello	Photo courtesy of Carolyn Candiello
183	Image of Jeneen M. Iwugo	Jeneen M. Iwugo	Photo courtesy of Jeneen M. Iwugo
185	Image of Alexa Kersting	Monica and Loren Kersting	Photo courtesy of Monica and Loren Kersting
187	Donate Life logo	Department of Health and Human Services	Public Domain

Page	Description	Source	Permission/Credit
191	Image of original artwork of an angel	Author	Artwork by Monica Kersting; photo provided by Dennis Wagner
193	Image of Phyllis Busansky	Wikipedia	Fair Use
195	Image of Diane M. Hill and Dennis Wagner	Author	Photo provided by Dennis Wagner
197	Map of Camino de Santiago journey by Wagner-Hill family	Kayla Renals	Fair Use
198	Image of Leonard Cohen	Wikimedia Commons	Rama, CC BY-SA 2.0 FR <https://creativecommons.org/licenses/by-sa/2.0/fr/deed.en>
198	Image of a man busking for Pilgrims on the Camino	Diane M. Hill	Photo by Diane M. Hill
199	Two images of the Wagner-Hill family	Author	Photos provided by Dennis Wagner
201	Image of Anne H. Hastings and John Scanlon	Anne H. Hastings	Image courtesy of Anne H. Hastings
202	Image of Anne H. Hastings and Father Joseph Philippe	Darcy Kiefel	© Kiefel Photography
204	Image of a bus on a country road in Haiti	Brian Gately	Photo courtesy of Fonkoze Foundation
209	Image of Fonkoze banking clients	Darcy Kiefel	© Kiefel Photography
211	Staircase Out of Poverty graphic	Brad Latham	Graphic courtesy of Fonkoze Foundation
211	Two images of Wilna's old and new houses	Anne H. Hastings	Photos courtesy of Fonkoze Foundation
217	Graphic of Fonkoze Bank Branches	Anne H. Hastings	Photo courtesy of Fonkoze Foundation
217	Image of villagers with Anne H. Hastings	Anne H. Hastings	Photo courtesy of Fonkoze Foundation
222	Image of Cesar Chavez	Wikipedia via donated collection of photos from US News and World Report to Library of Congress	Public Domain photo by Marion S. Trikosko
234	Image of To Err is Human report cover	National Academies Press 978-0309261746	Used with permission of National Academies Press, from To Err is Human: Building a Safer Health System by the Institute of Medicine, Committee on Quality Healthcare in America, edited by Molly S. Donaldson, Janet M. Corrigan, and Linda T. Kohn, 2000; permission conveyed through Copyright Clearance Center, Inc
238	Image of Tracy Washington Enger	Tracy Washington Enger	Photo courtesy of Tracy Washionton Enger
249	Diagram: Influence Pyramid	Principle Centered Leadership by Steven Covey	Adapted from Principle Centered Leadership by Stephen Covey
252	Image of Dennis Wagner with Jean Moody-Williams and Paul McGann MD	Partnership for Public Service	Courtesy of the Partnership for Public Service
272	Image of Jade Purdue	Jade Purdue-Puli	Reprinted by permission of Jade Purdue-Puli
273	Image of Jade Purdue-Puli's children, Benjamin and Indie	Jade Purdue-Puli	Reprinted by permission of Jade Purdue-Puli
284	Image of Paul O'Neill	Department of the Treasury	Public Domain

299	Image of the abundance of the Milky Way galaxy	iStock	den-belitsky/iStock
299	Image of Susan McVey Dillon	Susan McVey Dillon	Image courtesy of Susan McVey Dillon
300	Image of Michael McVey	Susan McVey Dillon	Image courtesy of Susan McVey Dillon
301	Image of Susan McVey Dillon, Santos Felix, John Edwards, and Avi Shaked MD	Janette Romano	Janette McVey, Photographer
302	Image of Howard Nathan	Howard Nathan	Reprinted by permission of Howard M. Nathan, DHL, Gift of Life Transplant Foundation, Philadelphia, PA
303	Image of Ginny McBride	Ginny McBride	Public Domain photo courtesy of the Health Resources and Services Administration, photographer Donald Coleman, reprinted with permission of Ginny McBride
303	Image of Tommy Thompson speaking	Donald Coleman	Public Domain photo courtesy of the Health Resources and Services Administration, photographer Donald Coleman
311	Image of Kevin O'Connor	Kevin O'Connor	Photo courtesy of Kevin O'Connor
332	Image of Vice President Al Gore and Mark Abramson	Mark Abramson	Photo courtesy of Mark Abramson
339	Segment on "Exercising Accountability Through 5 Dimensions of Action"	Mark Abramson and John Scanlon	Adapted from the original work of Mark Abramson and John Scanlon, Council for Excellence in Government
341	Image of Mark Abramson	Mark Abramson	Photo courtesy of Mark Abramson
356	Graphic of GBMC Leadership System	Adapted from original by John Chessare	Courtesy of Dr. John Chessare, President, CEO, Greater Baltimore Medical Center
358	Graphic of GBMC Integrated Management Systems	John Chessare	Courtesy of Dr. John Chessare, President, CEO, Greater Baltimore Medical Center
363	Graphic of GBMC's Systematic Approach to Caring for a Population of Patients	Adapted from original by John Chessare	Courtesy of Dr. John Chessare, President, CEO, Greater Baltimore Medical Center
364	Chart showing Total Primary Care Patients - Growth	John Chessare	Courtesy of Dr. John Chessare, President, CEO, Greater Baltimore Medical Center
365	Chart showing Best Health Outcome: Improvement in Diabetic Care	John Chessare	Courtesy of Dr. John Chessare, President, CEO, Greater Baltimore Medical Center
366	Image of the Malcom Baldridge National Quality Award	Wikipedia	Public Domain photo by U.S. Department of Commerce
394	Image of Dennis Wagner, and Kimberly Green-Goldsborough	Author	Photo provided by Dennis Wagner
395	Image of Mae Moh Powerplant, Thailand	iStock	tampatra/iStock
402	Graphic of Rapid National Reductions in Early Elective Deliveries	Healthy Moms, Healthy Babies, 2020 Leapfrog Hospital Survey	Graphic courtesy of The Leapfrog Group For further information: https://www.leapfroggroup.org/influencing/early-elective-deliveries
403	Two images from the Partnership for Clean Indoor Air 2009 Biennial Forum	Author	Photos provided by Dennis Wagner
405	Graphic of Results and Data Summary from 87+ Organizations	Adapted from graphic provided by John Mitchell, U.S. Environmental Protection Agency	Partnership for Clean Indoor Air Biennial Forum, 2009

Page	Description	Source	Permission/Credit
406	Graphic showing that Bold Aim in Uganda Propels Worldwide Results	Adapted from graphic provided by John Mitchell, U.S. Environmental Protection Agency	Partnership for Clean Indoor Air Biennial Forum, 2009
407	Image of Brenda Doroski & John Mitchell	Partnership for Public Service	Courtesy of the Partnership for Public Service
409	Steven Chen with a patient	Michelle Keller	Photo by Ed Carreon/USC Mann
434	Dennis Wagner speaking	Marcia Coleman	Photo provided by Dennis Wagner
436	Image of HRSA Administrator Elizabeth "Betty" Duke	AllGov.org	Public Domain
443	Image of Larry Minnix and Secretary Thompson	Christopher Smith	Public Domain photo courtesy of the US Department of Health and Human Services, photographer Christopher Smith
443	Image of Jim Low, Camile Haney, Secretary Thompson and Amy Luxner	Christopher Smith	Public Domain photo courtesy of the US Department of Health and Human Services, photographer Christopher Smith
446	Image of Frank Zampiello MD	Donald Coleman	Photo courtesy of Donald Coleman
449	Image of Helen Bottenfield with transplant recipient	Author	Photo provided by Dennis Wagner
452	Image of Ginny McBride, Donald Coleman, Jade Purdue, Elizabeth Duke, and Dennis Wagner	Author	Photo provided by Dennis Wagner
474	Image of John Scanlon	Author	Photo provided by John Scanlon
475	Image of Dennis Wagner	Author	Photo provided by Dennis Wagner

www.ingramcontent.com/pod-product-compliance
Lightning Source LLC
Chambersburg PA
CBHW080532300426
44111CB00017B/2685